Southwestern Historical Quarterly, Volume 24...

Eugene Campbell Barker, Herbert Eugene Bolton, Texas State Historical Association, University of Texas at Austin. Center for Studies in Texas History

Nabu Public Domain Reprints:

You are holding a reproduction of an original work published before 1923 that is in the public domain in the United States of America, and possibly other countries. You may freely copy and distribute this work as no entity (individual or corporate) has a copyright on the body of the work. This book may contain prior copyright references, and library stamps (as most of these works were scanned from library copies). These have been scanned and retained as part of the historical artifact.

This book may have occasional imperfections such as missing or blurred pages, poor pictures, errant marks, etc. that were either part of the original artifact, or were introduced by the scanning process. We believe this work is culturally important, and despite the imperfections, have elected to bring it back into print as part of our continuing commitment to the preservation of printed works worldwide. We appreciate your understanding of the imperfections in the preservation process, and hope you enjoy this valuable book.

THE SOUTHWESTERN HISTORICAL QUARTERLY

VOLUME XXIV

JULY, 1920, TO APRIL, 1921

EDITORS:

EUGENE C. BARKER, HERBERT E. BOLTON.

ASSOCIATE EDITORS:

CHAS. W. RAMSDELL, E. W. WINKLER, EDGAR L. HEWETT.

MANAGING EDITOR:

EUGENE C. BARKER.

THE TEXAS STATE HISTORICAL ASSOCIATION

AUSTIN, TEXAS

1921

1224
.898 V. 24 (1920-21)

The Texas State Historical Association

Organized 1897

PRESIDENT:

MRS. ADELE B. LOOSCAN

VICE-PRESIDENTS:

ALEX. DIENST,
LEWIS R. BRYAN,
R. C. CRANE.
GEORGE W. LITTLEFIELD,

RECORDING SECRETARY AND LIBRARIAN:

EUGENE C. BARKER.

CORRESPONDING SECRETARY AND TREASURER:

CHARLES W. RAMSDELL.

EXECUTIVE COUNCIL:

LEWIS R. BRYAN,
Z. T. FULMORE,
ALEX. DIENST,
GEORGE W. LITTLEFIELD,
R. C. CRANE,
MRS. ADELE B. LOOSCAN,
EUGENE C. BARKER,
CHARLES W. RAMSDELL,
E. W. WINKLER,
JOHN C. TOWNES,
MRS. MATTIE AUSTIN HATCHER;
S. H. MOORE,
ADINA DE ZAVALA,
E. T. MILLER,
J. W. BARTON,
MRS. PEARL CASHELL JACKSON.

PUBLICATION COMMITTEE:

MRS. ADELE B. LOOSCAN,
EUGENE C. BARKER,
HERBERT E. BOLTON,
E. W. WINKLER,
Z. T. FULMORE.

CONTENTS

Number 1: July, 1920

Number 2: October, 1920

Number 3: January, 1921

Number 4: April, 1921

185154

THE SOUTHWESTERN HISTORICAL QUARTERLY

VOL. XXVI JULY, 1920 No. 1

The publication committee and the editors disclaim responsibility for views expressed by contributors to THE QUARTERLY

THE QUESTION OF TEXAN JURISDICTION IN NEW MEXICO UNDER THE UNITED STATES, 1848-1850

WILLIAM CAMPBELL BINKLEY

Practically every student of American history has heard of the boundary controversy between Texas and New Mexico because of its connection with the famous Compromise of 1850. Most of the general histories of the United States mention the question and its final adjustment,[1] and it has even been intimated that had not President Taylor died at the time he did a civil war would have been precipitated in 1850 as a result of this issue alone. These accounts, however, emphasize only the national phase of the subject, while the local activities of the parties interested in the controversy have been left in the background. This is unfortunate, inasmuch as these local activities played a part in shaping the national phase of the question.

During her short life as an independent republic, Texas claimed the Rio Grande from mouth to source as her western boundary, and even seriously considered the possibility of extending her jurisdiction to include the valuable bay of San Francisco. But the boundary actually claimed meant a direct encroachment upon the territory of the neighboring Mexican states. Since the northern part of the territory thus claimed had long been under the jurisdiction of New Mexico, and even included the capital of that province, the people of the region naturally resented any attempted encroachments. As a result, the first Texan efforts at occupation

[1]The fullest accounts are McMaster, *History of the People of the United States*, VIII, 40-41, and Schouler, *History of the United States of America*, V, 180-184.

ended in failure. But the sting of failure was soon alleviated through the annexation of Texas to the United States, and while that government was planning to adjust the claims it had thus inherited, the question changed from the status of a revolutionary movement under the Mexican government to an international situation. The climax of this transitory stage was reached in the Mexican War, as a result of which New Mexico also became a part of the United States. Thus the question was once more an internal problem, but under a different government, and here it took the form of a three cornered quarrel between Texas, New Mexico, and the central government, in which Texas assumed the aggressive.

The Problems Involved Under the United States.—The first problem which presented itself was that of ascertaining the attitude of the United States government, and in this both Texas and New Mexico were naturally interested. Before the American occupation of New Mexico in 1846, the boundary question had not seriously troubled the people of that department. The Santa Fé expedition had, of course, brought an awakening to the possibilities of an encroachment from the east, and its outcome left them opposed to a division of their province by Texas. But they had considered the issue to be between Texas and Mexico rather than between themselves and Texas, and therefore had looked to the supreme government of Mexico to keep their domain intact. Consequently, for them the treaty of Guadalupe Hidalgo meant that the Mexican government was no longer responsible for their territory, and in spite of the declaration of General Kearny that he would hold the department with its original boundaries,[2] they feared that the attitude of the new government under which they found themselves was favorable to Texas. These apprehensions were increased as a result of statements made by President Polk, and they began to feel that unless they took active steps to assert their rights, they were facing territorial disintegration.

For the Texans also, the trend of events in connection with the military occupation of New Mexico and the maintenance of the military government had brought uneasiness. Even before the establishment of peace, President Polk had been compelled to face a question from Texas concerning the jurisdiction of the military

[2]Kearny's proclamation of August 22, 1846, in *House Ex. Doc.* 60, 30th Cong., 1st sess. (Ser. no. 520), p. 170.

government in New Mexico. Information concerning the nature of Kearny's occupation had reached the state officials of Texas through the newspapers, and after looking in vain for a contradiction of the statement that the general government claimed the right of jurisdiction over the region as a conquered country, the authorities began to feel apprehensive over their claims. Accordingly, Governor J. Pinckney Henderson wrote to Secretary Buchanan, asking to be informed concerning the accuracy of the newspaper accounts, especially in regard to any claims of the general government to any portion of the territory lying within the limits of Texas as named in her boundary act of December 19, 1836. He solemnly protested against any action on the part of the United States which might interfere with the rights of Texas, but concluded by saying:

> Inasmuch as it is not convenient for the State at this time to exercise jurisdiction over Santa Fe, I presume no objection will be made on the part of the government of the State of Texas to the establishment of a territorial government over that country by the United States, provided it is done with the *express* admission on their part that the State of Texas is entitled to the soil and jurisdiction over the same, and may exercise her right whenever she regards it expedient.[3]

This letter reached Washington early in February, and in the meantime information was also arriving concerning the attitude in Texas which had impelled the sending of the protest. Through their press the Texans denounced the establishment of a separate territorial government over Santa Fé and the surrounding country as a violation of the "compact of annexation," and they professed inability to understand how Polk could reconcile his military movements with his assumption of the Rio Grande as the boundary. They argued that "Santa Fe is equally a part of our annexed territory [on this assumption] as that opposite Matamoros," and yet General Taylor was sent to occupy and defend the latter as United States soil, while General Kearny was sent to conquer and establish a government over the former.[4] A spirit of this nature had to be placated, and in reply to Governor Henderson's letter Polk assured him that the military government in New Mexico was only

[3]Henderson to Buchanan, January 4, 1847, in *Sen. Ex. Doc.* 24, 31st Cong., 1st sess. (Ser. no. 554), p. 2.

[4]*Niles' Register*, LXXI, 305.

such as must necessarily exist under the laws of nations and of war to preserve order and protect the rights of the inhabitants, and that it would automatically cease upon the conclusion of a treaty of peace with Mexico.

But he was now forced to take a stand upon the boundary claims, and he appeased the Texans by stating that nothing could be more certain than that the temporary government would never injuriously affect the right which he believed to be justly asserted by Texas to the whole territory east of the Rio Grande, whenever the Mexican claim to it should be extinguished by treaty. He now absolved himself from any further responsibility on the question by adding that the solution of the problem belonged more properly to the legislative than to the executive branch of the government.[5] This assurance had the desired effect in Texas, with the result that so far as the local boundary question was concerned, all moves toward securing a settlement were suspended until it could be determined what effect the war would have upon the international line of demarcation.

Polk later explained to Congress that under the circumstances a postponement of the settlement was the most plausible solution. It would obviously be impracticable, if not impossible, to determine a boundary line between two nations while they were at war with each other. Therefore, in spite of the fact that New Mexico was under the control of the United States army, since it had never actually been occupied by Texas, and was still claimed by Mexico, it was not yet an undisputed portion of the United States; and even were the Texas claim admitted, no part of the disputed territory could be delivered to it until the international question of ownership was settled.[6] This point of view, as well as the promise in the President's statement to Governor Henderson that the military government legally ceased to exist as soon as peace should be established, led to the expectation in Texas that the territory east of the Rio Grande would immediately be turned over to the jurisdiction of the Texas government. But the practical conditions required the maintenance of some definite form of government over the newly acquired territory, until a legalized civil

[5]Buchanan to Henderson, February 12, 1847, in *Sen. Ex. Doc.* 24, 31st Cong., 1st sess. (Ser. no. 554), p. 3.

[6]Polk's message to Congress, July 24, 1848, in *House Ex. Doc.* 70, 30th Cong., 1st sess. (Ser. no. 521), p. 4.

government could be set up; and for this reason the existing military control was allowed to continue, with no provisions for a change in the extent of its territorial jurisdiction.

In the establishment of a civil government for the acquisition, the problems which had to be met were numerous. In the first place, it was not expedient to attempt to establish a civil government in territory which was claimed by one of the states, while that claim was still unsettled. Moreover, while the territory east of the Rio Grande was conceded in executive circles to rightfully belong to Texas, the fact remained that no constituted authorities from the government of that state were on the ground to establish and maintain her jurisdiction. And since the Mexican population of the region was openly hostile, there was no alternative left for the United States army but to maintain control until either Texas or the central government acted, or else to withdraw, and thereby leave New Mexico in a state of anarchy and without control.[7] From the standpoint of the central government, the power to organize the civil government of the territories of the United States rested solely in Congress. In addition, the President had placed upon the legislative branch of the government the responsibility for settling the question between the United States and the state of Texas. Congress, therefore, had become the potent force which was to determine the nature of the development of the vast southwestern area which had just been acquired, and at this particular period in the history of the United States, no question which came before Congress was able to remain free from an entanglement with the all-pervading issue of slavery extension.

This one was to be no exception, for almost as soon as it became evident that the Mexican War would bring the accession of new territory, the slavery question was introduced by means of the Wilmot Proviso, attempting to prohibit the extension of slavery to any territory which might be acquired with the funds then being granted to the President. The Proviso failed to pass, but it had the effect of bringing the Southern congressmen to openly demand definite legislation establishing the right to carry slaves into any territory which was to be added or organized. The continual recurrence of the sentiment of the Proviso, not only during the war, but also after peace was established, brought a fear that it might ultimately succeed, and consequently limit all possibility of fur-

[7] *Idem*, 4.

ther extension westward by the slavery interests. This led to tactics for delay on the part of the slaveholders, and as a result it was impossible to agree upon the organization of the civil government for New Mexico and California. The military government established by General Kearny continued, therefore, to hold control.

The Texan Movement to Establish Jurisdiction in 1848.—As long as this state of affairs existed, the New Mexicans were apparently upheld in their boundary desires, and there was no incentive for immediate action on their part. But since Texas had expected to receive jurisdiction over the territory east of the Rio Grande, she was not inclined to acquiesce in the arrangement. Under the circumstances, therefore, it seemed necessary that she should take the first step toward securing a settlement of the boundary question. No immediate action had followed the activities of Governor Henderson in January, 1847, because of the conciliatory attitude of the administration at Washington. But during its next session the legislature of Texas began to act concerning western jurisdiction.

Early in the session, and even before the status of the territory between the Nueces and the Rio Grande was settled by the treaty of Guadalupe Hidalgo, the new counties of Nueces, Webb, Starr, and Cameron, all of them within this region, were created.[8] The actual work of organizing these counties had already been begun under the supervision of Mirabeau B. Lamar, a former president of the republic, who was now a captain of Texan troops stationed in the region, and considerable opposition had been encountered.[9] The terms of the treaty confirmed the legality of this action, but the legislation soon advanced another step. In a special message to the legislature, on March 2, 1848, Governor George T. Wood, who had succeeded Henderson, called attention to rumors of efforts to establish a state government in New Mexico, and asserted that had the United States government assigned Texan troops to that region, such a move would never have occurred. He warned the legislators that silent acquiescence might be construed into a submission to unauthorized encroachments, and, therefore, he recom-

[8]Gammel, *Laws of Texas*, III, 18, 24, 26, 27, 484.

[9]Lamar to Bliss, July 10, 1847, in *Lamar Papers*, Texas State Library. The election returns from Nueces county showed a total of forty votes, and the list discloses the fact that thirty-seven of the voters possessed Spanish names.

mended that the legislature take some action so that the Texan representatives in Congress might feel authorized to protest against an infringement of Texan rights or a usurpation of any portion of her territory. In addition, he suggested that suitable action be taken for the immediate enforcement of the civil and political jurisdiction of the state over the Santa Fé region.[10]

As a result, on March 15, the county of Santa Fé was created, with boundaries

> beginning at the junction of Rio Puerco, with the Rio Grande, and running up the principal stream of the Rio Grande to its source; thence due north to the forty-second degree of north latitude; thence along the boundary line as defined in the treaty between the United States and Spain to the point where the one hundredth degree of longitude west from Greenwich, intersects Red river; thence up the principal stream of Red river to its source; thence in a direct line to the source of the principal stream of the Rio Puerco, and down said Rio Puerco to the place of beginning.[11]

This included practically the entire region of New Mexico to which Texas had laid claim by the boundary act of 1836, and was the first actual legislation since that act that directly affected the territory. Two weeks previously, an act had been passed providing for the control of the militia of the Santa Fé district,[12] and other acts were speedily passed, allowing it one representative in the Texas house of represcntives, and establishing the eleventh judicial district of the state, to be composed of the new county.[13] It was provided that court should be held twice a year at Santa Fé, and Spruce M. Baird was sent there to serve as judge for the newly created district, with additional instructions that part of his duty was to be the organization of the new county, and the formal establishment there of the Texan jurisdiction.[14]

In addition to this legislation a resolution was adopted on March 20, which stated that since the people of Santa Fé, which was an integral part of Texas, were believed to have attempted to estab-

[10] *Senate Journal*, 2nd Texas Legislature, 465-468.

[11] Gammel, *Laws of Texas*, III, 95; see also Batts, *Defunct Counties of Texas*, in THE QUARTERLY, I, 91.

[12] *Ibid.*, III, 50.

[13] *Ibid.*, III, 96; see also *Niles' Register*, LXXIV, 224.

[14] Davis, *El Gringo*, 110; *Niles' Register*, LXXIV, 211. Bancroft. *History of Arizona and New Mexico*, 455, follows the *Register* by giving this name as Beard, but his own correspondence shows that Baird is correct.

lish a separate government in direct violation of the rights of Texas, the government of the United States was to be requested to issue orders to the military officers at Santa Fé to aid the officers of Texas in organizing the region, and in enforcing the laws of Texas in case resistance should be offered.[15] Governor Wood at once asked that this be done, "to the end that the State of Texas may in no wise be embarrassed in the exercise of her rightful jurisdiction over that territory."[16] After waiting for what he considered a reasonable time for a reply, Wood wrote again in October, expressing the surprise of the people of Texas at the efforts of the United States government to deprive them of territory which had previously been conceded to them. He claimed that the sole reason for leaving the question of boundaries open at the time of annexation was that the United States "might not have to approach the settlement of her actual or prospective difficulties with Mexico, clothed with only a qualified and imperfect power of adjustment." In his opinion, the United States government was simply an agent and trustee for Texas, and as such she could not acquire a right to any territory within limits even claimed by Texas. He pointed out that for Texas the question was one of honor, since she was forced to look to her public domain as her only source of revenue for the payment of the debt she had contracted in the course of her revolution, and for this reason no measure to obtain any portion of her territory south of forty-two degrees or east of the Rio Grande, without ample compensation, would be considered.[17]

When it was learned in Santa Fé that Texas had begun a new movement to extend her jurisdiction over the territory, steps were taken by the authorities to arouse opposition among the people. The principal newspaper of the region, the Santa Fé *Republican,* was controlled by the officers of the military government,[18] and through its columns an effort was made to secure an exciting reception for Judge Baird. It says:

We would now inform our Texas friends that it is not necessary to send us a judge, nor a district attorney, to settle our affairs

[15]Gammel, *Laws of Texas*, III, 218-219.

[16]Wood to Polk, March 23, 1848, in Austin *State Gazette*, November 10, 1849.

[17]Wood to Polk, October 6, 1848, in *Idem.*

[18]Washington to Baird, November 23, 1848, in *Santa Fé Papers*, Texas State Library.

. . . for there is not a citizen, either American or Mexican, that will ever acknowledge themselves as citizens of Texas, until it comes from higher authorities. New Mexico does not belong, nor has Texas even a right to claim her as a part of Texas. We would so advise Texas to send with her civil officers for this country, a large force, in order that they may have a sufficient body-guard to escort them back safe. . . . Texas should show some little sense, and drop this question, and not have it publicly announced that Texas' smartest men were tarred and feathered by attempting to fill the offices assigned them.[19]

Baird started from Texas on May 24, 1848,[20] going by way of St. Louis,[21] and arrived in Santa Fé on November 10.[22] After investigating the situation, he wrote to Colonel John M. Washington, the commanding officer at Santa Fé, and ex-officio civil and military governor of New Mexico, expressing his surprise at finding the military authorities still in control there. He inquired if the government established by General Kearny had not come to an end with the ratification of the treaty with Mexico, thereby giving Texas the right to assume civil jurisdiction over the region. At the same time he presented his commission from Governor Wood, together with the laws upon which his authority was based, and added that for the future "the State of Texas must regard all judicial proceedings, and the exercise of all civil functions inconsistent with her laws and constitution, null and void."[23] Washington at once replied that the government established by General Kearny had been declared by the President to continue to exist after the ratification of the peace terms, and added that it was his intention to maintain its existence "at every peril" until ordered by either the executive or the legislative power of the United States to desist.[24]

On the following day he returned the documents which had been submitted by Baird, with an accompanying statement that when they appeared at the proper time before the proper tribunal they would undoubtedly receive consideration in the way of estab-

[19]*Niles' Register*, LXXIV, 224.

[20]Nacogdoches *Times*, May 27, 1848.

[21]Baird to Miller, September 22, 1848, in *Santa Fé Papers*, Texas State Library.

[22]Baird to Miller, November 10, 1848, in *Ibid.*

[23]Baird to Washington, November 22, 1848; Baird to Miller, September 21, 1849, in *Ibid.*

[24]Washington to Baird, November 22, 1848, in *Ibid.*

lishing the Texan claims. Then in reply to a suggestion from Baird that he would publish a proclamation announcing the purpose of his mission, Washington stated that the press of Santa Fé "belongs to the General Government and must of course be under its control."[25] Baird now felt that further progress was blocked, and reported to the officials in Texas that he could do nothing until the question of jurisdiction could be settled in Congress, unless he received further instructions from the governor, or Washington received new orders from the President.[26] Consequently he turned his attention to the natural resources of the region, and in company with seven other Texans and Americans, applied to the governor of Texas for authority to operate certain valuable saline deposits lying in the territory between the Rio Grande and the Pecos, below Santa Fé.[27] To Governor Wood he explained that this was for the purpose of recovering the financial loss he had suffered in going to Santa Fé. At the same time he submitted a report upon the conditions in the region, together with a suggestion for opening a direct route from San Antonio to Santa Fé in order to facilitate communications between the two portions of the state.[28]

He then began to make plans to leave Santa Fé early in the spring of 1849,[29] but in March the preparation by some of the army officers stationed in New Mexico, of newspaper articles which he considered to be derogatory to the claims of Texas, led him to reopen a correspondence with Colonel Washington. He warned Washington that if these were published, he would hesitate no longer to assert the Texan claims, and would inform the people of New Mexico as to the correct situation.[30] His subsequent reports indicate that the information which he planned to divulge to the people was the fact that they were being received concerning the real aims of the Texans, simply because the men who had "grown into officials in the breath of a moment" as a result of the establishment of the Kearny government were reluctant to give up the influence of the patronage which they now possessed.[31] In

[25]Washington to Baird, November 23, 1848, in *Ibid.*

[26]Baird to Miller, December 10, 1848, in *Ibid.*

[27]McNees, Baird, and others to Miller, December 7, 1848, in *Ibid.*

[28]Baird to Wood, December 18, 1848, in *Ibid.*

[29]Boyers to Miller, February 6, 1849, in *Ibid.*

[30]Baird to Washington, March 21, 1849, in *Ibid.*

[31]Baird to Miller, September 23, and October 20, 1849, in *Ibid.*

order to prevent this, Washington attempted to persuade Baird that the articles in question could not be considered as having any effect upon the Texan claims, and expressed a wish that the matter should rest until they could act jointly, "when the thing can be arranged without difficulty."[32] Baird proceeded, however, to print proclamations claiming exclusive jurisdiction for Texas,[33] but in the end allowed himself to be persuaded by the military governor to suspend their circulation until Congress could be heard from.[34] The absence of new instructions from his own government was also a factor in bringing about his decision to wait. His activities at this time, however, did have the effect of causing the suppression by Washington of the articles in question.[35]

The receipt of this information in Texas led Governor Wood to appeal once more to the chief executive of the nation. He reviewed the situation once more, complaining at the failure of Polk to answer his earlier letters urging President Taylor to offer to Baird such assistance as might seem consistent with the obligations of the federal government and the rights of Texas; and concluding with a request for an early reply in order that the views of the general government might be submitted to the Texas legislature in the following November.[36]

During the first week in April, Baird received indirect information which led him to believe that Congress had agreed to Texan jurisdiction over New Mexico, and immediately notified Washington that all judicial proceedings under the military authorities would be void if continued under these circumstances.[37] He was once more prepared to proceed to accomplish the organization of the region, but once more Washington was equal to the occasion, and succeeded in persuading him to postpone action until the arrival of official information.[38] This left the advantage on the side of the military authorities when authentic reports disclosed the fact that Congress had failed to reach a decision, and once

[32]Washington to Baird, March 21, 1849, in *Ibid.*

[33]Baird to Miller, November 6, 1849, in *Ibid.*

[34]Baird to Wood, March 30, 1849, in *Ibid.* Also Nacogdoches *Times*, June 23, 1849.

[35]Baird to Miller, November 6, 1849, in *Ibid.*

[36]Wood to Taylor, June 30, 1849, in Austin *State Gazette*, November 10, 1849.

[37]Baird to Washington, April 5, 1849, in *Santa Fé Papers*, Texas State Library.

[38]Washington to Baird, April 5, 1849, in *Ibid.*

more Baird found himself waiting for a new opportunity to move.

In the meantime his communications of the previous fall were beginning to reach the officials in Texas, and on April 14, Washington D. Miller, secretary of state in Texas, informed him that it was expected that the obstacles presented as a result of the military occupation would soon be removed. He was therefore told to "labor to conciliate the people of that remote frontier," in order that they would be ready to consent to the organization of the region as soon as the military officials were out of the way.[39] A new proclamation for calling an election in Santa Fé county was then forwarded to him, and on June 18, he prepared this for circulation. In it the people were informed of the legislative act creating the county, and were told that "henceforward, the civil and criminal jurisdiction over said county, legitimately, will be assumed and exercised by the authorities of the State of Texas only, and the citizens will be required to yield obedience thereto."[40] Before circulating the proclamation, however, he notified Colonel Washington of its receipt, and of his plans to issue writs of election immediately. In the personal conference which followed, Washington convinced him that he could not possibly make the returns of an election in time to prevent all except the votes for county officers from being null, and that this fact would have a bad effect upon those who voted.[41] He agreed, therefore, to suspend operations until he could be further advised,[42] and in return, Washington assured him that nothing should be authorized by the military governor "which would wrongly prejudice the claims of Texas."[43]

Feeling that he had accomplished all that was possible under the circumstances, and relying upon Washington's assurances, Baird now decided to leave Santa Fé for a time. To his own government he reported that the men who were opposed to the claims of Texas in the region were "actuated solely from a desire

[39]Miller to Baird, April 14, 1849, in *Ibid.*

[40]A copy of this proclamation is in the *Santa Fé Papers.*

[41]Baird to Miller, September 21, 1849, in *Ibid.*

[42]Baird to Washington, July 4, 1849, in *Ibid.*

[43]Washington to Baird, July 4, 1849, in *Ibid.* In reporting this answer to Miller, Baird says, "I felicitate myself that I am advanced in the Colonel's estimation since my first communication, from an Esquire to a Judge, and from that you may form perhaps a correct estimate of the rise of Texas stock during the winter." Baird to Miller, September 21, 1849, in *Ibid.*

to figure as public functionaries themselves," and therefore, that he entertained no doubt as to his ability to organize under the jurisdiction of Texas when the military government established by Kearny should be removed.[44] In support of his opinion he stated that General Armijo, whom he considered as the leading man of the region, "espouses our cause with great zeal."

The Struggle for Civil Government in New Mexico.—During this same period the people of New Mexico had likewise become active. When it was found that the legislature which had been provided for in the Kearny Code was powerless if any of its measures did not meet the approval of the military commander, no effort was made to hold a second meeting, and dissatisfaction began to develop.[45] It was felt that the stipulations of the code and of the treaty of Guadalupe Hidalgo had given them the right to a civil government, and a movement was begun to have the military control replaced by a territorial form of government. The President had advised that they should live peaceably and quietly under the military government until Congress could act deliberately and wisely.[46] Senator Thomas H. Benton assumed a different point of view, however, and in August, 1848, he addressed a letter to the people of both California and New Mexico, suggesting to them that since they had no civil government, the best move to make would be to provide for themselves a simple form of government until Congress should provide one for them. He believed that they would need only a governor, judges, and peace and militia officers, and very little in the way of laws.[47]

Following this suggestion, a convention met at Santa Fé on October 10, 1848, and formulated a petition to Congress, asking for the establishment of a civil government of a territorial nature, and stating, among other subjects, that they were opposed to slavery, and that they firmly protested against the dismemberment of their territory in favor of Texas, or for any other cause.[48] It was exactly one month later that Baird arrived in Santa Fé, and he reported that even then "the convention excitement was still alive, and there was much dissatisfaction as to the manner in which

[44]Baird to Miller, September 21, 1849, in *Ibid.*
[45]Baird to Miller, September 23, 1849, in *Ibid.*
[46]Prince, *New Mexico's Struggle for Statehood*, 6.
[47]*Niles' Register*, LXXIV, 244.
[48]*Congressional Globe*, 30th Cong., 2nd sess., 33.

it had been gotten up and conducted, both among the Mexicans and Americans."[49] According to the accounts given to him by the people, the movement was planned in secret by those holding, or desiring to hold office under the military government. Only five days notice was given for the election of delegates, and "poll books were made out and distributed to the various precincts headed with the names of those whose election was desired by the conclave." It was to this cause that Baird attributed the protest against the Texan claims. He accounted for the anti-slavery statement on the grounds that discord in the convention caused the withdrawal of enough delegates to reduce the number below a quorum, and thus disappointment caused those remaining to draw up this resolution in the hope of enlisting the abolitionist sympathies on their side.[50]

But at the same time that these New Mexicans were engaged in formulating this petition, opposing the division of their territory, Secretary of War Marcy, following instructions from President Polk, was writing to the commanding officer of the United States forces at Santa Fé, to inform him that the national government had not contested the claim of Texas to all the territory east of the Rio Grande. He also stated that any civil authority which Texas had established, or might establish in the region, was to be respected, and in no manner interfered with by the military forces in that department, unless their aid might be needed to sustain it.[51] In giving these instructions, Polk stated that he deemed them necessary because of the danger that the military officers at Santa Fé might come into collision with the authorities of Texas. He added also that he had not changed his opinion as expressed in his message of July 24, to Congress, concerning the right of Texas to jurisdiction over all that part of New Mexico east of the Rio Grande.[52] Two months later these same instructions were sent to General William J. Worth, who was in command of the eighth and ninth military departments, composed of Texas and New Mexico, respectively.[53]

[49]Baird to Miller, September 30, 1849, in *Santa Fé Papers*, Texas State Library.

[50]Baird to Miller, September 23, 1849, in *Ibid.*

[51]Marcy to Commanding officer at Santa Fé, October 12, 1848, in *House Ex. Doc.* 17, 31st Cong., 1st sess. (Ser. no. 573), p. 261.

[52]Quaife (editor), *Diary of James K. Polk*, IV, 150-151.

[53]Marcy to Worth, December 10, 1848, in *House Ex. Doc.* 17, *op. cit.*,

But on March 4, 1849, a new administration came into power, and among the early acts of the new Secretary of War, George W. Crawford, was the writing of a letter to the commanding officer at Santa Fé, reproving him for failure to report to the department concerning the management of affairs in New Mexico. He then repeated the instructions sent out by Secretary Marcy, concerning the boundary question, but added that it was not expected that Texas would undertake to extend her civil jurisdiction over the remote region designated.[54] This letter indicates that the new secretary was not informed as to the actual situation which had already developed in connection with the Texan activities of the previous year. A warning was added, however, that in case Texas should make a move to occupy the region, the commanding officer should be careful not to come into conflict with her authorities, and should likewise refrain from expressing an opinion upon the validity of her claims. This meant a slight change from the policy of the preceding administration. Marcy's instructions had indicated that if it seemed necessary, the military authorities were to aid in sustaining Texan jurisdiction, or in other words, they were to remain neutral only so long as the Texan interests seemed to be safe.

While the Marcy instructions were still the order to follow, Colonel Washington had written to the adjutant general that "To avoid embarrassment in regard to recognizing the jurisdiction of the authorities of Texas over a large portion of this territory, it is very desirable that Congress should act in the matter before the demand is made."[55] He was already facing the problem as a result of the presence of Baird, and was divided between his interest in maintaining his position with the office holders of the region, and the possible necessity of assisting Baird in accordance with the Marcy orders. His own inclinations apparently led more strongly toward the former, so for this reason Crawford's letter

p. 271. The general orders to the War Department had made the division between the two departments, a line running from the Rio Grande near El Paso, directly to the Red river at the mouth of Choctaw creek, in the vicinity of the one hundredth meridian, thus dividing the territory claimed by Texas. See *House Ex. Doc.* 1, 30th Cong., 2nd sess. (Ser. no. 537), p. 178.

[54]Crawford to Commanding officer at Santa Fé, March 26, 1849, in *Ibid.*, 272.

[55]Washington to Jones, February 3, 1849, in *House Ex. Doc.* 5, 31st Cong., 1st sess. (Ser. no. 569), p. 105.

absolving him from the responsibility of rendering sustenance to Texas, was a relief for him, even though he was to maintain a neutral position.

During the summer of 1849 the movement to secure a civil government in New Mexico was renewed, and in September, in answer to a call issued by Lieutenant-Colonel Benjamin L. Beall, who was acting governor in the absence of Colonel Washington, a convention met at Santa Fé to draw up a new petition to Congress. Beall made this call as a result of a series of resolutions drawn up on August 22, and presented to him by a group of Americans,[56] and on September 10, each of the seven counties of New Mexico[57] named delegates who were to meet on September 24. A considerable faction of the population, led by the military officers, was in favor of establishing a state government, but to this the civil officials were opposed, and here the influence of the instructions from the War Department was felt. The advocates of state government feared that the raising of the question at this time might bring a recognition of the Texan claims, and in order to decrease the probability of a forced connection with that state they were willing to postpone action.[58]

This convention, therefore, declared itself in favor of a territorial, rather than a state form of government, drew up a territorial code of laws, and elected Hugh N. Smith, a Texan, as delegate to Congress, with instructions to secure some sort of Congressional action. The members voted that the division of counties should not be changed except by action of their own legislature. But their definition of the boundaries of the territory is significant. A resolution was passed instructing the delegate to Congress to define the territory as bounded on the north by the Indian

[56]Accounts of these proceedings were copied from the Santa Fé *Republican* by Baird, and enclosed with Baird to Miller, October 20, 1849; in *Santa Fé Papers*, Texas State Library.

[57]By a decree issued July 17, 1844, the department of New Mexico had been divided into the counties of Bernalillo, Rio Arriba, San Miguel, Santa Ana, Santa Fé, Taos, and Valencia, all of which included territory on both sides of the Rio Grande. *Sen. Ex. Doc.* 41, 30th Cong., 1st sess. (Ser. no. 505), p. 478; also Bancroft, *History of Arizona and New Mexico*, 311-312. In the *Bancroft Collection*, University of California, is a "Map of New Mexico with Pueblos as noted by Calhoun, 1850." which shows the boundaries of these counties as conceived by James S. Calhoun, the United States Indian agent in New Mexico.

[58]Calhoun to Brown, November 2, 1849, in Abel (editor), *Official Correspondence of James S. Calhoun*, 70.

territory, on the west by California, on the south by the boundary line between the United States and Mexico, and on the east by the state of Texas.[59] When it is recalled that to the leaders in New Mexico the question of how far to the west the state of Texas extended, was one of the important issues, this failure to specify a definite boundary on that side would indicate that the inhabitants were now ready to follow the suggestion which had been made by President Polk, and to turn the question of the disputed jurisdiction over to Congress to be settled.

But before any results could be obtained from this movement, President Taylor had announced himself as favoring the granting of statehood to both California and New Mexico. Acting upon this policy, Secretary Crawford wrote to Lieutenant-Colonel George A. McCall, who was leaving Washington to join his regiment in New Mexico, informing him that if the people of New Mexico desired to take any steps toward securing admission as a state, it would be his duty, and the duty of others with whom he would be associated, "Not to thwart but advance their wishes," since it was their right to ask for admission.[60]

Two months later, in complying with a request from the House of Representatives for information on the subject of California and New Mexico, President Taylor took advantage of the opportunity to state his views officially, and here he expressed regret that New Mexico had not already been admitted as a state, in order that the boundary question with Texas might be settled by a judicial decision. Since that had not been done, however, he agreed with his predecessor that Congress alone possessed the power of adjustment, and he questioned the expediency of attempting to establish a territorial government there before making such an adjustment.[61] But Congress was already deeply involved in debate over the question, and this message had little effect, other than to furnish new fuel for discussion.

The Question of Control in the El Paso District.—In spite of the attitude which was being manifested in New Mexico, however, new troubles over the jurisdiction were close at hand; for almost

[59]The proceedings of the convention are in *House Ex. Doc.* 17, 31st Cong., 1st sess. (Ser. no. 573), pp. 93-104; available also in Historical Society of New Mexico, *Publications*, No. 10.

[60]Crawford to McCall, November 19, 1849, in *Ibid.*, 280-281.

[61]Taylor's message to Congress, January 21, 1850, in *Ibid.*, 3.

at the same time that the convention of September, 1849, was in session at Santa Fé, Major Jeff Van Horne, a new officer, stationed opposite El Paso, was writing for information as to whether the laws of New Mexico should be enforced at his post. This region was included in the ninth military department, which had its headquarters at Santa Fé, but under Mexican control it had been in Chihuahua, and was now in territory which was included in the Texas boundary act of 1836. It was now a part of the county of Santa Fé, as organized by the Texas legislature, and a group of Texans under the leadership of R. Howard, who claimed to be a legally appointed surveyor for the Texas government, was busy locating Texas claims in the salt deposits of the region. These men claimed the exclusive right to use the salt, or to levy a tax on any others who used it, while at the same time the New Mexican prefect for this district was asking Van Horne to aid him in enforcing the collection of taxes there for New Mexico.[62] Being new to the district, Van Horne was not familiar with the facts of the controversy between Texas and New Mexico, nor with the instructions which had been issued, and he therefore refused to pass judgment until he could receive instructions from the commander of the department.

By the time his inquiry reached Santa Fé, Colonel Washington had been superseded as commander and ex-officio governor of New Mexico, by Colonel John Munroe,[63] and the new commander seems to have been as thoroughly ignorant of the situation, and of the attitude of the government, as was Van Horne himself. He sent the data to the adjutant general of the army, that they might be submitted to "the proper department of the government at Washington, with the view of having the question of jurisdiction determined."[64] Instead of waiting for a reply from the government, however, he wrote to Van Horne that since there was a portion of the territory in question over which no civil authority had been established by either Texas or New Mexico, he deemed it advisable, in order that the people might have the protection of civil laws and magistrates, that the military authority should sustain

[62]Van Horne to Munroe, September 23, 1849, in *Sen. Ex. Doc.* 56, 31st Cong., 1st sess. (Ser. no. 561), p. 3.

[63]General Order No. 3, War Department, May 26, 1849, in *Sen. Ex. Doc.* 60, 31st Cong., 1st sess. (Ser. no. 561), p. 2.

[64]Munroe to Jones, November 21, 1849, in *Sen. Ex. Doc.* 56, *op. cit.*, pp. 2-3.

the civil jurisdiction of the territory of New Mexico, and aid her officials in the execution of their duties until such time as Texas should assume civil jurisdiction, or until the boundary between Texas and New Mexico should be finally settled.[65]

It seems incredible that Munroe could not have had access to Secretary Crawford's letter enjoining strict neutrality, but this letter to Van Horne indicates a complete lack of knowledge that such instructions had ever been issued to the department under his command. In answer to his letter to the adjutant general, he was curtly informed that "The jurisdiction over the soil east of the Rio Grande, claimed by Texas and New Mexico, cannot be settled by this department. The commanding officer must refer to and abide by instructions previously given on this subject."[66] This letter and one from Munroe to the War Department, enclosing a copy of his instructions to Van Horne,[67] seem to have passed each other somewhere between Santa Fé and Washington, and the receipt of the latter by the department officials brought prompt action in the form of a caustic letter to Munroe, which virtually amounted to a reprimand for "manifestly assuming to decide the question of the territorial jurisdiction of Texas," and informing him that "it is deemed necessary distinctly to repeat, for your guidance on this occasion, what the department has often stated, that the executive has no power to adjust and settle the question of territorial limits involved in this case."[68]

A glance at the dates of the letters in this set of correspondence will reveal the lack of promptness on the part of the government agents of this period, as well as some of the handicaps to which the officers in the remote outposts were subjected. Van Horne's letter to Munroe, asking for instructions, was written from the El Paso district, September 23, 1849. It was not forwarded from Santa Fé to the War Department until November 21, while it was not until December 28 that Munroe wrote his answer to Van Horne, and still another week passed before he sent a copy of this letter to Washington. In the meantime, until the arrival of Munroe's second letter, action was equally slow in Washington, for the answer to the letter of November 21 is dated February 15, 1850,

[65]Munroe to Van Horne, December 28, 1849, in *Ibid.*, 4-5.
[66]Jones to Munroe, February 15, 1850, in *Ibid.*, 3-4.
[67]Munroe to Jones, January 3, 1850, in *Ibid.*, 4.
[68]Jones to Munroe, March 8, 1850, in *Ibid.*, 5-6.

and in all probability it did not reach Van Horne for at least six months after his request for instructions. Much could take place in that period of time; and as a matter of fact, much had happened before the correspondence was ended.

The Renewal of Activities by Texas.—During the fall of 1849, while these developments were in progress in New Mexico, Texas had no official agent in the region. Baird was now in Missouri, and from there was sending reports to the officials in Texas concerning the results of his mission, together with such information as he could secure upon the course of events after his departure from New Mexico in July.[69] Earlier information which had come from him aroused considerable resentment in Texas, and in the campaign of 1849 for the election of a governor, Wood was opposed for re-election by P. Hansborough Bell, who advocated action by Texas. Bell was elected, and almost immediately he began to receive applications for permission to raise companies of soldiers for the purpose of occupying New Mexico.[70]

In his final annual message to the Texas legislature, on November 6, 1849, Governor Wood referred to the opposition which Baird had received in New Mexico, but stated that no official report had been received from him at that time, nor had he received a reply for his letters to either Polk or Taylor.[71] This situation, he told the legislators, "imposes upon you the necessity of adopting energetic and efficient measures to protect the rights of your State and acquit herself of what is due to her honor and dignity." Since a previous effort to legislate Texas into possession had apparently failed, he felt that the question had now become one "with which there should be no temporizing, for the sooner the issue is made the sooner will the question be adjusted." He therefore recommended that the governor be given ample power and

[69]These reports were made in seven letters to Washington D. Miller, Texan secretary of state, written at irregular intervals from September 21 to November 6, 1849, and are now in the *Santa Fé Papers*, Texas State Library.

[70]Copies of these letters are in the *Santa Fé Papers*. By the fall of 1850, Bell had received dozens of such letters, many of them from other southern states. Most of them are checked as having been answered October 18, 1850, by C. A. Harrison, private secretary to the governor.

[71]This would indicate that Bancroft, *History of the North Mexican States and Texas*, II, 398, is in error in stating that Wood was notified by the authorities at Washington that any attempt at forcible occupation of New Mexico would be considered as an intrusion.

means to raise the proper issue and contest it, "not by demonstrating in argument the justice of our claims, nor by reference to our statutes, but with the whole power and resources of the State."[72] In addition to this, he suggested that a commissioner be sent to Washington as soon as some plan should be adopted, in order to show the federal government that Texas was in earnest.

This portion of the message was submitted by the lower house of the legislature to its committee on federal relations, and this group, on November 13, reported a resolution giving the governor the power and means to send a special commissioner to Washington, to "ascertain the exact views of the Federal Government, in relation to the county of Santa Fe, in time to lay the same before the Legislature during their present session." Further action upon the subject was to be suspended until this report could be received.[73] Before action could be taken upon this resolution, the senate, on November 14, began the consideration of a resolution providing for a special joint committee of the two houses to prepare a protest against the further continuance of the military government at Santa Fé, to be laid before Congress.[74] This resolution was adopted, and was agreed to by the lower house on November 23.[75] Wood's plans for action were thus checkmated, in spite of the fact that newspaper comment upon his attitude was favorable at this time. Hopes were expressed that the legislature would comply with his recommendation,[76] while one editor went so far as to say that the "banner of the Lone Star shall be again unfurled; not for *offence,* but for *defence,* and those who were foremost to cry aloud for annexation, will be foremost to sever the country from a *Union* that embraces but to crush and destroy."[77]

Just at this juncture a letter from Major P. J. Pillans, whom Baird had left in charge of his affairs in Santa Fé, was made public in Texas. In it Pillans stated that the opposition to Texas

[72]Austin *State Gazette,* November 10, 1849.

[73]*Ibid.,* November 17, 1849. No bound voume of the House Journals for the third legislature is available, but the *Gazette* printed the journals of both houses, in full.

[74]*Ibid.,* November 24, 1849; also *Senate Journal,* 3rd Legislature, 117.

[75]*Ibid.,* December 1, 1849.

[76]See Houston *Telegraph and Texas Register,* Austin *State Gazette,* Nacogdoches *Times,* and Marshall *Texas Republican,* for this period.

[77]Austin *State Gazette,* December 1, 1849.

in Santa Fé could never be overcome.[78] At the same time Baird's reports had begun to arrive, and in one of them he stated that one of the secrets of opposition on the part of the people in New Mexico was a fear that grants of land which had been made previously would become void under Texan jurisdiction.[79] In order to counteract this feeling, the lower house of the legislature, on December 3, adopted a resolution looking toward the passage of a law under which the citizens of Santa Fé might be granted land within the limits of Santa Fé county as it then existed.[80] During this same week, however, news reached Texas concerning the New Mexican convention which had been called by Colonel Beall. Intense excitement was manifested, and an immediate forcible occupation of the region was advocated.[81] But Governor Wood's administration was too near its close for any definite steps to be taken, and his final act in the matter was the submitting of Baird's correspondence, to the legislature, on December 11.[82] Baird, himself, had by this time become disheartened because of criticism of his work by the newspapers, and expressed his determination to resign as soon as possible.[83]

In his first message to the legislature, Bell referred to the repeated disregard by the federal authorities for the Texan rights in New Mexico, and agreed with Wood that the question should be brought to an issue at once. The failure of the legislature to support Wood's recommendations, however, led him to suggest that it was not necessary that the whole power and resources of the state should be placed at the disposal of the governor, but that he should be authorized "to send to Santa Fé, if the necessity for doing so shall continue to exist, a military force *sufficient* to enable the civil authorities to execute the laws of the State in that part of the territory, without reference to any anticipated action of the Federal Government, or regard to the military power of the United States stationed at Santa Fe." In his opinion this force should be used only in case the citizens of Santa Fé continued reluctant

[78]*Ibid.*, December 29, 1849, quoting from the Bonham *Advertiser*.

[79]Baird to Miller, September 23, 1849, in *Santa Fé Papers*, Texas State Library.

[80]Austin *State Gazette*, December 22, 1849.

[81]*Ibid.*, December 8, 1849.

[82]*Senate Journal*, 3rd Legislature, 223.

[83]Baird to Evans, December 11, 1849, in Marshall *Texas Republican*, January 24, 1850.

to submit to the civil jurisdiction of Texas, after the military forces of the United States ceased to exercise such functions. He also concurred with Wood on the question of sending a commissioner to Washington, but felt that Texas should first decide upon the course to be pursued in case the mission proved futile, in order that the commissioner might at once make known the position of his state.[84] This same message also included a suggestion that the territory lying north of the parallel of thirty-six degrees, thirty minutes, be sold to the United States government for the purpose of liquidating the public debt of the state.[85]

The legislature now became active once more, and on December 31, 1849, new boundaries were designated for Santa Fé county, decreasing its size, and from the remainder of the original county, as organized in 1848, the three new counties of Presidio, El Paso, and Worth were created.[86] Presidio county was to include all the territory between the Rio Pecos and the Rio Grande, from the junction of the two rivers north to a line running straight northeast to the Pecos from a point on the Rio Grande where the Ford and Neighbors trail first touches that stream, "as defined by a map compiled by Robert Creuzbaur, date of 1849." This map shows the trail as striking the Rio Grande about one hundred miles south of El Paso.[87]

El Paso county included the territory between the two rivers from the northern boundary of Presidio county to a line extending from a point on the Rio Grande, twenty miles above the town of San Diego, due eastward to the Pecos. This line was also to form the southern boundary of Worth county, which was to cover the

[84]Bell's message to the legislature, December 26, 1849, in *Senate Journal*, 3rd Legislature, 285-287; also in Austin *State Gazette*, December 29, 1849.

[85]Similar suggestions had been made previously by both Henderson and Wood, but these seem to have been for an indiscriminate sale of any unoccupied lands within the state. See Miller, *Financial History of Texas*, 118. Memucan Hunt, attorney for a number of the creditors, in 1849, published a pamphlet entitled *The Public Debt and Lands of Texas*, and in this he seems to have originated the idea of selling a definite portion of the territory claimed by the state. For a reference to the pamphlet and a brief sketch of its contents, see *De Bow's Commercial Review*, VII, 273. A copy of the pamphlet itself, is in the *Bancroft Collection*, University of California.

[86]Gammel, *Laws of Texas*, III, 462-463.

[87]The map is in Creuzbaur, *Guide to California and the Pacific Coast*. See also a letter from James S. Ford to the editor of the *Texas Democrat*, written June 18, 1849, in *Ibid.*, 4-5.

region northward to a line running directly east to the Pecos from a point on the Rio Grande twenty miles above the town of Sabine. The remainder of the region which had formerly been allotted to Santa Fé county was now designated as the new county of Santa Fé.[88] The four counties were specified as the eleventh judicial district,[89] and in the reapportionment of representatives in the Texas legislature, the four were combined into one senatorial district, while Santa Fé county was allowed a representative in the lower house, and the other three counties together were given a representative.[90]

On January 4, 1850, an act was passed providing for the appointment of a commissioner to organize each county, by laying it off into convenient districts, or precincts, and by holding elections for county officers, and notifying the proper state official of the result of these elections.[91] On the following day Governor Bell drew up an address to the citizens of these four counties, in which he explained that their territory had long been included in the limits of Texas, but that the necessity of centering her attention upon the struggle for independence had rendered it impracticable to organize the region earlier. They were now informed that organization had been provided for, and that Robert S. Neighbors had been selected by the governor to accomplish this organization, the principal motive being to extend to them the advantages which other Texans held; and they were therefore invited to "hold the most free and unrestricted intercourse with him and . . . to lend him such assistance and protection" as his presence among them might require.[92]

Neighbors was instructed to proceed as quickly as possible to the counties which were to be organized, and to circulate this address, which, it was thought, should prepare the people for ready acquiescence. His method of procedure upon arrival was explained, and he was especially warned that while he should act with firmness and decision, he should also "observe that mildness and courtesy of manner which is so well calculated to inspire confidence and esteem, and remove all prejudices which may hereto-

[88]Gammel, *Laws of Texas*, III, 459-460.

[89]*Ibid.*, III, 462.

[90]*Ibid.*, III, 479, 481.

[91]*Ibid.*, III, 464-465.

[92]*Senate Journal*, 3rd Legislature, 2nd sess., appendix, 69-71; also Houston *Telegraph and Texas Register*, March 7, 1850.

fore have existed in respect to the government, and our people as a race."[93] He was already familiar with the country which he was to organize, having been a special Indian agent for the United States government in the El Paso region, and he set out at once to begin his work.[94] His salary as commissioner was voted to him in advance,[95] and at the same time the legislature resolved that all the territory east of the Rio Grande was included in the rightful civil and political jurisdiction of the state, and that she was determined to maintain the integrity of this territory.[96]

Baird at once began to make preparations for returning to Santa Fé in order to be on hand to hold court as soon as Neighbors succeeded in organizing the region. Before leaving Austin, however, he submitted to Governor Bell a series of suggestions, covering numerous points which had been omitted in the plans for organization, and which he deemed to be necessary, in order to gain the confidence of the people of that region. Among other things, he felt that the territory should have been divided into seven counties, corresponding with the ones then existing under the Mexican law; that the Pueblo Indians should be induced to settle on the frontiers; that the Mexican laws with regard to irrigation, mining, and herding cattle should be perpetuated; that the wood and the salt deposits should be reserved from private appropriation and declared to be the common property of the people for their free use; and that English schools should be established there to the full extent of the means that could be raised by Texas.[97] During his previous stay in the region, he had apparently been studying the situation, but the officials in Texas failed to recognize the soundness of his suggestions, and therefore no changes were made in the plans for organization.

[93]Webb to Neighbors, January 8, 1850, in *Senate Journal*, 3rd Legislature, 2nd sess., appendix, 72-74.

[94]Bancroft, *History of Arizona and New Mexico*, 455, purports to give the personnel of the Neighbors party, but the party named was one which accompanied him in the spring of 1849, on one of his trips as Indian agent. See Ford to the editor of the *Texas Democrat*, June 18, 1849, in Creuzbaur, *Guide to California and the Pacific Coast*, 4.

[95]Gammel, *Laws of Texas*, III, 773. Neighbors was later granted the sum of $1256.51 to reimburse him for expenditures made while on this mission. *Ibid.*, III, 786.

[96]*Ibid.*, III, 645-646; also Bancroft, *History of the North Mexican States and Texas*, II, 399.

[97]Baird to Bell, February 27, 1850, in *Senate Journal*, 3rd Legislature, 2nd sess., appendix, 74-81.

El Paso was reached by Neighbors about the middle of February, and he began his work of organization there. On February 23, Major Van Horne reported to the authorities at Santa Fé that the Texas commissioner was busy holding elections and circulating messages from the governor of Texas.[98] Van Horne felt that according to Munroe's instructions of December 28, which were the last he had received, one of the two conditions had come upon when the civil jurisdiction of his command could be surrendered to Texas, and therefore, he offered no opposition. On the same date, Neighbors himself wrote to Munroe, stating that since he had found no opposition to the extension of the Texan jurisdiction in the El Paso region, he had issued writs of election, and expected to accomplish the organization there in a short time. He added that as soon as was possible he would proceed to Santa Fé, and upon his arrival there he would submit to Munroe his instructions from the governor of Texas, and ask for his "friendly co-operation in organizing all the territory belonging to this state, into counties, and to extend over the inhabitants, the civil laws of the state."[99]

One month later, he reported to Governor Bell that El Paso county was fully organized, and that the officers who had been elected had entered upon the discharge of their duties.[100] According to other reports which reached Austin, the people of El Paso were highly gratified at being organized under the laws of Texas, and 765 votes were cast in the election for county officers.[101] Neighbors now reported that it was impossible to go to Presidio county without an armed escort, because of the enmity between the Indians and the few white inhabitants of the region, and also that the organization of Worth county would depend upon that of Santa Fé, since both were under the same influence. In the accomplishment of the latter, he felt that he faced two handicaps: first, a lack of necessary funds, and, second, the absence of proper pledges to the people in regard to their lands. He com-

[98]Van Horne to McLaws, February 23, 1850, in Abel (editor), *Official Correspondence of James S. Calhoun*, 163.

[99]Neighbors to Munroe, February 23, 1850, in *House Ex. Doc.* 66, 31st Cong., 1st sess. (Ser. no. 577), p. 2.

[100]Neighbors to Bell, March 23, 1850, in *Senate Journal*, 3rd Legislature, 2nd sess., appendix, 1-6.

[101]Austin *State Gazette*, April 27, and May 4, 1850. William Cockburn arrived from El Paso, April 26, and brought this information.

plained that Howard and his party, concerning whom Van Horne had been inquiring, were already located on land belonging to others, thus causing prejudice against Texas.[102]

At the time that Neighbors' letter of February 23 reached Santa Fé no answer for Colonel Munroe's letter of the previous November had as yet come from Washington, but he had at least found the earlier instructions. He at once issued orders to all officers commanding posts in and near the territory claimed by the state of Texas, to "observe a rigid non-interference" with Neighbors "in the exercise of his Functions and equally avoid coming in conflict with the Judicial authorities created by that State."[103] When the reports began to reach Santa Fé that a Texas commissioner was on his way to organize New Mexico, there was talk of resistance,[104] and this spirit was encouraged by a proclamation published on the next day after Munroe issued his orders for strict neutrality, by Joab Houghton, one of the judges of the superior court in New Mexico under the military government. In this proclamation, Houghton advised the people not to go to the polls which the Texas commissioner would open, for they should be neither loyal nor obedient to Texas, but on the contrary, were in duty bound to resist any attempt on her part "for the unjust usurpation of our land and boundaries." He proposed that each county hold meetings on the following Monday for the purpose of drawing up resolutions upon the Texan claims, and felt that if the people would observe his directions, "the present mission of the Commissioner of Texas will be as useless as that of Judge Baird."[105]

Thus when Neighbors arrived in Santa Fé on April 8, he not only found that he would be forced to work without the assistance of the military officers, but also that he would receive little encouragement from the people themselves. He reported, however, that he was courteously received by the inhabitants, but that he

[102]Neighbors to Bell, March 23, 1850, *op. cit.*

[103]Munroe to Beall and others, March 12, 1850, in *House Ex. Doc.* 66, 31st Cong., 1st sess. (Ser. no. 577), p. 2; also in Abel (editor), *Correspondence of James S. Calhoun*, 164.

[104]Calhoun to Brown, March 16, 1850, in Abel, *op. cit.*, 163. A similar report was carried to St. Louis by traders from Santa Fé. See Austin *State Gazette*, May 25, 1850.

[105]Houghton's proclamation, March 13, 1850, in *Senate Journal*, 3rd Legislature, 2nd sess., appendix, 11-12; also in Austin *State Gazette*, June 8, 1850.

found Munroe favorable to the existing state of affairs, while Houghton expressed a determination to imprison any person who should attempt to enforce the laws of Texas. He was told by members of the original state party that they were now willing to aid him in the organization, but that they believed that it would be necessary for Texas to send a military force to New Mexico before she could exercise jurisdiction.[106] Feeling, however, that those inhabitants who were favorable to Texas were in the minority under the existing state of affairs, Neighbors now decided to defer the calling of an election for Santa Fé county as organized by the legislature of Texas.[107]

But at about the same time that Neighbors reached Santa Fé, Colonel McCall also arrived with information concerning the attitude of the President toward statehood, and in the new possibilities, Neighbors was ignored. As a result of McCall's message notices were posted, on April 13, calling the citizens of Santa Fé county, New Mexico, to a meeting to be held a week later for the purpose of passing resolutions in favor of a state form of government, and of requesting the governor of the territory to call a convention to form a state constitution.[108] As soon as Neighbors had seen these notices, he protested to Colonel Munroe against such an action, on the basis of the constitutional provision that no state should be formed within the jurisdiction of another state, without the consent of the legislature of the state concerned. He held that since the government of Texas had expressed its determination to maintain inviolate all the territory within her boundaries, which had been guaranteed to her by the annexation resolution, the move for a state government in New Mexico would be a violation of that provision.[109]

Munroe was now confronted with a dilemma. He had not only received instructions to maintain neutrality in the boundary dispute, but he had also been told through Colonel McCall to give assistance to any steps which the people of New Mexico might desire to take toward securing a state government. Under ordi-

[106]Neighbors to Bell, June 4, 1850, in *Ibid.*, 7-10.

[107]*Idem;* Davis, *El Gringo*, 110-111, states that he issued a proclamation calling an election, but no evidence of this is to be found in Neighbors' own reports.

[108]*Sen. Ex. Doc.* 56, 31st Cong., 1st sess. (Ser. no. 561), p. 14.

[109]Neighbors to Munroe, April 14, 1850, in *Ibid.*, 15; also *Senate Journal*, 3rd Legislature, 2nd sess., appendix, 12.

nary circumstances, these instructions would have caused no trouble, but owing to the fact that the Texas government was at the time attempting to organize the region, the move for a state government in New Mexico meant a direct conflict with the Texan claims. But he did not hesitate long. Just three days after the meeting was held to formulate the petition to him, he issued a proclamation naming May 15 as the date for the desired constitutional convention.[110]

None of his actions in connection with the question seemed destined to receive the full approval of the various departments of the government, however, for before the summer was over his course was questioned from three different causes, by as many different parties. His order of March 12, enjoining non-interference on the part of the commanders under him, brought a resolution from the House of Representatives, asking the President for an explanation. In reply, the Secretary of War referred the members to the letters of instructions written by both himself and his predecessor to the commanding officer at Santa Fé.[111] A short time afterward, the Senate took up the matter from another angle, and demanded of the President, information concerning the orders which had authorized Colonel Munroe to oppose or prevent the exercise of Texan jurisdiction over the Santa Fé region. Aside from Munroe's mistake of December 28, which had by this time been corrected by the order of March 12, this was a deliberate disregard for the actual happenings. President Taylor answered that no such orders had been given, and submitted to the Senate the correspondence in connection with Van Horne's inquiry of September 23. He then brought up the question of the activity of Neighbors in the New Mexico region, and stated that although he had "no power to decide the question of boundary, and no desire to interfere with it," he believed that the territory in question was actually acquired by the United States from Mexico, and had since been held by the United States. For this reason, it was his opinion that it "ought so to remain until the question of boundary shall have been determined by some competent authority."[112] And he had stated earlier what he deemed this competent authority to be. This meant another step in the adminis-

[110] *Sen. Ex. Doc.* 60, Part II, 31st Cong., 1st sess. (Ser. no. 561), p. 2.
[111] *House Ex. Doc.* 65, 31st Cong., 1st sess. (Ser. no. 577), p. 1.
[112] *Sen. Ex. Doc.* 56, 31st Cong., 1st sess. (Ser. no. 561), p. 1.

tration's attitude on the question. The policy had developed from the instructions under Polk, that neutrality was to be broken only in case of need from Texas, through the early policy of the Taylor administration, of non-interference with the Texan efforts; and now non-interference was made to apply the other way. Texas should not attempt to interfere with the possession of the territory by the United States.

The question which caused the greatest excitement, however, came from the governor of Texas. As soon as Munroe issued his proclamation calling a constitutional convention, Neighbors withdrew from Santa Fé, and immediately upon his arrival at the Texas capital he submitted to Governor Bell a detailed report upon his mission.[113] When the contents of this report became public, the anger of the Texans was at once aroused. It was held that the action of Munroe was an insult of the grossest character, and committed upon the rights and dignity of the people of Texas "an outrage beyond which it was not possible to go." They felt that the matter had now been brought to a definite issue, and suggestions were made that the claim should be enforced by military power,[114] while it was also claimed that when Texas was admitted into the Union as a state, her people believed that the limits as defined by the government of the republic would be respected. If they had been in error when they voted for annexation, it was but just, according to their belief, that the whole question should be reconsidered, and in that case they were represented as being as willing to leave the Union as they had been to join it. A mass meeting which was held at Austin on June 8 gave voice to these sentiments,[115] and during the months of June, July, and August, similar meetings were held throughout the state, all of them expressing the same sentiments.[116]

Governor Bell at once took steps to meet the situation. On June 12, he wrote to Baird, who had returned to Santa Fé, urging him to leave that place immediately, and proceed to El Paso

[113]Neighbors to Bell, June 4, 1850, *Senate Journal*, 3rd Legislature, 2nd sess., appendix, 7-10.

[114]Austin *State Gazette*, June 8, and 15, 1850.

[115]*Ibid.*, June 15, 1850; also *Niles' Register*, LXXV, 156-157.

[116]*Ibid., passim.* On August 14, the La Grange *Texas Monument* states: "There has been but one solitary meeting in the State, we believe, which has passed a resolution declaring the opinion that the time has not arrived for action."

in order to check any attempts which might be made to shake the allegiance of that region to Texas. At the same time he was to keep the governor advised concerning the developments at Santa Fé.[117] On June 13, he wrote to the Texan delegation in Congress, stating the situation, and voicing his intention to act,[118] while on the following day he wrote to President Taylor, demanding an explanation of the steps taken by Munroe, especially as to whether he had acted under orders from his government, and whether his proclamation met the approval of the President.[119] In addition to this, a special session of the legislature was called for August 12, in order that the methods for meeting the situation might be properly determined upon.[120]

The letter to the President did not reach Washington until after Taylor's death, and therefore went to his successor, who placed it in the hands of Daniel Webster, the new Secretary of State, to be answered. Webster answered the first of the two questions asked by Governor Bell, by quoting from the instructions of November 19, to Colonel McCall, thus upholding Munroe's action. In answer to the second question, he stated that if the call for a convention intended to settle the boundary question, it was not approved by President Fillmore, for the oft repeated reason that the power of making that settlement belonged solely to Congress. But he held that such was not the intention of the convention, and pointed out that it could not make such a settlement because its acts were ineffectual until they were ratified by Congress. And he added that since "it is the right of all to petition Congress for any law which it may constitutionally pass, this people were in the exercise of a common right when they formed their constitution with a view to applying to Congress for admission as a state," and for this reason the President felt bound to approve the conduct of Colonel Munroe in issuing the proclamation.[121] Throughout the letter there can be seen a veiled suggestion that Texas had as little authority to interfere in the boundary question, as had the President; and there is also a carefully worded hint that unless she

[117]Bell to Baird, June 12, 1850, in *Senate Journal*, 3rd Legislature, 2nd sess., appendix, 81-83.

[118]Austin *State Gazette*, July 13, 1850.

[119]Bell to Taylor, June 14, 1850, in *House Ex. Doc.* 82, 31st Cong., 1st sess. (Ser. no. 579), pp. 6-7.

[120]Austin *State Gazette*, July 6, 1850.

[121]Webster to Bell, August 5, 1850, in *House Ex. Doc.* 82, *op. cit.*, 7-12.

refrained from interfering, it would be the duty of the President to see that the treaty of Guadalupe Hidalgo, as a part of the supreme law of the land, was sustained in every particular, down to the maintaining of the inhabitants of the territory in the free enjoyment of their liberty and property.

In submitting this correspondence to Congress, however, President Fillmore was less guarded than Webster had been in his language. He reiterated the claim, on the New Mexican side, that the territory had always been regarded as an integral and essential part of New Mexico, and after stating that the Texas legislature had been called into session for the purpose of establishing her own jurisdiction, and her own laws over the region by force, he added:

> These proceedings of Texas may well arrest the attention of all branches of the government of the United States; and I rejoice that they occur while the Congress is yet in session. It is, I fear, far from being impossible, that in consequence of these proceedings of Texas, a crisis may be brought on which shall summon the two houses of Congress—and still more emphatically the executive government—to an immediate readiness for the performance of their respective duties. . . . The constitutional duty of the President is plain and peremptory, and the authority vested in him by law for its performance, clear and simple. . . . If Texas militia, therefore, march into any one of the other states, or into any territory of the United States, there to execute or enforce any law of Texas, they . . . are to be regarded merely as intruders; and if, within such state or territory, they obstruct any law of the United States, either by power of arms, or mere power of numbers, constituting such a combination as is too powerful to be suppressed by the civil authority, the President of the United States has no option left to him, but is bound to obey the solemn injunction of the Constitution, and exercise the high powers vested in him by that instrument and by the acts of Congress.[122]

In sending this message to Congress, the President submitted no other evidence than Governor Bell's letter and Webster's reply, and the meagerness of the information furnished concerning the probability of forceful measures in Texas made the tone of the message decidedly alarmist. That government officials had more information concerning the actual developments in Texas than they cared to divulge, however, is shown in the work of General Winfield Scott, who was at the time acting Secretary of War. On the same day that Fillmore's message was written, General Scott

[122]Fillmore's message to Congress, August 6, 1850, in *Ibid.*, 1-6.

notified Colonel Munroe that about 750 additional troops were being sent to Santa Fé, for the double purpose of protecting against Indians, and against "another and more painful contingency" which might be apprehended. This new contingency, he explained, was the probability that unless the disputed boundary between Texas and New Mexico was soon established by Congress, a large body of troops would be raised by Texas and sent to New Mexico to effect by force of arms the extension of the Texan civil and political jurisdiction over that part east of the Rio Grande. In order that Munroe might be able to meet the demands in event this should happen, Scott proceeded to give him full instructions as to the necessary course of action under the various probable methods of procedure which might be used by the Texan invaders. Munroe was told, however, to profit by all opportunities to avoid a resort to violence; but a warning was also added, not to lose any advantage by delaying, and to resist the encroachment vigorously when it became necessary to protect the people of New Mexico against violence and the destruction of their property.[123]

During the same time that this official correspondence was being carried on, developments were also under way in the region which was being discussed. The convention for the formation of a state constitution, which had met on May 15, in accordance with Munroe's call, completed its work on May 25, and within a month the constitution had been adopted by practically a unanimous vote.[124] The limits prescribed for the state were to begin at the Rio Grande just north of El Paso, and extend from there east to the one hundredth meridian; thence north along the one hundredth meridian to the Arkansas river; thence up that stream to its source; thence in a direct line to the Colorado river of the West at its intersection with the one hundred and eleventh meridian; thence south on that meridian to the boundary between the United States and Mexico, and along that boundary back to the Rio Grande, down which it was to run to the point of beginning.[125] The notable feature in this boundary is the fact that just as the Texas boundary act of 1836 had included territory which by right of occupation belonged

[123]Scott to Munroe, August 5, 1850, in Abel (editor), *Official Correspondence of James S. Calhoun*, 164-165.

[124]The vote was 6,771 for the constitution; 39 against it. *Sen. Ex. Doc.* 74, 31st Cong., 1st sess. (Ser. no. 562), p. 2.

[125]*Ibid.*, 2-3.

to New Mexico, so did this constitutional provision reciprocate by laying claim to territory which Spanish decrees unquestionably included in Texas. But it was at last a definite boundary claim on the part of New Mexico—the first tangible limits which had ever been named for a province established 250 years previously.

The adoption of a state constitution did not, however, bring an end for the complications in New Mexico. In the election of state officers, Henry Connelly was chosen governor, and Manuel Alvarez, lieutenant-governor.[126] In the absence of Connelly, Alvarez assumed charge of the government and proceeded to nominate such officers as the constitution required. Here Colonel Munroe interposed with the declaration that the military authority remained in force until Congress agreed to the admission of New Mexico as a state, or substituted some other form of government, and that he would consider any move to appoint officers "as an act, on the part of all concerned, in direct violation of their duties as citizens of the United States."[127] Alvarez proved obstinate, however, and refused to concede that the military government could continue to exist without the consent of the people, and on July 20, he issued a proclamation, in accordance with an act of the legislature established by the constitution, ordering elections to be held on the second Monday in August for the purpose of choosing county officers in each of the eight counties[128] of the state.[129]

On the same day, Baird, who, not having received Governor Bell's letter of June 12, was still in Santa Fé, issued a proclamation for the holding of an election in Santa Fé county, Texas, for the purpose of choosing both state and county officers under the Texas rule. This election was to be held on the first Monday in August, in accordance with a proclamation of the governor of Texas, calling for a general election throughout the state.[130] This situation seemed to forebode trouble for Colonel Munroe, and as a result, three days later, on July 23, he issued a proclamation announcing his purpose of maintaining the military organization

[126]Bancroft, *History of Arizona and New Mexico*, 448.

[127]Munroe to Alvarez, July 12, 1850, in Austin *State Gazette*, September 14, 1850.

[128]Socorro county had been created from a part of the territory of Valencia county, by a legislative act, approved July 5. 1850.

[129]This proclamation appears in Abel (editor), *Official Correspondence of James S. Calhoun*, 234.

[130]*Ibid.*, 233.

in New Mexico until he was otherwise instructed from Washington.[131] Not much excitement seems to have been aroused over these three conflicting efforts,[132] and Munroe's disposition of his troops effectively prevented either of the two elections from being held.[133] Thus with the military government once more firmly in control of affairs in New Mexico, there was nothing to be done in that region but to await the decision of Congress upon the question of organization and of territorial jurisdiction. Baird moved on to El Paso, therefore, and announced his intention of holding court in that place on the first Monday in October.[134]

In Texas, however, during this same period, developments of a different nature were in progress. The legislature met on August 12, in accordance with the call of the governor, and on the following day he submitted his message. In it he reviewed the most prominent facts and circumstances connected with the Texan relations with Santa Fé, and described the development of opposition, both local and national, stating at the same time his belief that the state had no choice but to meet the situation. He said:

> It must be met boldly and fearlessly and determinedly. Not by further supplication or discussion with the Federal authorities. Not by renewed appeals to their generosity and sympathy. Not by a longer reliance on the delusive hope that justice will yet be extended to us; but by action, manly and determined action on our part, by a prompt assertion of our rights, and a practical maintainance of them with all the means we can command *'at all hazards and to the last extremity.'*

He repeated, therefore, his request of the previous December that he be authorized to raise a force sufficient to occupy Santa Fé, and made suggestions as to the methods of securing the necessary funds for financing such a move.[135] As a preparatory measure, Bell made plans to issue commissions for the raising of such a force, in order that it might be ready in case the legislature granted the

[131] *Ibid.*, 234-235.

[132] Calhoun to Brown, July 31, 1850, in *Ibid.*, 232.

[133] Calhoun to Brown, August 13, 1850, in *Ibid.*, 252-253.

[134] La Grange *Texas Monument*, September 25, 1850.

[135] Bell's message to the legislature, August 13, 1850, in *Senate Journal*, 3rd Legislature, 2nd sess., 1 ff. In commenting upon this message the La Grange *Texas Monument*, August 21, 1850, states that at least two regiments should be raised.

authority, and it was estimated that at least five thousand men were ready to volunteer for the undertaking.[136]

The legislature spent the first two weeks of the session in a general discussion, but on August 26, Webster's letter of August 5 to Governor Bell arrived in Austin, and was immediately submitted to both houses.[137] Action began at once. On the same day the senate took up a bill to provide for organizing the militia of Texas, and requiring the governor to call into the service of the state three thousand mounted volunteers, for the purpose of suppressing the insurrection in the counties of Worth and Santa Fé.[138] Other bills were also introduced, providing the necessary funds, by setting aside special amounts from the school fund of the state; by levying a special tax upon the assessments of that year; and by allowing the use of the proceeds which might arise from the sale of lots to be placed at the disposal of the government in the city of Austin.[139] News was also received at the same time that Congress seemed likely to reach a decision soon,[140] and on the following day an effort was made to add to the bill authorizing the raising of a military force, a clause providng that if the United States government should make a proposition to Texas, before January 1, 1851, for the purchase of any portion of the territory of the state, including the whole, or any part, of the counties of Worth and Santa Fé, the governor should submit this proposition to the voters of the state for their rejection or acceptance. In case of their acceptance, the legislature was to be convened to confirm the sale; in case of their rejection, the governor was to proceed to call together the troops.[141] This was finally passed as a separate bill, and was vetoed by Bell for technical reasons. The legislature then adjourned on September 6, without taking any other definite action upon the question, much to the disappointment of a large proportion of the people of the state.[142] This left nothing for the Texans, themselves, but to follow the example of the New

[136]Austin *State Gazette*, August 24, and 31, 1850.

[137]*Senate Journal*, 3rd Legislature, 2nd sess., 36.

[138]*Ibid.*, 44-45.

[139]*Ibid.*, 48-50. These bills followed the suggestions made by Bell in his message of August 13.

[140]Austin *State Gazette*, August 31, 1850.

[141]*Senate Journal*, 3rd Legislature, 2nd sess., 56.

[142]Austin *State Gazette*, September 7, 1850.

Mexicans in waiting for news of Congressional action upon their boundary claims.

Congressional Action upon the Question.—Throughout the entire period of two years in which these local developments were taking place, Congress was also deeply involved in discussing exactly the same problem.[143] Even before the close of the war, in 1848, the question of boundaries had been brought up in that body, and the discussion had gradually changed from a partisan to a sectional character as a result of the slavery question. By the early months of 1850 the situation had become sufficiently acute to alarm such a leader as Henry Clay, with the result that he included the question of the western boundary of Texas in his series of resolutions which he hoped would bring about "an amicable arrangement of all questions in controversy between the free and the slave states, growing out of the subject of slavery."[144] Two months of discussion failed to bring about a settlement, and on April 19 the Senate selected a committee of thirteen members, with Clay as chairman, to work out a scheme of compromise which would adjust all the questions with which slavery was connected.[145] On May 8, this committee submitted the series of measures which came to be known as the Compromise Bill of 1850, and included in the proposals was a new provision for the settlement of the Texas boundary.[146]

The suggestions naturally brought further discussion, and it was while this debate was in progress in Congress that Neighbors reported to the governor of Texas concerning his failure in organizing the New Mexican region for his state. Governor Bell's protest reached Washington in July, and President Fillmore's message of August 6 found the discussion at fever heat. The danger which this message implied, of a conflict in the southwest, together with reports which were reaching the capital concerning the attitude of Texas, brought an awakening to the absolute necessity of a speedy settlement of the issues involved, in order to prevent a

[143]This phase of the question is better known, and therefore a brief summary is sufficient for the purpose of the present paper. The fullest statement of the activities of Congress during 1850 in connection with the subject, is Spillman, *Adjustment of the Texas Boundary, 1850,* in THE QUARTERLY, VII, 177-195.

[144]*Congressional Globe,* 31st Cong., 1st sess., 244-245.

[145]*Ibid.,* 774, 780.

[146]*Ibid.,* 944-948.

general rebellion.[147] In order to hasten the settlement of the slavery question, James A. Pearce, of Maryland, had already moved in the Senate to strike out of the compromise measure all that related to Texas and New Mexico.[148] This motion was adopted, thus bringing the first step in the break up of the compromise, and Pearce then introduced a bill providing for the establishment of the northern and western boundary of the state of Texas, and for the relinquishment of the territory claimed by her outside of the limits which he defined. The lines suggested by him form the present boundary of Texas, and in consideration of the reduction of her boundaries from those previously claimed, Texas was to receive ten million dollars.[149]

The new dangers which had arisen brought about the immediate consideration of this bill, and it was passed by Congress, after an amendment was added, providing for the organization of New Mexico as a territory, and was signed by President Fillmore on September 9. In November the legislature of Texas voted to accept its provisions, thus bringing to a close a controversy which had brought grave dangers for the national government. The boundary thus agreed upon was far enough west to conciliate the Texans; far enough north to please various interests in the United States; and far enough east to satisfy the advocates of the New Mexican rights; while the sum offered to Texas was almost the exact amount needed to cancel her public debt. Each of the three interested parties had been forced to make concessions, and yet each had gained its fundamental aims, and therefore the settlement made would seem to present the nearest possible approach to the establishment of justice for all.

[147]Alexander H. Stephens, of Georgia, declared in the House that "The first Federal gun that shall be fired against the people of Texas without the authority of the law will be a signal for the freemen from the Delaware to the Rio Grande to rally to the rescue." *Ibid.*, appendix, 1083. Clay expressed a similar fear. *Ibid.*, appendix, 1412.

[148]*Ibid.*, appendix, 1473, 1479, 1487.

[149]*Ibid.*, 1555.

MIRABEAU BUONAPARTE LAMAR

A. K. CHRISTIAN

CHAPTER IV

FRONTIER DEFENCE

I. *Relations with Miscellaneous Indian Tribes*

In order to make clear the policy of Lamar in dealing with the Indians, it will be necessary to discuss in some detail the methods used by his predecessors in attempting to keep the peace. It will not be necessary, however, to give a detailed history of the various tribes which occupied Texas. It will suffice at this point to say that the usual classification used during the days of the Republic depended upon the degree of civilization adopted, and the terms "Wild Indians" and "Civilized Indians" were considered as sufficiently descriptive. Another grouping that was made was the indigenous and immigrant, the latter term meaning the more civilized tribes which had come from the United States, and including the Cherokee and associated bands.[1]

There was an Indian question in Texas from the time that the first Anglo-Americans began to arrive. For a dozen years after Austin brought his first colonists to Texas, the chronicles are full of Indian atrocities. The year 1832, Yoakum tells us, was the first in which the settlers had not been attacked often by the Indians, and their failure to attack that year was due to the fact that the Comanches and Shawnees had had a great battle in which so many were killed that they were unable to undertake a war against the whites.[2] In April, 1833, a convention met at San Felipe to petition for a separation of Texas and Coahuila. It was asserted that Texas was such a great distance from the center of government that no adequate means of protection against the Indians presented themselves, and this was considered a sufficient reason for the establishment of a separate state government for

[1]H. E. Bolton, *Athanase de Mézières and the Louisiana-Texas Frontier, 1768-1780*, pp. 17-122. has an extensive discussion of the indigenous Indians of Texas. T. M. Marshall, *A History of the Western Boundary of the Louisiana Purchase*, 124-140, is a convenient brief account of the location and history of the tribes.

[2]Yoakum, *History of Texas*, I, 310.

Texas. The memorial forwarded to Congress by the Convention, which closed April 13, 1833, is a gloomy one. It was written by David G. Burnet. After enumerating many evils from which the people were suffering, due to the lack of a strong local government, it declared:

We do not mean to attribute these specific disasters to the union with Coahuila, for we know they transpired long anterior to the consummation of that union. But we do maintain that the same political causes, the same want of protection and encouragement, the same mal-organization and impotency of the local and minor faculties of the government, the same improvident indifference to the peculiar and vital interests of Texas, exists *now* that operated then. Bexar is still exposed to the depredations of her ancient enemies, the insolent, vindictive, and faithless Comanches. Her citizens are still massacred, their cattle destroyed or driven away, and their very habitations threatened, by a tribe of erratic and undisciplined Indians, whose audacity has derived confidence from success, and whose long-continued aggressions have invested them with a fictitious and excessive terror. Her schools are neglected, her churches desolate, the sounds of human industry are almost hushed, and the voice of gladness and festivity is converted into wailing and lamentation, by the disheartening and multiplied evils which surround her defenceless population. Goliad is still kept in trepidation; is paralyzed in all her efforts for improvement; and is harassed in all her borders by the predatory incursions of the Wacoes, and other insignificant bands of savages, whom a well-organized local government would soon subdue and exterminate.[3]

Santa Anna, who was, in effect, dictator in Mexico when Stephen F. Austin presented this memorial, refused the request, imprisoned Austin, and in October, 1834, announced his purpose to send four thousand troops to San Antonio, "for the protection of the coast and frontier."[4] In March, 1835, Congress decreed the reduction of the militia throughout the Republic to one man for every five hundred inhabitants, and the disarming of the remainder.

Troops dispatched to Texas began to arrive early in 1835, and conflicts with the settlers soon began. At Anahuac a collector, backed by a small body of troops, attempted to collect tariff duties, which the Texans resented.[5] This situation, together with the

[3]Yoakum, *History of Texas*, I. 475.

[4]E. C. Barker, in Texas Historical Association *Quarterly*, VII, 250; Brown, *History of Texas*, I, 275.

[5]Barker, *op. cit.*, 250.

hostility of the Indians throughout the year, led to the creation of committees of safety and correspondence, which led to the calling of the Permanent Council in October. The Columbia committee wrote to J. B. Miller, the political chief of the Brazos Department suggesting that each municipality be required to furnish twenty-five men for use in an Indian campaign, to which Miller replied that he was already taking steps to punish the Indians.[6] The committee of San Felipe issued a circular on September 13, in which it was stated that the committee considered it important that the just and legal rights of the civilized Indians should be protected, "but not having any certain information on the subject, they can only recommend it to your consideration."[7]

The spirit exhibited in the letter of the San Felipe committee of safety became the spirit of the Permanent Council, and was adopted by each of the revolutionary bodies that governed Texas until March, 1836. The Permanent Council on October 18 adopted the report of a committee for appointing three commissioners to the civilized Indians. The commissioners appointed were Peter J. Menard, Jacob Garrett, and Joseph L. Hood. Several of the Indian chiefs had been invited to convene with the whites in their Consultation for the purpose of having their claims to lands properly adjusted by that body, but they failed to attend, and the three commissioners were therefore instructed to proceed to their villages and ascertain the cause of their grievances, and to assure them that their case would receive prompt attention as soon as the Consultation should reconvene. "This committee are of the opinion," said the report,

> that there have been unwarrantable encroachments made upon the lands occupied by the said Indians; therefore be it resolved by the permanent council of Texas now in session, that Peter J. Menard, Jacob Garrett, and Joseph L. Hood, be appointed commissioners for the purpose of holding consultations with the different tribes of Indians, and giving them such assurances as may be necessary for the advancement of their rights and privileges as citizens of Texas, and for the purpose of transacting such other business as may be necessary to promote the cause of the people of Texas.

[6] "Texas Revolutionary Documents," in Southern Historical Association *Publications*, VII, 89, 90.

[7] *Ibid.*, VIII, 20.

It was made the duty of the commissioners to co-operate at all times with the local committees of safety.[8]

At the same time, however, the Permanent Council provided a system of ranger service to keep the Indians in check. On October 17 a resolution was adopted authorizing Silas M. Parker to employ and superintend twenty-five rangers to guard the frontiers between the Brazos and Trinity rivers; Garrison Greenwood was authorized and required to employ and superintend ten rangers on the east side of the Trinity; and D. B. Fryar to employ twenty-five rangers for service between the Brazos and Colorado rivers. A committee of five men was appointed to report on the details of this scheme. The committee reported on the same day, and their report was adopted by the Council. The superintendents of the rangers from the Colorado to the Brazos and from the Brazos to the Trinity were to make their place of rendezvous at the Waco village, on the Brazos; those on the east of the Trinity were to rendezvous at Houston. The superintendents were to be vigilant in carrying the provisions of the resolution into effect, and were to have the authority to contract for ammunition, and to draw on the general council for payment. The companies were to select officers, whose duty it was to make reports to the superintendents every fifteen days, and the superintendent was to report to the General Council every thirty days. The companies ranging from the Colorado to the Brazos and from the Brazos to the Trinity were to rendezvous at the Waco village every fifteen days unless engaged in pursuing Indians, and the companies were to unite whenever their officers considered it necessary. Finally, the officers were to be "particular not to interfere with friendly tribes of Indians on our borders."[9]

The Consultation, which succeeded the Permanent Council on November 3, took further steps to secure the good will of the Indians. On the day before it adjourned a resolution was adopted in which the claims of the Indians to the lands they occupied in East Texas was recognized, and the Governor and General Council were advised to send commissioners to form a treaty with them. On November 15, Henry Smith, who had been elected provisional governor, advised the carrying into effect of the recommendation

[8]Texas Historical Association *Quarterly*, IX, 288.

[9]"Journal of the Permanent Council," in Texas Historical Association *Quarterly*, VII, 260-262.

of the Consultation. On the 22d Smith was empowered by the General Council to appoint Sam Houston, John Forbes, and John Cameron as commissioners to the Indians. The commissioners proceeded to the village of Bowl, military chief of the Cherokees, and on February 23, 1836, a treaty was drawn up agreeable to the wishes of the Cherokees.[10]

During the progress of the War of Independence the western frontier was evacuated by the people before the advancing Mexican army, hence there is no record of Indian wars in the West. In the East the civilized tribes were kept quiet partly through the promises held out to them by the Permanent Council and the Consultation for a definite settlement of their claims. At the same time, however, the Texans deliberately attempted to create the impression in the minds of officers of the United States that there was danger of an Indian uprising in the East, and it was their success in this propaganda that caused General Gaines to send some United States troops to Nacogdoches in the summer of 1836. By the treaty between the United States and Mexico both nations were to undertake to keep their Indians quiet, and it was this treaty that made possible the intervention of the United States in the affairs of Texas. It is interesting to notice that the colonists had attempted to form an alliance with the Indians in the spring of 1836.[11]

With the defeat of the Mexicans in the battle of San Jacinto, April 21, 1836, and the subsequent withdrawal of all enemy forces from Texas, those who had fled before the invaders returned to their homes. Besides, the settlers in search of new lands pushed out into territory regarded by the Indians as their hunting grounds, and the surveying parties early became an object of suspicion, the surveyor's compasses being known by the Indians as "land stealers."[12] The Indians were very troublesome and threat-

[10]Marshall, *A History of the Western Boundary of the Louisiana Purchase*, 139.

The relations with the Cherokees, their claims to lands in East Texas, and their final expulsion from Texas, is so different from the relations with the other Indian tribes that I shall treat it in a separate section, contenting myself here with a reference to that tribe only when they come into the natural development of the subject.

[11]E. C. Barker, "The United States and Mexico, 1835-1837," in *The Mississippi Valley Historical Review*, I, 20, 21.

[12]W. D. Wood, "History of Leon County," in Texas Historical Association *Quarterly*, IV, 204.

ening in the latter part of 1836 and throughout 1837. President Burnet had placed Captain Robert M. Coleman in charge of a ranging force divided into three or four detachments. One detachment was on the Trinity, one at the Falls of the Brazos, one at the Three Forks of Little River, and one near the mouth of Walnut Creek on the Colorado. These detachments fought numerous battles with the Indians.

On January 7, 1837, a detachment of fourteen men and boys under Lieutenant George B. Erath fought one hundred Indians eight miles west of Cameron, killing fifteen. A short time later a battle was fought near where Austin now stands, in which the Indians were defeated. Several men were murdered at different times in Lavaca County. In Fayette County John G. Robison, a member of Congress, and his brother, who was visiting him from the United States, were killed. On the Trinity, west of Palestine, David Faulkenberry, his son Evan, and Columbus Anderson, were killed. Massacres occurred during this year at various places in East Texas.[13]

The attitude of President Houston, in spite of the evident unpopularity of that policy, was one of conciliation throughout his administration; and in the early part of his administration he had the sympathy and support of Congress. In a message to the Senate, November 6, 1836, shortly after his inauguration as President, he said,

> The friendship and alliance of many of our border Tribes of Indians will be of the utmost importance to this Government, keeping them tranquil and pacific, and if need shall require it, affording us useful auxiliaries.

He suggested the advisability of entering into commercial treaties with them, and announced the appointment of commissioners to conclude articles of peace, friendship, and intercourse.[14]

In an act to protect the frontier, approved on December 5, 1836, the Congress took a middle ground between the advocates of extermination and conciliation. The President was required to raise, with as little delay as possible, a battalion of mounted riflemen, to consist of two hundred and eighty men for the pro-

[13]Brown, *History of Texas*, II, 129.

[14]*Secret Journals of the Senate of the Republic of Texas* (First Biennial Report of the Texas Library and Historical Commission), 19. Hereafter this is referred to as *Secret Journals*.

tection of the frontier. The term of service was to be twelve months. The President was also authorized to order out such number of the militia as the exigencies of the case might require. He was further directed to have such block houses, forts, and trading houses erected, as, in his judgment, might be necessary to prevent Indian depredations. And finally, it was to be the duty of the President to enter into such negotiations and treaties as might secure peace to the frontiers; he was to have power to appoint agents to live among the Indians, and to distribute presents as he deemed necessary, not to exceed in amount twenty thousand dollars.[15] That no steps had been taken for the organization of the mounted battalion before the middle of the following year, is indicated by a resolution, approved June 7, 1837, authorizing the President to absent himself from the seat of government for thirty days "to organize and set on foot the corps of mounted gun men, authorized to be raised by the act passed the present session of congress for the protection of our northern frontier."[16] On December 10, 1836, a joint resolution was approved authorizing and requiring the President to take such measures "as in his judgment will effect the release or redemption of our unfortunate prisoners, captured by and in the possession of hostile Indians, said to be on the waters of Red River, either by calling for and sending volunteers against said Indians, or by purchase, treaty or otherwise."[17]

In the spring of 1837 some Mexican agents visited the various Indians on the frontier, promising them arms, ammunition, all the booty taken, and peaceful possession of the frontier after the Americans were driven out, and by these promises many Indians were induced to join the Mexicans. Houston attempted in June to organize a mounted force for the punishment of the Indians. He ordered Lieutenant A. C. Horton, of San Augustine, to raise a force of one hundred and twenty men and as many more volunteers as were necessary to proceed against the Indians. Nothing seems to have come of this, however.[18] On November 10, a body of eighteen rangers fell in with a band of one hundred and fifty hostile Indians, and after a long battle the Indians were defeated, leaving fifty dead, while the loss of the Texans was only Lieu-

[15] *Laws of the Republic of Texas*, I, 53-54.

[16] *Ibid.*, 244.

[17] *Ibid.*, 74.

[18] Yoakum, *History of Texas*, II, 228.

tenant Miles and eight men.[19] That was the most serious attempt to chastise the Indians during the year.

In spite of the constant reports of Indian attacks on defenceless settlers, Houston showed by his message to Congress, November 21, 1837, that he still considered conciliation the best policy to pursue. It was of interest to the country, he said, that the relations with the Indians be placed upon a basis of lasting peace and friendship. Convinced of that truth, it had been his policy to seek every possible means to accomplish that object, and give security to the frontier; and he considered the indications more favorable than they had been at any time before Texas assumed that attitude. "Measures are in progress with the several tribes," he continued,

> which with the aid of suitable appropriations by Congress, may enable us to attain the objects of peace and friendly intercourse. Apprised of these facts, it is desirable that the citizens of Texas should so deport themselves, as to become the aggressors in no case, but to evince a conciliatory disposition whenever it can be done consistently with justice and humanity. . . . The undeviating opinion of the Executive has been, that from the establishment of trading houses on the frontier (under prudent regulations), and the appointment of capable and honest agents, the happiest results might be anticipated for the country. The intercourse between the citizens and Indians should be regulated by acts of Congress which experience will readily suggest.[20]

In carrying out this policy he insisted on the ratification by the Senate of the treaty drawn up with the Cherokees in 1836, and the running of the boundary line under that treaty.[21] He advised the settlers to stay at home and not tempt the Indians to hostile attacks; and it was charged by a newspaper in the heat of a political campaign in 1841, that when a committee of men from Robertson and Milam Counties asked for protection for the frontier, he answered that "he hoped every man, woman and child that settled North of the San Antonio Road would be tomahawked."[22]

The year 1838 was not different from the preceding year. A committee on October 12, 1837, had reported that several of the tribes of Indians were at peace, and advised the President to at-

[19]*Telegraph and Texas Register*, December 23, 1837.

[20]Crane, *Life and Select Literary Remains of Sam Houston*, 292.

[21]*Secret Journals*, 35, 36, 37.

[22]*Telegraph and Texas Register*, August 25, 1841.

tempt to make a treaty with the Comanches. At the same time they denied the right of the Cherokees to the land which they occupied.[23] This was not done, however, and the Comanches continued to harass the western frontier. A few instances are here given to illustrate the conditions. On August 10 Captain Henry W. Karnes with twenty-five men was attacked by 200 Comanches, and after a furious fight drove them off with a loss of twenty of the assailants. On the Rio Frio, about the same time, a surveying party was attacked, and several of the party wounded. On October 19 a surveying party seven miles west of San Antonio was attacked and the surveyors killed. In October also occurred the surveyors' fight in Navarro County, when twenty-three men fought several hundred Indians from 9 o'clock in the morning till 12 o'clock at night.[24]

In the summer of 1838 the Indians of the East became restless, due partly to the efforts of Mexican agents, and partly to the failure of the Senate to ratify the treaty with the Cherokees. In August took place the curious Nacogdoches rebellion. On August 4 a party of citizens who went in search of some horses that had been stolen found the trail of a large number of Mexicans. On the 7th it was reported that there were a hundred or more Mexicans encamped about the Angelina under the command of Nathaniel Norris, Vicente Cordova, and Cruz. On the 10th it was reported that the Mexicans had been joined by 300 Indians, and that their force then amounted to 600. The same day they sent a letter to President Houston disclaiming allegiance to Texas, and set out for the Cherokee nation. Major Augustin was detached with 150 men to follow the rebels, while General Rusk marched with the main force of the Texans to the village of Bowl, military chief of the Cherokees. Before reaching there he found that the insurgents had dispersed.[25]

No satisfactory explanation has ever been made of the purposes that the Mexicans had in mind in this rebellion. On August 20, a Mexican by the name of Pedro Julian Miracle was killed on the Red River, and on his body were found instructions from General Vicente Filisola directed to the Mexicans and friendly Indians in

[23] *Secret Journals*, 75-79.

[24] Brown, *History of Texas*, II, 143.

[25] Yoakum, *History of Texas*, II, 245-246; Bancroft, *North Mexican States and Texas*, II, 320; Brown, *History of Texas*, II, 143.

Texas, together with a diary which Miracle had kept during his journey into Texas. The instructions and the diary taken together would indicate that Miracle was visiting the Mexicans and Indians in the region of Nacogdoches for the purpose of fomenting a conspiracy, and it was probably due to his activities that the Mexicans decided to revolt. One of the documents found on the body of Miracle was entitled "Private instructions for the captains of friendly Indians of Texas, by his Excellency the General-in-chief Vicente Filisola," and it was apparently aimed to control his activities with the Indians. He was to invite the principal chiefs to a meeting and propose to them that they and their friends should take up arms in defence of the Mexican territory in Texas. Afterwards, he was to meet several from each tribe, and distribute among them powder, lead, and tobacco, "in the usual manner."

> You will make them understand that as soon as they have agreed in taking up arms, they will be rewarded according to their merits; and that so soon as they have taken possession of the places that I have mentioned to you, you will advise me by an extraordinary courier, giving me a detailed account of the strength of the Mexican force, and of the Indian tribes, with the plan of attack, that I may be enabled to direct the forces that are to leave from this place to the assistance of those who are to operate in that quarter. Make them understand that as soon as the campaign is over, they will be able to proceed to Mexico, to pay their respects to the Supreme Government, who will send a commissioner to give to each possession of the land they are entitled to.

A second document, apparently written by Miracle himself, was addressed, "Companions and friends." In it he called upon the Indians to give their service to their country during the campaign which was about to take place, and declare that he had been instructed by the general-in-chief to pay particular attention to their behavior during the campaign and report it to him. "As soon as the news of our operations are made known in Matamoras," he ended, "his excellency the general-in-chief will make a forced march towards the point where our troops may be, so that in the event of any sudden reverse, you will be aided, and a central position fixed upon for your reunion, to be headquarters during the remainder of the campaign."

According to the memorandum book which was found on the body of Miracle, he left Matamoras on May 29, and after a leisurely journey, accompanied by Mexican and Indian followers, he arrived on the Trinity and made camp on July 2. An extract from his diary will explain to some extent his activity.

July 4. Started for "Plazeta creek." Soon after we discovered the farms of the Choctaw Indians; we directed our course towards the rancho of Buenavista.

July 5.—Don Vicente Cordova presented himself and read the communication of his excellency the general-in-chief, Don Vicente Filisola.

July 7.—We expect to meet the Indian chiefs or captains.

July 8.—About three o'clock in the afternoon Guimon, Boll, and their interpreters, made their appearance; but, on account of the rain, nothing was done.

July 9.—At seven o'clock we started to a rancho to hold a consultation with the Indians. We read the communication of his excellency the general-in-chief; the interpreters being inefficient, nothing was done. They left us without any understanding, but are to meet them in ten days, when they will determine. They left an Indian to conduct me to Boll's house; which was done, and we reached that place drenched with rain. I am to take the first opportunity to speak to Boll, to show him by private instructions; but I can do nothing as yet. He has sent me to another of his houses where I could conceal myself; for he said that some Americans were coming with a communication from Houston, the contents of which I have not learned. Nothing can be done without trouble. [From the ninth until the seventeenth Miracle remained concealed.]

July 17 and 18.—In the afternoon of these days several Indians made their appearance for the meeting.

July 19.—Boll, Dillmoor, and several other captains, came in; but the non-arrival of the Kickapoos delayed our meeting.

July 20.—The meeting took place. War was agreed upon as soon as circumstances would permit, and as speedily as possible; the amount of our force to be taken immediately; including Nacogdoches we have 540 men. At five o'clock p. m. Capt. Saguano began to raise objections to the making of any movement until the arrival of the army in the country when war could be carried on with energy; but finally it was resolved that our force should be in readiness at a moment's warning. At five o'clock Boll left us, and all went away, including Cordova and the people of Nacogdoches, about eight o'clock in the morning.

The remainder of the diary records visits to the other tribes, and comes to an end with an entry for August 8.[26]

[26]Copies of these documents found upon Miracle were sent to the American State Department by the Texan Minister, Anson Jones, on December 31, 1838, with a claim that the conditions were made worse on the border

Lamar was aware of the conditions on the frontier, and of the unpopularity of Houston's Indian policy, being informed both by his own interest as a presidential candidate and by the reports of his friends. On June 26, 1838, he received a letter from Reuben H. Roberts of Aransas, supporting his candidacy for the presidency, saying that the cry of the people was for a President who would protect the frontier.[27] On July 29, William McCraven wrote from San Antonio, telling of the dangers from Mexicans and Indian marauders, and expressing the popular hope that Lamar's administration would defend the frontier.[28]

On August 24, General Rusk wrote to Lamar from Nacogdoches concerning the Cordova rebellion, as follows:

> Dear Genl
> I have received your letter by Col Bee for which please accept my thanks You must excuse me for not having written you before but recent events have crowded on me so fast that I have had very little time. I will in a few days give you a full account of the recent rebellion here it was a deep and well laid scheme to involve the country in a general Indian war I have had great difficulty in preventing it His Excellency has acted strangely indeed had I been governed by his peremptory orders I have not the least doubt that an Indian war would have been now raging here but a timely demonstration of force by marching six hundred horsemen through their Country excited strongly that which can only be depended upon in Indians their fear.[29]

Two days later Hugh McLeod, adjutant to General Rusk, wrote, saying that the Mexicans had plotted for a general uprising of Indians, and but for Rusk's promptness they might have brought it about. He criticised President Houston severely for his conduct during the rebellion. "He cramped Genl Rusk in ever way," he said, "with his orders, written here, where one could not judge what was the true state of affairs at HdQrs."[30] Besides these, there were other letters strongly criticising the policy of Houston and hoping that Lamar would adopt a different policy with regard to the Indians.

On October 22 McLeod reported a renewal of Mexican hostili-

by the failure of the two governments to run the boundary line. They appear printed in 32 Cong., 2 session, *Senate Documents*, No. 14, pp. 11-17.

[27]*Lamar Papers*, No. 753.

[28]*Lamar Papers*, No. 772.

[29]Rusk to Lamar, August 24, 1838, *Lamar Papers*, No. 797.

[30]McLeod to Lamar, August 26, 1838, *Lamar Papers*, No. 800.

ties, giving an account of the battle of Kickapoo on the 16th, and on the 25th he wrote that Rusk had become convinced that the time had come for a campaign of extermination against all Indians except the friendly ones.[31] On November 17, General Rusk wrote, suggesting the creation of a permanent force of five hundred men to operate against the Indians. At the same time he suggested that Lamar demand the removal of all United States Indians under the treaty of 1831 between the United States and Mexico.[32]

The inauguration of Lamar was to take place on December 10, and the stage was set for a declaration of policy different from that of Houston, who continued to insist that his policy was the only one that promised success. Houston delivered his valedictory message on November 19, and to illustrate the contrast of the attitude of the outgoing to that of the incoming President, I shall give his policy as he expressed it. Criticising the whites for their aggression on the Indian lands, Houston said:

> The great anxiety of our citizens to acquire land induced them to adventure into the Indian hunting grounds in numbers not sufficient for self-protection, and inasmuch as they met with no serious opposition in the commencement of their surveying, they were thrown off their guard, which afforded the Indians an opportunity of taking them by surprise, and hence they became victims to their own indiscretion and temerity.

The executive anticipated the consequences that would result from penetrating into the Indian hunting grounds, he said, and had done everything in his power to prevent such a course. His personal remonstrances were insufficient to control the determination of those whose opinions set at naught admonitions that could not be legally enforced. The Indians, by gaining partial advantages, were induced to form more numerous associations, that had rendered them formidable; and occasionally acquiring spoil, they had been induced to advance upon the settlements in marauding parties, while the continued surveys within their hunting grounds had so much exasperated their feelings that their invasions had become formidable to the frontier. He went on to say that the system of surveying lands had involved the country in all the calamities that had visited the frontier, and suggested that for

[31]McLeod to Lamar, October 22 and 25, 1838, *Lamar Papers*, Nos. 846, 852.

[32]Rusk to Lamar, November 17, 1838, *Lamar Papers*, No. 876.

some time to come restrictions should be placed on surveying beyond the settlements. He concluded by censuring General Rusk for alleged encroachments on the Presidential power during the Cordova rebellion, and claimed that that revolt was brought about by violation of the rights of the Mexicans and Indians.[33]

Lamar did not leave the country long in doubt as to his policy in dealing with the Indians. "It is a cardinal principle in all political associations," he said in his first message to Congress, December 21, 1838, "that *protection* is commensurate with *allegiance,* and the poorest citizen, whose sequestered cabin is reared on our remotest frontier, holds as sacred a claim upon the government for safety and security, as does the man who lives in ease and wealth in the heart of our most populous city." He was not anxious to aggravate the ordinary calamities of war by inculcating the harsh doctrines of *lex talionis* toward debased and ignorant savages. War was an evil which all good people ought to strive to avoid, but when it could not be avoided, it ought to be so met and pursued as would best secure a speedy and lasting peace. The moderation hitherto extended to the Indians on the border had been answered by all the atrocious cruelties that characterize their mode of warfare. His solicitude for the due protection of the frontier had partially overruled his habitual repugnance to standing armies; and in the disturbed state of their foreign and Indian relations, the proper security of the country at large, especially the peace and safety of the border settlements, seemed to require the organization of a regular, permanent, and effective force.

He showed himself in harmony with the popular sentiment in his remarks concerning the Indians in the East. He referred to the trouble around Nacogdoches in August, and said that it was not all clear to him, but that he was far from conceding that the Indians, either native or immigrant, had any just cause of complaint. He proceeded to discuss the nature of their claims to lands in East Texas, showing to his satisfaction that they were worthless. He was particularly severe on the Cherokees and clearly foreshadowed stern measures with them. He suggested the establishment of a line of military forts, announced that agents were to be appointed to live in the Indian settlements, and that Indians were to be required to submit to Texan criminal laws.[34]

[33]Kennedy, *Texas*, II, 316.

[34]*Telegraph and Texas Register*, December 26, 1838; *Lamar Papers*, No. 361.

On the day that he sent this message to Congress he received from Congress, and approved, an act "to provide for the protection of the Northern and Western Frontier." It created a regiment comprising 840 men, rank and file, divided into fifteen companies of fifty-six men each. The term of service was to be three years, at a compensation of sixteen dollars a month, and with a bounty of thirty dollars. The regiment was to be divided into eight detachments, stationed as follows: at or near Red River; at or near the Three Forks of the Trinity; at or near the Brazos; at or near the Colorado River; at or near St. Marks River; at the headwaters of Cibolo; at or near Rio Frio; and at or near the Nueces River. At each of these posts fortifications were to be constructed. These posts were to become the center of frontier settlement. As soon as the positions were selected, three leagues of land were to be laid off and surveyed into lots of 160 acres each. Two of the lots were to be reserved for the government for the purpose of constructing fortifications, one lot was to be given to the soldiers obeying the term of enlistment, and the remainder was to be given in lots of 160 acres to bona fide settlers in fee simple who would live there two years. The act further provided for the establishment of sixteen trading posts.[35]

On January 1, 1839, two other acts for the further protection of the frontier were approved. The first authorized the President to accept eight companies of mounted volunteers for a period of six months, and appropriated $75,000 to maintain that force. The second appropriated the sum of $5,000 for a company of fifty-six rangers for a three months period.[36] A little later another act was approved providing for three companies of militia for the protection of the frontier;[37] and an January 24, the sum of $1 000,000 was appropriated for the protection of the frontier.[38]

In October conditions had become unsettled in the East again, and on the 16th the army under Rusk fought a battle with a mixed force of Mexicans and Indians at Kickapoo. Shortly afterwards the Caddos in the Red River valley became threatening, and just before Lamar's inauguration, Rusk had followed them into the United States and disarmed them, thereby incurring a

[35]Gammel, *Laws of Texas*, II, 15.

[36]*Ibid.*, II, 30, 31.

[37]*Ibid.*, II, 74.

[38]*Ibid.*, II, 84.

protest from the government of the United States.[39] These activities made necessary the use of the whole army in the East, and the West was left unprotected. On January 2, 1839, Joseph Baker, Indian agent at San Antonio, reported that the Comanches, Lipans, and Tonkawas were active, and that several children had been captured at Gonzales; on the 16th, several citizens sent a circular announcing Indian attacks in Robertson County, and appealing for aid.[40]

It is not worth while to enumerate all the Indian attacks during this period. It is sufficient to say that a lack of interest in frontier protection had caused the depletion of the army, and a lack of funds at the outset of Lamar's term made impossible the carrying into effect of the ambitious program that he had announced. His response to the appeals for help coming from the western counties was that the lack of funds made him unable to do anything effective in defending the frontier, but that an agent was then in New Orleans attempting to sell bonds, and that he would apply all the proceeds from the sale to the purchase of ammunition and the payment of soldiers.[41] On February 28 he called for volunteers from eight counties in western Texas for an Indian war. Edward Burleson had been appointed a colonel in the regular army and stationed at Bastrop, but recruiting was very slow, and practically the only defence for the western frontier during the year was by volunteer bodies, supported by what there was of a regular army. It is likely, however, that the endorsement of an aggressive policy by Lamar gave encouragement to the citizens in their local warfare with the Indians.

By far the most troublesome Indians to the Texans were the Comanches, who had established themselves on the headwaters of the Colorado before the American occupation. Throughout the period of the Republic, and even after annexation, they made frequent attacks on the western settlements. President Houston was authorized by the Senate to make a treaty with them in 1837, and he invited a number of their chiefs to Houston where he had a conference with them, giving them presents, and accepting their

[39]*Indian Affairs*, 1831-1841; McLeod to Lamar, November 21, 1838, *Lamar Papers*, No. 882; 32d Cong., 2d sess., *Senate Document*, No. 14, p. 17.

[40]*Lamar Papers*, Nos. 982, 1016.

[41]Lamar to Inhabitants of Robertson's Colony, February 22, 1839, *Lamar Papers*, No. 1084.

promise to keep the peace. In 1838, during the closing year of Houston's administration, no effort was made by the government to protect the frontier from the Comanches, and the President went so far as to criticise the whites for provoking attacks from the Indians by their imprudence. Lamar gave to the local movements the moral support of the administration, and as far as possible the actual physical support. I shall follow out, as far as possible, the relations with the western tribes, particularly the Comanches, reserving a discussion for the relations with the immigrant tribes of East Texas until later.

In the latter part of January, 1839, three companies of volunteers were organized and placed under the command of Captain John H. Moore, and ordered to move against the Comanches. They marched up the Colorado. On the 14th of February they came to within ten miles of the Indian village, and after dark attacked a vastly superior force. After killing about thirty of the Indians and losing one killed and six wounded, the Texans drew off and did not renew the fight. In the latter part of February, a party of Indians committed several murders in the vicinity of Bastrop, and were attacked by about fifty Texans. The Texans were forced to fall back, but were reinforced by General Burleson with thirty men, and after a sharp battle the Indians fled. In May, a force of thirty-five men under Captain John Bird discovered a party of twenty-seven Indians on Little River. They pursued them until the Indians came up with the main body of from two hundred and fifty to three hundred. The Texans managed to secure an advantageous position, and beat the Indians off with severe losses.[42]

The punishment that the Indians received in these engagements caused them to be more wary in their attacks, and early in the following year an effort was made to enter into a treaty with the Texans. In February, 1840, some of the Indians came to San Antonio for the purpose of making peace with Texas, and were told by the commissioners to bring in the captives they had taken. The Indians promised to do this, and on March 19, appeared with only one captive. Twelve of the chiefs met the commissioners, and when called upon to produce their captives produced only one little girl. The Texans knew that the Comanches had other cap-

[42]Yoakum, *History of Texas*, II, 261-263; Report of Secretary of War, November, 1839.

tives and demanded that they be brought before any treatv would be signed. When the chiefs claimed that they had no other captives, General McLeod, who was in command of the Texans, ordered a company of soldiers into the house and told the Indians they were under arrest, and that they would be detained until they sent the rest of their company for the prisoners and brought them in. This statement immediately precipitated a fight in the council room, which spread to the warriors outside. All the chiefs and warriors were killed, and twenty-seven women and children were taken prisoner, the Texans losing seven killed and eight wounded. The women were kept prisoners while one of their number was sent to inform the Comanches what had taken place and to say that the Texans were willing to exchange prisoners. A few days later she returned with two white captives and four or five Mexicans, and proposed to exchange them for her people and pay the difference in horses. She was informed that all the white prisoners must be brought in.[43]

In revenge for this battle at San Antonio, the Indians planned an extensive campaign. Aided bv the Mexicans and some Kiowas, a band estimated at from four hundred to a thousand Indians suddenly attacked Victoria on the evening of August 6. The citizens had had no notice of their coming, but they managed to take refuge in the center of the town, and put up an effectual resistance, losing only a few persons and a considerable number of horses. They made another attack the next day, which also failed, and then they crossed the Guadalupe River and attacked Linnville on the coast. The inhabitants took refuge in a lighter on the Gulf, but the Indians burned the town and carried away most of the goods and cattle that they could find. In the meantime volunteers had been collecting, who, joined by regulars and rangers, intercepted the Indians at Plum Creek. Here under General Felix Huston, the Texans fought and defeated the Indians, killing from fifty to eighty, and recovered all horses and prisoners. The Indians were pursued for some distance, but the main body made its escape.

Not content with the defeat of the Indians at Plum Creek, the Texans determined to send an expedition into the Comanche coun-

[43]Report of McLeod to Secretary of War, March 20, 1840; *Telegraph and Texas Register*, April 15, 1840; Bancroft, *North Mexican States and Texas*, II, 324; Yoakum, *History of Texas*, II, 298; Brown, *History of Texas*, II, 175.

try and chastise them so that they would make no more attacks on the frontiers. Colonel John H. Moore, who had followed the Comanches up the Colorado to their village in February, 1839, was chosen to lead the expedition. Setting out about the first of October with ninety men, besides twelve friendly Lipans, he went up the Colorado about three hundred miles to where Colorado City now stands. Here the Lipans found the Comanche village in the bend of the river, with a bluff to cut off their retreat. McLeod sent thirty men to occupy the bluff, and with his main force made a surprise attack, which proved fully successful. Only two warriors escaped, and a hundred and thirty-four were found dead on the field. Thirty-four squaws and children were captured. The Texans had a few wounded but none killed. This ended the organized attacks of the Comanches during Lamar's administration, though they continued to annoy outlying settlements.[44]

II. Relations with the Cherokees

A group of Indians that furnished a special problem to the Texans from their first immigration, consisted of the semi-civilized tribes which had emigrated from the United States, consisting of the Cherokees, the Coshattoes, the Kickapoos, the Choctaws, the Shawnees, the Biloxis, and the Caddoes. Most of these had no claim to the soil on which they had settled, and contemporaries and historians have agreed on the justice of their removal from Texas. The Cherokees did have some claim, however, or thought they did, to the occupancy and government of the region where they were settled. The refusal of Lamar to recognize their claims as valid, and his determination to treat them as other immigrant tribes, make necessary a full discussion of their claims, both under the Mexican régime and after the Texans had won their independence.

In the winter of 1819-20, the first party of Cherokees, consisting of sixty warriors, left their settlements among the Caddoes north of Red River, and came into Texas, settling somewhere along the boundary between the Caddoes and the Prairie Indians.[45] By

[44]Accounts of this campaign can be found in Yoakum, *History of Texas,* II, 302-305; Bancroft, *North Mexican States and Texas,* II, 325-326; Brown, *History of Texas,* II, 178-183. Brown as a young man was present as a volunteer in the battle of Plum Creek, and writes an interesting account of the battle.

[45]E. W. Winkler, "The Cherokee Indians in Texas," in Texas Historical

the latter part of 1824 they were claiming the region lying between the Sabine and Trinity Rivers north of the San Antonio Road, which continued to be their claim until driven from Texas in the summer of 1839. Whether or not they had permission from the Spanish authorities to settle in Texas it is impossible to say. A letter from Richard Fields, their chief, to James Dill, alcalde at Nacogdoches, just after the revolution which freed Mexico from Spanish rule in 1822, indicates that probably some Spanish governor had given them the right to locate there for hunting purposes. The letter, addressed to the "subsprem Governor of the Provunce of Spain," February 1, 1822, asked what was to be done with the poor Indians. They had some grants, it said, which were given them when they lived under the government of Spain, and they wanted to know whether or not the grants would be recognized by the new government. This letter was forwarded to the governor by Dill, but it elicited no response.[46]

Early in November, 1822, Fields with twenty-two more Indians, visited Don José Felix Trespalacios, the governor of the province of Texas, and asked permission for all belonging to his tribe to settle upon the lands of the province. Trespalacios entered into a temporary agreement with Fields, and sent him to the commandant general of the Eastern Interior Provinces at Monterey, Don Gaspar Lopez, who, if agreeable was to send him on to the court of the Empire, for the purpose of securing a confirmation of the grant given by Trespalacios. This agreement constitutes the main documentary evidence of the claims of the Cherokees in Texas prior to the declaration of the Consultation in 1835, and I shall quote it in full.

Article 1st. That the said chief Richard [Fields] with five others of his tribe, accompanied by Mr. Antonio Mexia and Antonio Walk, who act as Interpreters, may proceed to Mexico, to treat with his Imperial Majesty, relative to the settlement which said chief wishes to make for those of his tribe who are already in the territory of Texas, and also for those who are still in the United States.

Article 2d. That the other Indians in the city, and who do not accompany the beforementioned, will return to their village in the

Association *Quarterly*, VII, 96; *National Intelligencer*, September 15, 1820.

[46]Winkler, in *Ibid.*, 99. The original of this letter is in *Bexar Archives*. It is printed in full in Mr. Winkler's article, as cited.

vicinity of Nacogdoches, and communicate to those who are at said village, the terms of this agreement.

Article 3d. That a party of the warriors of said village must be constantly kept on the road leading from this province to the United States, to prevent stolen animals from being carried thither, and to apprehend and punish those evil disposed foreigners, who form assemblages, and abound on the banks of the river Sabine within the Territory of Texas.

Article 4th. That the Indians who return to their Town, will appoint as their chief the Indian Captain called Kunetand, alias Tong Turqui, to whom a copy of this agreement will be given, for the satisfaction of those of his tribe, and in order that they may fulfill its stipulations.

Article 5th. That meanwhile, and until the approval of the Supreme Government is obtained, they may cultivate their lands and sow their crops, in free and peaceful possession.

Article 6th. That the said Cherokee Indians, will become immediately subject to the laws of the Empire, as well as all others who may tread her soil, and they will also take up arms in defense of the nation if called upon so to do.

Article 7th. That they shall be considered Hispano-Americans, and entitled to all the rights and privileges granted to such; and to the same protection should it become necessary.

Article 8th. That they can immediately commence trade with the other inhabitants of the Province, and with the exception of arms and munitions of war, with the tribes of Savages who may not be friendly to us.[47]

Fields and his party arrived in Saltillo, the headquarters of the commandant general, early in December, and after being entertained by him for a few days were sent on to Mexico City, arriving there early in 1823, at the time when the revolution against the power of Iturbide was taking place. During the progress of the revolution Fields and his companions remained in Mexico, awaiting a settlement of their claims. On April 27, 1823, the minister of relations in the provisional government, announced the decision of the government to recognize the agreement between Fields and Trespalacios until a general colonization law could be passed. "The Supreme Executive Power," wrote Alaman to Don Felipe de la Garza, who had succeeded Lopez as commandant general of the Eastern Interior Provinces,

has been pleased to resolve that Richard Fields chief of the Cher-

[47]*Record of Translations of Empresario Contracts*, 85. General Land Office of Texas.

okee Tribe of Indians, and his companions now in this Capital, may return to their country, and that they be supplied with whatever may be necessary for that purpose. Therefore, Their Supreme Highnesses have directed me to inform you, that although the agreement made on the 8th November 1822 between Richard Fields and Colonel Felix Trespalacios Governor of Texas, remains provisionally in force, you are nevertheless, required to be very careful and vigilant, in regard to their settlements, endeavoring to bring them towards the interior, and at places least dangerous, not permitting for the present the entrance of any new families of the Cherokee tribe, until the publication of the General Colonization law, which will establish the rules and regulations to be observed, although the benefits to arise from it, can not be extended to them, in relation to all of which, Their Highnesses intend to consult the Sovereign Congress. That while this is effecting, the families already settled, should be well treated, and the other chiefs also, treated with suitable consideration, provided that those already within our territory respect our laws, and are submissive to our Authorities; and finally, Their Highnesses order, that in future neither these Indians, nor any others be permitted to come to the City of Mexico, but only send their petitions in ample form, for journeys similar to the present, are of no benefit, and only create unnecessary expense to the State. All of which I communicate to you for your information and fulfillment.[48]

With this understanding Fields seemed fully satisfied and returned to Texas.

It is apparent from these documents that Fields received no more than a temporary concession, and that a permanent grant was left in abeyance. Besides, he was conceded no more than the right to sow his crops, and till his fields without interference from the authorities. A year later we find Fields claiming considerably more than this. In calling a council of all the Indian tribes for the purpose of forming a treaty with them, he said:

The superior government has granted to me in this province a territory sufficient for me and that part of the tribe of Indians dependent on me to settle on, and also a commission to command all the Indian tribes and nations that are in the four eastern provinces.

In the council he was to propose treaties with all Indians who would agree to submit themselves to the orders of the government, and if there were any who would not agree, he was to use force to

[48]Alaman to De la Garza. April 27, 1823, *Record of Translations of Empresario Contracts,* 85, 86; Winkler, as cited, 105, 106.

subdue them.[49] This letter of Fields's was transmitted to the government at Mexico City, and Alaman responded immediately that no such commission and no such grants had been made, stating that the only agreement was for an extension of the provisional treaty between Trespalacios and Fields of November 8, 1822.[50]

On August 18, 1824, the general colonization law was passed, giving to the States the right to make regulations for the distribution of lands within their boundaries. The State of Coahuila and Texas passed their colonization law on March 24, 1825. Less than a month later, April 15, 1825, the State granted three contracts for the settlement of two thousand families in the region claimed by the Indians. Robert Leftwich was to settle eight hundred west of the Cherokee claim, Frost Thorn four hundred north of their villages, and Edwards eight hundred on the lands claimed and occupied by the Cherokees. These grants do not, of course, prove that the Indians had no claim to the lands. It is more likely that the authorities of the State of Coahuila and Texas knew nothing of the temporary grant by Trespalacios and confirmed by the authorities in Mexico. The granting of their lands to others, however, led to a threatened revolt, which was prevented only by earnest efforts on the part of friends of Texas.[51] At the same time Fields was assured that he would get suitable lands, and he continued to assert all the powers he had claimed before.

On March 20, 1826, when a general Indian war was threatening, Fields wrote to the political chief at San Antonio promising help against those Indians, the Comanches and others, who were refusing to come to terms with the Mexicans. A little later Stephen F. Austin was ordered by the *commandante* at San Antonio to attack the Wacoes, Tehuacanos, and other tribes, and he called upon Fields for assistance, stating that it would be the means of securing the lands which the Cherokees desired. Fields asserted his willingness to assist the whites, but said the waters of the Neches were too high for them to get across. The attack was postponed at that time, but in the autumn Fields asked permission to make war on the same Indians, which was granted. Before it could take place, however, other matters entirely changed the aspect of affairs, and the Cherokees were ready to attack the Mexicans.[52]

[49]Winkler, "The Cherokee Indians in Texas," *op. cit.*, 108.

[50]*Ibid.*, 110.

[51]*Ibid.*, 117-120.

[52]*Ibid.*, 126.

In the summer of 1825, about the time that Fields was preparing to secure his lands by force, John Dunn Hunter, a white man who had spent several years of his youth in captivity with the Indians, and who had wonderful schemes for civilizing the Indians, made his appearance among the Cherokees of Texas. Hunter counselled friendship with the Mexicans, and proceeded to Mexico City to petition for lands for the Indians, arriving there on March 19, 1826. It seems to have been the purpose of Hunter to secure from the government a grant of land in the vacant parts of Texas and Coahuila for the settlement of nearly 20,000 warriors, who were to adopt the Catholic religion, take the oath of allegiance to the Mexican Government, devote themselves to agricultural labor, and defend the frontiers.[53] Hunter returned about September and announced the failure of his mission, and the Cherokees immediately began preparations to gain by force what they had not been able to get peaceably.

A council was called, and addressed by Hunter and Fields. The speech of Fields, as reported to Stephen F. Austin by P. E. Bean, indicates that he was willing to demand perhaps more than he believed had been granted. In the language of Bean, it was as follows:

> In my old Days I travilid 2000 Miles to the City of Mexico to Beg some lands to setel a Poor orfan tribe of Red Peopel that looked up to me for Protasion I was Promised lands for them after staying one year in Mexico and spending all I had I then came to my Peopel and waited two years and then sent Mr. hunter again after selling my stock to Provide him money for his expenses when he got there he Staited his mision to Government they said they New nothing of this Richard fields and treated him with contampt I am a Red man and a man of onor and Cant be emposid on this way we will lift up our tomahawks and fight for land with all those friendly tribes that wishes land also if I am Beaten I will Resign to fait and if not I will hold lands By the forse of my Red Warriors.[54] . . .

It was at first the purpose of the Cherokees to attack the Americans in Texas, and they were to begin with Edwards's colony, which included the lands occupied by them. At about that time, however, Edwards had become involved in a controversy with the

[53] *Ibid.*, 123.

[54] P. E. Bean to S. F. Austin, December 30, 1826, in *Austin Papers*. Winkler, "The Cherokee Indians in Texas," *op. cit.*, 133.

authorities and in the end this resulted in the revocation of his grant. Rather than submit to the loss which this would entail, Edwards and some of his followers raised a rebellion against the authority of Mexico, declaring the colony independent under the name of Fredonia. Hunter thought it best to consult with the colonists under these circumstances, and he went to Nacogdoches for the purpose. Hunter's visit resulted in a treaty of alliance between the Cherokees and the rebels under Edwards.

The treaty of alliance as drawn up by Hunter and Fields on the part of the Indians and Harmon B. Mayo and Benjamin W. Edwards as Agents of the Committee of Independence provided that the contracting parties bound themselves into a solemn Union, League and Confederation, in peace and war, to establish and defend their independence against the Mexican United States. The boundary between the whites and the Indians was outlined, and it was agreed that the territory apportioned to the Indians was intended as well for the benefit of those tribes living in the territory apportioned to the whites as for those living in the former territory, and that it was encumbent upon the contracting parties for the Indians to offer those tribes a participation in the territory.[55]

It is not my purpose to follow the events connected with this rebellion. The other American settlers in Texas not only refused to give any assistance to the rebels, but joined the authorities in putting them down. The Cherokee chiefs were unable to form a league of the Indians in Texas, or even to secure the united support of their own people. Mexican agents went among the Indians and promised them land if they would refuse to join in the movement for independence. Among these agents P. E. Bean was the most active. Through his influence the political chief wrote a letter to Fields attempting to explain the failure of the government to grant the lands desired, and promising that the grants would be made as soon as possible. He failed, however, to detach Fields and Hunter from the alliance; but the activity of the agents among the Indians themselves was more successful, and the greater part of them under the leadership of Bowl and Big Mush went

[55]Foote, *Texas and the Texans*, I, 253-256; Winkler, "The Cherokee Indians in Texas," *op. cit.*, 142.

over to the Mexicans and killed Fields and Hunter in January, 1827.[56]

In spite of the promise of lands to Bowl and Big Mush, in order to secure their co-operation against the rebels during the Fredonian rebellion, no steps were taken to put them in possession of the lands selected until 1831, though there was no effort to interfere with their peaceful possession. Instead of putting them in possession of the Edwards grant, the legislature divided that territory between David G. Burnet and Joseph Vehlein.[57]

On April 6, 1830, a Federal act prohibiting the further immigration of Americans into Texas was passed. As an alternative to American settlement of Texas, the law proposed the settlement of Mexican families around the Americans already there, thus overcoming the isolation of the Americans. General Teran, who had become commandant general of the Eastern Interior States, appealed to the governor of each State to furnish a certain number of Mexican families to settle upon the Texas frontier. The governors failed to respond to this request, and no Mexican families were sent. This determined Teran to attempt to settle Indians to keep the Americans in check. He decided to begin this by settling firmly the Cherokees on the land which they claimed and had occupied for several years, hoping thus to stop the American advance in this manner. On August 15, 1831, he wrote to Letona, the governor of Coahuila and Texas, as follows:

> In compliance with the promises made by the Supreme Government, to the Cherokee Indians, and with a view to the preservation of peace, with the rude tribes, I caused them to determine upon some fixed spot for their Settlement, and having selected it on the head waters of the Trinity, and the banks of the Sabine, I pray your Excellency may be pleased, to order that possession be given to them, with the corresponding Titles, with the understanding, that it will be expedient, that the commissioners appointed for this purpose, should act in conjunction with Colonel José de las Piedras, commanding the military force on the frontier of Nacogdoches.[58]

The local officials fell in with the suggestions of the commandant

[56]Winkler, "The Cherokee Indians in Texas," *op. cit.*, 146-150.

[57]Bancroft, *North Mexican States and Texas*, II, 110.

[58]*Record of Translations of Empresario Contracts*, 89. Translation by Thomas G. Western. Winkler, "The Cherokee Indians in Texas," *op. cit.*, 154.

general, and on March 22, 1832, the governor instructed the political chief to cause the commissioner, Piedras, to be furnished with such stamped paper as he might require for that purpose.[59] Before Piedras could carry out his instructions he had been expelled from Nacogdoches by an uprising of the American settlers, and this ended the efforts of the government to put the Indians in possession of their lands. Shortly after this Teran committed suicide and was succeeded as commandant general by General Vicente Filisola, the holder of an empresario grant himself. Governor Letona, bitterly hostile to the Americans, fell a victim of yellow fever and was succeeded by Beramendi, a warm friend of Texas.[60]

In 1833 the Cherokees with the assistance of the Americans took steps to secure the titles to their lands. A number of the Indians proceeded to San Antonio to lay before the political chief a petition expressing their desires, and giving the boundary of the lands that they wanted. On July 20, he gave them a pass to visit the governor at Monclova. On August 21, Governor Beramendi gave them a document which promised that they would not be disturbed until the supreme government could investigate; but because the time limit for the settlement of David G. Burnet's grant had not expired he could not put them in full possession.[61]

The matter was still unsettled in 1835. On March 10, the political chief wrote that the supreme government of the State would not let the Cherokees, Coshattoes, and other Indians be disturbed until the supreme government could pass on the subject. On May 12, the congress of Coahuila and Texas passed a resolution declaring:

Art. 1. In order to secure the peace and tranquility of the State, the Government is authorized to select, out of the vacant lands of Texas, that land which may appear most appropriate, for the location of the peaceable and civilized Indians which may have been introduced into Texas.

Art. 2. It shall establish with them a line of defense along the frontier to secure the State against the incursions of the barbarious tribes.[62]

This was the last act of the Mexican government with regard to

[59]Winkler, "The Cherokee Indians in Texas," *op. cit.*, 155; *Record of Translations of Empresario Contracts*, 90.

[60]Winkler, "The Cherokee Indians in Texas," *op. cit.*, 156, 157.

[61]*Ibid.*, 163.

[62]*Laws of Coahuila and Texas*, 300.

Indian claims. On November 11 the Consultation adopted articles for a provisional government, and declared all land offices closed until a government could be formed and a land office established under that government capable of issuing valid land grants. The Indian claims were left as they had been throughout the decade. Fields had obtained a shadowy temporary right to land. He had claimed much more for this grant than can be allowed. When the Mexican authorities failed to put him in possession of the land, denying knowledge of him in 1825, he joined with the Fredonian rebels against Mexican authority. In order to overthrow this rebellion, the Mexicans promised land to Bowl and Big Mush, without specifying what lands. The Indians insisted on receiving title to the lands lying between the Trinity and Sabine Rivers north of the San Antonio Road, though it had been officially granted to Burnet, Filisola, and others. During 1831-1832 the authorities contemplated putting the Cherokees in actual possession of that territory, but failed, as we have seen. When Bowl appealed to the governor of Coahuila and Texas in 1833, he was given the same evasive assurances as had been received before, but Beramendi threw some doubt on his right to the lands occupied. Finally, the congress of Coahuila and Texas proposed to remove them from their homes and establish them on the frontiers for defense against the hostile Indians.

The Mexican control of Texas passed with the question in this situation. The Indians had been promised land on numerous occasions, but not the land on which they were located. That land had been granted to others, so that the Mexican government could not legally grant it to the Indians. The period closed with the Indians having no legal claim, and knowing that they had no legal claim, to lands anywhere in Texas.

The Americans in the beginning of their revolt in 1835 recognized the importance of keeping the Indians quiet. The committees of safety had suggested the desirability of coming to some agreement with the Indians, and the Permanent Council had appointed three commissioners to proceed to the Indian villages and discover the cause of their grievances and attempt to settle them. The Consultation, which succeeded the Permanent Council, went further and recognized the rights of the Indians to the lands they had occupied and claimed. "We solemnly declare," said the declaration passed by the Consultation the day before adjournment, that the boundaries of the claims of the said Indians are as follows, to wit, being north of the San Antonio road and the Neches, and west of the Angelina and Sabine rivers. We solemnly declare that the Governor and General Council immediately on its organization shall appoint commissioners to treat with the said Indians to establish definite boundaries of their territory and secure their confidence and friendship. We solemnly declare that we will guarantee to them the peaceable enjoyment of their rights and their lands as we do our own. We solemnly declare that all grants, surveys and locations within the bounds hereinbefore maintained, made after the settlement of the said Indians, are and of right ought to be utterly null and void, and the commissioners issuing the same be and are hereby ordered immediately to recall and cancel the same, as having been made upon lands already appropriated by the Mexican government. We solemnly declare that it is our sincere desire that the Cherokee Indians and their associate bands should remain our friends in peace and war, and if they do so we pledge the public faith to the support of the foregoing declaration. We solemnly declare that they are entitled to our commiseration and protection, as the first owners of the soil, as an unfortunate race of people, that we wish to hold as friends and treat with justice.[68]

On December 22, 1835, the Council, as we have seen, acting upon the recommendation of Governor Henry Smith, appointed Sam Houston, John Forbes, and John Cameron commissioners to treat with the Indians under the instructions to be drawn up by the governor, which was done on the 30th. The commissioners were to proceed to Nacogdoches as soon as possible and enter upon the discharge of their duties, in which they were in nowise to transcend the instructions of the Declaration of the Consultation. "You will in all things pursue a course of justice and equity towards the Indians," Governor Smith said,

and protect all honest claims of the Whites, agreeably to such Laws compacts or treaties, as the said Indians may have heretofore made with the Mexican Republic.

You will provide in said treaty with the Indians, that they shall never alienate their Lands, either separately or collectively, except to the Government of Texas, and to agree that the said Government, will at any time hereafter purchase all their claims at a fair and reasonable valuation. You will endeavor, if possible, to secure their effective co-operation at all times when it may be necessary to call the effective forces of Texas into the field and agreeing for their services in a body for a specific time. If found expedient and consistent, you are authorized and empowered to exchange other Lands

[68]*Journal of the Consultation*, 51-52.

within the limits of Texas not otherwise appropriated in the room of the Lands claimed by Said Indians and as soon as practicable, you will report your proceedings to the Governor and Council for their ratification and approval.[64]

On February 23, 1836, the commissioners entered into a treaty with the Cherokees. By this treaty the Indians were to receive title to the land they claimed, and which under the declaration of the Consultation was adjudged to be theirs. The rights of those who settled before the Cherokees were to be respected, but all who had been once removed and had later returned were to be considered intruders. All bands or tribes mentioned in the treaty were to be required to remove within the boundary fixed. The lands were not to be sold or alienated to anyone except the government of Texas, and the Cherokees agreed that no other tribes should be allowed to settle there. No individual Indian was permitted to sell land, and no Texan to buy from an Indian. The Indians were to be governed by their own laws. The government of Texas had power to regulate trade and intercourse between the Indians and others, but should levy no tax on the trade of the Indians. Property stolen from citizens or from the Indians was to be restored to the persons from whom stolen, and the offender or offenders were to be punished by the tribe to which he or they belonged.[65]

A ratification of this treaty would have resulted in the establishment of a separate Indian state with practical independence. It would have been a nation living within definitely fixed boundaries, under their own laws, punishing their own citizens for theft of horses from the whites, exempt from taxation by the Texan government, and under no more restriction than would be involved in a control over foreign affairs and the appointment by Texas of an agent to live among the Indians. The Convention which met in March, however, refused to ratify the treaty, though Houston and the Indians considered the government morally bound to do so.

Acting upon the theory that the declaration of the Consultation was sufficient authority for his action in drawing up the treaty with the Indians, Houston, while he was attempting to secure a ratification of the treaty by the Senate of the Republic after he became President, deliberately gave the Indians to understand that ratification was not necessary, and that they would get their lands.

[64]MS. *Indian Affairs*, 1831-1841. Texas State Library.
[65]*Secret Journals*, 35, 36, 37, 38.

Writing to Bowl on April 13, 1836, during the retreat from Gonzales, and after the refusal of the Convention to ratify the treaty, Houston said:

> My friend Col Bowl.
>
> I am busy, and will only say, how da do, to you! You will get your land as it was promised in our Treaty, and you, and all my Red brothers, may rest satisfied that I will always hold you by the hand, and look at you as Brothers and treat you as such!
>
> You must give my best compliments to my sister, and tell her that I have not wore out the mockasins which she made me; and I hope to see her and you, and all my relations, before they are wore out. Our army are all well, and in good spirits. In a little fight the other day several of the Mexicans were killed, and none of our men hurt. There are not many of the enemy now in the Country, and one of our ships took one of the enemy's and took 300 Barrels of flour, 250 Kegs of powder, and much property—and sunk a big warship of the enemy, which had many Guns.[66]

The purpose of this letter was probably to keep the Indians quiet by promising them their lands under the treaty and by making it appear that the Mexicans were making only a slight effort to subdue the Texans. In December, however, when there was no danger of the return of the Mexicans, he sent a message to the Senate urging its ratification. "You will find upon examining this treaty," he said,

> that it is just and equitable, and perhaps the best which could be made at the present time. It only secures to the said Indians the usufructuary right to the country included within the boundary described in the treaty, and does not part with the right of soil, which is in this Government; neither are the rights of any citizen of the Republic impaired by the views of the treaty, but are all carefully secured by the third article of the same. In considering this treaty, you will doubtless bear in mind the very great necessity of conciliating the different tribes of Indians who inhabit portions of country almost in the center of our settlements as well as those who extend along our frontier.[67]

The Senate took no action at that time; but at the next session appointed a committee to consider the treaty and the general Indian question, and this committee reported on October 12, 1837. It declared the opinion that the rights with which Indians might have been invested by the Mexican government previous to the

[66] *Lamar Papers*, No. 352.

[67] *Secret Journals*, 35.

declaration of independence should be respected, but was not able to find that any such right had been acquired. The premises assumed by the Consultation were false, and acknowledged rights based on false premises "are of no effect and void, which your committee conceive to be the case in this instance." The territory mentioned in the treaty formed part of the grant to David G. Burnet for the purpose of colonization, the colony was filled, or nearly so, prior to the declaration of the Consultation, and the committee was satisfied that the grant of the territory to Burnet for colonization many years after the settlement of the Indians on the soil, was sufficient evidence that no obligation was created which could be considered binding in favor of the Cherokees, or any other Indians. Finally, the committee reported the following resolution:

> Resolved by the Senate of the Republic of Texas that they disapprove and utterly refuse to ratify the Treaty or any artickles thereof concluded by Sam Houston and Jno. Forbes on the 23rd day of February, 1836, between the provisional Gov[ernmen]t of Texas of the one part, and the "Head Chiefs" Head men and warriors of the Cherokees on the other part. Inasmuch as that said treaty was based on premises that did not exist and that the operation of it would not only be detrimental to the interests of the Republic but would also be a violation of the vested right of many citizens, . . .
>
> Resolved that the President of this Republic be authorized and advised to appoint commissioners and furnish them with instructions such as he may deem most expedient to bring about friendly relations between the Comanches and this Republic; Provided that no fee simple right of soil be acknowledged by this Gov[ernmen]t in favor of those Indians.[68]

On December 16 a resolution was adopted declaring null and void the treaty with the Cherokees, and no further attempt was made by Houston to secure ratification.[69]

There was considerable unrest among the Indians in the East in the summer of 1838 at the time of the Cordova rebellion. There is an indication from the diary of Miracle referred to above that Bowl had foreknowledge of the plans of the Mexicans. He managed to hide his knowledge, however, and received assurances from Houston that the treaty was being observed by the Texans, and

[68] *Secret Journals*, 75-79.
[69] *Ibid.*, 100.

calling upon him to keep the treaty. Houston promised the immediate appointment of some one to run the boundary line between the white and Indian possessions, and on August 16, sent Bowl another letter promising that the white warriors would not hurt the Indians.[70] On August 18, after the dispersal of the rebels, Houston issued an order for mustering out the army, in which he urged the soldiers in falling back to respect the Indians and their property. avoiding injury to every species of property.[71]

The promises of Houston that the treaty would be observed and the boundary line run kept the Cherokees from taking active part with the Mexicans. Later, in the month of August, Rusk asked Bowl to influence the Shawnees, Kickapoos, Delawares, Kaosatis, and other friendly tribes to keep the peace. After the battle with the Kickapoos on October 16, Rusk complained to Bowl that a Cherokee had been found among the dead Kickapoos, which Bowl explained by saying he was a renegade Indian.[72]

In the latter part of the summer of 1838 Houston appointed Alexander Horton to run the line between the Indian territory and that of the whites. On account of the opposition of the whites, and the quarrels among Horton's men, nothing was accomplished before the end of Houston's administration. A letter from Bowl to Horton on October 27, is interesting and enlightening as regards the relations of the whites and Indians at that time. He wrote:[73]

Mr Horton Dear Sir I have accomplished my Desir in rasing my men for to guard and aid you while you are running the Line in so much I understand that some of the white people are against it which I am sorry to hear that, for we wish to do write ourselves, and we hoped that white people wanted to do the same as for your disputes among yourselves I have ordered my men to have nothing to do with it. My express orders is to my men is to guard you and your property from the enemy I hope that you will be particular with us in consequence of us not understanding your tongue and also we will pay that respect to you I hope you will let us know when you need us and where and I will be at your service I will detain Gayen till I get a line from you so as he may read our writing I have twenty-five volunteers to send to you so nothing more only your Friend Bole.

[70]Originals in *Lamar Papers*, Nos. 781, 782, 783, 784, 785, 786.

[71]*Ibid.*, 792.

[72]*Lamar Papers*, Nos. 801, 839.

[73]*Lamar Papers*, No. 855.

Early in December, just before his inauguration as President, Lamar received a long letter from Archibald Hotchkiss of Nacogdoches. It cannot be shown to have influenced Lamar in determining his course toward the Cherokees, but it was not calculated to change his belief that they had no real right to the soil which they occupied. After tracing in a general way the history of the Cherokees in Texas, Hotchkiss said:

> In the year 1833 I became the agent of Burnet for the purpose of carrying out the terms set forth in his contract; to wit: to settle the land . . . a short time subsequent to my receiving this it became necessary for me to repair to the seat of Government for the purpose of transacting business for my [principal,] the principle object of which was to induce them to remove the Indians who had settled within [the bounds] of our grant, and by so doing had to a very great extent impeded the settling of the lands. [I received] assurances from the Government that they [would be removed] immediately; but that promise was not realized [on account] of the increased internal difficulties of the country.
>
> In the early part of 1835 I entered into a correspondence with the Gov[ernmen]t of the State of Coahuila and Texas upon the subject of removing the Indians representing the extreme difficulty we had in obtaining colonists, who were willing to settle in the vicinity of such dangerous neighbors as the Cherokees had allways proved themselves to be in the United States; In answer to which the Governor informed me that he was very sensible of the difficulties under which I was laboring, but that the finances of the State were at such a state of exhaustion that it was extremely doubtful whether they would be able to do anything until the ensueing year, whereupon I offered upon behalf of my principals to advance the means necessary for removing if the Government would afford its countenance and authority for the undertaking, and the corresponding order was sent to the political chief of Nacogdoches for their removal forthwith sometime in the Spring of 1835 which order was never executed but suppressed at the instigation of designing men, the war of Independence which succeeded shortly after put an end to all further action upon this subject.[74] . . .

Lamar's message of December 21, 1838, with regard to the Indian, has been mentioned. Further notice at this point is necessary for an explanation of the attitude he assumed concerning the rights of the Cherokees to the lands they occupied. He said that the immigrant tribes had no legal or equitable claim to any portion of the territory of Texas; that their immigration to Texas

[74]Hotchkiss to Lamar, December 5, 1838, *Lamar Papers*, No. 905.

had been unsolicited and unauthorized, and had always been a source of regret to the more enlightened population; that the Federal Government of Mexico neither conceded nor promised them lands or civil rights; that they came as intruders, and were positively forbidden to make any permanent abidance, and had continued in the country up to that time against the public wish and at the sacrifice of public tranquility. The offer made to bordering tribes in the colonization law of Coahuila and Texas contained precedent conditions which had in no wise been carried out. The pledge of the Consultation and the treaty drawn up under it had never been ratified, and, if it had been, the Indians had violated it time and again.[75]

In the latter part of 1838 and early part of 1839 the Indians in the West were active, and the government made preparations to punish them. To keep the Indians in the East quiet, Lamar appointed Martin Lacy agent to the Cherokees, Shawnees, and other tribes. The special object of the appointment, said the instructions, was to cultivate and preserve the friendly relations existing between the frontier inhabitants of Texas and the "Cherokees, Shawnees, etc., which have emigrated from the United States to Texas, but whose claim to territory or even its occupancy has not yet been recognized, and is now a subject of grave deliberation on the part of the Texian Government." The Cherokees could not better evince their friendly intentions, he suggested, than by prohibiting intercourse with the hostile Indians.[76]

On March 10, 1839, the Texan minister in Washington informed the government of the United States that the President of Texas was determined to act with great energy towards those Indians of the East who had been consistently hostile, and suggested that the United States take steps to restrain their Indians from assisting the kindred tribes in Texas. Before entering on a general war, however, Bowl, chief of the Cherokees, was allowed to visit the various chiefs and attempt to bring about an adjustment of the differences with them. Bowl reported that there was a sincere

[75]*Lamar Papers*, No. 361; *Telegraph and Texas Register*, December 26, 1838.

[76]Lamar to Martin Lacy, February 14, 1839, *Indian Affairs, 1831-1841*, Texas State Library.

desire on the part of the Indians to resume peaceful relations with the Texans.[77]

This change in the attitude of the Indians was probably produced by the destruction of the party of Cordova, March 26, 1839. Cordova had been active in the rebellion at Nacogdoches in 1838, and was at the time of his defeat by Burleson probably on his way to Matamoras to get supplies for another outbreak similar to that of 1838. On March 26, 1839, he was discovered with a party of sixty or seventy Mexicans, Indians, and negroes, encamped at the foot of the Colorado Mountains. Colonel Burleson collected eighty men and started on his trail, overtaking him on the Guadalupe, where a battle was fought resulting in the defeat of the Cordova party with the loss of about thirty men. Cordova himself escaped, but this ended his efforts to stir up revolution in Texas.[78]

Albert Sidney Johnston, Secretary of War, writing to Bowl on April 10, referred to this action, and said that the recent developments went to show incontestably that the Cherokees, or a part of them, the Delawares, Shawnees, Kickapoos, Caddoes, Wacoes, "Tewankanees," Bedies, and Kechies, about the time he was with them had entered into a compact with Cordova to carry on the war as soon as he should return from Matamoras. The assertion that Cordova had been driven off when he attempted to agitate a revolt, he said, was probably to gain time and to conceal the object of the journey to Matamoras.

> The President grants peace to them but is not deceived. They will be permitted to cultivate undisturbed as long as they manifest by their forbearance from all aggressive acts and their friendly conduct the sincerity of their professions or until Congress shall adopt such measures in reference to them as in their wisdom they may deem proper. With a clear view of all matters connected with their feeling and interests It should not surprise the Cherokees to learn that such measures are in progress under the orders of the President as will render abortive any attempt to again disturb the quiet of the frontier nor need it be any cause of alarm to those who intend to act in good faith. All intercourse between the friendly indians & those at war with Texas must cease. The President directs that you will cause the contents of this communication to be made known to all the chiefs who were present at the council.[79]

[77]Thirty-second Cong., 2nd. sess., *Senate Documents*, No. 14, p. 20. A. S. Johnston to Bowl, April 10, 1839, *Lamar Papers*, No. 1188.

[78]Yoakum, *History of Texas*, II, 261.

[79]A. S. Johnston to Bowl, April 10, 1839, *Lamar Papers*, No. 1188.

Some time in April or early in May Major B. C. Waters was ordered to construct a military station on the Great Saline, which was in territory claimed by the Cherokees. Bowl mobilized his warriors and ordered Waters to leave, which he did, since he was not supported by a military force of his own large enough to resist the Indians. This naturally aroused the whites, particularly of the East. The San Augustine *Red Lander* called on the citizens to respond to the call of Major Waters for aid in carrying out the orders of the Secretary of War.[80] The *Telegraph and Texas Register* stated that there were constant complaints of Indian aggressions; that the Cherokees had been a source of trouble since 1836, and that they could not be tolerated longer in Texas.[81]

The action of Bowl called forth a stern letter from Lamar. He had learned with surprise, he said, that Bowl had compelled Major Waters to leave his post on the Great Saline. That officer was acting under the authority and orders of the government, and any attempt to interfere with him or to impede the execution of his duty could be regarded in no other light than as an outrage upon the sovereignty of Texas. "You assume to be acting under a Treaty negotiated at your village on the twenty-third day of February 1836 with commissioners appointed by the Provisional Government of Texas." No doubt there were those who would impress him with the belief that by virtue of that treaty the Cherokees had a right to maintain within the limits of the Republic an independent government bearing no responsibility to the whites as though they were a foreign nation. But the Texans had acquired their sovereignty by many rightful and glorious achievements, and would exercise it without division or community with other people. The Indians could never be permitted to exercise a sovereignty which would conflict with the rights of the Texans. He charged that Bowl was at the center of all conspiracies, and concluded with this ultimatum:

> I therefore feel it my duty as the Chief Magistrate of this Republic to tell you in plain language of sincerity, that the Cherokees will never be permitted to establish a permanent and independent jurisdiction in the limits of this government—that the political and fee simple claims which they set up to our territory now occupied by them will never be allowed—and that they are permitted

[80]Quoted in *Telegraph and Texas Register*, June 19, 1839.

[81]*Telegraph and Texas Register*, June 19, 1839.

at present to remain where they are only because this government is looking forward to the time when some peaceable arrangement can be made for their removal without the necessity of shedding blood; but that their final removal is contemplated is certain and that it will be effected is equally so. Whether it will be done by friendly negotiating, or by the violence of war, must depend on the Cherokes themselves.[82]

Shortly before this, May 14, 1839, Manuel Flores, who had been active the year before in the Cordova rebellion, with a party of twenty-five marauders committed some murders between Seguin and Bexar. They were pursued by several Texans under Lieutenant James O. Rice, and were overtaken on the San Gabriel fifteen miles from Austin. In the battle which followed Flores and two others were killed and the others put to flight. On the body of Flores were found papers which convinced Lamar and his cabinet that the Cherokees were again in treasonable correspondence with the Mexicans. These documents were sent to the Secretary of War by Colonel Burleson on May 22, reaching him about the time of Lamar's letter to Bowl.[83]

These papers consisted of letters addressed to Manuel Flores, Vicente Cordova, and to the friendly tribes of Texas, by the commandant general for the Eastern Interior States, Canalizo, who had succeeded Filisola. The letter to Flores, February 27, 1839, stated that it was impossible for the Federal Government to take any steps for the recovery of Texas on account of the war with France. It was possible, however, he said, that the Indians and loyal Mexicans could defend their homes by joining together against the Americans. They ought not to depend on flying invasions, but on operations of a more continuous character, causing perpetual alarm and inquietude to the enemy. To obtain these objects it was necessary "to burn their habitations, to lay waste their fields, and to prevent them from assembling in great numbers, by rapid and well-concerted movements, so as to draw their attention in every direction, and not offer to them any determinate object at which to strike."

Another letter was addressed by Canalizo to the chiefs of the tribes. As it was the principal basis for the claim that the Chero-

[82]Lamar to Bowl, May 26, 1839, *Indian Affairs, 1831-1841*, Texas State Library.

[83]Yoakum, *History of Texas*, II, 259.

kees and other tribes were plotting with the Mexicans for the extermination of the whites, it is given in full:

> Don Manuel Flores, and the chiefs of the friendly tribes accompanying him, will make known to you my sentiments towards yourself and my friends, the Indians of your tribe; and also what you have to expect as regards your remaining in quiet possession of the land selected by you within the Mexican territory for settlement. And these individuals are informed in relation to what has to be done.
>
> Have an understanding with said Flores in order that you may act in such a manner as to be secured in the peaceable possession of your lands, and to prevent any adventurer again destroying the repose of your families, or again treading the soil where repose the bones of your forefathers, and be careful not to deviate from his instructions.
>
> Act under the full assurance of our generosity, of which we have given so many proofs, and that nothing can be expected of the greedy adventurers for land, who wish to deprive you even of the sun which warms and vivifies you, and who will not cease to envy you while the grass grows and the water flows.[84]

This letter was addressed to Captain Ignacio of the Guapanagues; Captain Coloxe of the Caddoes; The Chief of the Seminoles; Big Mush, civil chief of the Cherokees; Captain Benito of the Kickapoos; Fama Sargento de los Brazos; Lieutenant-Colonel Bowl of the Cherokees.

On receipt of these papers Lamar decided to arrange for the immediate removal of the Cherokees from Texas, and sent the Vice-President, David G. Burnet, and the Secretary of War, A. S. Johnston, to negotiate with them. The commissioners were to offer to buy their produce and pay for their removal to the United States. At the same time he announced in a letter to the Shawnees the intention to expel the Cherokees, in a friendly manner if possible, but by force if they resisted, and warned the Shawnees to have nothing to do with the Cherokees or the Mexicans.[85]

The commissioners reached the Cherokee village about the first of July and entered into negotiations with Bowl and Big Mush. Bowl acknowledged that they were intruders and had no legal

[84]This correspondence was sent by the Texas State Department to the Texan minister at Washington, and presented by him to the American Secretary of State, June 29, 1839. It is published in 32 Congress, 2d session, *Senate Document*, No. 14, pp. 29-35.

[85]Lamar to Linnee and other chiefs and headmen of the Shawnees, June 3, 1839, *Lamar Papers*, No. 1321.

rights to the soil they occupied. He agreed to return to Arkansas in return for payment for their improvements and transportation, but he delayed on one pretext after another putting his agreement in the form of a treaty, using the delay, it was supposed, to get his forces together preparatory to resist the Texans. Even up to the morning of July 15, Bowl assured Adjutant General McLeod that he was willing to abide by his agreement, but again asked for delay in signing the treaty. The Texan forces had assembled by that time, and wearying of the procrastination of the Cherokee chief, orders were given for the battle.

The council-ground was about five miles below the Indian camp. When the Texans arrived at the camp they found that the Indians had mobilized seven miles above. When the Texans approached their rendezvous they were fired on by the Indians, upon which the Texans attacked and drove the Indians from their position, killing a number. The next day they followed their retreating enemies, and in another battle completely defeated them, killing almost a hundred, among the dead being Bowl. The Indians continued their flight, pursued by the Texans, until the 25th, when the pursuit was given up. The main body of Cherokees reached their friends in Arkansas, and save for occasional marauding parties the Texans were free of them as neighbors permanently.[86]

The Shawnees, to whom Lamar had sent a warning on June 3, decided to accept the offer of the Texan government to pay their transportation and to pay for all improvements, consequently the commissioners were able to sign a treaty with them, and they left peaceably for the United States.[87] The Coshattoes and Alabamas, who had accepted the proposal of the Congress of Coahuila and Texas in 1835, were removed to other lands in the Republic.

In his message to Congress on November 12, 1839, Lamar reviewed the whole Cherokee question up to their removal from Texas. He gave as his reasons for expelling them from Texas: (1) that they were immigrant tribes, asserting political rights; (2) that they were a most enlightened and most wily foe, and through their superior intelligence were able to control the wild Indians; (3) that they had committed atrocities on the inhabitants of Texas;

[86]Report to Secretary of War, *Telegraph and Texas Register*, July 24 and August 14, 1839; Yoakum, *History of Texas*, II, 270.

[87]*Indian Affairs, 1831-1841*, Texas State Library. Lamar's message to Congress, November 12, 1839, *Telegraph and Texas Register*, November 27, 1839.

and (4) that they had been in collusion with the Mexicans. He reviewed the efforts of commissioners to secure their friendly removal by agreeing to pay for the transportation of the women and children and for all improvements, but said that in the face of these offers they flew to arms. And finally he expressed it as his opinion that the proper course to pursue with all the barbarian race was expulsion or extermination.[65]

The expulsion of the Cherokees was naturally not accomplished without serious criticism of Lamar, and an earnest defense by his contemporaries; and some historians have seen fit to claim that the action of Lamar was unjustified. It is perhaps not worth while to enter into the discussion of this question. The history of Texas in relation to the Indians is too similar to that of Georgia and other American States to require justification here. Lamar's instincts and training naturally led him to sympathize with the settlers as against the Indians. He was secretary to Governor Troup of Georgia while that State was attempting to extend her jurisdiction over the territory of the Creeks in response to a demand of the would-be settlers. And it may have been that he was too ready to listen to tales of conspiracies between the Mexicans and Indians. But sufficient evidence has been presented to prove that the Cherokees did not have any vested rights in the soil they occupied. The Mexican government might have been culpable for promising lands and then not giving them, but the Indians certainly understood that they had not secured title to the lands. The government of the Republic might have been culpable for using the promise of lands in return for a guarantee of neutrality during the War of Independence, but again the Indians knew that they had not secured title to the lands under the Republic.

The charge that the Cherokees were engaged in a conspiracy with the Mexicans is not important in this connection. The important question is as to whether or not sufficient evidence was presented to Lamar to justify his believing that they were so engaged. And this seems to be answered in the affirmative. The papers taken from the body of Miracle had shown him in consultation with Bowl before the Cordova rebellion in 1838, and Bowl must have known before hand of the proposed rebellion. The papers addressed by Canalizo to the Indian chiefs, including Bowl and Big Mush, while not proving any connection of the Cherokees with the

[65] *Telegraph and Texas Register*, November 27, 1839.

proposed war, could be taken by Lamar in the light of the earlier documents as at least indicating some connection, especially as they came at a time when Bowl was ordering the military agent of the government out of his territory and mobilizing his warriors to prevent the building of a fort.

The whole problem comes back to whether or not the Indians should have been permitted to establish in Texas a government of their own, independent of the Texan government. A ratification of the treaty drawn up on February 23, 1836, under the Provisional Government would have guaranteed the perpetuation of such a government. It was inevitable that the whites should encroach on the Indians, and it was unlikely that a white population would have tolerated an independent Indian state within their borders. Lamar, therefore, acted legally and justly, and what is perhaps more important, logically, in forcing the withdrawal of the Cherokee Indians from Texas.

This story ends with the passage on February 1, 1840, of an act for sectionizing and selling the lands which had been occupied by the Cherokees.[89] The act made no provision for the settlers who had come into the territory since 1822, and because of this and the desire of many to locate claims in that region, there was bitter opposition to the passage of the bill. Houston, who was now a member of Congress, led the advocates of the bill, while the opposition was led by David S. Kaufman, Speaker of the House. The advocates of the measure claimed that the Cherokee lands did not come under the general land act, as they had been won from the Indians only in the preceding July, and that they actually belonged to the government for disposal as it saw fit. The opponents of the measure claimed that the lands had always belonged to the Republic, hence they should come under the terms of the general land act and be disposed of as other lands of the Republic. The argument that the sale of the lands would bring much needed revenue into the treasury overcame the objections of many who held that the Indians had no legal right to the land or of occupancy, and the measure became a law.

(*To be continued.*)

[89]Gammel, *Laws of Texas*, II, 358.

MINUTES OF THE AYUNTAMIENTO OF SAN FELIPE DE AUSTIN, 1828-1832

XI

EDITED BY EUGENE C. BARKER

[p. 18] In the Town of San Felipe de Austin on the 6th day of June 1831. At a regular meeting of the Ayuntamto. of this Jurisdiction present Francis W. Johnson Prest. Walter C. White 1st Regidor Randall Jones 2d Regidor and Pleasant D. McNeil 3rd Regidor Absent Wm Robinson 4th Regidor and Robt M. Williamson sindico procurador. The meeting was opened by the acts of the last meeting being read which were approved.

The following resolutions were then adopted first—that F. W. Johnson prest. W. C. White first regidor and Citizen Wm. H. Jack be appointed a committee to draw up and report to the body at the next regular session, a system for the regulation of Municipal surveying, to regulate the fees and emoluments which the Municipal surveyors shall receive and collect and also to propose a division of the jurisdiction into surveying districts.
second—The return of the election held on the Colorado being informal ordered that a new election be held at the house of Wm. Robertson and Wm. Bartons on the 25th of this month for the election of Militia officers for that company.
third—That the Alcalde of the jurisdiction and the Comisarios of the various precincts be recommended to call on or send for the Chiefs of the various rambling and other tribes of Northern Indians and represent to them the great injury and inconvenience experienced by the inhabitants of the Colony by their destroying the game and burning or firing the prairies, and request them to remove with their tribes beyond the limits of the Colony.

fourth—That in conformity with the provisions of [p. 19] the 8th Chapter of the Municipal ordinance and the authority vested in the Ayunto. by decree No. 180 of the State Legislature. All storekeepers, retailers or venders of goods wares and merchandise be required to come forward on or before the first day of July next, and take out the licence necessary for them to exercise their professions agreeably to the provisions of said chapter of the ordinance. Lawyers or those persons who exercise the profession of public agents for individuals before the Alcaldes will also prior to the sd. 1st July apply for Licence. As all those who fail to comply with this order will be fined agreeably to the provisions of said law. Tavern keepers must also under the provissions of said law take out a licence on or before first July next.

fifth—That the Comisarios of precincts and Sindicos be ordered to take the census of their respective precincts and report the same to the Ayuntamto. of this jurisdiction at their next regular session and that they be also furnished with instructions how to proceed to take a list of the taxable property of each resident of the jurisdiction, and that blank forms be furnished them.

sixth That it shall be the duty of every ferryman or owner of a ferry boat to post up in some conspicuous place the rates of ferriage as established by this body, and every ferryman who exacts more than the said rates shall be liable to a fine of five dollars recoverable before the Comisario of any precinct or before the Alcalde of the jurisdiction.

seventh That the Alcalde be authorized to have some blank licences printed for the purpose of issuing [p. 20] to those persons who may apply for them agreeably to the provissions of the — chapter of the municipal ordinance, for which a sum equivalent to the printing and paper shall be exacted.

That S. M. Williams agent of the Empresario Austin be requested to furnish the body with a list of the land granted to individuals in this Colony.

It having come to the knowledge of the Ayuntamto. that C. G. Cox and J. B. Walls are exercising the profession and practice of medicine without having previously complied with the ordinance regulating the practice of medicine within this jurisdiction. Ordered, that they be notified to attend at the next regular meeting of the Ayunto. on the first Monday in July next. And show cause why they should not be fined agreeably to the provissions of said ordinance.

The report of the Committee to whom was referred the formation of a fee bill to regulate the charges of licenced Physicians was read and approved, and the fee bill ordered to be engrossed in the book of Ordinances (for which see sd book pages —)

A petition from Gail Borden, jr praying to be appointed Municipal Surveyor was read and the appointment made subject to such special regulations as may hereafter be adopted.

A petition from Laughlin McLaughlin praying that the title for Town Lot No. — be made to John M. Allen, for the reasons set forth in the petition—prayer granted.

[p. 21] A petition from S. A. Brown was presented read, and rejected by the unanimous vote of the body.

BOOK REVIEWS AND NOTICES

Kino's Historical Memoir of Pimería Alta: A Contemporary Account of the Beginnings of California, Sonora, and Arizona, by Father Eusebio Francisco Kino, S. J., Pioneer Missionary Explorer. Cartographer, and Ranchman, 1683-1711. By Herbert Eugene Bolton, Ph. D. (Cleveland, The Arthur H. Clark Co., 1919. 2 vols. Pp. 379, 329.)

The history and bibliography of the Spanish Southwest has been notably enriched by the publication of Professor Bolton's two volumes on Father Kino. The author and editor has rescued from oblivion what may be justly characterized as one of the most valuable sources in the field of which he is the acknowledged pioneer and master, and has given to the scholarly world a final and authoritative picture of the great missionary whose name will always be intimately associated with the northward expansion of New Spain. "Bolton's 'Kino'" will doubtless become as well known a phrase as is "Parkman's 'La Salle'," "Fiske's 'Las Casas'" and other similar works.

The major portion of this work consists of a carefully edited translation of Father Kino's lost history known as "Favores Celestiales." The original manuscript was discovered by Professor Bolton during his researches in the Mexican archives. There had been a few vague references made and much speculation indulged in by earlier writers as to the existence of a formal history by Father Kino, but Professor Bolton was the first to locate and definitely identify such a work. The text of the translated manuscript comprises a total of 567 pages in the two volumes, and contains Kino's personal account of his labors in the region of Pimería Alta, roughly corresponding to present northern Sonora and southern Arizona.

In the sixty-page introductory essay that precedes the text Professor Bolton has made an important contribution to the early history of North America. It is not only an interpretation of Kino's manuscript, but also an excellent biographical sketch of that interesting personage. Kino's labors and personality may best be described in the words of Professor Bolton:

> He was great not only as a missionary and church builder, but also as an explorer and ranchman. By him or directly under his supervision missions were founded on both sides of the Sonora-Arizona boundary, on the Magdalena, Altar, Sonóita, and Santa Cruz Rivers. The occupation of California by the Jesuits was the direct result of Kino's former residence there and of his persistent efforts in its behalf, for it was from Kino that Salvatierra, founded of the permanent California missions, got his inspiration for that work. To Kino is due the credit for first traversing in detail and accurately mapping the whole of Pimería Alta. . . . During his twenty-four years of residence at the mission of Dolores, between 1687 and 1711, he made more than fifty journeys inland, an average of more than two per year. . . . In the course of them he crossed and recrossed repeatedly all of the two hundred miles of country between the Magdalena and the Gila and the two hundred and fifty miles between the San Pedro and the Colorado. When he first opened them nearly all his trails were either absolutely untrod by civilized man or had been altogether forgotten. . . . One of his routes was over a forbidding, waterless waste, which has since become the graveyard of scores of travelers who have died of thirst because they lacked Father Kino's pioneering skill. . . . In the prosecution of these journeys Kino's energy and hardihood were almost beyond belief.

In addition to all of this, as Professor Bolton points out, Kino was very active in his literary work and map-making. The editor has also given us the personal, subjective side of the great missionary, and draws a picture that constitutes a new tribute to the sincerity and value of Spain's civilizing work in America. Kino's perseverance, piety, resourcefulness, business ability, personal courage, and medieval asceticism bespeak an unusual character worthy of close study. The sympathetic enthusiasm of the editor adds charm and interest to the entire work.

The translation is unusually accurate and painstaking. The volumes abound in helpful footnotes indicative of Professor Bolton's marvelous familiarity with his field. A number of contemporary maps are reproduced for the first time, and the editor has compiled a detailed map of the scene of Father Kino's labors which locates accurately for the first time all of the principal frontier settlements of northwestern New Spain. The typographical excellence of the work is worthy of mention, and the modern scholarly aids in the way of bibliography and index are unusually complete. The work may well be considered a masterpiece in the historical literature relating to the Spanish régime in the Americas.

W. E. DUNN.

NEWS ITEMS

John N. Simpson, prominent business man of Dallas, died in that city June 26, 1920.

Mr. H. W. McGee of Marshall presented to the Association a copy of a *National Register* extra, published at Washington, April 16, 1845, and containing the proclamation of President Anson Jones, convening the congress of the Republic in extra session.

Rev. Johannes Mgebroff, author of *Geschichte der ersten deutschen evangelisch-Lutherischen Synode in Texas,* died at his home near Brenham, May 22, 1920.

Edgar Rye, author of *The Quirt and the Spur: Vanishing Shadows of the Texas Frontier,* died at Los Angeles, California, June 7, 1920.

John W. Sansom, author of a pamphlet entitled *Battle of Nueces River,* died at his home in San Antonio, June 19, 1920.

Who Was "Democrat"?—During an investigation by the State Printing Board, at Austin, September 5, 1882, of certain charges filed against the State Printer, the following facts were brought out concerning a pamphlet addressed "To the people of Texas" and signed "Democrat." It was written by Adjutant-General W. H. King, and printed by the State Printer during August, 1882. The pamphlet embraces twelve octavo pages, and presents an interesting, though partisan, resume of the political history of Texas from 1870 to 1882.

E. W. WINKLER.

Authorship of a Pamphlet by Curtius.—The library of the University of Texas recently acquired a pamphlet entitled: "Texas.

A brief account of the origin, progress and present state of the colonial settlements of Texas; together with an exposition of the causes which have induced the existing war with Mexico. Extracted from a work entitled, 'A geographical, statistical and historical account of Texas,' now nearly ready for the press. Some of these numbers have appeared in the New Orleans Bee and Bulletin. Nashville: Printed by S. Nye & Co., 1836." 8vo., 16 pp. The preface is signed "Curtius"; this pseudonym also appears at the end of the text. The text is addressed "to an impartial world," and is divided into numbers I-IV.

A comparison of the text of this pamphlet with the text of the first twelve pages of an "Address of the Honorable Wm. H. Wharton, delivered in New York, on Tuesday, April 26, 1836," shows that entire paragraphs in the two publications are substantially identical in language. Without further proof one would conclude that Wm. H. Wharton and "Curtius" are the same. In a letter from Wm. H. Wharton to Henry Smith, dated Nashville, February 7, 1836, he says, "I have also published and sent on my Curtius pamphlet."

The "Curtius" pamphlet was written in December, 1835, and was published at Nashville about February 1, 1836. Several errors in the pamphlet are corrected in the address, and in one instance a misprint in the address is cleared up by the pamphlet.

In a note to the statement, quoted from Wharton's letter to Smith, Dr. Garrison says, "For what was doubtless the matter of this pamphlet, see *Telegraph and Texas Register* for February 27, 1836." The number of the *Telegraph* referred to had transferred to its columns from those of the New Orleans *Bee* Number 1 only of the four numbers constituting the complete pamphlet.

What became of the "work entitled 'A geographical, statistical and historical account of Texas,' now nearly ready for the press," cited in the title of the Curtius pamphlet?

E. W. WINKLER.

THE SOUTHWESTERN HISTORICAL QUARTERLY

VOL. XXIV OCTOBER, 1920 No. 2

The publication committee and the editors disclaim responsibility for views expressed by contributors to THE QUARTERLY

MIRABEAU BUONAPARTE LAMAR

A. K. CHRISTIAN

CHAPTER V

THE SANTA FE EXPEDITION

Perhaps of all the things undertaken or accomplished by Lamar, the project of sending a mercantile expedition to Santa Fé accompanied by a military aid has caused most adverse criticism. Most historians have followed contemporaries, particularly Houston, and near contemporaries, as Yoakum, and are content to refer to Lamar's scheme as visionary. As it was one of the policies that gripped him throughout his whole administration, and as its failure has led to so much criticism, a full examination of his purposes in sending such an expedition, and the obstacles confronted by those who undertook it, is necessary.

It should be understood, in the beginning, that Texas claimed, whether rightly or wrongly, all the territory to the east of the Rio Grande, and Santa Fé was about twelve miles east of that river in New Mexico. Shortly after the constitutional government was established in October, 1836, Stephen F. Austin, Texan Secretary of State, in his instructions to William H. Wharton, the envoy to the United States, said that as regarded boundary, the question could not be settled at that time, but that Wharton might explain to the Government of the United States that Texas claimed possession to the Rio Grande. He traced the boundary as follows: Beginning at the mouth of said river on the Gulf of Mexico, thence up the middle of the river, following its main channel, including the islands, to its most northerly source, then in a straight line to the United States boundary, and along that boundary to the starting point.[1]

The First Congress took early action in proclaiming the boundaries of the new republic, and on December 19, 1836, the President approved an act providing that the civil and political jurisdiction of Texas should extend to include the boundaries as Austin had outlined them to Wharton, at the same time the President was directed to open negotiations with the United States to ascertain and determine the boundary between those two countries.[2] And from that time on the Rio Grande to its source was officially considered as the western boundary of Texas.

Just when Lamar conceived the idea of establishing the authority of Texas over the territory included in this claim, it is not possible to say; nor can we determine positively what motive chiefly influenced him in adopting the policy which he ultimately carried out. It is likely that he began his administration as President with some idea of taking possession of the Santa Fé country, though it was not until the last year of his administration that he was able actually to undertake the measure. There is no doubt that he desired to establish control, partly because he was convinced that the people of New Mexico desired to live under Texan sovereignty, and partly because he wished to create a nation reaching ultimately to the Pacific; but chiefly because he understood the commercial benefits that would accrue to Texas through a diversion of the trade between St. Louis and Santa Fé to the ports of Texas.

The importance of this trade to Texas was early recognized. On August 27, 1829, Stephen F. Austin wrote to Henry Austin, stating that he contemplated opening a road to El Paso and to Santa Fé with a view to diverting the Missouri trade to Galveston.[3] Later, in 1835, Austin recommended to the Mexican government that two companies of riflemen be stationed on the Colorado and Brazos rivers for the purpose of defense and for opening a road to Chihuahua.[4] One cannot say whether these suggestions in-

[1]Garrison, *Diplomatic Correspondence of the Republic of Texas*, I, 132. American Historical Association *Report*, 1907, II.

[2]Gammel, *Laws of Texas*, I, 1193-1194.

[3]*Austin Papers*, file of July, 1836. University of Texas.

[4]Stephen F. Austin to James F. Perry, March 4, 1835, in *ibid.*

fluenced Lamar, but he was acquainted with them, and, as will appear, he adopted a policy in keeping with the ideas of Austin.

At the same time that the commerce with Santa Fé was becoming attractive to the Texans, it seemed that the people of New Mexico were about to throw off their yoke of allegiance to the Mexican government, and there was reason to suppose that Texan rule would not be objectionable. In 1835, when a strong central government was established in Mexico, resulting in the secession of Texas from the Mexican government, Colonel Albino Perez was sent to take charge of the province of New Mexico. The people up to that time had been ruled by native governors and resented the appointment of a stranger as governor. The new governor introduced a system of direct taxation which proved unsatisfactory, but the populace took no active steps in opposition until a native *alcalde* was imprisoned by the *Prefecto* of the northern district. The *alcalde* was released by a mob, upon which the governor called out the militia to put down the mob. It developed that the militia were in sympathy with the mob, however, and, only a few adhering to the governor, he was easily taken by the mob and put to death. The mob proceeded to elect a governor of their own, and managed to hold out as an independent government until put down by Armijo in January, 1838.[5]

The Texan authorities knew of the rebellion, but they were not aware that it had been put down. On January 5, 1838, the secretary of state wrote the Texan minister in London, as follows:

> The Californias continue independent of Mexico, and recently a rebellion in Santa Fé resulted in the death of the Governor and a number of the principal officers of the Government, and the appointment on the part of the revolutionists, of commissioners to apply to the U. States for admission; not knowing, I suppose, that they are included within the limits claimed by Texas.[6]

Shortly after the inauguration of Lamar an act was passed for the creation of a regiment of regular soldiers for warfare against the Indians.[7] Colonel Edward Burleson, with a full staff of subordinate officers, was stationed at Bastrop, an outlying settlement

[5]Josiah Gregg, *Commerce of the Prairies*, I. 130-136.

[6]Garrison, *Dip. Cor. Tex.*, III, 838. The secretary of state was wrong in saying that application for annexation to the United States was considered.

[7]Gammel, *Laws of Texas*, II, 15.

on the Colorado. On January 14, 1839, an act was passed for the permanent location of the seat of government, and this location was to be limited to some point between the Trinity and the Colorado, north of the San Antonio Road.[8] The connection between these two acts will appear presently.

Among the officers under the above act, William Jefferson Jones was appointed as a lieutenant. He had taken part in the campaigns against the Indians in the East in the summer of 1838. He was in Houston in December, 1838, or January, 1839, and it appears that he was the first to outline a program for taking possession of the Santa Fé country. He had a conversation with Lamar on the subject, but whether he initiated the proposal, there is no present way of knowing. The only record of the conversation is contained in a letter from Jones to Lamar a short time later, and this would indicate that the originator of the scheme was Jones. It is necessary to quote at length from this letter in order to make clear the connection of Jones with the enterprise.

Genl M. B. Lamar. Bastrop Feby 8th, 1839,
My dear Sir,

In a letter, which I addressed to the Secretary at War a few days since relative to the contemplated expedition against the Comanches, I took occasion to refer to the importance of the Santa Fe trade and of the facilities of diverting it to the Colorado Valley, the natural outlet for all commerce of the North Western Territory of Texas, at this moment the most productive portion of it. The lowest estimate of the trade of what was formerly New Mexico has been placed at $20,000,000 (millions), consisting of gold & silver and the rich furs of the mountains, which now pass out by the Red River valley and the Rio Grande, building up the towns of St. Louis and Matamoras. . . .

Whilst in the City of Houston and at the time of my appointment to the Regiment against the Comanches, I suggested to you the importance of a politico-military mission to Santa Fe with a view to the introduction of the trade of New Mexico thro' the natural outlet within the limits of this Republic.

. . . I have every reason to believe the seat of government will be located on the Colorado between this place and the mountains, probably at their foot and I have no doubt, the selection will be the most judicious which can be made within the limits assigned the Commissioners by the law. In that event the Capital of the Nation may command the entire trade of New Mex-

[8] *Ibid.*, II, 163.

ico. . . . With a view to the immediate diversion of this trade to the Colorado I would suggest the early establishment of a trading house at the highest point on the river known to be navigable, say at the junction of the Pasigona & Colorado, with a small force to protect it. [He went so far as to suggest conciliation with the Prairie Indians, who were the most troublesome of the Indian neighbors, and continued,]

As the government of Texas claims to extend its territory to the utmost limits of Santa Fe, it is desirable that the people should be brought under our direct political control. The great distance of Santa Fe from the government of Mexico has left that territory entirely dependent upon itself for protection, and the people only feel the authority of the political power thro the weight of taxation imposed by the central head. They are prepared to unite with us, and this is the favorable moment to cement the friendship they have offered. The revolutionary spirit is warm in New Mexico, and the people are determined to throw off the despotic yoke of the present government. We should at once demonstrate our sympathies with them.

I hope, if possibly in your power, that you will order an immediate military escort for a company of traders to Santa Fe, and that a portion if not the entire adventure may be undertaken by the government itself. Immense profits must result from it, and the introduction of 75 or 100 thousand dollars of specie from Santa Fe thro' the Colorado Valley will give confidence to individual enterprize and the route will soon be lined with traders able to protect themselves, who will introduce the riches of New Mexico into the lap of Texas. . . .[9]

It is a striking fact that the five commissioners charged with the location of the permanent seat of government came to the conclusion anticipated by Jones. I have found no direct connection between Jones and the commissioners, but it is unlikely that the harmony of his ideas with the report of the commissioners was accidental. Unfortunately there is no record of the instructions given to the commissioners by Lamar other than the statement of his secretary referred to above; hence, it is not possible to indicate how far the desirability of the point selected as a way station between Santa Fé and points on the Gulf was a part of the in-

[9]W. J. Jones to Lamar, February 8, 1839, *Lamar Papers*, No. 1049. This letter is endorsed by Lamar, "Thos J Jones Bastrop 8th Feby 1839. Upon Santa Fee trade &c Received 20th Feby." This indicates a strange lack of knowledge of Jones' real name. The letter was autographed, "Wm. Jefferson Jones," but the first abbreviation is difficult of interpretation. Certainly Jones must have been little known by Lamar previous to this, though he became better known later.

structions. The commissioners left while Jones was in Houston, or shortly after, and there seems no doubt that there was a general understanding among the commissioners and the President that a location was to be selected favorable to the proposed occupation of New Mexico. The report of the commissioners, among other things, stated:

> The Commissioners confidently anticipate the time when a great thoroughfare shall be established from Santa Fe to our Sea ports, and another from Red River to Matamoras, which two routs must almost of necessity intersect each other at this point. They look forward to the time when this city shall be the emporium of not only the productions of the rich soil of the San Saba, Puertenalis Hono and Pecan Bayo, but of all the Colorado and Brassos, as also the Produce of the rich mining country known to exist on those streams. They are satisfied that a truly National City could at no other point within the limits assigned them be reared up, not that no other sections of the Country are not equally fertile, but that no other combined so many and such varied advantages and beauties as the one in question. The imagination of even the romantic will not be disappointed on viewing the Valley of the Colorado, and the fertile and gracefully undulating woodlands and luxuriant Prairies at a distance from it. The most sceptical will not doubt its healthiness, and the citizens bosom must swell with honest pride when standing in the Portico of the Capitol of his Country he looks abroad upon a reigon worthy only of being the home of the brave and free. Standing on the juncture of the routs of Santa Fe and the Sea Coast, of Red River and Matamoras, looking with the same glance upon the green romantic Mountains, and the fertile and widely extended plains of his country, can a feeling of Nationality fail to arise in his bosom or could the fire of patriotism lie dormant under such circumstances.[10]

For a while Lamar seriously considered the sending of an immediate military expedition to Santa Fé. This would have been justified on the grounds that Texas was still technically at war with Mexico, though no actual hostilities had occurred since the Mexican defeat at San Jacinto. In March, 1839, he addressed the Harrisburg Volunteers on the defence of the frontier, and congratulated them on their prospects for "honorable station in the select Regiment which is to be placed under the command of Colonel Karnes in the anticipated expedition to Santa Fee."[11]

[10]Report of Seat of Government Commissioners, April 13, 1839, *MS. Seat of Government Papers*, Texas State Library.

[11]*Lamar Papers*, No. 1162.

Letters from correspondents also indicate that there was some activity looking toward such an expedition.[12] Lamar was unwilling, however, to adopt the suggestion of Jones that the Prairie Indians be conciliated, especially since he had repeatedly expressed himself as favoring their extermination or expulsion from the republic. And the warfare begun early in his administration continued until the close of 1840, leaving little opportunity to divert any of the forces for an expedition to Santa Fé.

It will be noticed that the letter of Jones mentioned a previous letter to the secretary of war on the subject of the Santa Fé trade, and the importance of securing it for Texas. It is interesting to notice that the secretary of war in his report, September 30, 1839, mentioned the fact that the government was constructing a military road from Red River to the presidio crossing of the Nueces river, and proposed the construction of a similar road from Austin to Santa Fé. He said that Santa Fé was situated about twelve miles east of the upper Rio Grande, and was included within the statutory limits of Texas. It was settled entirely by Mexicans, and never having been conquered by Texas was still under the Mexican government. The country between Austin and Santa Fé, he said, was wholly unoccupied save by roaming bodies of Indians. For many years the traders of the United States had carried on a successful commerce with Santa Fé, of the annual value of four or five million dollars. Santa Fé was not the consumer of all the goods, but was rather the depot for trade with the interior of Mexico. He thought that the trade might be diverted to Texas if a military road were constructed, since the distance from Santa Fé to Texas ports was much less than to St. Louis; and Texas would be the recipient of the vast profits realized. He suggested, also, that a military road would serve to conciliate the western part of the Texan territory, and the two sections would be bound closely together.[13]

Lamar, in his message to Congress, November 12, 1839, referred to this subject, and discussed the importance of the Santa Fé trade without recommending any action by Congress at that time.[14]

[12]J. S. Jones to Lamar, April 14, 1839, *Lamar Papers*, No. 1198; W. J. Jones to Lamar, April 15, 1839, *Ibid.*, No. 1199.

[13]Yoakum, *History of Texas*, II, 313.

[14]*Lamar Papers*, No. 1529.

Lamar was intensely interested in extending the trade of the republic. In his inaugural address in December, 1838, he had expressed himself in favor of free trade; and in the instructions to the various ministers sent to Europe, he always suggested the policy of offering favorable commercial privileges in return for recognition of independence. In February, 1839, he issued a proclamation, after Congress had passed an act to that effect, opening trade between the western settlements of Texas and the Mexicans on the Rio Grande.[15] This action was a result of the revolt of Canales against the centralists, and did not carry any recognition of Mexican rights to the east of the Rio Grande.

A considerable trade had developed between Santa Fé and St. Louis on one side, and between Santa Fé and Matamoras on the other. This had its beginning after the expedition of Pike, though it was not until 1821 or 1822 that any appreciable success attended the efforts of merchants to open trade—at the time that Stephen F. Austin left Missouri with his colonists and settled in Texas. In 1833 and 1834 the government of the United States found it necessary to give military aid to the expeditions on account of the hostility of the Indians.[16] In 1839 an effort was made to open direct trade between Van Buren, Arkansas, and Chihuahua, Mexico, an account of which appeared in the *Telegraph and Texas Register* on July 17, 1839, probably stimulating the interest of the government and people of Texas in trade with Mexico.

During the fall and winter of 1839-1840, the possibility and desirability of getting control of the Santa Fé trade was under discussion by the people and newspapers. The editor of *The Sentinel,* published at Austin, said that he had frequently been asked as to the feasibility of establishing direct communication with Santa Fé. He estimated that the distance from Austin to Santa Fé was about four hundred and fifty miles. The road, he said, was through a rich, rolling, well-watered country. The distance from Austin to the old San Saba fort was estimated at one hundred and twenty-five miles, and the writer said that the old Spanish road could be followed from Gonzales to that place. The Santa Fé road, it was stated, passed through a beautiful country

[15] *Lamar Papers*, No. 1079.

[16] Gregg, *Commerce of the Prairies*, I, 24, 31.

at the headwaters of the Red River, where there was good grazing. A small force would be sufficient, as there were no enemies except the Comanches, and fifty well-armed men would suffice for protection against them. Finally, the Texan traders would have every advantage over those from St. Louis.[17]

About the time this was published, and just before it appeared in the *Telegraph and Texas Register,* William G. Dryden, who had spent a number of years in Santa Fé appeared in Texas. He was sent on April 1, 1840, to Lamar with a letter of introduction by William H. Jack of Brazoria.[18] Jack introduced him as a former officer in the Mexican service who was well acquainted in Santa Fé, Dryden's report of the conditions in Santa Fé must have been favorable, as we find Lamar issuing an address to "The Citizens of Santa Fee" two weeks later.

In this letter, which was probably carried to Santa Fé by Dryden, he saluted the citzens of Santa Fé as "Friends and Compatriots." He referred to the revolution which had emancipated Texas from the "thralldom of Mexican domination." The revolution was forced upon them by circumstances too imperative to be resisted. The Anglo-American population of Texas had left the comforts and the enlightened liberty of their own country, and had migrated to Texas under the guarantee of the Constitution of 1824. They had witnessed many civil wars, and had hoped that calamities would harmonize the government, and teach the authorities of Mexico that frequent political changes and domestic discords were destructive of the prosperity and character of a people. Texas had resolved to be free, when a military despotism arose with the forcible abrogation of the Constitution of 1824. Impelled by the highest considerations, which a benignant providence had sanctified by conferring an unexampled prosperity upon them, they had asserted and achieved their independence, and had entered the great family of nations. They had been recognized by "the illustrious Government of the United States, and by the ancient Monarchy of France," and other powers of Europe were ready to extend the right hand of fellowship. Their natural resources were in rapid progress of development; the population was increasing by numerous accessions from Europe

[17]*Telegraph and Texas Register*, April 8, 1840.

[18]Jack to Lamar, April 1, 1840, *Lamar Papers*, No. 1757.

and the United States, and their commerce was extending with a power and celerity seldom equalled in the history of nations.

All this was introductory to what follows. "Under these auspicous circumstances," he said,

> we tender to you, a full participation in all our blessings. The great River of the North, which you inhabit, is the natural and convenient boundary of our territory, and we shall take great pleasure in hailing you as fellow-citizens, members of our Young Republic, and co-aspirants with us for all the glory of establishing a new and happy and free Nation. Our constitution is as liberal as a rational and enlightened regard to human infirmities will safely permit. It confers equal political privileges on all; tolerates all Religions without distinction, and guarantees an even uniform and impartial administration of the laws.

He hoped the communication would be received by them and the public authorities in the same spirit in which it was dictated. And then he announced that if nothing intervened to change his resolution, he would despatch in time to arrive "in your section of Country about the ninth of September proxima, one or more commissioners, gentlemen of worth and confidence to explain more minutely the condition of our country, of the seaboard and the co-relative interests which so emphatically recommend and ought perpetually to cement the perfect union and identity of Santa Fee and Texas." The commissioners were to be accompanied by a military escort for the purpose of repelling any hostile Indians that might infest the passage, and with the further view of ascertaining the opening of a safe and convenient route of communication between the two sections of country, "which being strongly assimilated in interest, we hope to see united in friendship and consolidated under a common Government." Until the arrival of those commissioners he was appointing some of their own citizens, William G. Dryden, John Rowland, and William Workman, to whom the views of the Texan government had been communicated, to confer with them upon the subject matter of the communication.[19]

In spite of this assurance, no action was taken to carry out the purposes expressed in the letter. For the whole of the summer and until October, all the Texan forces were engaged in warfare with the Comanches. Besides, a total lack of funds prevented

[19]Lamar to the Citizens of Santa Fé, April 14, 1840, *Lamar Papers*, 1773.

the carrying out of the policy of Lamar at that time. Under these circumstances, he appealed to Congress, which met in November, to supply the funds and take the necessary steps to bring Santa Fé under the political and commercial control of Texas.

The Congress had been elected on an issue of retrenchment, and was by no means warm to the plans of Lamar from the beginning. Besides, Sam Houston had succeeded in making himself a leader of the anti-administration forces in Congress, and, as will be seen, was able to defeat appropriations for the project.

On November 9, 1840, Representative Usher, a friend of the administration, introduced a resolution requesting the committee on the state of the republic to take into consideration the propriety and expediency of passing a law with the view to inform the inhabitants of Santa Fé of their privileges as citizens of the republic of Texas.[20] On the same day Representative Miller of Austin, a friend of Houston's, introduced a resolution instructing the committee on finance to inquire into the expediency of laying off and setting apart so much of the public domain intermediate and equidistant between Austin and Santa Fé, as might be adapted to the establishment of a colony of actual settlers, with a view to opening, facilitating, and securing the trade of Santa Fé.[21] Out of this second resolution grew the notorious "Franco-Texienne" bill, which was ardently supported by the French minister, Saligny, and the opponents of the administration, led by Sam Houston. As this was an alternative measure to the policy of the administration, a somewhat full examination is necessary.

This bill proposed to create a corporation headed by two Frenchmen, Jean Pierre Hippolyte Basterreche, and Pierre Francois de Hassauex, which contracted to introduce within the republic eight thousand families by January 1, 1849. For this purpose three million acres of land were granted to the corporation, on the condition that all the terms of the contract were carried out. The land was to be divided as follows: 512,000 acres fronting one hundred miles on the Rio Grande, above the Presidio road, and eight miles in depth; 192,000 acres on the Nueces, above the Presidio road, on both sides of the river, six miles in width and twenty-one in length; 194,000 acres on the Rio Frio; 128,000 acres ex-

[20] 5 Tex. Cong., 1 Sess., *House Journal*, 45.
[21] *Ibid.*, 43.

tending from the Arroyo Seco to the Arroyo Uvalde; 128,000 acres on the Guadalupe above the mouth of Sabine Creek; 1,000,000 acres, in three tracts between the Colorado and San Saba; 192,000 acres from the Colorado to the Pasegoña river, three miles and one hundred miles along the old Santa Fé road; 294,000 acres on Red River, next above the Cross Timbers, fronting forty-six miles and two miles in depth; 50,000 acres at the head of the Nueces; 50,000 acres at the head of the Colorado; 50,000 acres on the Aguila river; 50,000 acres near the source of the Little river; 50,000 acres on the Brazos, thirty miles above the Palo Pinto creek; 50,000 acres on the Noland river, fifty miles above its mouth; 50,000 acres in the forks of the Trinity, west of the Cross Timbers. The company was also to maintain a line of military posts from a point thirty miles above the town of Presidio, and extending to the Red River, at some point near the Cross Timbers. This line was to consist of twenty posts, which were to be maintained for a period of twenty years. They were also to keep up lines of communication between the posts, and were to appoint a sufficient number of geologists, mineralogists, and botanists to explore the whole country and report on all mines found. They were to open and work all mines found, and give fifty per cent of the proceeds to the Republic of Texas.

Practical autonomy was granted to the colonists by the provision that they might make by-laws not in violation of the Texas Constitution. Another attractive feature from the standpoint of the colonists was that the lands were to be exempt from taxation until January 1, 1845.[22]

This remarkable bill actually passed the House of Representatives, and came near to passing the Senate. It is likely that it would have passed the upper House except for the opposition of Lamar.[23] The defeat of this bill aroused the bitter opposition of Saligny to the Government, and unfortunately, he was abetted by the opponents of the administration in denouncing those who voted against the bill.

President Lamar had been in poor health during a good part of his administration, and on December 12, he had become so ill that he found it necessary to apply to Congress for a leave of

[22]*Austin City Gazette*, July 21, 1841; Brown, *History of Texas*, II, 187.

[23]See Mayfield to Saligny, March 29, 1841. and Mayfield to McIntosh, May 12, 1841, Garrison, *Dip. Cor. Tex.*, III, 1315; 1326.

absence so that he could go to New Orleans for treatment. He did not return to his duties until February, 1841, after Congress adjourned. In his absence, however, the Senate passed the administration bill providing for the opening of communications with Santa Fé.[24] This bill was received by the House on January 15, whereupon Representative Murchison introduced a substitute bill authorizing the President to raise volunteers to make an expedition to Santa Fé. This principle was accepted by the committee on the state of the republic, and five days later was reported to the House as a substitute for the Senate measure. On January 26 the House defeated the Senate bill by a vote of sixteen to nineteen, and passed the substitute measure by a majority of two, Houston working against both bills.[25] The Senate failed to agree to the substitute measure, and the session came to a close without legislative approval of the expedition to Santa Fé, but apparently the principle was accepted by both Houses, and they were only unable to agree to the particular method to be used in carrying out the project.

Lamar returned to the Capital in February, 1841, and immediately began preparations to despatch an expedition to Santa Fé in spite of the failure of Congress to make provision for it. He issued a long proclamation to the people of Santa Fé, calling upon them peacefully to accept Texan rule, and guaranteeing them the privileges mentioned in his letter of April, 1840.[26] He appointed Hugh McLeod military commander of the expedition, and, since Congress had failed to make appropriations for the regular army, authorized him to raise volunteers to accompany the expedition. He took upon himself the authority to order the secretary of the treasury to instruct the comptroller to open on his books an appropriation for fitting out the Santa Fé expedition,[27] and Major George T. Howard was sent to New Orleans to purchase supplies.

The volunteers for the expedition began to arrived in Austin early in May, and went into camp on Brushy Creek, about twenty miles north of Austin.[28] The party was collecting for the next

[24]5 Tex. Cong. 1 Sess., *House Journal*, 509.

[25]*Ibid.*, 518, 555, 610.

[26]A copy of the proclamation is in *Lamar Papers*, No. 1942.

[27]Lamar to Chalmers, Secretary of the Treasury, March 24, 1841, Yoakum, *History of Texas*, II, 323, note.

[28]*Austin City Gazette*, May 12, 1841.

month, the last group leaving Austin on June 18, accompanied by President Lamar, and the secretary of the treasury, J. G. Chalmers; and on June 21, the whole body set out on the long march to Santa Fé.

The expedition consisted of a military escort consisting of two hundred and seventy volunteers under the command of General Hugh McLeod, and about fifty other persons, consisting of General McLeod's staff, merchants, tourists, servants, and the civil commissioners who were to take over the civil government of the province in case of success.[29]

The commissioners, William G. Cooke, J. Antonio Navarro, Richard F. Brenham, and William G. Dryden, being expected to take over the civil affairs, the instructions of the state department were directed to them. According to these instructions, the commissioners were appointed to accompany the military expedition about to start for Santa Fé, and they were to have the chief directions of the expedition. The expedition had been organized by the President, the acting secretary of state said, for the purpose of opening a communication with that portion of the republic known as Santa Fé, and of closely uniting it with the rest of the republic, "so that the Supremacy of our constitution and laws may be asserted equally over the entire tract of country embraced within our limits; but as that portion is inhabited by a people strangers to our institutions and to our system of Government, speaking a different language, and deriving their origin from an alien source, whose religion, laws, manners and customs, all differ so widely from our own, the greatest circumspection will be necessary, in making known to that people the object of your mission, on your first arrival in Santa fe and subsequently in conducting your intercourse with them."

The great object of the President, he said, was to attach the people of the district of Santa Fé to the Texas system of government, and to create in their minds a reverence for the Texan Constitution; and to spread among them a spirit of liberty and independence, which would alone qualify them for good citizens, under a government, the very existence of which, depended upon the will of the people.

The President had no illusions as to the possible manner of

[29]Kendall, *Texan Santa Fé Expedition*, 72.

reception of the expedition; and the commissioners were instructed to conduct themselves with caution, and to require the same of the military command entrusted to their charge. It was expected that they would meet with opposition from narrow-minded persons, but the President believed that patience and good judgment would accomplish their purpose.

Their first object upon entering the city of Santa Fé was to attempt to get possession of all the public property; but they were to hesitate to use force if the property were not surrendered peaceably. "The people of Santa fe are our fellow citizens," said the Secretary of State,

> and it cannot be long before they will be fully incorporated with us, partaking of all the advantages and benefits which we enjoy, under our form of government. . . . If they can be brought with their own free will and consent, to submit quietly and cheerfully to an incorporation with us, acknowledging themselves a constituent portion of the Republic, and setting into operation our constitution and laws, then may we confidently expect of them, fidelity and patriotism; but if they are awed into submission by threats, or still worse if they are driven to it by the application of Military power, the disasterous consequences that must inevitably follow, cannot well be foreseen.

The commissioners were to be left largely to their own resources in accomplishing the purposes of the government, but several arguments were submitted for their guidance. In the first place, they were to assure the people of Santa Fé of the protection of the government in the enjoyment of life, liberty, trial by jury, freedom from forced loans, and from all taxes levied without their consent; at the same time they were to hold before their eyes the folly of resistance. Emphasis was to be placed on the fact that by coming under the government of Texas they were to have equal representation in Congress as based upon population.

In case all obstacles were overcome, after taking possession of the custom-houses, books, money, archives, they were to appoint such persons as they might think proper for the government of the city; and were advised to appoint local men as far as possible. After familiarizing themselves with the conditions, they were to propose the sending of three commissioners to Austin, who were to have a seat in the Congress, with the right to discuss any proposition coming before the body, but without a right to vote.

In view of the fact that some of the Texan politicians of the day, and many people in the United States, understood it to be Lamar's intention to conquer with a force of two hundred and seventy men a province of Mexico lying hundreds of miles from the frontier of his own government, the following quotation from the official instructions is inserted, which indicates that no such purpose was in his mind. After stating that the foregoing instructions were based on the supposition that no force would be opposed by the citizens of Santa Fé, and that in case of opposition the commissioners must rely upon their own discretion, the instructions continued:

> The President anxious as he is to have our National flag acknowledged in Santa fe, does not consider it expediant at this time to force it upon that portion of the Republic. If the Mexican authorities are prepared to defend the place with arms, and if you can satisfy yourselves that they will be supported by the mass of the people, no good result can come from risking a battle; for if our arms are successful, a strong Military force would be necessary to hold possession of the place, the cost of keeping which, to say nothing of other objections equally forcible, would of itself be sufficient; and if they are unfortunate, the evils that would flow from it are sufficiently apparent. In this case therefore, you will not be authorized to risk a battle.

It was to be expected that much would be made of the commercial possibilities of the expedition, yet we find that little attention was paid to that subject. "As valuable as their trade is," said the instructions,

> and solicitous as the President is to open its advantages to the citizens of this country, he yet owes a paramount duty to the constitution, and has directed me to instruct you, that you are to make no arrangement, stipulation or agreement whatever with the inhabitants, for the admission of Texan goods into that District of country, by which Texan Citizens will be required to pay any duties to them. We claim the jurisdiction, and consequently the right to demand the revenue, and if we cannot enforce our right, we must at least do nothing to impair it. . . . The object of the expedition being to conciliate the people of Santa fe, to incorporate them with us, and to secure to our citizens all the benefits arising from the valuable trade carried on with them. It may be necessary to diminish the tariff to a

still lower rate to effect these objects; but nothing short of necessity will justify any interference with the rates established by Congress, and of this necessity the collector of customs must be the Judge.[30]

At the same time that the above instructions were given to the four commissioners, a separate list was given to Cooke, who was to be resident commissioner and have charge of the government after the other commissioners had returned to Texas. These instructions constituted Cooke the ruler of Santa Fé under the laws of the Republic of Texas, and of course were to be effective only in case the expedition accomplished its purpose.[31]

As I have said, the last detachment of volunteers and guests left Austin for the camp on Brushy Creek. Among these was George Wilkins Kendall, editor of the New Orleans *Picayune,* who had decided to join the expedition when he became acquainted with Major George T. Howard, who was purchasing supplies in New Orleans, and who was invited to join the expedition as a guest of the government. Kendall has given us an extensive account of the trip from its beginning to his release from a Mexican prison.[32] Also with this last detachment rode the President of the republic. During their ride to Brushy Creek from Austin they stopped for lunch in the middle of the day, and Kendall was very much impressed by the fact that Lamar groomed his own horse and cooked his own dinner. "There was a specimen of Republican simplicity," he said, "the chief magistrate of a nation cooking his own dinner and grooming his own horse." He then paid this tribute to Lamar: "In all my intercourse with General Lamar I ever found him a courteous and honorable gentleman, possessing a brilliant intellect, which has been highly cultivated; and if Texas ever had a warm and untiring friend, it was and is Mirabeau B. Lamar."[33]

Lamar and his party spent the night in camp, reviewed the various companies, and delivered an address to the assembled party, and then returned to Austin. The expedition got under way June 21, a month later than had been originally planned.[34]

[30]Acting Secretary of State Roberts to William G. Cooke, etc., June 15, 1841. Garrison, *Dip. Cor. Tex.*, II, 737-743.

[31]Roberts to Cooke, June 15, 1841, in *Ibid.*, 743-747.

[32]*Narrative of the Texan Santa Fé Expedition.*

[33]Kendall, *Narrative*, I, 69.

[34]*Ibid.*, I, 71.

In writing a biography of Lamar, we might perhaps leave the expedition here; for the group of men who set out with such confidence and so blithely on June 21 were not heard of again until several months after the close of Lamar's administration, and then they were prisoners of the Mexicans, on their way to Mexico City. But the failure of the expedition was made the excuse for bitter attacks on Lamar, and since historians have accepted the more or less superficial judgments of the time, it will be well to give a somewhat complete history of the expedition, and try to arrive at the causes for its failure.

The first incident after leaving that contributed to the failure of the enterprise occurred only a few days after departure from the camp on Brushy Creek. Anticipating a journey of only six weeks or two months, provisions had been prepared for that length of time; but the long delay in getting under way had caused the consumption of the cattle to a large extent, and when the party pitched camp on Little River, June 24, only about sixty miles from Austin, it was found necessary to send back for more beef cattle. The main body waited five days for these supplies, and, in the meantime, continued to consume the provisions which were not too plentiful.[35]

They left the camp on Little River on June 29, and traveling almost due northward, were almost a month in traversing the valley of the Brazos. On July 21, they came to the Cross Timbers, about two hundred miles from their starting place. About ten days were consumed in cutting their way through the Cross Timbers, the wagons of the merchants which accompanied the expedition making necessary roads of some description. At this point, it was necessary to cross the Brazos, which was accomplished with much difficulty.

The purpose of the leaders was to go north to the Red River, and to follow that river to its source, whence only a short distance would remain to Santa Fé, and that along the well marked trail from Santa Fé to St. Louis. The distance was much greater than a direct route, but they were unable to secure guides who knew the country to the northwest. It was to prove that they were no more fortunate in securing a guide for the longer journey. After leaving the Cross Timbers, July 31, their next destination was

[35]Kendall, *Narrative*, I, 85.

Red River. They soon came to the Wichita River which they mistook for the Red River, and followed it for several days, until they found slightly to the south, the headwaters of the Brazos, the river which they had crossed a month before. When this was discovered, a detachment was sent northward to explore for the Red River, and it was located about seventy-five miles north of where the main body was encamped.[36] From this point I shall quote freely from the official report of William G. Cooke, the resident commissioner.

After many unexpected delays and embarrassments, that retarded our march beyond the time anticipated for our arrival in Santa Fé, we at length on the 29th August, reached a point on the Palo Duro a tributary of Red River beyond which there was apparently no further means of progressing with the wagons accompanying the Command. Previous to this time, on the 11th, Mr. Howland our guide, was sent forward with two men, bearing a communication to Mr. Dryden our colleague in Santa Fé; we being at the time under the impression that we were within one hundred miles of that city—judging from the information of a Mexican whom we had also employed as a guide, who was a native of Taos and appeared to be familiar with the country through which we were passing. A few days after the departure of Howland the Mexican suddenly deserted in company with a private—an Italian named Brignoli. On our arrival at the Palo Duro the Commissary reported but five days ration of beef, other rations exhausted—the country in advance of us appeared impassable for wagons—and Indians in large numbers had made their appearance in the vicinity of our camp. Under these embarrassing circumstances, when further progress with the entire command and train seemed impracticable, it was concluded that the undersigned, and a majority of the Commission should proceed forward with one-third of the escort to the nearest settlement to procure supplies and guide to furnish and conduct the troops into New Mexico. We left camp accordingly on the 31st August with 75 soldiers under the command of Capt Sutton—who with the merchants and others formed a body of 97 men. It was our expectation on leaving camp that we should arrive at settlements or strike a road that had been described to us leading to San Miguel, in five days march—but we saw no human being nor any sign of civilization until we reached the Moro a branch of Red River on the 11th Sept, where we met with some Mexican traders—they informed us that we were about 80 miles distant from San Miguel and that there was a wagon road leading from that place to within

[36]Kendall, *Narrative, passim.*

a short distance of our camp. We immediately sent back two of them with orders to Genl. McLeod to destroy the baggage wagons and follow us with all despatch. We continued our march and on the 14th Mr. G. Vanness our Secretary was despatched ahead to San Miguel to communicate with Mr. Dryden whom we expected to meet there and to gain some information respecting the condition of the country—he was also directed to make arrangements for procuring supplies—he was accompanied by Maj. G. T. Howard, Capt W. P. Lewis, Mr. Fitzgerald a merchant of San Antonio and Mr. Kendall of New Orleans.

The main body were forced to travel slowly on account of the condition of their horses, and arrived on the Pecos on September 15 at a small town named Anton Chico, twenty miles from San Miguel. Here they were visited by a Mexican officer accompanied by seventy armed men, who informed them that the Governor of New Mexico was advancing to meet them with a large force, and ordered them to surrender their arms. "We declined holding any communication with him in regard to the object of our visit. . . . but informed him that we came with no hostile intentions toward the citizens of the country and positively refused to lay down our arms."

They decided to remain at Anton Chico until they had received some intelligence from Van Ness, who was supposed to have proceeded to meet the governor. On the 16th they had another interview with the Mexican officer, and told him that unless they received some news from Van Ness by the following morning, they would proceed to San Miguel. The officer said that he would send a courier to Van Ness and order his return, and said that on the following day he would cross the river with his men and encamp near the Texans in order to prove their friendliness. "Up to this time," said the report, "no event had occurred that could justly excite feelings of hostility against us among the people we had met who had been treated by our men with the utmost courtesy, the provisions we had received had been paid for at double their customary value."

On the following day the officer called on them with an express from the governor requesting them to pause until that functionary could arrive. He stated that the governor was approaching with five thousand men and would be in Anton Chico the following day. In the meantime the Mexican forces began to take positions favorable to attack, and the Texans assumed a posture of defence, expecting every moment to be attacked by the forces under Salezar. "There was no longer any doubt as to the intentions of the Mexicans," continued the report,

> and we were momentarily expecting a conflict, when Capt Lewis galloped over to us in company with Don Manuel Chavis kinsman and confidential agent of the Governor with authority to demand our surrender upon the following terms—That we should immediately give up our arms and remain at Anton Chico as prisoners of war on parole, until such time as supplies could be obtained for the subsistence of our troops in returning to Texas—that on no condition could we be allowed to proceed further into Mexican territory, but that as soon as provisions were procured we should be escorted beyond the frontier, where the arms, horses and private property of the officers and men should be restored to them.—These terms were offered by Mr. Chavis, with the most solemn pledges for their fulfillment, seconded by the assurances of Capt Lewis in whom at that time we reposed the utmost confidence.

And then follows the story of Lewis's treachery. Lewis informed the commissioners that he had gone with Van Ness and Howard to execute the orders of the commissioners, when all three were surrounded and taken prisoners by the Mexicans. They were about to be shot when some explanations Lewis made caused the Mexicans to release them; and they were conducted to the governor. The governor, Lewis said, released him and sent him back on parole. He stated that the people of the country were all arrayed in arms against the invaders, and greatly exasperated against them on account of the false reports that had been circulated as to the object of the expedition by the deserter Brignoli. He then told them that he had left the governor within twelve miles of Anton Chico with two thousand troops, and that he would shortly be joined by two thousand more, all well armed and disciplined. As a result of this, and on account of his argument that the lives of the whole party depended upon surrendering their arms at once, "Under these circumstances," said Cooke's report,

> without provisions for our men, our horses broken down by long and weary marches, deprived of any hope of aid from our main body by a distance of two hundred miles, with an enemy before us with more than five times our numbers and should we be victorious in the present fight of which we had no doubt, the prospect

of being attacked by several thousand fresh troops in less than twenty four hours—in this situation and considering that we were specially instructed to avoid hostilities should the people themselves be opposed to us, we concluded the best and most prudent course we could adopt was an acceptance of the terms proposed, and consequently we surrendered.

Governor Armijo arrived at Anton Chico on the 18th with less than one thousand men, and immediately distributed the arms of the Texans among the Mexicans, and started the Texans on their long march to Mexico City. At the same time he moved forward to meet the body which had been left behind on August 31 under General McLeod. Efforts had been made to inform McLeod of the fate of the advance party of ninety-seven men, but they failed, and McLeod received the same treatment as the others, being forced to surrender one hundred and eighty-two men, who were sent after the first group to Mexico City.[37]

It is not my purpose to follow the prisoners on their painful journey on foot to the city of Mexico, nor to follow the negotiations for their release. It is sufficient here to say that in the spring, after seven months in prison, through the intervention of the foreign ministers in Mexico, all the prisoners who could show themselves to be citizens of the United States or some European country were released. The Texans, with the exception of Navarro, who was bitterly hated by Santa Anna, were released in the summer, and by the close of 1842 most of them were again in Texas.[38] I shall, however, examine the various causes given for the failure of the expedition, and consider the criticisms and defence of the administration for undertaking the enterprise.

For the sake of clearness let me summarize at this point the developments connected with the sending of the expedition. The Texans claimed, partly as a result of the treaty of May 14, 1836, with Santa Anna, and partly on account of a statute, passed in December, 1836, that the boundary extended along the Rio Grande to its source, which would include Santa Fé. Lamar, on coming into office, was advised by his friends and received favorably their

[37]W. G. Cooké and R. F. Brenham to Secretary of State, November 9, 1841. *Santa Fé Papers.* This report was sent from Allende, Chihuahua, Mexico, as they were on their way to Mexico City. It did not arrive in Texas until February of the following year, after Lamar's term of office had expired.

[38]Garrison, *Texas*, 246.

advice to undertake a politico-military expedition to Santa Fé, partly for the purpose of establishing commercial connections, but also for the purpose of establishing political control over that part of New Mexico. Various other interests prevented the undertaking until the summer of 1841. In the meantime, however, Lamar had been in communication with men who had lived at Santa Fé, and had received assurances that the populace were very much dissatisfied with the rule of Armijo, the governor, and would welcome a Texan force. As a result of this he sent a letter to the citizens of Santa Fé, and appointed three commissioners to prepare the ground for the coming of the Texans. He attempted to secure some authorization from Congress for the expedition during the session of 1840-1841, but due to an economizing spirit, and on account of the opposition of Houston, and as a result of a difference of opinion as to how military aid should be extended to the merchants, nothing was done by Congress. In spite of this, Lamar called for volunteers, ordered an appropriation opened on the books of the comptroller for fitting out the expedition, and on June 21, 1841, it left with his blessing, but to be taken captive in September, before ever they reached Santa Fé.

Nothing having been heard of the expedition when the next Congress met in November, 1841, a reaction had set in, and the members were free in their criticism of the President's action. The House of Representatives appointed a select committee to investigate the whole subject. This committee reported on December 6, and found that the President had violated the Constitution in ordering money paid out of the treasury without an appropriation by Congress, and that his action in enlisting an army of volunteers without the sanction of Congress was in violation of the Constitution. They found that for the expenses of the expedition $89,549.69 had been expended.[39] The quarter-master-general, on the other hand, reported the sum of $78,421.51.[40]

The committee did not find that any of the rights of Mexico had been overridden, and there is every evidence that it was considered purely as a matter of domestic concern, and the question was one merely of constitutionality. Houston held the same view,

[39] *Austin City Gazette*, December 15, 1841.
[40] *Army Papers*, 1840-1841. Texas State Library.

as instanced by his letter to Santa Anna, March 21, 1842. In this letter he defended the claims to the Rio Grande as a western boundary, and insisted that the prisoners should be released, since it was no concern of Santa Anna. At the same time, he said that Lamar had acted unconstitutionally in sending the expedition without the approval of Congress.[41]

This criticism was probably justified. It must be remembered, however, that Lamar had considered sending the expedition on his own account ever since the matter first came into his mind, and he did not consider the approval of Congress necessary. Normally the regular army was under his command, and could be sent anywhere in the republic that he wished to send it; and he conceived it to be a legitimate use of the army to protect merchants in opening up trade which all public men favored. It was the failure of Congress to make any provision for the regular army in the session of 1840-1841, that made it necessary for Lamar to take the matter into his own hands. He justified himself in this, however, by saying that the principle had been accepted by both houses, and it was only the details on which they could not agree.

Assuming that the claims of Texas to the Rio Grande were just, and nobody in Texas denied it at that time, was Lamar justified in his assumption that the people of Santa Fé would accept Texas sovereignty without a struggle? The instructions to the commissioners prove that Lamar had no grandoise schemes of conquest, and that he was not under the illusion that he was able at that distance to maintain control over New Mexico in case there was resistance on the part of the people of New Mexico themselves. The whole expedition was planned on the assumption that the people of Santa Fé would welcome the Texans. And Lamar was not alone in this assumption. The revolt of 1837-1838 against the central authorities, and the complaints which had come to Texas concerning the rule of Armijo, who had put down the revolt, together with the assurances of Dryden, who was in Texas in 1840, convinced the people of Texas that no difficulty would be encountered in taking possession of Santa Fé. "The universal impression in Texas was," says Kendall,

that the inhabitants of Santa Fé were anxious to throw off a yoke,

[41]Houston to Santa Anna, March 21, 1842, *Niles Register*, LXII, 98.

which was not only galling, but did not of right belong to them, and rally under the "lone star" banner; and events which have since transpired, and which I shall refer to hereafter, have convinced me that such was the feeling of the population. Should any opposition be made to the peaceable entry of the Texan pioneers, it was thought that it would come from the few regular troops always stationed at Santa Fé by the government of Mexico; and this force would have easily been put down if a large majority of the residents were in favor of such a course.

William G. Dryden, who had been in Austin in March and April, 1840, returned to Santa Fé on September 17, and immediately began holding conferences with the people and governor of Santa Fé. On March 10, 1841, he wrote:

Ever since I arrived on the 17th of last Septr., we have been looking for some news from Texas—Because every American, and more than two thirds of the Mexicans, and all the Pueblo Indians are with us heart and soul; and whenever they have heard of your sending Troops, there has been rejoicing: and indeed I have talked many times with the Governor, and he says he would be glad to see the day of your arrival in this country, as he feels well assured that no aid will be sent from below, as they have no means, and he himself will make no resistance

I assured all my friends you would send last fall—I now have pledged myself, this summer; and I shall never lose hope as long as life shall last. I trust, if all things are right, before you receive this, the force will be under march, and near here. It will but be a trip of pleasure.[42]

This letter did not reach Lamar until August, after the expedition had left, but indicates that this man who had lived long among them thought the people of Santa Fé would welcome the Texan expedition.

An interesting testimony to the same effect is contained in a letter of an American Santa Fé trader to the *St. Louis Bulletin* in the fall of 1841. The writer related some of the incidents of the trip which he had just completed from Santa Fé, and with regard to the Texan expedition said:

No news had been received at the time of the departure of the Texan expedition. A ready submission on the part of the inhabitants is to be anticipated; but the number sent from Texas, with-

[42]Dryden to Lamar, March 10, 1841, *Santa Fé Papers*, Texas State Library; *Austin City Gazette*, August 25, 1841.

out reinforcements, is entirely too small to retain possession of the country. Should they arrive at all in Santa Fé it is said they must suffer for want of supplies, as great scarcity of food in that quarter is looked for for the coming winter.[43]

Unquestionably the reception accorded to the expedition was not in accordance with the hopes or expectations of the Texans, of Dryden, and of the anonymous American writer. Was this due to the fact that the observers misunderstood the attitude of the people of Santa Fé, and that there was never the willingness to change allegiance that was ascribed to them; or was it due to a change in sentiment before the Texans arrived, and before the agents in Santa Fé could communicate to the authorities of Texas? Both were partly true, it seems. Apparently no secret was made of the plans of the Texans, either in Texas, or by the commissioners residing in Santa Fé; so ample opportunity was given for counter-preparations in case the Mexican government opposed Texan occupation of Santa Fé. Dryden had been discussing the subject since September, 1840, and there had been ample time for Armijo to communicate with his home government; but in case the governor were disloyal, the central authorities had ample opportunity to learn of the project from other sources.

On the day after the Santa Fé party took their departure from the camp on Brushy Creek, Rafael Uribe, an emissary of General Mariano Arista, commander of the Northern Army of Mexico, arrived in Austin with a letter from his commander to "Mr. Mirabeau Lamar." The substance of this letter was that Arista was anxious to come to some agreement with the Texan authorities with regard to the border brigandage which was taking place. Lamar refused to receive this emissary because the letter was improperly addressed, but he took the opportunity of sending two commissioners to the camp of Arista empowered to treat on the subject.[44] The rejected commissioner was able to learn of the departure of the Santa Fé expedition, and to give information to his government regarding it. Governor Armijo and the other authorities had been advised that an invasion from Texas was probable, and after the departure of McLeod and his party, special warnings had been sent from the city of Mexico ordering him to keep a constant look-

[43]Copied from *St. Louis Bulletin* in *Niles Register*, LXI, 100.
[44]Garrison, *Dip. Cor. Tex.* II, 748.

out for the party. Reinforcements were promised him in case of need.[45]

Twitchell is of the opinion that while some dissatisfaction did exist among the native people owing to the official abuses of Armijo, still the great majority of New Mexicans were not ready to hail the Texans as deliverers; and naturally Armijo, who was well settled in power himself and left to his own devices by the central authorities, was opposed to any change of government. As a consequence, every precaution was taken, and among the common classes the Texans were represented as being a "choice assortment of reckless and desperate men, from whom nothing other than pillage, murder and outrage could be expected."[46] That the governor should be averse to accepting Texan control and giving up his own office is entirely reasonable; but I cannot accept the view of Mr. Twitchell that there was not a large majority of the people of Santa Fé willing if not anxious to change to Texan sovereignty.

It will be recalled that Dryden wrote to Lamar on March 10, and April 18, 1841, showing with what favor his mission had been received, and with what enthusiasm the people anticipated the coming of the Texans. Kendall, who with the advance guard was taken prisoner before arriving in Santa Fé, was convinced that the great majority of the people were anxious for the success of the Texans, and that the failure was due to fortuitous circumstances over which the Texan authorities had no control. I feel constrained to quote in full the explanation given by Kendall for the failure of the enterprise.

In the first place, the expedition began its march too late in the season by at least six weeks. Had it left Austin on the 1st of May, the grass would have been much better, and we should have had little difficulty in finding good water both for ourselves and cattle. In the second place, we were disappointed in obtaining a party of the Lipan Indians as guide, and were consequently obliged to take a route some three hundred miles out of the way, and in many places extremely difficult of travel. Thirdly, the government of Texas did not furnish wagons and oxen enough to transport the goods of the merchants, and this, as a matter of course, caused tedious delays. Fourthly, cattle enough on the hoof were not provided, even with the second supply sent for by the com-

[45]Twitchell, *Leading Facts of New Mexican History*, II, 74.
[46]*Ibid.*, II, 74.

missioners from Little River. Again, the distance was vastly greater than we had anticipated in our widest and wildest calculations, owing to which circumstance, and an improvident waste of provisions while in the buffalo range, we found ourselves upon half allowance in the very middle of our long journey—a privation which weakened, dispirited, and rendered the men unfit for duty. The Indians also annoyed us much, by their harassing and continual attempts to cut off our small parties and steal our horses. Finally, the character of the governor of New Mexico was far from being understood, and his power was underrated by all. General Lamar's estimate of the views and feelings of the people of Santa Fé and the vicinity was perfectly correct; not a doubt can exist that they all were and are anxious to throw off the oppressive yoke of Armijo, and come under the liberal institutions of Texas; but the governor found us divided into small parties, broken down by long marches and want of food, discovered a traitor among us, too, and taking advantage of these circumstances, his course was plain and his conquest easy.[47]

Granting that there was sufficient evidence of the friendly feeling of the people of Santa Fé, there is still sufficient grounds, even among the causes of failure listed by Kendall, for serious criticism of Lamar for undertaking the enterprise. It would seem that a careful executive would have so planned the expedition that the causes contributing to failure would be reduced to a minimum. Why did the expedition not start by the first of May? It was intended by the President that it should, and the delay was caused by the slowness with which men volunteered for the expedition. Why was not more known as to the distance? The actual distance in an air line from Austin to Santa Fé was only a little less than a thousand miles, and the indirect route taken by the Texans was near thirteen hundred. Nobody in Texas at that time thought it was more than five hundred miles, however, and Lamar can hardly be blamed for adopting the universal view. Jefferson purchased Louisiana with less knowledge of that territory than Lamar possessed of the upper Rio Grande. The failure to provide sufficient supplies is natural when we consider the mistaken idea as to the distance. It does seem that Lamar should have known enough of the character of the Mexicans not to place too much confidence on the word of one of their rulers, and for this failure he was justly criticised.

[47]Kendall, *Texan Santa Fé Expedition*, I, 365-366.

Lamar seems to have had a single-track mind, and when once he became convinced that an expedition to Santa Fé should be undertaken for the two-fold purpose of bringing that region under subjection to Texas and securing the valuable trade for Texas, he was unable to consider the effect of success or failure on the relations of Texas with Mexico. In fact, it seems that he considered the question as entirely foreign to the interests of Mexico, and even while he was preparing the expedition, he was sending a minister to Mexico to treat on all questions at issue between Mexico and Texas, and, as we have seen, two days after the expedition left he was sending commissioners to the camp of General Arista for the purpose of arranging some means of stamping out brigand border warfare, and in order to keep open the commerce of Texas with the western settlements of Mexico on the Rio Grande.[48] Andrew Jackson, who had continued his interest in Texas, understood the importance of this phase of the question, and on May 25, 1842, wrote to Houston as follows:

> The wild goose campaign to Santa Fé was an ill-judged affair; and their surrender without the fire of a gun has lessened the prowess of the Texans in the minds of the Mexicans, and it will take another San Jacinto affair to restore their character.[49]

The expedition failed, and it is easy to criticise a venture that has failed. It is easy to see how certain conditions should have been anticipated and guarded against, but none of Lamar's critics pointed out any of these things before the enterprise was undertaken, the only cause of opposition being the expense. Since it failed, however, there were many who were willing to criticise the plans and the policy, and one critic went so far as to demand that Lamar be sent to Mexico and be sacrified for the prisoners who were in Mexico at that time.[50] But if it had succeeded, and there were strong evidences that it would succeed, Lamar would have added to Texas a tremendous territory, and would have secured valuable trade for Texas ports. It may be well enough to judge of its expediency from its failure, but to judge rightly the policy, one should take into consideration the plans and purposes

[48]Garrison, *Dip. Cor. Tex.*, II, 748.

[49]Jackson to Houston, May 25, 1842, Yoakum, *History of Texas*, II, 329, note.

[50]Lamar Papers, No.

of Lamar, and the seeming justification in his own mind at the time for the enterprise.

Chapter V

FOREIGN AFFAIRS DURING LAMAR'S ADMINISTRATION

When Lamar assumed the presidency the independence of Texas had been recognized only by the United States. This recognition had been extended just before the close of Jackson's administration. The Texan offer of annexation, which had been adopted by an almost unanimous vote in the summer of 1836, had been definitely rejected by the United States in August, 1837, and in October, 1838, the minister of Texas to the United States, acting on instructions from President Houston, withdrew it. This action was commended by Lamar in his inaugural address. Shortly after this address the Congress adopted resolutions endorsing the withdrawal of the offer, though the preceding Congress had refused to take such action.

The withdrawal of the offer of annexation immediately gave Texas a better standing among the nations of the world. As long as England and France believed that Texas was only waiting for annexation to the United States, they were not materially interested in its affairs, but now there seemed to be a favorable opportunity for friendly relations or for exploitation, and the European countries became more interested in the development of Texas. Lamar made deliberate use of the changed attitude, advising Congress to levy only nominal tariff duties in order to draw the trade of the European countries, and instructing the various representatives of Texas in Europe to offer favorable commercial concessions in return for recognition of Texan independence. Partly as a result of this policy, and partly from other causes which I shall show in the proper place the first year of Lamar's administration saw the recognition of Texan independence by France, and during 1840 England, Holland, and Belgium extended recognition.

In the policy of standing aloof from the United States while pursuing friendly relations with England and France, Lamar was following in part the policy suggested by his predecessor though he gave vitality to it because of his well known and strong opposition to annexation. The policy of direct negotiation of peace with Mexico on the basis of the purchase of her territory by Texas began with Lamar, however, and during his administration he sent three separate agents to Mexico for this purpose, while numerous secret agents kept him informed of the developments. At the same time, while remaining officially neutral, he gave some countenance to the various revolts of the federalists against the centralists in power at that time. I shall follow out with some detail these efforts to negotiate with Mexico, and also discuss the relations between Texas and the United States, France, and England.

I. Efforts to Negotiate Peace with Mexico

Just who was responsible for the idea of sending an agent to Mexico for direct negotiations, it is impossible to say. Lamar had nothing to say with regard to this policy in his inaugural address or in his message to Congress a few days later. In fact, the first time that he took Congress into his confidence was in November, 1838, when he told the Congress in a secret session the result of the first mission, and announced that he had sent another. On September 12, 1838, James Morgan, an old friend of Lamar, sent him a confidential letter from a friend in New York, and asking his opinion of the project set forth.[1] This enclosure has not been found, but a letter of December 27 from Morgan indicates that the friend in New York was James Treat, who afterward became a secret agent of Texas to Mexico, and that his suggestion was that a secret agent be sent from Texas to bring about overtures of peace from Mexico on a basis of the purchase of her own territory by Texas. Morgan advised the adoption of this policy.[2] A short time afterward George L. Hammeken, who was also well acquainted with conditions in Mexico, wrote suggesting a peace commission to Mexico.[3] This was followed by a letter from Samuel Plummer, another man who was acquainted with conditions in Mexico, advising similar action.[4]

There was apparently no connection between these men, but all knew intimately the conditions in Mexico, and all advised the sending of a peace commission. All of them had lived in Mexico for some time or had just been there, and spoke with a full knowledge of conditions. It did not take their statements, however, to in-

[1] *Lamar Papers*, No. 814.

[2] Morgan to Lamar, December 27, 1838, *Lamar Papers*, No. 959.

[3] Hammeken to Lamar, January 2, 1839, *Lamar Papers*, No. 984.

[4] Plummer to Lamar, February 16, 1839, *Lamar Papers*, No. 1068.

dicate to Lamar and his advisers that if there was ever to be a propitious time for a negotiated peace, that was the time.

For the greater part of 1838, and until March, 1839, the Mexican ports were blockaded by a French squadron. For several years there had been complaints on the part of French subjects in Mexico on account of unfair treatment, and the government of France had demanded a settlement of the claims of her citizens against Mexico. Despairing of an amicable settlement, the French minister withdrew from Mexico City on January 16, 1838, leaving the legation in charge of a *chargé d'affaires.* Upon leaving Vera Cruz he was met by a French squadron under Bazoche, who had been instructed to support the demands of the minister with force. On March 21 Bazoche sent an ultimatum to the Mexican government demanding the immediate payment of $600,000 to be applied to the claims of French citizens. Four days later the Mexican government announced its refusal to accede to the demands, and refused to discuss the matter unless the French squadron retired.[5] On April 16 Bazoche acted upon his threat and announced that diplomatic relations were suspended and the ports blockaded, not against the nation, as he said but against the government. This was probably to weaken the government of Bustamante, which was already growing unpopular.[6] A French squadron stood off Vera Cruz and effectively prevented the entrance or egress of any vessels, thus seriously crippling the finances of the country. This blockade continued throughout the summer with the acquiescence of Great Britain, and to the delight of the Texans.

While the French were blockading the ports of Mexico, the federalists used the opportunity to break out in revolts in various parts of the country. The adoption of the centralized constitution in 1835, which had resulted in the Texas revolution, and which had caused an outbreak in New Mexico in 1837, had never been universally accepted. In the summer of 1838 the discontent made itself felt in uprisings in Sonora, Sinaloa, California, Tamaulipas, and Yucatan. The most serious of these was in Sonora and Sinaloa, headed by Urrea. Urrea seized the custom-house at Guaymas and restored the federalist system. He was defeated at Mazatlan on May 6, 1838, but went to Tampico and stirred up a re-

[5]Bancroft, *History of Mexico*, V, 187, 188; C. M. Bustamante, *Cabinete Mexicana*, I, 112.

[6]Bancroft, *History of Mexico*, V, 189.

volt there in October, 1838. The government of Bustamante was very weak, and no effective steps were taken to put down and punish the rebels. The cutting off of imports left the country without funds, and Congress took no steps to remedy matters.[7]

Late in October Admiral Baudin arrived at Vera Cruz with additional ships and took over command of the French squadron. He was authorized by his government to enter into negotiations for the settlement of the difficulties. He at once got into communication with Cuevas, the Mexican Minister of Foreign Affairs, and made the same demands that had been made by Bazoche in March. The failure of Cuevas to give proper guarantees that the demands would be granted or considered led to the sending of an ultimatum by Baudin on November 21, in which he stated that if the demands were not granted by the 27th he would begin hostilities by an attack on the castle San Juan de Ulua. No adequate response was made, and on the day set San Juan de Ulua was bombarded, and although the Mexicans considered it impregnable, it was captured after a few hours bombardment. The French took possession the following day, promising to restore the fortress as soon as all differences were adjusted. The commander of the Mexican forces agreed to reduce the garrison of Vera Cruz to one thousand men, and to receive back and indemnify the expelled Frenchmen. The French on their part agreed to lift the blockade for eight months.

The Mexican cabinet refused to confirm the agreement of the commander of the forces at Vera Cruz and prepared for fighting. This led to a battle at Vera Cruz early in December, when the Mexicans under the command of Santa Anna were severely defeated. Shortly after this the British minister offered his services to mediate the difficulty, and both sides accepted. This resulted in the signing of a treaty on March 9, 1839, by which the Mexicans agreed to everything demanded by the French.[8] San Juan de Ulua was restored on April 7, and the French fleet retired.[9]

These conditions, as I have said, were known to Lamar and influenced him to send a peace commissioner to treat with the Mexican authorities. Besides, Lamar and his cabinet had heard that Santa Anna was again at the head of the government in Mexico,

[7] Rives, *United States and Mexico, 1821-1848*, I, 435.

[8] Dublan and Lozano, *Legislacion Mexicano*, III, 617.

[9] Bancroft, *History of Mexico*, V, 204.

probably because he was appointed to the command of the army at Vera Cruz, and they considered that as favorable to Texas. It will be recalled that Santa Anna, while a prisoner in Texas after the battle of San Jacinto, entered into a secret treaty with the Texan authorities by which he agreed not to take up arms against Texas during the war for independence; that he would prepare the cabinet in Mexico for the favorable reception of a minister when Texas saw fit to send one; and that a treaty of amity, commerce, and limits should be agreed to, the limits of Texas not to extend beyond the Rio Grande.[10] It is apparent that this belief also influenced Lamar to send the mission.

The information that several towns in the north had declared for the federalist system was contained in a letter dated December 17, 1838, from Canales, a federalist leader, who prophesied that within a short time the whole republic would come over to the Federalist party.

The information that Santa Anna was at the head of the government as a supporter of the Federalist party was contained in the letter of Plummer, referred to above. It was this letter that determined Lamar to send immediately an envoy to Mexico, and he considered it of enough importance to send his secretary of state Barnard E. Bee. Bee had been intended for appointment as minister to the United States, and had been instructed to get in touch with the minister from Mexico and attempt to form a treaty of peace through him; at the same time he was to seek the mediation of the United States. When it was decided to send Bee to Mexico, Richard G. Dunlap was sent as minister to the United States with the same instructions as were given to Bee. Both were to do everything in their power to come to an agreement with Mexico.[11]

Bee was given two commissions, one as minister plenipotentiary to be used in case he was received by the Mexican government, and one as agent in case he was not received. He was given full powers to negotiate for peace, and sign a treaty securing it, but he was to require the unconditional recognition of the independence of Texas, and was to admit no limits less than those prescribed by the act of Congress of December 19, 1836, which provided that

[10]Garrison, *Dip. Cor. Tex.*, II, 434; *Niles Register*, LXIX, 98.

[11]Webb to Dunlap, March 13 and 14, 1839, Garrison, *Dip. Cor. Tex.*, I, 368-378.

the Rio Grande to its source was the boundary between Texas and Mexico. If Mexico was willing to establish peace and recognize the original boundaries of Texas—which included only to the Nueces—he was empowered to propose a compromise by offering to purchase all included between the original boundary and the Rio Grande at a sum not exceeding five million dollars.[12]

The commission and instructions to Bee were dated February 20, 1839, but for some reason he did not get away from Texas until April 1. He then went to Mobile, where he hoped to secure passage to Vera Cruz. Failing there he proceeded to New Orleans, where he got into communication with James Hamilton, Loan Commissioner of the Republic of Texas, and with a Mr. Gordon of the house of Lizardi and Company, the chief holders of Mexican bonds. It was probably here that the idea was conceived to use the indemnity which Texas offered Mexico for recognition to redeem the Mexican bonds held by English investors. Bee remained in New Orleans until May 2, when he embarked for Vera Cruz, arriving there on May 8.

This was the most inauspicious time that could have been chosen to arrive in Mexico with such an object. The difficulties with France, which had been counted upon to expedite negotiations, had been settled and the French fleet had sailed away a month before. Besides, with the withdrawal of the French the authorities had been able to give some attention to the Federalist risings, and one of the most formidable—that of Tampico—had been put down by Santa Anna and Urrea had been captured. Santa Anna was temporarily in charge of the executive office while Bustamante was absent in the north on a campaign against the Federalists there, and certainly nothing could be hoped for from him. So, while Bee set forth on his mission with high hopes, he arrived when an entirely new situation had developed, and there was no chance of success.

While remaining on board the schooner Woodbury at Vera Cruz he communicated with various officials requesting that he be allowed to go to Mexico City to lay his case before the Council. This was peremptorily refused, if he had come to treat for independence. He was informed by General Victoria, the commandant at Vera Cruz, who had acted as the agent of the government in

[12]Webb to Bee, February 20, 1839, Garrison, *Dip. Cor. Tex.*, II, 434.

communicating with Bee, that the French question was settled, the Federalists put down, that reform was about to take place, and that with the great resources at her command Mexico would be forced to wage an efficient war on Texas in order to bring her back into the fold—all this in urging that Texas come back to her allegiance to Mexico. Failing to interest the Mexican authorities in his mission, and receiving threatening letters from several of the people of Vera Cruz, Bee took refuge on the French frigate *Phaeton* on May 28, and wrote letters to several members of the cabinet suggesting that negotiations for peace and recognition be held in Washington.[13]

While Bee was still waiting at Vera Cruz to hear from Mexico City as to the possibility of his reception, Pakenham, British minister in Mexico, received a letter from Gordon in New Orleans, written April 29, 1839, stating the purposes of Bee's mission, and advising that Pakenham give assistance to his project. He stated that Bee was prepared to offer five million dollars for the land between the Nueces and the Rio Grande, and suggested that Mexico should satisfy the claims of English bondholders by locating lands for them within the disputed territory, accepting the five million dollars from Texas, and then agreeing to the line claimed by Texas.[14] Pakenham reported this plan to the Mexican authorities, but was informed that Bee had been rejected without hearing what he had to propose.

Pakenham had been absent on leave in England in 1838, and in October, just before leaving for his return to Mexico, he had been instructed by Palmerston to urge upon Mexico the importance of a prompt recognition of Texas. He now used the opportunity presented by Gordon's suggestion and insisted upon the acceptance of that policy. He laid stress upon the advantage to Mexico of having a barrier state between her and the United States. Gorostiza, the foreign minister, replied that he realized the value of such an arrangement, but that the Mexican government dared not risk so unpopular an act, and hinted that as a preliminary to recognition Mexico would welcome from England a suggestion of an armistice. With regard to the boundary desired by Texas, Gorostiza said that Mexico would never consent to the claims of Texas.

[13] *Lamar Papers*, No. 1255.

[14] Gordon to Pakenham, April 29, 1839; Adams, *British Interests and Activities in Texas*, 26.

"Reconquest is admitted to be impossible," said Pakenham in reporting the conversation to Palmerston, "and yet a feeling of mistaken pride, foolishly called regard for the national honor, deters the government from putting an end to a state of things highly prejudicial to the interests of Texas and attended with no sort of advantage to this country."[15]

Bee had left for his mission not over-sanguine as to its success, believing that Washington was the proper place to treat. After his failure to get in touch with the authorities in Mexico, he was naturally still convinced that he should have gone to Washington. He wrote just before leaving for Vera Cruz: "We made a merry move in coming so suddenly upon these people, the first plan was the true one. It ought to have opened at Washington."[16] He continued firm in the belief that with less publicity Mexico would be willing to come to terms. He was further convinced of this when, after his arrival in New Orleans, he received a letter from Almonte, Mexican secretary of war, stating that the President was willing for him to open his views to the government. At this point James Treat enters into the negotiations.[17]

James Treat had lived in Mexico for a number of years, was well acquainted with Santa Anna, and for some time had been in correspondence with the secret agent of the Mexican government in New Orleans. It was he who had outlined a scheme for pacification in December, 1838, and who had been recommended by James Morgan for a peace mission to Mexico. In the summer of 1839 he became acquainted with James Hamilton,[18] and on June 22

[15]Pakenham to Palmerston, June 3, 1839, British Foreign Office, Mexico, 125; Adams, *British Interests and Activities in Texas*, 27.

[16]Bee to Webb, May 28, 1839, Garrison, *Dip. Cor. Tex.*, II, 449.

[17]Bee to Webb, July 6, 1839, Garrison, *Dip. Cor. Tex.*, II, 456.

[18]James Hamilton played such an important part in the history of Texas during this period that some notice of his activities is required. He was a native of South Carolina who had early become interested in Texas. He was a member of Congress from South Carolina from 1822 to 1829, and governor of the state from 1829 to 1830, retiring when Hayne became governor. His first correspondence with Lamar was in June, 1836, when he wrote a letter of introduction for Barnard E. Bee, who was just then coming to Texas. From that time on he was a steady correspondent, and after Lamar was elected president in 1838 he wrote frequent and long letters giving his advice as to public policy, and probably more than anyone else he influenced Lamar's actions. Just before the close of Houston's administration an effort had been made to secure the appointment of Hamilton as loan commissioner. Upon the refusal of Houston to appoint him, Bee had resigned from the cabinet, probably

Hamitlon wrote to Lamar advising that Treat be appointed to assist Bee in the negotiations in New Orleans. Without waiting for a reply, he took the liberty of sending Treat to New Orleans with instructions to assist Bee by getting into communication with the Mexican secret agent.[19] Before anything was done, however, Hamilton, acting on the advice of Poinsett, American secretary of war, advised that Treat be sent direct to Mexico City. This advice was acquiesced in by Bee, and Lamar decided to act upon the advice and send Treat as secret agent with full powers to negotiate a treaty.[20]

The instructions to Treat were in part a duplicate of those to Bee. The unconditional acknowledgment of the independence of Texas within the statutory boundaries was to be demanded as a *sine qua non*. The Texas authorities were now willing to go further in territorial claims, however, and Treat was instructed to propose as the boundary, a line commencing at the mouth of the Rio Grande and running midway of its channel to El Paso, and from that point due west to the Gulf of California, and along the southern shore of that gulf to the Pacific Ocean. "This boundary will not be strenuously insisted upon," said the instructions, "but may be intimated as a counterpoise to any extravagant expectations on the part of Mexico and as a premonition to that government of the ultimate destination of that remote territory." He was authorized to offer up to five million dollars for a recognition of the first claimed boundary, any part of which might be in Mexican bonds.[21]

Treat left Austin immediately upon receiving his instructions and proceeded to New Orleans, where he arrived on August 13, He left there two days later for New York, arriving on the 29th. Here he was detained for two months while waiting for transportation and attempting to secure funds for the trip. He finally left New York in the latter part of October, and arrived, after a

determining Lamar to appoint Bee as secretary of State. He visited Texas in March, 1839, and was appointed by Lamar as loan commissioner, and was sent to France and England to assist Henderson in securing recognition while negotiating for a loan. He was sent on various diplomatic missions after this, which will appear when I discuss the relations of Texas with Europe.

[19]Hamilton to Lamar, June 28, 1839, Garrison, *Dip. Cor. Tex.*, II, 453.

[20]Garrison, *Dip. Cor. Tex.*, II, 459, 466, 470.

[21]Burnet to Treat, August 9, 1839, Garrison, *Dip. Cor. Tex.*, II, 470.

long journey, at Vera Cruz on November 28. He reached Mexico City on December 11 and began his negotiations.

The internal conditions in Mexico throughout the greater part of 1839 were unsettled. The Federalist movement, which had gained considerable strength in 1838, was still flourishing in Tampico and various parts of the north. With the French difficulties settled, the government decided to proceed with vigor against the insurgents under Urrea at Tampico, and Santa Anna, whose loss of a leg in the battle of Vera Cruz had restored him to favor with the populace, urged the president, Bustamante, to lead the expedition against them. Bustamante reluctanatly agreed. The executive authority would normally have fallen upon the vice-president, Nicolás Bravo, but the populace demanded Santa Anna, and Bravo gracefully stepped aside, and the Council appointed Santa Anna. Santa Anna assumed the executive power on March 18, 1839, and Bustamante set out for Tampico.[22]

Bustamante traveled leisurely towards Tampico and allowed the insurgents to get between him and Mexico City. Santa Anna, who was in the capital, raised a force and advanced to meet them, and defeated them at Acajete on May 3, 1839. In June Tampico was taken. In July Bustamante returned to the capital and assumed the executive authority. As he had seen no fighting he was discredited and his government was weaker than ever. Santa Anna was the popular hero, but he did not consider that conditions were ripe for his return to power, so he retired to his ranch and left the control of affairs to Bustamante.[23] A complete reorganization of the cabinet took place, however. Juan de Dios Cañedo succeeded Gorostiza as foreign minister, Luis Gonzales Cuevas became secretary of the interior, Xavier de Echeverria, secretary of the treasury, and J. N. Almonte, secretary of war.[24]

Before proceeding with Treat's negotiations it will be necessary to notice the efforts of the Texan minister in Washingtan to negotiate with the Mexican minister, and also his efforts to secure the mediation of the United States. It will be remembered that Dunlap had been instructed to treat if possible with the Mexican min-

[22] Bustamante, *Cabinete Mexicana*, I, 176; Rives, *United States and Mexico*, I, 450.

[23] *Ibid.*, I, 451.

[24] Treat to Burnet, (Enclosure) September 21, 1839, Garrison, *Dip. Cor. Tex.*, II, 488.

ister in Washington, and if necessary he was to secure the mediation of the United States. To Dunlap's suggestion that the United States mediate between Texas and Mexico, Forsyth gave a half-hearted assent, and instructed Ellis, the new minister to Mexico, to be ready, while observing strict neutrality, to interpose his good offices between Mexico and Texas, but not until Mexico should ask for them.[25] The Mexican minister, Martinez, was made aware of the purposes of Dunlap, but it was not until October that the two ministers got together. During the second week of October they held several conferences, and Dunlap submitted to Martinez a formal request that negotiations be undertaken. The Mexican minister responded that he had no authority to enter into a treaty, but that he would send Dunlap's suggestions to his home government. This was the end of efforts to negotiate a treaty in this manner.[26]

Great Britain had, on her own initiative, taken some steps towards mediation before Treat's arrival in Mexico. As I have already stated, Palmerston had given verbal instructions to Pakenham in October, 1838, urging the recognition of Texan independence, which instructions were submitted after Bee's failure. On April 25, 1839, Palmerston sent his first written instructions to Pakenham on the subject of Texas. In this letter Palmerston argued at length as to the impossibility of a reconquest of Texas. In supplementary instructions enclosed in this letter, Palmerston said that it was not likely that Mexico would listen at once to the suggestion for recognition, but he did hope that she would be willing to accept the good offices of Great Britain.[27] Cañedo had become foreign minister when these instructions were received, and to him Pakenham communicated the substance of them. Cañedo responded that he realized the importance of the recognition of Texan independence, but that the government could not risk so unpopular an act. He stated that Mexico might welcome from Great Britain a suggestion for suspension of hostilities; and Paken-

[25]Forsyth to Ellis, May 3, 1839, MS., Archives. See also Reeves, *American Diplomacy under Tyler and Polk*, 87; Dunlap to Lamar, May 16, 1839, Garrison, *Dip. Cor. Tex.*, I, 383.

[26]Dunlap to Burnet, October 12, 1839, (Enclosing Martinez to Dunlap, October 8, 1839) *Dip. Cor. Tex.*, I, 421-424.

[27]Adams, *British Interests and Activities in Texas*, 28-29.

ham was convinced in September that such an arrangement could be made preparatory to pacification.[28]

From that time forward Pakenham was active in the interest of the recognition of Texas independence by Mexico. On December 12, 1839, he addressed a letter to James Hamilton, who was about to set out on a diplomatic mission to Great Britain, in which he gave an account of his activities. After acknowledging a letter from Hamilton written November 18, he said:

It is some time since I received from Viscount Palmerston Instructions to tender the good offices of Her Majesty's Government towards effecting an arrangement between this Country and Texas; but I regret to say that all my exertions to induce this Government to entertain the question of recognition have hitherto proved unavailing. Not but that the more enlightened Members of the present Administration appear to understand that to continue the contest with Texas would be worse than useless, but there is no man among them bold enough to confront the popular opinion, or, I should rather say the popular prejudice upon this point, which is strongly pronounced against any accommodation with Texas. Besides which they fear, and not without reason,, that, for the sake of Party objects, an attempt would dishonestly be made to crush by the unpopularity which would, very certainly, attend such a measure, any Government which should be bold enough to advocate the policy of alienating what is still talked of as a part of the National Territory.

Under these circumstances it appeared to me that the next best thing to propose was a mutual suspension of hostilities as a preparatory step to the ulterior measure of absolute recognition at a future period. . . .

Some time ago Senor Cañedo, the Minister for Foreign Affairs, who, to speak the truth, strongly inclines to the course which wisdom and sound policy recommend with regard to the question of Texas, informed me that after repeated and arduous discussions with his Colleagues he had succeeded in obtaining their consent to place on the records of their deliberations a minute to the effect that if Commissioners from Texas should present themselves, they would be listened to, with the distinct understanding, however, that no proposition for the alienation of the right of Sovereignty would be entertained. But as he would not take upon himself to put into my hands any written communication to that effect, or even convey to me a more definite understanding of what his Government might be disposed to accede to in the way of armistice, or otherwise, I did not think myself at liberty to recommend to Colonel Bee, with whom, on the occasion of his late Mission, I

[28]*Ibid.*, 32-33.

had had some communication, to undertake a fresh journey to this country upon such vague and uncertain grounds.

On receipt of your letter[29] I again entered into communication with the Mexican Government upon the important subject to which it relates, but I am sorry to say, as far as regards the question of recognition, with no better success than before. Nevertheless I have obtained from Senor Cañedo a written communication, . . . stating that this Government are disposed to listen to proposals from the Inhabitants of Texas; but that on no account will they relinquish the right of Sovereignty over that Territory.[30]

Both the Bee mission and the Treat mission were undertaken by President Lamar without consulting Congress. On December 10, 1839, however, he sent a special message to a secret session of Congress giving a full account of the proceedings so far, including the reasons for sending Bee, the causes of his failure, and the reasons for his sending a secret agent. He also mentioned the terms on which the agents were instructed to make peace.[31] As a result of this, Congress passed a joint resolution endorsing his acts, as follows:

1. Congress views with entire approbation the present policy of the Executive.

2. [Boundary as in the Act of December 19, 1836.]

3. That should such a Treaty be passed between the Commissioner on the part of the Government of Texas and Mexico, and

[29]Written November 18 and received December 4. 1839. Hamilton had proposed that Mexico acknowledge the independence of Texas and receive from Texas the sum of five million dollars, with the understanding that the money go directly into the pockets of the bondholders. The bondholders were then to release the lands that had already been granted to them by the government of Mexico. He also informed Pakenham that Treat was on his way to Mexico, but suggested that peace negotiations be begun in London, so that the Mexican bondholders could be present and look after their interests.—Adams. *British Interests and Activities in Texas*, 37.

[30]Pakenham to Hamilton, December 12, 1839, (Copy enclosed in Hamilton to Burnet, January 5, 1840) *Dip. Cor. Tex.*, III, 879-880.

Pakenham enclosed a copy of the written communication by Cañedo, the important part of which was as follows: "V. E. se sirve manifestarme su deseo de saber si por se ha tomado por este Gobierno alguna resolucion en virtud de las propuestas amistosas que en cumplimiento de sus citidas instrucciones ha hacho; y en contestacion tengo la honra de decirle que los Commissionados de los habitantes de Texas seran oydos por el Gobierno Mexicano, bajo la condicion indispensable de que este no ha de desistir de la Soberania nacional sobre aquel Departamento de la Republica."—*Dip. Cor. Tex.*, II, 505.

[31]Winkler, editor, *Secret Journals of the Senate of the Republic of Texas*, 148.

after the same may have been ratified and confirmed by the President and Senate of this Republic, our Commissioners of loans in Europe are authorized to borrow the amount which may be stipulated in said Treaty, at an interest not exceeding six per cent.

4. Be it further resolved, That the said Commissioners appointed on the part of Texas shall if practicable procure the Guaranty of Great Britain for the faithful performance of the Treaty by both parties.[32]

One of the first things that Treat had to report after arriving in Mexico was the promulgation of a proclamation by the President announcing the renewal of hostilities with Texas, and the consideration by Congress of ways and means for financing a military campaign.[33] In fact, A. S. Wright, a secret correspondent of the Texan government was convinced that Mexico was making preparations to invade Texas and kept the Texan authorities informed for some months before Treat arrived.[34] Public or political sentiment would probably have demanded some effort to subdue Texas at any rate; but the news that Texans had joined with the insurgent Federalists on the Rio Grande led to the proclamation of a renewal of the war, and special efforts to secure action by Congress in support of the campaign.[35]

The Texan authorities had shown a marked partiality for the Federalists, partly because they were fighting for the same principles for which the Texans had fought in 1835 and 1836, but chiefly because they felt that the Federalists would regard with more favor the claims of Texas to independence. On December 17, 1838, the Licentiate Antonio Canales, commander of the Third Division of the Federal army, wrote a letter to Lamar announcing the capture of several towns by the Federalists.[36] In this letter he addressed Lamar as "President of the Republic of Texas," which was thereafter cited as an indication that the Federalists recognized the claims of Texas in advance of their success in the revolution. As a result of the friendly feeling engendered by this letter, Congress passed a joint resolution providing for the open-

[32]*Ibid.*, 166.

[33]Treat to Burnet, November 29, 1839, Garrison, *Dip. Cor. Tex.*, II, 501.

[34]Wright to Bee, August 29 to November 18, 1839, in *Ibid.*, 615-632.

[35]Wright to Bryan, November 21, 1839, in *Ibid.*, II, 496.

[36]Canales to Lamar, December 17, 1838, in *Ibid.*, II, 430.

ing of trade with the Rio Grande settlements, and the President issued his proclamation to that effect in February, 1839.[37]

In the spring of 1839 General Anaya, later put to death after the capture of Tampico in June, 1839, who was looked upon as the chief of the Federalist party, visited Texas and promised the Texan authorities that if they would allow him to transport troops across Texas and raise troops in Texas, he would, in case of success, recognize their independence. This permission was refused. Later the Federalists of the northern states sent Francisco Vidaurri, governor of Coahuila, to make overtures for an alliance between Texas and the states of Nuevo Leon, Tamaulipas, Coahuila, Chihuahua, New Mexico, Durango, and the Californias.[38] In spite of the strong sentiment in favor of such an alliance, the authorities refused to entertain the idea.

After the overthrow of the insurgents in Tampico in June, General Canales, Colonels José Maria Gonzales, and Antonio Zapata with a small force fled to Lipantitlan on the Nueces river. Here Canales issued a proclamation inviting the Texans to join him, promising them an equal division of the spoils, twenty-five dollars per month, and a half league of land to those who should serve during the war.[39] Though the government had refused to join Canales, about one hundred and eighty Texans under Colonels Reuben Ross and S. W. Jordan joined the Federalists. On September 30, 1839, the Federalist forces, consisting now of six hundred men, crossed the Rio Grande and marched against Guerrero, which was held by General Pavon with five hundred regulars and four pieces of artillery. Pavon retreated toward Mier and was followed by Canales. On October 3 was fought the battle of Alcantro, in which the Texans distinguished themselves by overwhelmingly defeating the enemy. This was the battle which caused the preparations for an active campaign against Texas.[40]

The Texans continued their operations in connection with Canales and the Federalists, participating in January, 1840, in the creation of the "Republic of the Rio Grande." It is not my purpose, however, to follow their activities. The President had, while

[37] *Lamar Papers*, No. 1079.

[38] Bancroft, *North Mexican States and Texas*, II, 327.

[39] *Ibid*; Yoakum. *History of Texas*, II, 274.

[40] Bancroft, *North Mexican States and Texas*, II, 328; Yoakum, *History of Texas*, II, 274.

treating their envoys with courtesy, refused to join the Federalists in their campaign against the central government. It is likely that he desired their success, as it would have made things better for Texas; but he did not trust the Mexicans. On December 21, 1839, he issued a proclamation warning the citizens of Texas not to invade Mexico, and not to take part in any marauding expedition or other acts of hostility against Mexico, until a renewal of hostilities should be announced by public notice. He declared that any citizen who should invade Mexico, or by any hostile act molest its inhabitants within their own territory, should be considered without the protection of the Texan government, which disclaimed all participation in their conduct, and could afford no countenance to their unauthorized acts.[41]

In his letter of November 29 from Vera Cruz Treat told of the impression created in Mexico by the Texan participation in the battle of Alcantro, but he dismissed the matter by saying the impression would blow over. Later in a letter to James Hamilton, a copy of which was sent to the Texas state department, he considered it more serious than he had at first thought. With regard to this matter and the action of the Mexican government upon it, he wrote:

> . . . You will have seen that the movement of Ross and his party, with other volunteers, to which they attribute the success of the Federalists, and the surrender of the troops in or near Mier, (some 600 men) have produced much excitement on the part of the Govmt as well as in the public mind. The Govmt. having taken all the measures in their power, have called on Congress for special powers to levy taxes to support the war against Texas, and to reunite that department to the national union, etc. etc. etc. Not satisfied with this measure initiated in Congress, and without waiting for the action of that body, another project of Law is sent down by the Secretary of War (Sr. Almonte) declaring it treason against the state for any one "to write act or speak in favour of the views and intentions of the Texans; or in favour of the views of any foreign power having for its object to dismember the territory of Mexico etc.[42]

These two proposals were sent to a special committee by the

[41] *Austin City Gazette*, January 1. 1840.

[42] Treat to Hamilton, December 16, 1839, Garrison, *Dip. Cor. Tex.*, II, 508-509. Treat had a peculiar habit of underscoring, entirely without meaning, many words in his despatches. I shall ignore his italics, using them only when it seems that emphasis is intended.

Chamber of Deputies. The committee reported against granting special powers, but recommended proceeding with the expedition under the ordinary powers of the government. Instead of reporting ways and means promptly, they recommended measures assessing taxes which could not be collected for three or four months.[43] The Deputies refused to accept the report of the committee, and sent it back to them for revision.[44] On January 1, 1840, the President, in his annual message to Congress, expressed surprise at the recognition of Texan independence by France, and urged upon the Congress the necessity of passing the laws asked for the prosecution of the war. After praising the soldiers who were operating against the Federalists in the north, he said:

> The Executive will not fail to use every effort in their power to secure our frontier by the recovery of the territory of Texas, usurped by the ungrateful foreigners, to whom we gave a generous hospitality in that part of the Republic.
>
> On the 18th June of last year, the Government presented to their Council the Bill which, with some modifications, they afterwards laid before the Chambers on the 26th November, demanding powers for making the necessary expenditure, and for carrying into effect the political and military measures requisite for reuniting the Department of Texas to the National Union, which Bill is now before the Chamber of Deputies, as well as another, having for its object to declare traitors to their country such persons who, by act or writing favour the views of any foreign Power, or of the usurpers of Texas, for the purpose of dismembering or making themselves masters of the Mexican territory. The Executive Government have the honor to recommend both these bills once more to your notice, hoping that you will take them into consideration, with the diligence and promptitude which the importance of their object requires of your patriotism.[45]

Apparently this was an unfavorable situation for negotiation, and for the next month Treat did not reveal himself or the objects of his mission to the authorities. Still he did not believe that any serious efforts would be made to subjugate Texas. He thought that by asking for political and military powers, they desired to secure authority to raise an army and at the same time negotiate with the Texans. During the next month, however, he was busily engaged in working secretly against the granting of the extraor-

[43]Treat to Lamar, December 20, 1839, in *Ibid.*, II, 513.

[44]Treat to Lamar, December 31, 1839, in *Ibid.*, II, 523.

[45]*British and Foreign State Papers*, XXIX, 1084 (Translation).

dinary powers. It was not until February 1, 1840, that he, through the intervention of Pakenham, had an interview with Cañedo, minister for foreign affairs.

Naturally, this first interview was introductory and nothing was accomplished. Cañedo explained to Treat the difficulty he had had in persuading the President and other members of the cabinet to receive him at all, explaining that the intervention of Pakenham had been the determining factor. He had been finally authorized by the President to listen to all that Treat might have to say, without committing himself in return. When Cañedo asked to see Treat's credentials it developed that he had no formal credentials, but only the letter of instructions signed by Burnet. Cañedo was willing to accept the letter as sufficient, but stated that the other members of the Government would not, and that it was necessary to secure proper credentials before proceeding. In the meantime, he was willing to accept the guarantee of Pakenham that Treat was officially accredited. The proper credentials were dispatched on March 12.[46]

On March 1, 1840, Treat got so far as submitting to Cañedo the formal *projet* of a treaty, in accordance with his instructions.[47] On April 15 he received his credentials. On the 18th he communicated this fact to Cañedo, and was informed that Cañedo was in sympathy with his desires. Cañedo also informed him as to the procedure he would advocate. The plan as outlined to Treat was as follows: A special cabinet meeting was to be held, when an effort would be made to pass the question along to the Council of the Government. If the Council recommended any action, the cabinet was to pass the matter along to the legislature for their action, where it was hoped that authorization would be given to treat with Texas.[48]

This procedure was followed exactly. On May 5 the cabinet ordered that all the papers, documents, and correspondence be submitted to the "Council of Government" for their opinion, with the question: Whether the Council concurred with the cabinet in their resolution to ask Congress for special powers to negotiate an amicable arrangement with the Government of Texas.[49] The mat-

[46]Treat to Lamar, February 1, 1840, Garrison, *Dip. Cor. Tex.*, II, 540.
[47]Garrison, *Dip. Cor. Tex.*, II, 592.
[48]Treat to Lamar, April 21, 1840." Garrison, *Dip. Cor. Tex.*, II, 606.
[49]Treat to Lamar, May 7, 1840. Garrison, *Dip. Cor. Tex.*, II, 634.

ter went to the Council, which on May 12 voted down by a vote of five to four the unanimous recommendation of a committee of the Council that the views of the cabinet be adopted. This was due to the influence of Gorostiza, Treat thought, who was a friend of Santa Anna and an opponent of the existing government. He announced his purpose of attempting to secure the submission of the whole question to Congress without recommendation. "I think that my efforts," he wrote,

> and those of some friends will prove Successful, as I am assured that whatever may be the range and tenor of the report, it will be such as will Square with the Resolution that will be proposed, viz: To transmit the whole Subject, without expressing an opinion themselves, to the consideration of Congress. With this, and some other timely measures, I think I can expect the result promised.[50]

The papers were submitted to Congress on July 3 for discussion, but on the night of the 14th one of the periodical revolutions in the Capital broke out and prevented their consideration.[51]

Lamar was becoming impatient at the delay in accomplishing any definite results. The threatening proclamations of the Centralist commander in Coahuila, General Arista, and the manifest efforts of the Mexicans to stir up the Indians made it difficult for the Government to restrain public sentiment which demanded a coalition with the Federalists. On March 27 Treat had notified the Texan Government that he had formally laid before the Mexican Government a proposal for peace. In response to that letter, May 7, 1840, the Texas secretary of state, Abner S. Lipscomb, wrote as follows:

> The President has directed me to instruct you, that if after the reception of your credentials, you can obtain no decisively favorable answer to your overtures for peace, that you will withdraw from your Agency. Should this be the result, you are instructed to make known to the Minister of Her Britanic Majesty in Mexico, that should this Government be constrained to change its position and commence offensive operations, it will not be with a view of extending our territory, beyond the *Rio Grande* and any occupation or military movement west of that River, will be temporary and solely with the view of forcing the enemy to make peace.[52]

[50] *Ibid.* to *Ibid.*, May 28, 1840, *Ibid.*, II, 636.
[51] *Ibid.*, II, 669; 670.
[52] Lipscomb to Treat, May 7, 1840. Garrison, *Dip. Cor. Tex.*, II, 635.

In June Lamar determined to send the Texas navy on a cruise in the Gulf. This was due to the threat of a blockade of the ports of Texas by the Mexicans, who were supposed to have secured a navy in England, to the desire of Lamar to establish communications with the Federalists of Yucatan and Tabasco, who had seemingly made good their secession from Mexico, and to communicate with Treat, who was expected to have completed his mission by that time. The commander of the navy, E. W. Moore, was instructed to proceed to some safe anchorage off Vera Cruz and send in the dispatches for Pakenham. He was to cause one of his vessels to stand off Point Maria-Andrea for thirteen days to receive any communication that might be sent by Treat. If he should receive notice that Treat had failed in his mission, he was instructed to cruise against the Mexican vessels and make prizes of them. He was not to commence hostilities until Treat had notified him of the failure of negotiations, but if attacked, he was to defend himself. Finally, he was to endeavor to ascertain the condition of the state of Yucatan, and the disposition of the functionaries administering the Government, "whether friendly or otherwise to us, any manifestation of friendship from them you will reciprocate."[58]

With Moore went a letter to Treat from the secretary of state in which he again called attention to the conduct of the Mexicans on the frontier and denounced the conspiracies of the Mexicans with the Indians. Lipscomb instructed Treat to inform the Texan Government as to the length of time necessary to come to some conclusion. He was also to inform the Mexican Government that Texas had about reached a decision to begin hostilities if no treaty were possible. "It would perhaps," he wrote,

be well for you to urge upon Mexico the moderation of this Government in not co-operating (thus far) with the Federalists on the Rio Grande as she has been strongly urged to do, and might have done with great benefit to herself and detriment to Mexico, that it is a forbearance we cannot practice much longer, lest we loose all the advantages which such a co-operation would give us, without gaining any thing from the Central Government of Mexico. The Federalists are still sanguine of Success, and unremitting in their overtures to us, to make a Common Cause in making war on

[58]Lamar to Moore, June 20. 1840. Garrison, *Dip. Cor. Tex.*, II, 651-652.

the Centralists, and in return, would grant every thing we could reasonably ask of them.[54]

This letter did not reach Treat until August 13. He had already, after the revolution in the Capital in July, communicated to the foreign minister Lamar's instructions of May 7, stating that he was under the necessity of hastening negotiations, and receiving a promise of immediate consideration from Cañedo. On August 21 he communicated a long memorandum in which he called attention to the various complaints against Mexico, and urged an immediate consideration of his mission. This receiving no consideration, on September 5 he addressed another letter to the secretary of foreign affairs, stating that if some official or formal assurance of the final determination of the Government with regard to his mission by the 18th, "which may satisfy him of the actual intentions of the Government to enter forthwith upon an amicable Negotiation" were not received, he would be compelled to ask for his passports and withdraw from his mission.[55]

Receiving no response of any kind to this memorandum, Treat on September 21 addressed a note to Cañedo requesting his passports. While waiting for his passports, Pakenham suggested to Cañedo that the only way to avoid a conflict with Texas was to arrange an armistice. Cañedo agreed that if Treat had authority to agree to an armistice, his Government would receive his proposals and act promptly upon them, or, at least, so Pakenham understood. Treat agreed to receive any proposals the Mexican Government might offer. He did, however, draw up a draft of an armistice which he authorized Pakenham to put before the Mexican Government. The plan called for a cessation of hostilities for three or four years, and six months notice were to be given before renewing hostilities. The virtual recognition of the Rio Grande as a boundary was contained in an article requiring any Mexican forces to the east of the river to pass to the other side.[56] On September 29 Cañedo sent Treat's passports by Pakenham without mentioning the matter of the armistice, and Cañedo quit office the following day. Almonte, the strong man of the cabinet, assured Pakenham that he favored an armistice and would

[54]Lipscomb to Treat, June 13. 1840. Garrison, *Dip. Cor. Tex.*, II, 645.

[55]Garrison, *Dip. Cor. Tex.*, II, 675; 688; 700.

[56]Treat to Lipscomb, September 29, 1840. Garrison, *Dip. Cor. Tex.*, II, 705, 707, 708.

use his influence to bring it about, so Treat determined to wait eight days longer before leaving the country.

On October 15, 1840, Pakenham informed Treat that the Mexican Government refused to entertain any proposal for an armistice which should not be presented with the previous sanction of the Texan authorities; and that in no case could they consent to a provisional line of demarcation to the south of the San Antonio river. Pakenham stated that he had reluctantly come to the conclusion that nothing could be gained by further overtures to the Government.[57] On account of ill health Treat was forced to remain in Mexico until some time in November, when he embarked on one of the Texan vessels for Galveston. He had been in bad health at various times during his stay in Mexico, and was handicapped in his negotiations on that account. He died on his way to Texas on board ship, November 30, 1840, so we do not have the benefit of his official report summing up the results of his mission, or giving suggestions for the future conduct of Texas. His reports to the Texas authorities were full, however, and make plain the chief Mexican traits of double dealing and procrastination. The following letter from Pakenham to Treat on the eve of his departure for Texas gives a summary from an impartial witness of the main facts connected with Treat's mission:

The Passport issued in conformity with your request accompanied Senor Cañedo's note; but you will perceive that he declines to enter into the explanation solicited by you respecting the transactions connected with your Mission, the fruitless issue of which he attributes to your not having confined your propositions to the basis originally put forth by this Government viz: "That Mexico would not consent to relinquish the sovereignty of the Territory of Texas."

It is true that in Senor Cañedo's letter of the 11th. Decr. 1839, a copy of which I transmitted at the time to Gen. Hamilton, and of the contents of which you are also informed, the non-alienation of sovereignty was stated to be an indispensable condition to any arrangement: but it is no less true that the introductory propositions, presented by you on the 23rd. March last, went directly to solicit the recognition of the independence of Texas, with such boundaries as might hereafter be agreed upon—that this proposition, so far from having been at once rejected by the Mexican Government as inadmissable, was referred to the Council of State, where the whole question with regard to Texas was made the sub-

[57]Garrison, *Dip. Cor. Tex.*, 726.

ject of more than one anxious discussion—and finally that in conformity with the resolution of the Council the correspondence which had passed between Senor Cañedo and myself, relative to your Mission and the proposition presented by you, were submitted to the consideration of the Congress, where, however, the matter appears to have remained altogether unnoticed.

It is therefore certain that the propositions submitted by you, although not confined to the basis originally announced by Señor Cañedo, were to all intents and purposes entertained by the Executive branch of the Government, and not, as Señor Cañedo would wish to have it inferred, rejected *in limine* because they went beyond the basis at first propounded by the Mexican Government.[58]

The news of the failure of Treat's mission came early in December, and President Lamar recommended to Congress the provision for a force sufficient to compel Mexico to acknowledge the independence of Texas. In the House a resolution was passed instructing the committee on military affairs to inquire into the expediency of authorizing the President to raise and equip five thousand men to invade Mexico and compel her to recognize independence. The men were to equip themselves and to have the spoils which they might take, and each was to be entitled to a league and labor of land, and further pay in land which might be taken on the west side of the Rio Grande.[59] On December 5 the Senate sent word that they had appointed a committee to act with the House committee to consider the expediency of a war with Mexico.

At this juncture President Lamar became seriously ill, and on December 12 he petitioned Congress for and received leave of absence to go to New Orleans for treatment. David G. Burnet, the Vice-President, became Acting-President, and continued to urge preparations for an offensive against Mexico. On December 19 he sent to Congress the information that Treat had died on his way to Texas, and that the mission had failed. In spite of the efforts of Burnet to secure the co-operation of Congress, nothing was done save to authorize the employing of three companies of spies.[60] On January 12, 1841, a select committee of the House brought in a report pointing out the poverty of the Republic, and advising against offensive war against Mexico. At the same time,

[58] *Ibid.*, II, 724.

[59] 5 Tex. Cong., 1 Sess., *House Journal*, 181-182.

[60] 5 Tex. Cong., 1 Sess., *House Journal*, 347.

they advised that Texas be put in a state of defense against invasion.[61] The whole matter ended by the two Houses failing to agree on the appropriation bill for the regular army, so even that instrument of defense was left without means of support, and was shortly after disbanded.

(*To be concluded.*)

[61] *Ibid.*, 473.

THE HAYES ADMINISTRATION AND MEXICO[1]

WILLIAM RAY LEWIS

On March 4, 1877, Hayes succeeded Grant as President of the United States, elected by a slight and uncertain majority. His inauguration at Washington occurred just thirty days after Porfirio Diaz had assumed charge in Mexico City by right of successful revolution against Lerdo, and ascendency over Iglesias, a counter aspirant. The two or three years ensuing were years of great upheaval and unrest in the border states of Mexico, pending the firm establishment of Diaz. They were years also of a peculiar weakness and indecision at Washington, due to the bitterly contested election and numerous factional intrigues. Consequently, the documents of this period tell of a most turbulent state of affairs between the two countries, and a season of border troubles similar to that more recent "reign of terror" along the Rio Grande, during the first term of Woodrow Wilson.

The Situation in 1877

President Hayes, in his first annual message, referred to "disturbances along the Rio Grande," and to "lawless incursions into our territory by armed bands from the Mexican side of the line for the purpose of robbery," stating that such had been of frequent occurrence and that in spite of the most vigilant efforts of our commanding forces, the marauders had generally succeeded in escaping into Mexico with their plunder.[2] At this time John W. Foster, then Minister to Mexico, wrote a letter to the state department in Washington, in which he told of "a series of raids into Texas from Mexico, resulting in murders, arson, plundering of Government Post Offices and Custom Houses, robberies and other outlawry.[3]

[1]This paper was prepared in the Seminar of Professor Thomas Maitland Marshall, at the University of Colorado.

[2]*Message from the President of the United States to the Two Houses of Congress at the Commencement of the second Session of the forty-fifth Congress with the Reports of the Heads of Departments and Selections from accompanying Documents, 1877-1878*, pp. 16-17. Hereinafter cited as *Mess. & Docs.*

[3]Foster to Evarts, April 24, 1877, *H. Ex. Docs.*, *For. Rel.*, 45 Cong. 2 Sess., I, 402.

To this same session of Congress, William Everts, Secretary of War, made the statement that in consequence of this state of things, the people in that portion of Texas bordering on the Rio Grande had suffered greatly and had with great reason, complained to his department for protection.[4] The picture is made more graphic in his letter to Foster, written about the same time in his official correspondence: "The continual harassing and apparently ceaseless turmoil—on our otherwise peaceful borders by these marauding bands of Mexicans which crossing secretly and in the darkness of the night from their own territory, emerge upon the farms and fields of American citizens, carrying perpetual alarm and dread."[5]

Before going further with the list of our own aggravations, it is only fair to cite references also to certain grievances held by Mexicans, which afforded some ground for retaliation, even aside from the crossing of the border by our troops under General Ord. President Diaz, very soon after coming into power, and about the time he borrowed three hundred thousand dollars with which to make good an installment of the claims award to the United States, referred the state department at Washington to the fact that there had been also, "Indian raids from the American Reservation in New Mexico into Chihuahua," also to alleged cattle stealing by bands organized in Texas.[6] These charges Foster replied to by asserting that the Indians in question had not returned to the United States, having rather abandoned their citizenship, or else never having owned allegiance.

There was, however, one episode on the Texas side of the line in 1877, which would seem to show that Mexican rights were trampled upon and Mexican blood shed at the hands of Americans. This was the Salt War, which took place in El Paso County, the trouble lasting from September until December. This war was in the nature of a personal feud, growing out of certain Texans interfering with Mexican rights to the free use of salt from the Guadalupe Salt Lakes, ninety miles east of San Elizaro. Louis Cardis, a popular Mexican leader, was killed by Charles H. Howard, who, with the county judge and justice of peace, was seeking to

[4]Sec. of War, *Rept.*, in *Mess. & Docs., 1877-1878*, pp. 373-374.

[5]Evarts to Foster, September 20, 1878, *H. Ex. Docs.*, *For. Rel.*, 45 Cong., 3 Sess., I, 612.

[6]Foster to Evarts, September 7, 1878, *Ibid.*, I, 593.

bluff the Mexicans out of their treaty-given rights. It would seem that Mexican sympathies had found redress in the fact that Howard and several of his associates were shot later by a mob of the Mexican populace. But such an incident furnished the Mexican press with a subject for "righteous indignation."[7]

Taken as a whole, it appears that the grievances of United States citizens far outweighed those of Mexicans. Perhaps the exact number of Americans slain at the hands of Mexican outlaws and accomplices will never be known, but it was so large as to prompt and to justify the most serious consideration on the part of the Hayes administration. One of the most notorious and most unjustifiable cases of murder was that of Walter Henry, an inoffensive and law-abiding citizen, on his way to Saltillo,—treacherously killed while asleep under one of his baggage carts, and robbed of his goods.[8] Again, "Three Mexican criminals—committed a murder near Hidalgo, Texas, and evaded the officers by hiding in the region of Matamoras."[9] About the same time, W. Berry, and his servant, Juan Diaz, were murdered in the Mexican judicial district of the Rio Grande.[10] Another typical raid was that of a band of Mexicans crossing the Rio Grande at Rio Grande City, breaking the jail, releasing two prisoners, and wounding the jailer, his wife and the city attorney.

To make the situation more serious, it was proven that the Mexican state and federal authorities were often implicated in these crimes. General Ord—and the civil authorities—asserted that they had undoubted evidence that the Kickapoos who participated in the most violent and havoc-working raids in Texas, were both harbored by and confederated with Mexican authorities.[11] The officer in command of the Mexican troops at Piedras Niegras was reported officially to be not merely cognizant of the repeated thefts of American cattle, but was positively protecting the raiders, furnishing them with arms, and on one occasion receiving a large portion of the booty so obtained.[12] The facts and

[7]H. H. Bancroft, *North Mexican States and Texas*, II, 519.

[8]Evarts to Foster, September 11, 1878, *H. Ex. Docs., For. Rel.*, 45 Cong., 3 Sess., I, 603-604.

[9]General Ord, *Rept.*, in *Mess. & Docs., 1877-1878*, p. 314.

[10]Evarts to Foster, August 13, 1878. *H. Ex. Docs., For. Rel.*, 45 Cong., 3 Sess., I, 573.

[11]Foster to Evarts, September 7, 1878, *Ibid.*, I, 593.

[12]Evarts to Foster, September 20, 1878, *Ibid.*, I, 612.

evidence discovered in the murder of Henry tended to implicate the customs officer at Piedras Niegras.[13]

In addition to those perils from raiders and murderers crossing the border into Texas, and waylaying our travelers in Mexico, another festering menace was that of the formation of bands of revolutionists and the fomentation in the border counties of these bands among themselves. These revolutionaries had centers at Eagle Pass, at Laredo and at six large ranches on the Texas side.[14] They were bent upon swooping over into Mexico and undertaking the overthrow of Diaz. On several occasions they crossed in large numbers, but were defeated and chased back and dispersed on Texas soil, in open violation of the treaty with the United States.[15] Something of the dimensions of this menace may be seen in the fact that in some instances the revolutionists numbered as high as three hundred men. These bands were organized in full view of the Texans, whose life and property were being continually outraged.[16]

These revolutionary leaders even purchased supplies in New York, twelve thousand dollars in one deal changing hands through a New York broker, and one thousand rifles and much ammunition being delivered through New York by way of Austin.[17] On May 25, 1877, one of these bands crossed the frontier, robbing travelers, kidnaping hostages, outraging women and children, both Mexican and American, and for twelve days destroying fields of grain. The terrorists were described as being "All the vagabonds of the neighbodhood of Laredo, all those criminals who, being unable to live in Mexico, desired to aid in the organization of a government which, when established, would grant them immunity from punishment." The president of the ayuntamiento of Nuevo Laredo reported that the rebels, including Garza, Hayos, Salinos, and others, were well known cattle thieves.[18] The documents point to similar multi-

[13]Evarts to Foster, September 14, 1878, *Ibid.*, I, 606.

[14]Zamacoma to Evarts, July 31, 1878, *Ibid.*, I, 679-682.

[15]Evarts to Foster, June 21, 1877, *H. Ex. Docs., For. Rel.*, 45 Cong., 2 Sess., I, 413.

[16]Cuellar to Evarts, May 3, 1878, *H. Ex. Docs., For. Rel.*, 45 Cong., 3 Sess., I, 674.

[17]Zamacoma to Evarts, July 31, 1878, *Ibid.*, I, 679.

[18]Pres. of the Ayuntiamento of Nuevo Laredo, *Rept.*, *Ibid.*, I, 681.

plied outrages committed by Mexicans in Arizona as well as in Texas and New Mexico.[19]

There were still other sources of aggravation. The evasion of promises by the Mexican authorities, and the putting off of remedial action until *"Mañana,"* was a continual source of exasperation to the United States officials.[20] An application for citizenship, by one Augustus Somner, an American, was suspended for sixteen months.[21] Mexican cunning and disregard of justice may be seen in the example of a jury, which acquitted a man for the reason that only two witnesses swore that they saw him commit the murder, while the defense brought in ten men who swore that they did not see him. There are many cases on record in which our officials were assaulted or insulted. The United States consul at Acapulco was once fired upon while on a vessel in the harbor, and although he was "not hit, he was exposed to great humiliation and peril."[22] A comparison of times and events is difficult, but it may be safely concluded that the state of affairs on the border in 1877 was fully as critical as it was in 1913.

Frendly Administrative Measures

On June 1, 1877, the United States Secretary of War issued an official order to the border troops under General Ord to cross the border if necessary to punish bandits and to recover property, in view of the growing boldness of the outlaws. This order was greeted by the entire Mexican press with great protest and denunciation, as an insult to Mexican sovereigntv.[23] There seems, however, to be little evidence that action taken by the United States government was anvthing more than that of friendly measures toward protection and relief. In President Lerdo's time, American troops had crossed the border more than once, in hot pursuit of raiders, always causing a similar protest.[24] The report of Secretary Evarts in 1878 states that United States troops had

[19]Evarts to Zamacoma, May 8, 1878, *Ibid.*, 675.

[20]Foster to Evarts, November 29, 1878, *H. Ex. Docs., For. Rel.*, 46 Cong., 2 Sess., I, 734.

[21]Foster to Evarts, September 20, 1878, *H. Ex. Docs., For. Rel.*, 45 Cong., 3 Sess., I, 613.

[22]Evarts to Foster, July 3, 1877, *H. Ex. Docs., For. Rel.*, 45 Cong., 2 Sess., I, 419.

[23]John W. Foster, *Diplomatic Memoirs*, I, 90.

[24]*Ibid.*, I, 88-90.

been engaged in the enforcing of neutrality laws by preventing the crossing of our border by organized bands of revolutionists and raiders from Mexico. His entire report is strong evidence of the sincerity of the United States in its claim that the order of June 1 was for protection and not aggression.[25]

President Hayes, in his second annual message, explained that General Ord had been directed to co-operate with Mexican authorities, and to be careful against giving offense to Mexico, so far as possible and yet put an end to invasion of our own territory by those lawless bands. He contrasted the nature of our armies crossing their border for punishment only, and that of the marauders from the Mexican side in their deliberate and terrorizing work of devastation, stating that our troops were to cross the border only when the Mexican forces were unable to reach the scene of the trouble. He declared that both the Diaz and Lerdo governments had assured the United States of their having both the disposition and the power to prevent and to punish such invasions and depredations.[26] Secretary Evarts, however, seems to have developed grave doubts as to this when he wrote in 1877: "These incursions cannot be stopped so long as the government of Mexico is either unable or unwilling to punish the marauders and the United States is prevented from crossing the border in pursuit." He further declared that Mexico had not been able to keep upon her frontier a force able and disposed to prevent the raids, or to punish the raiders upon their return with booty.[27] Evarts interpreted the order of June 1 more explicitly by stating that General Ord was "to follow marauders either when the troops are in sight of them, or upon a fresh trail, across the Rio Grande and until they are overtaken and punished and the stolen property recovered. Whenever Mexican troops are present and prepared to intercept retreating raiders he is to leave the performance of that duty to them." Evarts also reported himself as being glad that, although the border had several times been crossed, in pursuance of the order, friendly relations of the two countries had not been disturbed. The secretary of state explained the order in a similar manner, and declared that no American force had ever gone over the Rio

[25]Sec. of War, *Rept.*, in *Mess. & Docs., 1877-1878*, pp. 314-319.
[26]*Mess. & Docs., 1877-1878*, p. 12.
[27]Sec. of War, *Rept.*, in *Mess. & Docs., 1877-1878*, p. 274.

Grande except in pursuit of the raiders who had invaded the soil of the United States and were escaping with booty.[28]

As to measures taken by the government, it was asserted by the state department that no effective step had ever been taken on the part of Mexico to check the raids, and that the United States, instead of receiving redress, had encountered always only delays, denials, and postponements at the capital of Mexico, while in the disturbed localities officers had met with active opposition in any attempt to enforce law and order.[29]

A fair example of the inefficiency of officers in the North Mexican army is set forth in the letter received by General Ord from a Mexican sub-commander, stating that "although animated with the best desires to be in accord with the civil and military authorities of the United States, yet the commander does not know where the Lipan marauders may be found; that he is actually indisposed (ill) at present, so that his condition prevents immediate action, but that, he believes many days will not pass before he recovers health and will occupy himself to commence with you the punishment of the said Lipans." It will be readily seen that before "many days," in such a matter as the chasing of bandits, time for action would be long past.

Another friendly measure taken by the Hayes administration was the great strengthening of the military posts in the southwest, at San Antonio, at Fort Brown, at Ringgold, and Fort Duncan, all of which occupied strategic position commanding the crossings of the Rio Grande. At San Antonio, an appropriation of $100,000 was used during 1878 in the erection of a building 624 feet square, enclosing a courtyard 558 feet square, this for a quartermaster's depot and the storage of large quantities of supplies.[30]

War Threatened in 1878

Bancroft says of the situation in 1878: "War in fact seemed imminent, there is little doubt that Foster would have fomented hostilities if he could, and President Hayes did not seem averse to such a course."[31] A perusal of then current newspapers of

[28]Evarts to Foster, August 13, 1878, *H. Ex. Docs.*, *For. Rel.*, 45 Cong., 3 Sess., I, 572-574.

[29]*Ibid.*, I, 573.

[30]Sec. of War, *Rept.*, in *Mess. & Docs.*, *1877-1878*, p. 280.

[31]H. H. Bancroft, *History of Mexico*, VI, 446.

Mexico City might verify this assertion as also some of the documents sent out by that government which decried the order of June 1 as a new invasion of Mexican territory.[32]

Was war seriously threatened by the United States Government, and if so, by what persons and classes, and for what purposes?

President Diaz responded to the popular clamor in Mexico City against the order of June 1 by issuing a counter order to his army of the north to "Repel with force any invasion of Mexican marauders.[33] This, if carried out, would inevitably have resulted in war. But because of a straightened treasury, and internal revolution nearer Mexico City, Diaz was utterly unable to carry out the order even if he ever intended to do so. As it was, the tone of the threat seems to have strengthened him greatly in the affection of the Mexican people.

But there were other and more serious steps taken by Mexico than that of the bluff military order. In one instance Diaz forces crossed the American border in pursuit of Revolutionary forces.[34] A statute was enacted whereby the United States citizens were prohibited from owning land in Mexico. A little later this was extended to include title to mining properties.[35] Furthermore, all proposed railroad connections between the two countries were officially discouraged.[36] In a number of cases, diplomatic intervention was denied.[37] The Mexican department of state kept on tantalizing Foster and Evarts with offers to stake all hopes for law and order on the plan for the extradition of offenders, a plan which had long been proven unavailing. Señor Mata, at this juncture, resigned his post at Washington, professing disgust over the attitude of our government in delaying recognition of the Diaz administration, and stating that he had little hope for a peaceful settlement.

An effort toward making a treaty at this time was finally rejected by Diaz because of the long delay of our government in tendering him recognition. This, indeed, gave Mexico a plausible

[32]Foster, *Diplomatic Memoirs*, I, 90.

[33]*Ibid.*, I, 90-91.

[34]Foster to Mata, July 15, 1878, *H. Ex. Docs.*, *For. Rel.*, 45 Cong., 3 Sess., I, 557-559.

[35]Foster to Evarts, August 20, 1879, *H. Ex. Docs.*, *For. Rel.*, 46 Cong., 2 Sess., I. 833.

[36]Foster to Evarts, May 31, 1879, *Ibid.*, I, 811-812.

[37]Foster to Evarts, December 14, 1878, *Ibid.*, I, 761.

ground for protest, as a year had elapsed since other powers had recognized his régime. Vallarta, the Mexican foreign minister, in an interview with Foster, charged the Hayes administration with a departure from the former policy of the United States in not recognizing Diaz, and declared also that he had private advices from Washington to the effect that a scheme was being concocted for the annexation by the United States of the north Mexican states. He charged that the order to General Ord was a step toward this, stating that an outright declaration of war against Mexico would have been much more honorable and considerate. Foster answered this insinuation of Vallarta by saying that the United States was waiting to recognize Diaz only until assured that his election was approved by the Mexican people and that his administration possessed stability and a disposition to comply with treaty regulations. He insisted that his government would recognize Diaz as soon as he proved able to settle the border troubles.[38]

The winter of 1877-1878 dragged through without the expected open clash of United States and Mexican troops, but Foster states that there was indescribable intensity of feeling in Mexico, and a general belief that the United States sought either to absorb and exterminate all Mexico or at least to annex her northern states, and every move of the United States was interpreted as a deliberate step in that direction. Foster admits that there was some foundation for the charge, pointing to a desire on the part of the faction at Washington to unify the administration and reconcile Tilden adherents by a war of conquest and the possible annexation of Mexican border territory. It is likely that President Hayes was influenced by this element about him to the point of delaying recognition of Diaz. But it is extremely doubtful whether he had any part whatsoever in the dispatching of Vallejo and Frisbe to Mexico City. It is certain that there were many Washington persons in the secret, and that these two gentlemen were empowered in some unofficial way.

Foster was called to Washington in January, 1878, having long desired to present in person the situation in Mexico and the merits of the Diaz régime as deserving of recognition. It was doubtless

[38]Foster to Evarts, June 20, 1877, *H. Ex. Docs., For. Rel.*, 45 Cong., 2 Sess., I, 410.

largely through this visit that the intriguing faction in Washington was broken up. On April 11, he returned to Mexico City announcing the official recognition of Diaz, which act served toward the settling, temporarily, of Mexican agitation, and for a little time great cordiality prevailed. But in the summer of 1878 another revolution broke out in Mexico and consequent border troubles again stirred up a suspicion on the part of both countries. On September 15, Foster retired from a public gathering in honor of the anniversary of Mexican independence, because of a poem's being recited which he considered insulting to his government. This seems to be the only ground upon which Bancroft could charge that Foster desired war. With great haste, however, Mexican authorities apologized to him for this poem, which had been declaimed by a radical agitator, without having had a place on the program as planned. Border conditions grew worse, however, and in October Foster reported to Washington his belief that the situation would end in war.[39]

A Study of Border Terrain

After a visit to the frontier along the Rio Grande, Foster wrote of the "wildness of the border country" as the primary source of all the trouble, because of its extreme handicap to army operations, and the chance it gave Mexican soldiers to desert their own troops and escape across the border uncaught. It is a fact all the more emphasized by recent troubles that disadvantages of terrain, to use a military term, have ever been the chief barrier to law and order there.

The Rio Grande frontier is, roughly speaking, divided into three sections, namely, the lowlands, the cañons, and the high, rugged mountains. Each of these is possessed of its own peculiar difficulties in the way of effect in border patrol.[40] The lowlands along the lower Rio Grande are fringed with lagoons and great, marshy swamps, all of which are breeding places of fever and plague. In the days before the advent of army sanitation the maintenance of forces there on either side of the line was a thing next to impossible. Chief Engineer Humphreys, writing in 1877, made reference to "these unhealthy marshes" as a great detriment to the

[39]Foster, *Diplomatic Memoirs*, I, 90-92.

[40]Gilbert and Brigham, *Introduction to Physical Geography*, 91.

health of the garrison, explaining that the lagoons filled with water at each overflow of its banks by the river. He pointed out, furthermore, that the "frequent changes continually taking place in the channel of the Rio Grande, the friable nature of the banks of the stream, and the encroachments of the river upon its banks" made it very difficult to plan the construction of a permanent fort.[41]

The topography of the central Rio Grande may be described as one vast waste of cañons, gorges, chasms and countless arroyos, both along the river and its many tributaries for several miles each way, all of them bounded by cañon walls rising abruptly in places to as high as one thousand feet. The river channels are choked by sandbars, difficult to bridge during the rainy season because of shifting beds of quicksand. Spasdomic rainfall results in sudden floods from the catchment areas, filling washes and arroyos, and carrying quick destruction to those who chance to be crossing. In this region the mesas and buttes are barren, rocky wastes, with basins and high tablelands almost void of vegetation. The country for miles on each side of the river offers to the visitor poison wells, alkali sinks, conglomerate beds of clay and lava-capped sandstone,—haunted by snakes, tarantulas, and beasts of prey. There are stretches of blinding salt marshes and dazzling, parched adobe which render camp life there extremely undesirable and prevent any movement of troops, either on foot or horseback. There were no railroads in those days, and no wagon roads even for hundreds of miles at a stretch, and disorders prevailed, as a rule, in direct ratio with the lack of good roads.[42]

Further westward the border is mapped out through high, rugged mountains, with unexplored wildernesses, lost rivers, gigantic caves, deep fissures, and underground passages affording no end of strongholds in which to hide. General Ord referred to an oak timber seven miles above San Felipe, in which Areola, a noted bandit, "terror of all parties," with thirty men was wont to take refuge. Ord declared that, at that time, there were no more than two hundred regular soldiers between Fort Clarke and Saltillo.[43] Even

[41]Humphreys, *Rept.*, in *H. Ex. Docs.*, *For. Rel.*, 45 Cong., 2 Sess., III, 473-476.

[42]United States Geological Survey, *12th Ann. Rept., 1890-1891*, Part II, *Irrigation*, 240-290.

[43]Ord to Shafter, June 4, 1878, *H. Ex. Docs.*, *For. Rel.*, 45 Cong., 3 Sess., I, 416.

minor disadvantages of terrain have been cited as the defeat of many an army. A true history of the Rio Grande border troubles must embody a keen appreciation of the difficulties in chasing bandits and outlaws who were, on their part, familiar with every square mile of the ground. The wisdom of both governments in the building of highways there is manifest, for such alone will overcome the main handicap.

THE GROWING STRENGTH OF DIAZ

Early in 1878, President Diaz, in announcing his policy toward the United States, declared himself to be "resolved to act with full justice, and animated by a friendly spirit, although decided at the same time to admit nothing which would wound the dignity of Mexico.[44] This statement is representative of all his official utterances and executive dealings with the Hayes administration. Anyone familiar with the temperament of the Mexican people will understand the defiant note in his expressions. But this must be interpreted in the light of his actual deeds, such as the borrowing of a very large sum of money, at a high rate of interest, in order to meet promptly an installment due the United States on the Claims Award, and especially his offering to pay this in the name of the Lerdo administration, to avoid diplomatic embarrassment. We might cite also his patient waiting for official recognition, his prompt apology for the "poem" of September 15, 1878, and his various steps towards mastering the border situation, taken just as rapidly as internal conditions in Mexico allowed.

Tension between the two countries remained high all through 1878 and well into 1879. The Hayes administration declined to withdraw the order of June 1, 1877, until in 1880. But little by little the frontier became better guarded, and no open conflict of the federal forces ever occurred. As time passed and all counter-revolutions against Diaz broke down, he was enabled more and more to grip the reins of power, and to enforce law and order in the north Mexican states. Largely due to his own native tact and good judgment, and to his firm stand in international affairs, his nation grew rapidly in the esteem of the world powers and large foreign capital became interested in the development of her re-

[44]Diaz, Address, in *H. Ex. Docs., For. Rel.,* 45 Cong., 3 Sess., I, 527-528.

sources. Being of native descent, Diaz represented the best Mexican traditions and was able to hold to an advanced and liberal policy and to keep his republic in the path of progress.[45]

By the close of 1878, General Ord reported the ousting of certain unfaithful public servants in the northern states and judicial districts and their replacement by men who were disposed to respect the orders of President Diaz. More prompt action against the raiders led to a gradual decrease in offenses along the Rio Grande. Late in 1879, Foster visited Matamoras while on his tour of Mexico, and great "hospitality and cordial expression of feeling toward the United States" was extended to him. Foster offers as evidence that the feeling of hostility had by that time dwindled away, the fact that even General Ord attended the festivities given at Matamoras by the Mexican authorities, and that Ord, as well as himself, was warmly welcomed.[46] By 1880, the consul of La Paz was able to report an increased trade in the way of imports such as flour, lard and rice from the United States, and that San Francisco companies were commencing operations in his province.[47] A similar report came also from Mazatlan.[48] And Consul Lespinasse of the province of Merido and Progreso stated that the consumption of American canned goods was increasing daily.[49]

We may conclude that President Diaz was, throughout his long administration, friendly to the United States. Even during the first trying period each and every diplomatic question arising with the sister republic was settled peaceably, satisfactorily, and in the spirit of true international friendship. It was largely due to his own growing power in all Mexico that the Hayes administration was spared even a much more lasting and complicated state of affairs, and indeed from a war which, at that time, and actuated by an inferior motive, on the part of an unworthy faction at Washington, might have proved a lasting blot on the fair page of the United States's foreign policy.

It must be concluded also that President Hayes and his admin-

[45]Hale, *Mexico*, 399.

[46]Foster, *Diplomatic Memoirs*, I, 135.

[47]Turner, *Rept.*, in *H. Ex. Docs.*, *Commercial Relations*, 45 Cong., 3 Sess., XVIII, 955.

[48]Kelton, *Rept.*, *Ibid.*, XVIII, 970.

[49]Lespinasse, *Rept.*, *Ibid.*, XVIII, 975.

istration were entirely friendly and sincere in their dealings with Mexico. There appears nothing in all the documents having to do with foreign relations, military affairs, commerce or any phase whatever of the home or foreign policy that would justify the assertions of Bancroft that "Foster would have fomented hostilities,— and that even President Hayes was not averse to such a course."[50] In his message of 1879 Hayes stated that "through the judicious and energetic action of the military commanders of the two nations on each side of the Rio Grande, under instructions of their respective governments, raids and depredations have greatly decreased."[51] He added that the third installment of the Claims award had been duly paid, and that the "satisfactory" situation led him to anticipate an expansion of our trade with Mexico and co-operation in developing the resources of that country. Again in 1880, in his last message to Congress, he paid tribute to the efficiency of the co-operative border patrol, relating how a band of outlaws, under the command of Chief Victorio, had disturbed the peace of the border with a "savage foray," but that by the combined and harmonious action of the military forces the band had been broken up and substantially destroyed.[52] By that time several important railway building enterprises were on foot, and much United States capital was invested south of the Rio Grande. A strong chain of forts and garrisons had been forged along the Texas frontier and there was some improvement in the main highways. So far as can be gathered from the records there was no activity on the part of the United States Navy along the coast of Texas or Mexico, and but little attention was paid to the upbuilding of a Gulf fleet.

[50]H. H. Bancroft, *History of Mexico*, II, 446.
[51]*Mess. and Docs., 1878-1880*, p. 14.
[52]*Ibid.*, 12.

MINUTES OF THE AYUNTAMIENTO OF SAN FELIPE DE AUSTIN, 1828-1832

XII

EDITED BY EUGENE C. BARKER

In the Town of San Felipe de Austin 4th July 1831. The Ayuntamto. of this jurisdiction this day met in regular session present the folowing members F. W. Johnson prest. W. C. White 1st Regidor P. D. McNeil 3d Regidor and R. M. Williamson Sindico procurador. Absent Randall Jones 2d Regidor and Wm. Robinson 4th Regidor. the acts of the last meeting were read and approved.

The report of the committee appointed to draw up an ordinance regulating the Municipal Surveying Department, was read and approved and the ordinance ordered to be published (for which see Book of ordinances pages —) and so much of the ordinance of 5th July 1830 as may be contrary to the provisions of this are hereby repealed.

On motion of R. M. Williamson Sindico procurador, ordered that Walter C. White Regidor be instructed and authorized to collect the amount due the Municipality on town lots in this Town.

On motion of the president the subject of the situation of the children of John Jones, who have been left by their parents in a helpless and starving condition was taken up and discussed and the Ayuntamto *ordered* that the treasurer be authorized to minister to their present wants and necessity from the municipal funds and until something can be done for their permanent support.

On motion of the prest. ordered that the Comisarios of the different precincts in the Municipality be required from their own observations and knowledge, and also on a report made to them by the sindicos of said precincts [p. 23] to make and transmit monthly to the Alcalde of the jurisdiction a report of all doctors, merchants, venders of Merchandise and retailers of liquor within their respective precincts, and all those who in any way exercise such professions or sell goods without having obtained a licence in conformity with the laws.

Ordered that Doctors S. B. Walls and C. G. Cox be fined each $25 for a breach of the municipal ordinances by practising medicine without having previously obtained a licence agreeably to said ordinances and also for a non compliance with the order of the Ayto. to present themselves before the body at this session.

Ordered that James Whiteside and Jonathan C. Peyton be fined each $5 for failing to comply with the provisions of the ordinances, regulating Tavern keepers, and also for a non compliance with the order of last meeting.

The report of the Committee appointed to draft rules and regulations for the government of the patrol guard, was read and adopted.

The petition of Asa Brigham praying for special privilege to collect for ferriage, at the ferry kept by him at Brazoria an amount equivalent to the former rates of ferriage to compensate him for his trouble and expence, was read and rejected on the ground of its being inadmissible to alter the present rates of ferriage to suit the special convenience of any particular person and to avoid a number of petitions from other ferries on the same subject.

The petition of John Peterson praying to be released from the effects of the order of this body by which he is prevented from receiving land as a colonist was read, [p. 24] in connection with the evidence of character presented by him, and was admitted, and the body ordered that the Empresario S. F. Austin be notified thereof in order that the said Peterson may obtain his land as a settler. A written application of Wm. T. Austin for a licence to keep a public house at Brazoria was admitted and the licence ordered to be issued.

A petition of Stephen Richardson praying that a title for Lot No. 565 purchased by him be made to Henry Cheves and Thomas Gay—prayer admitted and title ordered to be made.

On Motion of the Prest. ordered by a unanimous resolution of the body that the amt. of tax due and arising from Town and out Lots in this Town, and also the amount due and arrising from the ferry at this place shall be peculiarly and specially appropriated to the payt. of the claims due by the Ayunto. and on which the body has passed special resolutions, a list of which the secretary is ordered to furnish the prest. for his information and government. And further that no claims, orders, drafts, etc. shall be accepted by the treasurer or tax gatherers as set offs or in payt. of Taxes which will be due under the provissions of the Municipal ordinance and by virtue of law No. 180 as the amt. arrising from that tax is to be appropriated solely to the purposes expressed in said law. The body then ordered an extra meeting on Monday the 18th inst and adjourned to that day.

[p. 25] In the Town of San Felipe de Austin 5th Septembr 1831. The Ayuntamto. this day met in regular session, present F. W. Johnson Alcalde W. C. White 1st Regidor Randall Jones 2d Regidor and R M. Williamson Sindico procurador. The acts of the session of 4th July were read and approved as the extra meeting of the 18th July and regular meeting of 1st August did not take place on account of the members failing to attend.

The following appointments were then made by the body for Surveyors of the different Municipal surveying districts, on the petitions presented by the applicants and the evidence of their qualifications.

Thomas H. Borden, Municipal Surveyor of district Number 1.

John P. Borden, Municipal Surveyor of district Number 4.

Byrd Lockhart, Municipal Surveyor of district No. 3.

Horacio Chrisman and Saml P. Browne, Municipal Surveyors of District No. 2.

Gail Borden jr. Municipal Surveyor of district No. 5.

S. C. Hirams, Municipal Surveyor of district No. 7.

A letter from Henry Smith praying for the appointment of Municipal Surveyor of district No. 6 was deferred on account of his having failed to comply with the requisition of furnisihng the body evidence of his capacity.

[p. 26] A petition from the Citizens of Harrisburg praying for the appointment of Frederick Rankin John W Moore and John W. Litle as commissrs to lay off a road from Harrisburg to New Kentucky and the Lake Settlement prayer granted and the report ordered to be made first Monday in Novembr next.

A petition of Robert Peebles praying that the title for out lots numbers 43, 44, and 46 purchased by him from the Ayunto. may be made to James B. Miller to whom he has sold them, prayer granted and title order to be made to said Miller in conformity with a former order of this body, authorising the title to issue to said Peebles.

On motion of the president it was ordered that Stephen F. Austin, F. W. Johnson, and William Williamson be appointed a Committee to draft a plan of Town house or Municipal Hall and a Jail—The Court House to be at least 50 ft long and 20 feet wide and one and a half story high.

A petition of William Williamson praying that the right to Town lots No. 87 and 112 which were formerly purchased by John Montgomery and Patrick Green be transferred and vested in him by virtue and on account of his having purchased said lots. Which petition was granted and the body further allowed the sd. Williamson until the first of March 1832 to improve the said lots in. The title to issue to him as soon as they may be improved if done prior to sd. 1st March next. The plan of a patrol law as drawn up by the Committee appointed for that purpose was read and [p. 27] approved and it was ordered to be engrossed in the Book of Ordinances (for which see said Book pages —)

A petition of Wm. Cooper was presented and read in which he prays that a certain league of land granted to the late Benj Eaton be by the body declared as forfeited for the want of improvement rejected by the body on account of the time allowed by law for the improvement of the land not having expired.

An account presented by L. F. Farley for boarding Spinks rejected for want of proper vouchers.

A petition of Oliver Jones praying for a title to certain town lots referred to next meeting.

G. F. Richardson was fined in the sum of seventy-five dollars for selling Merchandise and Liquors without a licence.

Nathl Lynch was fined $112 50/100 for selling Merchandise and Liquers without a Licence.

Luke Lesassier appointed prosecuting attorney for the next 6 months.

[p. 28] In the Town of San Felipe de Austin 3d of October 1831. At a regular meeting of the Ayuntamto. of this jurisdiction the following members were present F. W. Johnson, prest, W. C. White 1st Regidor. Randall Jones 2d Regidor P. D. McNeil 3d Regidor and Wm. Robinson 4th Regidor absent R. M. Williamson Sindico procurador. The session was opened by reading the acts of the preceeding sessions which were approved.

A petition was presented by Moses Cummins praying to be appointed Municipal surveyor of surveying district Number 8 and the body being satisfied with the evidence of qualifications offered by said Cummins appointed him surveyor of said district.

A petition from E R Wightman for the appointment of partition surveyor in District number 5 and recommending Thos J. Tone for the same appointment, was presented and read and Thomas J. Tone was appointed Municipal Surveyor and authorized to do partition work in sd. district No. 5.

A claim presented by L. F. Farley for boarding and attendance of J. Spinks (a pauper) and after fully discussing the subject in its merits the body unanimously resolved that Ten Dollars be paid said Farley on his said acct.

On motion of the prest. it was ordered that William Pettus, Walter C. White and Samuel M. Williams be appointed a committee to investigate the true situation of the unimproved lots in this Town and report such as they may deem forfeited, to the body at the next meeting

[p. 29] Ordered that inasmuch as it has come to the knowledge of this body that Thomas Powell has been vending merchandise in this jurisdiction without having previously obtained a licence in conformity with the provisions of the Municipal ordinance that he be fined in conformity with said ordinance in the sum of $37 50/100 Thirty seven dollars and four bits.

A plan for the building of a town house or Municipal hall and a jail was submitted and approved ordered that inasmuch as it is reported that E. Winston has violated the provissions of the Municipal ordinance by vending merchandise in this municipality without a licence, that he be notified to show cause to this body if any he has at the next meeting why he should not be fined agreeably to the provissions of said ordinance—and it is further ordered that Randall Jones 2d Regidor be authorized to take the deposition of Wm. Little relative to the above fact of the sale, and present the same to this body at the next meeting.

A licence for the sale of dry goods issued in conformity with the provissions of the Municipal ordinance to James C. Carr had by said Carr been transferred to Henry Cheves to whom the said Carr had sold the remaining stock of his goods. The question then arose before this body whether or not licences are transferable, and after considerable discussion the question was put to vote and their being two Regidors in favor and two against the question the prest. by the ordinance had the right of voting and gave the casting vote against the question, whereupon it was ordered that licences for the sale of Merchandise etc. [p. 30] are not transferable

The subject of the propriety of taking a certain description of property in part payment of taxes due and to be collected from the inhabitants of this Municipality was discussed whereupon it was resolved by the body that good second rate cows and calves and good yearling heifers shall be recd from each individual who may desire to pay them under such special regulations as may hereafter be adopted for collecting the Taxes provided however that in no instance shall the amt of property so taken or recd exceed two thirds of the whole amount of tax due by such individual. And further that the price which is authorized to be allowed for such property is 10$ ten dollars for each cow and calf as aforesaid and five dollars for each heifer at least one year old.

The body then took up the subject of the appointment of a Collector whose duty it shall be to collect the amt. of Tax due and that it shall be the duty of whomsoever may be appointed for that purpose to make a correct return of all the amts. which he may have collected and recd in payment of taxes as well the amount of property as also the amt. of money and deliver them to the treasurer of this Municipality in this town on the first day of may next and that he shall give bond and security in the sum of Ten thousand dollars for the full and faithful performance of his duty as collector and for the delivery of the amt. collected and further be subject to such general instructions relative to the collections as this body may deem expedient to form for his government. [p. 31] And it was further ordered that the collection of the taxes for the present year shall be farmed out to the lowest bidder on the first day of November next at the office of the Alcalde in this town.

On motion of the president ordered that so much of the plan for the building of a town house approved at the meeting on the first Monday of last month, as relates to the heighth of said building be repealed, and that it be two stories high and further that the said building be constructed of brick and agreeably to the plan filed in the records of this body.

And it was further ordered that the plan for a jail as submitted be approved and that the building of it be farmed out to the lowest bidder on the first Monday in November next at the office of the Alcalde in this town the undertaker will be bound to give bond and sufficient security for the fulfilment of the contract.

A petition was presented from Dr. C. G. Cox praying the body to remit a fine imposed on him for a breach of the Municipal regulations which was rejected on the ground that the body has not the power of remitting fines (see article 147 of Law No. 37—of this state).

The excuse of Pleasant D. McNeil 3d Regidor for non attendance being heard was declared by the body good and reasonable.

[p. 32] In the town of San Felipe de Austin 7th Novr 1831 At a regular meeting of the ayuntamto. in consequence of the sickness of the Alcalde Walter C. White 1st Regidor presided. present R. Jones 2d Regidor William Robinson 4th Regidor and R. M Williamson sindico procurador—The acts of the last session were read and approved—

A petition from Nathaniel Lynch praying to be released from a fine imposed on him by this body—which was rejected and the fine ordered to be collected—

A petition from the inhabitants of the precinct of Bastrop living up on the Colorado praying for a division of the precinct and for permission to open a road from the crossing of the San Antonio road to this town. the body decided that it was impracticable to acceed to the prayer for a divission of the precinct but granted the privilege of opening the road.

A petition from Oliver Jones praying for a title to certain town lots Numbers 139-140-141-184-185 and 186 which was granted and the title ordered to be made.

Satisfactory evidence being before the body that E. Winston has violated the municipal ordinance by vending merchandise without a licence, it was ordered by the body that the said E. Winston be fined in conformity with said ordinance thirty seven dollars and a half.

Samuel C. Haddy, Martin Allen and Isaac Best were appointed commissioners to open a road from this town to the prairie on the opposite side of the river.

The body then entered into the discussion of the approaching election and the propriety of augmenting the number of electoral assemblies in the municipality for the convenience of the inhabitants, and [p. 33] also the number of members necessary for the

Ayuntamto. of the next year in conformity with the population of the jurisdiction, and inasmuch as article 98 of Law 37 provides that where the number of inhabitants exceeds 5000 the Ayuntamto. shall be composed of 2 Alcaldes 6 Regidors and 2 sindico procuradors there must be elected at the ensuing elections 2 Alcaldes 4 regidors and 2 sindicos procuradors, and that elections shall be held at the hereinafter described places—

Precinct of San Felipe—At the Town of Austin to be presided by the Alcalde—at the house of Wm. Robinson to be presided by sd. Robinson—at the house of Wm. Andrews to be presided by Randall Jones—at the house of Henry Jones, to be presided by W. C. White—at the house of Abner Kuykendall—to be presided by said Kuykendall.

Precinct of Viesca—At the house of Walter Sutherland to be presided by Jesse Grimes—at the house of Francis Holland to be presided by sd. Holland—At the house of Fredk Rankin to be presided by M. Herbert.

Precinct of Bastrop—At the house of Richard Andrews to be presided by sindico Mays—At the house of Wm. Barton to be presided by said Barton—At the house of John P. Coles to be presided by Nestor Clay—

Precinct of Victoria—At the house of Wm. Stafford to be presided by Mills M. Battle—At the house of Alexander Hodge to be presided by Asa Brigham sindico—at Brazoria to be presided by Henry Smith comisario—

Precinct of Mina—At the Town of Matagorda to be presided by James Norton—at the house of Robt H. Williams to be presided by P. D. McNeil—At the house of L. Ramey to be presided by said Ramey—At the house of George Sutherland to be presided by said Sutherland.

Precinct of San Jacinto—At Harrisburg to be presided by S. C. Hirams comisario—At the house of N. Lynch to be presided by sindico Bundick.

Gonzales—At the town to be presided by comisario Patrick. The [p. 34] election to be held at the before mentioned places on Sunday and Monday 11th and 12th Decemr next for the offices of the Ayuntamto. for the ensuing year and comisarios and sindicos of precincts in conformity with the provisions of the state constitution and law No. 37.

[p. 34a] **In the town of San Felipe de Austin, December 18, 1831. The ayuntamiento of this jurisdiction met in the Town Hall, as provided by Article 164 of the Constitution of the State and Article 100 of Law No. 37. The following members were present: Francis W. Johnson president, Walter C. White first regidor, and Robert M. Williamson sindico procurador—and in the presence of the presidents, tellers, and secretaries of the municipal electoral assemblies, the president declared the session opened. They formed the three general lists, as required by said Article 100 of Law No. 37, and in accordance therewith the president declared the following officers constitutionally elected: Horatio Chriesman first alcalde; John Austin second alcalde; Josiah H. Bell, Jesse Grimes, Martin Allen, and Abner Kuykendall regidors; and Henry Cheves and Rawson Alley *sindicos procuradores.* It was ordered that two copies of these lists be made immediately and posted in a public place. The ayuntamiento then passed to the formation of the lists for *Comisarios* and *sindicos procuradores* of precincts as required by Article 158 of the Constitution and Article 106 of Law No. 37. According to these the president declared the following citizens constitutionally elected:

For the precinct of Viesca: John Bowman, *comisario,* and Peter Whitaker *sindico.*

[p. 35a] For the precinct of Bastrop: Richard Andrews, *Comisario,* and Mosea Rousseau, *sindico.*

For the precinct of Mina

For the precinct of Victoria: Asa Brigham, *comisario,* and Thomas Westall, *sindico.*

For the precinct of San Jacinto: John W. Moore, *comisario,* and William Laughlin, *sindico.***[46]

[p. 37] List of Individuals who were voted for for Alcaldes at the Municipal elections held on the 11th and 12th of the present month in conformity with the 164th article of the constitution and articles 97 and 100 of Law No. 37.

Horacio Chriesman	recd 254 votes
John Austin	recd 243 votes
Florence Stack	recd 88 votes

*Port of the English is missing, and that part of the text between the asterisks is translated from the parallel Spanish.

John P. Coles	recd 77 votes
Samuel C Hirams	recd 75 votes

Town of Austin 18 Decr 1831

F. W. Johnson
John Jones
John W. Moore
Wm. Barton
Rich. Andrews
John Bowman
Henry Smith
A. Brigham

[p. 38] List of Individuals who were voted for for regidors at the municipal elections held on the 11th and 12th of the present month in conformity with articles 164 of the constitution and 97 and 100 of Law No. 37.

Josiah H. Bell	recd	227	votes
Jesse Grimes	"	189	"
Abner Kuykendall	"	140	"
Martin Allen	"	145	"
Byrd Lockhart	"	105	"
James Kerr	"	92	"
William Kincheloe	"	47	"
James Knight	"	25	"
William Robbins	"	20	"
John Jones	"	20	"
James Whiteside	"	19	"
Joel Leakey	"	17	"
Thomas Westall	"	13	"
James W. Jones	"	9	"
Thomas Davis	"	2	"
James Small	"	2	"
John Brown	"	2	"
John F. Webber	"	2	"

Town of Austin 18th Decr 1831

F. W. Johnson
John Jones
John W. Moore

Wm. Barton
Rich. Andrews
John Bowman
Henry Smith
A. Brigham

[p. 39] List of the individuals who were voted for sindico procuradors at the Municipal election held on the 11th and 12th of the present month in conformity with the 164th article of the constitution and 97 and 100 of Law No. 37.

Henry Cheves	recd 117 votes
Rawson Alley	recd 84 idem
R. H. Williams	recd 9 idem

Town of Austin 18th Decr 1831

F. W. Johnson
John Jones
John W. Moore
Wm. Barton
Rich. Andrews
John Bowman
Henry Smith
A. Brigham

[p. 40] List of the individuals who were voted for for Comisarios of precinct and Sindicos in the Municipal elections held on the 11th and 13th of the present month in conformity with article 158 of the Constitution and 106 of Law No. 37.

Precinct of Viesca

for comisario	John Bowman	recd 21 votes
	Francis Holland	recd 6 do
for sindico	Peter Whitaker	recd 22 votes
	Danl Millican	id 4 do

Precinct of Bastrop

for comisario	Richard Andrews	recd 33 votes
for sindico	Mosea Rousseau	recd 15 votes
	——— Tannehill	recd 14 do

Precinct of Mina

for Comisario	James Norton	recd 25 votes
	John Huff	recd 13 votes
for sindico	Daniel Decrow	recd 35 votes

[p. 41] *Precinct of Victoria*

for Comisario	A. Brigham	recd 88 votes
	M. Henry	do 75 do
for sindico	Thomas Westall	recd 27 votes
	Edwin Waller	do 16 do

Precinct of Sn Jacinto

for Comisario	John W. Moore	recd 56 votes
for sindico	William Laughlin	recd 49 votes
	Andrew Robinson	" 3 votes

[p. 42] In the Town of San Felipe de Austin on the 1st Jany 1832. The Ayunto. met in regular public session composed of the following members F. W. Johnson Alcalde Randall Jones 2d Regidor, William Robinson 4th Regidor and R. M. Williamson Sindico procurador In conformity with the provissions of art 101 of Law No. 37 and the 1st article of the Municipal ordinance The following members of the new Ayunto presented their credentials of election, and the president of last year administered the oath required in article 220 of the State Constitution to the Alcalde of the highest vote C. Horatio Chreisman who immediately administered the oath to the following members elected as Regidors Citizens Josiah H. Bell Jesse Grimes, Martin Allen, and Abner Kuykendall and to Citizen Henry Cheves, as sindico procurador. John Austin Alcalde of the 2d vote not being present and Rawson Alley sindico procurador likewise absent. and the act was then closed.

[p. 44][46] F. W. Johnson
R. Jones
Wm. Robinson
R. M. Williamson

[p. 45] In the town of San Felipe de Austin on the 2d of January 1832. At a meeting of the Ayuntamto pursuant to the order of the Presidt. yesterday composed of the 1st Alcalde C. Horatio Chreisman, Pleasant D. McNeil 2d Regidor William Robinson 2d Regidor Josiah H. Bell 3d Regidor Jesse Grimes 4th Regidor and Abner Kuykendall 6th Regidor and William Cheves sindico procurador, absent C. John Austin 2d Alcalde, Martin Allen 5th Regidor and Rawson Alley sindico procurador. The

[46]Page 43 is blank, and page 44 is blank, except for these signatures. It was probably intended to insert election returns above the signatures.

presidt. appointed as a special committee 2d Regidor Wm. Robinson 4th Regidor Jesse Grimes and the procurador sindico Henry Cheves to examine into and report the situation of the ferry flat at the ferry at this town and make said report at 2 o'clock this evening and the body adjourned.

2 o'clock in the afternoon—the body met pursuant to adjournment, the same members being present and also C. Martin Allen 5th Regidor who appeared and took his seat. The report of the committee appointed to inspect the ferry boat was read and approved.

ordered that the President of the body rent out the ferry at this town on tomorrow at 12 o'clock.

ordered that William Robinson, Martin Allen, Henry Cheves and S. M. Williams be appointed as a committee of finance.

ordered that Josiah H. Bell, Jesse Grimes and Pleasant D. McNeil be appointed a committee to examine into and report relative to the situation of the prisoners now in confinement which report they will present to the body on their meeting tomorrow at 10 oclock and the body adjourned.

[p. 46] Act continueing 10 oclock 3d January 1832. The report of the committee appointed to report relative to the situation of the prisoners now in confinement presented to the body their report which was read and on the final question, shall said report be adopted the vote stood thus, for the adoption P. D. McNeil 1st Regidor Wm. Robinson 2d Regidor J. H. Bell 3d Regidor Jesse Grimes 4th Regidor Martin Allen 5 Regidor Henry Cheves sindico procurador Abner Kuykendall 6th Regidor opposed on the ground that it was a subject that did not belong to the body. and the report was consequently adopted by the majority being in favor of it.

Ordered that the Alcalde be authorized to provide for the support of John Jones Children in the manner least expensive to the funds of the municipality, at the same time to prevent them from suffering and to pay for the same out of the said funds.

The body then proceeded to the appointment of a treasurer and Henry Cheves sindico procurador was unanimously elected treasurer. And the body adjourned to the next regular session.[47]

[47]The available record of the ayuntamiento of San Felipe de Austin ends here.

NEWS ITEMS.

The Littlefield Collection of Southern History in the University of Texas Library recently received important accessions of newspaper files: *Louisville (Ky.) Courier Journal,* 1865-1868, *Banner of Peace,* Nashville, 1840-1874, *Daily Picayune,* New Orleans, 1837-1861, *Texas Presbyterian,* 1846-48 and 1851-56, *Texas State Gazette,* Austin, 1849-1854, and *Tri-Weekly State Times,* Austin, 1853-1854.

Mr. Waddy Thompson, of Atlanta, Georgia, grandson of Waddy Thompson, of South Carolina, who was American minister to Mexico from 1842 to 1844, recently presented to the Texas State Historical Association sixteen original letters, being personal letters to or from Waddy Thompson during the years 1842 to 1848. Among the writers are Andrew Jackson, John Tyler, Daniel Webster, John C. Calhoun, Reverdy Johnson, Waddy Thompson, Hugh McLeod, José Maria Tornel, and Santa Anna. The subjects touched upon are the liberation of the Texan prisoners at Perote, American claims, peace between Mexico and Texas, acquisition of California, the prospect of war between England and Mexico, and the presidential campaign of 1848.

The Old Trail Drivers' Association, whose membership is composed of pioneer stockmen, held the sixth annual convention at San Antonio, September 28 and 29, 1920. The following officers were re-elected: George W. Saunders, president; J. B. Murrah, vice-president, and R. F. Jennings, secretary-treasurer. All officers are residents of San Antonio. The Association voted to publish a second and enlarged edition of Saunders' book *The Old Trail Drivers of Texas,* and to erect a monument to commemorate the part played by the Old Trail Drivers in the development and upbuilding of the State.

Dr. J. O. Dyer published in the Galveston *News* of July 11, 1920, an article on the history of the Tonkawai Indians, accompanied by a map. In the *News* of July 31 he published an article on "The medicine man at Anahuac."

Mrs. Jessie Briscoe Howe, daughter of Captain Andrew Briscoe, a San Jacinto veteran, died at the home of her son in Houston, July 9, 1920. The *Post* of July 11 contains a brief sketch of her life.

Colonel William Lewis Moody, banker and cotton factor of Galveston, died in that city, July 17, 1920. Colonel Moody was a life member of the Texas State Historical Association.

Judge Harris Masterson, a prominent lawyer of Houston, died in that city, July 29, 1920.

J. M. Polk, Company I, Fourth Texas Infantry, died at the Confederate Home, Austin, August 15, 1920. In 1907 Mr. Polk published a pamphlet, entitled *Memories of the Lost Cause and Ten Years in South America*. Several editions of this pamphlet with variations in the title, have been published.

Branch T. Masterson, formerly a prominent member of the Galveston bar, died at Denver, Colorado, August 16, 1920.

Chester H. Terrell, speaker of the House of Representatives of the 33d Legislature, died at his home in San Antonio, September 13, 1920.

Judge James L. Autry, a prominent lawyer of Houston, died in that city, September 29, 1920. His grandfather perished in the Alamo. Judge Autry was a life member of the Texas State Historical Association.

THE SOUTHWESTERN HISTORICAL QUARTERLY

VOL. XXIV JANUARY, 1921 No. 3

The publication committee and the editors disclaim responsibility for views expressed by contributors to THE QUARTERLY

THE LOUISIANA BACKGROUND OF THE COLONIZATION OF TEXAS, 1763-1803

MATTIE AUSTIN HATCHER

By the Treaty of 1763 Spain secured possession of Louisiana; and, almost immediately, she was besieged by English, Irish, French, Dutch, German, and American colonizers who, anxious to secure lands, desired to introduce settlers into the rich but undeveloped region. This met with the hearty approval of Carlos III, who, contrary to the usual custom of Spanish sovereigns, was so eager to settle his new possessions that he permitted the entry of Anglo-Saxons, most of whom, of course, were Protestants. He intended, however, to have Irish priests instruct the new comers in the faith professed by the Spanish nation. The only condition imposed upon them was that they should take the oath of allegiance to Spain. In 1798 the natural distrust of the Spaniards for all foreigners began to assert itself and more stringent immigration laws were passed mainly for the purpose of keeping out the Americans and the English who were at war with Spain's ally, France. But before this change in policy took place many foreigners had settled in Louisiana and, in time, many of them became accustomed to the Spanish laws and institutions. Hence it was that, when Louisiana was sold to the United States in 1803, some of these immigrants, desiring to follow the Spanish flag, moved across the border into Texas where, being vassals of the king of Spain, they were welcomed by the authorities who wished, by their aid, to form a new barrier against the United States and to force the

Indians to keep the peace. The story of the movement into Texas will be given in a subsequent paper.

Immigration into Lower Louisiana, 1765-1768.—Among the first immigrants to arrive in Louisiana after the Treaty of 1763 had converted it into Spanish territory were a number of Acadians who, as early as 1755, had temporarily taken refuge in Maryland. Between January and May, 1765, about six hundred and fifty of these unfortunate people arrived at New Orleans and, later, were sent to form the statements of Attakapas and Opelousas; while, in the spring of 1766, two hundred and sixteen others arrived and received permission to settle on both sides of the German Coast[1] as far up as Point Coupée. The reports which they made in regard to their new homes reached the ears of Henry Jernigham, an Englishman in Maryland. He at once opened up a correspondence with the governor of Louisiana and despatched an agent to New Orleans to make arrangements for the reception of a large number of English Catholics who were discontented because of their treatment by the Colonial government, and who, therefore, desired to follow their former neighbors and friends. This agent was kindly received and assisted in exploring the country as far north as the new trading post just established at St. Louis, since the governor believed that this movement would lead to the settlement of the country by a people hostile to the English government. He even believed that a "torrent" of immigration would flow in, not only from Maryland, but also from neighboring territories.[2] But a careful search of the *Archivo General de Indias* has failed to disclose any evidence of a general movement of English toward Louisiana. Indeed, everything seems to indicate that the plan was never carried out. Nevertheless, the correspondence and the report of the agent must have spread abroad information in regard to the advantages offered immigrants by Louisiana.

Beginning of Settlement in Upper Louisiana, 1767.—Spain was

[1]The German coast embraced the present parishes of St. Charles and St. John. It was founded in 1723 by some two hundred and fifty Germans who had been sent to Law's concession in Arkansas and who were granted lands on the Mississippi as a compensation for their losses due to the failure of Law's financial schemes. Fortier, *History of Louisiana*, I, 70.

[2]Documents contributed by James A. Robertson, *The American Historical Review*, xvi, 319-327.

slow to grasp the opportunity offered her on the Upper Mississippi by the cession of Louisiana. Indeed, beyond permitting the establishment of the trading post at St. Louis, encouraging the exploration just mentioned, and allowing a number of French families to locate at St. Genevieve, she made no effort to hold that portion of the country until after 1767, when she established two forts at the mouth of the Missouri river to prevent the English from penetrating into the adjacent region westward, which abounded in valuable furbearing animals.[3]

Admission of Acadians, Canadians, Italians, Spaniards, and Germans, 1777-1783.—In 1777, the lieutenant-governor of Louisiana received instructions to offer aid, from a fund set apart for the increase of population, the development of commerce, and the cultivation of friendly relations with the Indians, to such Acadians as still lived among the English but who now desired to take refuge among the Spaniards. In reply, he promised to make every effort to attract the Acadians, and discussed the ease with which French Canadians, who were Catholics, could be induced to follow the example of certain of their countrymen who had recently come to St. Louis "to escape the direst poverty and the grossest oppression." The king approved this suggestion and also gave orders or the admission of Spaniards, Italians, and Germans. To ensure an enthusiastic response to this invitation, the lieutenant-governor offered to reputable immigrants, houses, lands, provisions, tools, etc., on condition that they take the oath of allegiance to the Spanish government. A few poor families, who had to be supported for a season, settled at Attakapas and Opelousas and a considerable number of Acadians came back from France, founded the new settlement of Feliciana and located near Plaquemines and at various other points in Lower Louisiana.[4] In 1783, upon the proposal of Conde de Aranda, it was decided to secure in France Acadian families for the purpose of cultivating the soil

[3]Houck, *The Spanish Régime in Missouri*, I, xvii.

[4]Conde de Gálvez to Marqués de la Sonora, March 22, 1786, in Archivo General de Indias, Sevilla, Sto. Dom., 86-6-15, March 22, 1876; Miró to Marqués de Sonora, June 11, 1787, in A. G. I., Sto. Dom., 86-6-16. June 1, 1787, and Miró to Valdez, May 15, 1788, A. G. I., Sto. Dom., 86-6-8, May 15, 1788-October 20, 1788. Transcripts of the University of Texas.

of Louisiana.[5] However, because of the expense involved, only a few families were actually brought over.

All colonists were required to be Catholics since, as late as 1786, a royal order forbade the admission to Louisiana of any person who could not prove beyond a doubt that he was a Catholic. Even those professing this faith but who were unwilling to take the oath of allegiance or who could not prove good characters were to be excluded.[6] In the meantime, however, the way had been paved for the entry of Englishmen and Americans.

Opening Wedge for the Entry of English and American Protestants, 1786.—By a royal order, dated April 5, 1786, the king granted temporary asylum in Louisiana to certain Americans and to such British royalists as had remained there after the peace of 1783, permitting them to locate wherever they might choose.[7] As a result, a large number settled at Natchez, while fifty-nine other English and American families located in the vicinity.[8] In the order providing for the protection of the English, the king announced that he had under consideration a plan for admitting other foreigners into the territory and for sending out Irish priests to convert such of them as were Protestants. Without awaiting he instructions—which the king declared were being drawn up—Diego Gardoquí, Minister from Spain to the United States, began to issue passports to foreign families who wished to share in the promised advantages.

Upon receiving an appeal for aid from New Orleans, after the disastrous fire of 1788, he sent one hundred and thirty persons from New York and Philadelphia. Among the number were four negroes and seventy-nine persons who were absolutely destitute. He paid their transportation expenses, but upon their arrival, the government was compelled to support them for a year and to furnish stock, tools, etc. Estevan Miró, who was governor of Louisiana at the time, objected to this step, claiming

[5]Morales to the King, June 30, 1797, A. G. I., Sto. Dom., 86-7-17, May 8, 1797-June 9, 1799.

[6]Miró to Marqués de Sonora, June 28, 1786, A. G. I., Sto. Dom., 86-6-15, June 28, 1786.

[7]Zepédes to Marqués de Sonora, August 12, 1786, A. G. I., Sto. Dom., 86-6-15, August 12, 1786.

[8]Zepédes to Las Casas, June 20, 1790, A. G. I., Sto. Dom., 86-6-13, June 20, 1790-August 14, 1790, and Miró to Marqués de Sonora, February 1, 1787, A. G. I., Sto. Dom., February 1, 1787.

that the government had been able to contract for families who were able to sustain themselves and who asked only for lands. He feared that Gardoquí's procedure would inspire thousands of indigent persons in Ohio and Kentucky to move into Spanish territory.[9] Nevertheless, he felt compelled to receive all applicants, even non-Catholics, but stipulated that in future they should pay their own transportation and consider themselves as temporary settlers until the king should fix the conditions under which they were to be received as vassals.[10] Many of these immigrants were men of means, and, disliking this uncertainty of a temporary status, immediately applied for citizenship; while a number of colonizers, several of whom were Irish, offered their services in filling the country with settlers.

Irish Colonizers, 1787-1789.—Among these colonizers was Bryan Browin or Bruin, a Virginian, who had spent some time in New Orleans. In 1787 he asked to be allowed to bring in twelve wealthy Irish families. He declared that the applicants in question desired to immigrate because they were Catholics and because they had heard of the liberal laws and beneficient government in Louisiana. He enquired particularly as to the amount of land that could be secured at Baton Rouge. Miró favored the plan, especially because the applicants offered to bring at their own expense their household goods, their slaves, and such tools as might be necessary for clearing and cultivating plantations. This was in line with the condition for admission imposed by the supreme government which stipulated that no foreigner could be received who did not, of his own free will, present himself and swear allegiance to the king. To such persons lands were to be granted in proportion to the number in the family. No settler was to be molested on account of his religion, but Catholics alone were to be allowed public worship. The immigrants were to be required to bear arms in defense of the province only in case of invasion by an enemy. No inducements were to be offered save lands, protection, and kind treatment. They might bring with them property of any kind, but in case they later exported

[9]Miró to Váldez, January 8, 1788, A. G. I., Sto. Dom., 86-6-8, January 8, 1788; Miró to Gardoquí, September 30, and Miró to Váldez, October 10, 1788, A. G. I., Sto. Dom., 86-6-8, May 15, 1788-October 20, 1788.

[10]Zepédes to Las Casas, June 20, 1790, A. G. I., Sto. Dom., 86-6-18, June 20, 1790-August 14, 1790.

it they were to pay a duty of 5 per cent.[11] Miró liked the idea of economizing the public funds and believed that the possession of property would ensure good behavior as it was usually the people who had nothing to lose who stirred up trouble. He, therefore, gave permission for the settlement of the families in question at the points indicated and named a plot twenty by forty *arpents*[12] as the amount to be distributed to each family, promising an addition of a similar amount as soon as the first plot had been cleared and cultivated. He permitted them to introduce their stock, etc., upon the payment of the required six per cent, but suggested that this be remitted in the future so that immigration might be stimulated. However, he issued a warning against the introduction of any goods for subsequent sale and objected particularly to sugar and brandy, since they were contraband goods. It is not possible to ascertain whether or not any of these applicants actually entered, but the Irish continued to be interested in the settlement of Louisiana.

Later in the same year, William Fitzgerald, who had secured recommendations from Gardoquí, was allowed an advance of 1000 *pesos* for the payment of the transportation of thirty families who desired to come to Louisiana from New York. He likewise expected the government to reward him for his services. The intendant of Louisiana, who at this time had charge of colonization, recommended that these requests be granted, lest the petitioner might direct his settlers to Ohio.[13] But no evidence has been found concerning the execution of their plan.

Among other Irishmen interested in colonizing Louisiana may be named William Butler. Having secured a recommendation from Gardoquí, he asked to be allowed to introduce forty-six families from the extreme eastern portion of the United States, the government paying for their transportation. Miró refused this because immigrants could be secured on better terms. Thereupon, Butler signified his willingness to introduce one hundred and fifty-four persons of the original number who were willing to pay their own expenses. It is probable that a considerable

[11]Martin, *History of Louisiana*, 253-254.

[12]According to Violette "The *arpent* was used for both surface and linear measurement among the French. As a unit of surface measurement, it varied from 5-6 to 7-8 of an English acre." *History of Missouri*, p. 58.

[13]Navarro to Váldez, October 10, 1787, A. G. I., Sto. Dom., 87-1-21.

number came, since those responding were to be allowed to introduce their goods free of duty.[14]

Another Irishman, Augustin Macarty, who had retired from the French army, desired to share in the commercial advantages of the decree of January 22, 1782, and to "aid in the defense of Louisiana." He, therefore, offered his help in inducing two or three thousand discontented Irish Catholics, located at various points in the United States, to settle in that province. He asked that his colonists be given the same privileges as those granted the Acadians and that Gardoquí be instructed to furnish money and vessels for their transportation. He also requested that a tract of land be given each head of a family and that the tools needed for clearing and cultivating the ground be furnished. Miró was delighted with the proposition, since he favored the old plan of admitting Catholics only. He believed, too, that the proposed settlers would be able to defend the province and he had no fear of receiving those who were willing to renounce their allegiance to the United States.[15] It is impossible, from the records available, to estimate the number of immigrants introduced by any one or even by all the Irishmen interested in the question at this time, since only incomplete census returns can be found. Martin declares[16] that few or no settlers immigrated from Ireland, but this does not, of course, preclude the possibility of a heavy Irish immigration from the United States. At any rate, Irish names occur frequently on the lists examined. In the meantime, however, other colonizers, and that, too, of a different nationality presented themselves.

French Colonizers, D'Arges, 1787.—Pierre Wouves D'Arges, who believed that it would be exceedingly easy to induce a large number of Kentuckians to move to Louisiana, presented himself in August, 1787, and secured permission to introduce 1582 families on condition that they should receive lands and be allowed to worship according to their own beliefs.[17] However, because of his

[14]Butler to Miró, June 28, 1789, and Miró to Váldez, July 31, 1789, A. G. I., Sto. Dom., 86-6-17, June 28, 1789-July 31, 1789.

[15]Miró to Marqués de Sonora, August 15, 1789, A. G. I., Sto. Dom., 86-6-16, August 14-16, 1789.

[16]*History of Louisiana*, 254.

[17]Miró to Váldez, October 20, 1788, A. G. I., Sto. Dom., 86-6-8, Mav 15, 1788-October 20, 1788, and Miró to Váldez, April 11, 1789, A. G. I., Sto. Dom., 86-6-17, October 14, 1787-April 11, 1789.

insistence upon free commerce between Kentucky and Louisiana—a concession which seemed implied in his contract—he incurred the displeasure of Gardoquí, who wished all efforts confined to the introduction of families, of Miró, who feared the results of religious toleration, and of Wilkinson, who had commercial and colonization schemes of his own.[18] Miró even tried to persuade D'Arges that he could serve Spain best by assuming command of a post to be established at the mouth of the Ohio river, so that he might be able the better to induce immigration from *Illinois,* since the mere publication of the order granting a concession to Wilkinson would attract a great number of settlers from Kentucky.[19] As a result, D'Arges was unable to accomplish any decisive results, although it is quite possible that some families came in through his influence.[20] As he was out-generaled by Wilkinson, an examination of the latter's colonization plans for Louisiana are necessary. However, another American preceded him in the field and demands prior consideration.

American Colonizers, Morgan and Wilkinson, 1788.—In September, 1788, Gardoquí arranged with Colonel George Morgan, of New Jersey, to select a location on the west bank of the Mississippi suitable for a colony of sober, industrious farmers and mechanics. Morgan induced several gentlemen farmers, traders, workmen, etc., to aid him in exploring the country and in convincing the people of the United States of the advantages to be secured by a transfer to Spanish territory. A number of prominent French royalists of Illinois promised to join the colony with their families as soon as it should be established. Morgan, who had served as United States Indian agent, wisely secured the good will of the red men by paying the expenses of a delegation which accompanied him. Along the circuitous route which he traveled, he secured promises from numerous Germans of Pennsylvania—many of whom were Catholics—to join his colony when established, while ten of them at once joined the exploring party. Morgan continued his journey through Kentucky, and, in spite of Wilkin-

[18]Miró to D'Arges, August 13, 1788, A. G. I., Sto. Dom., 86-6-8, August 12-21, 1788.

[19]Miró to D'Arges, March 4, 1789, A. G. I., Sto. Dom., 86-6-17, March 4-15, 1789.

[20]Miró to Váldez, January 8, 1788, A. G. I., Sto. Dom., 86-6-8, January 8, 1788.

son's commercial schemes and of the oppositon of British agents, he secured many enthusiastic followers by promising them religious freedom and commercial advantages such as they had never dreamed of before. After examining the country, he chose a point of land on the west bank of the Mississippi opposite the mouth of the Ohio as "the most important spot in his Majesty's North American dominions both in a military and a commercial view." He suggested that this place be made an *entre-pôt* for the trade of Kentucky and all the future American settlements of the Ohio, thus rendering the navigation of the Mississippi perfectly unnecessary or indifferent to the United States. He predicted that the new subjects would soon be sufficient in number and possess enough capital to transact all the business of the country, and suggested that trial by jury and legislation on purely local matters be allowed, subject, of course, to the approval of the king. Without waiting for his recommendations to be acted upon, he established the town of New Madrid and laid out tracts of three hundred and twenty acres for three hundred and fifty families. To those with him and to other friends who were expected to join him, he actually granted lands and promised donations to still others who should make immediate settlement. They were required to take the oath of allegiance and to promise to pay the sum of forty-eight Mexican *pesos* with interest on deferred payments. He believed that a shiftless class of settlers would enter if lands were granted absolutely free. He also wrote to the inhabitants of Fort Pitt inviting them to join him. He feared that Miró's extreme anxiety to be considered "the first proposer and promoter of the settlements opposite the mouth of the Ohio," his opposition to religious toleration, and his subservience to Wilkinson would retard the execution of the plans just described.[21] And true to expectations, Miró did oppose a part of Morgan's plans. He objected to the sale of the lands and defended the schedule upon which the king had made free grants. This provided for a minimum grant of twenty-four *arpents* to families composed of two or three workmen; four hundred *arpents* to families containing between three and ten workmen; 600 *arpents* to families of ten to fifteen workmen; and 800 *arpents* to families of more than fifteen workmen. Wilkinson did all in his power to handicap Morgan's

[21]Houck, *The Spanish Régime in Missouri*, I, 286-309.

work, declaring the plan dangerous and unbefitting the crown. Nevertheless, Miró finally approved the plan for selling to families from Fort Pitt three hundred and twenty acres each, and recommended an increase in case the grantee were capable of bringing negroes or of hiring help. He promised not to interfere in matters of religion but insisted that Catholics alone hold public worship. To strengthen the Catholics he proposed to establish a number of forts and churches. He permitted immigrants to bring into the country free of duty goods bought with the proceeds of the sale of their property in the United States. He required them to take the oath of allegiance and bind themselves to bear arms in defense of the crown. He rejected the recommendation for trial by jury and legislation in local matters, but confirmed the grants of three hundred and twenty acres already made.[22] In spite of fair promises, Miró managed to embarass Morgan by placing a military commandant of his own choosing at New Madrid and granting to Wilkinson permission to encourage the entry of such Kentucky families as desired to immigrate to Spanish Dominions with permission to introduce their goods free of duty while all others were to be required to pay a duty of 15 per cent. Wilkinson's immigrants, likewise, were to be undisturbed in their private worship, and to be given free lands. Miró promised himself that, as a result of these concessions, both banks of the Mississippi would soon be settled.[23] Because of these handicaps Morgan failed to accomplish any striking results; but Houck pays tribute to his efforts by declaring that he was "the first person to set in motion the stream of American immigration into Spanish Dominions." His success was attributed to the gift of lands and exemption from taxation. As a result, it was but a few years until "the American population almost equaled the French population."[24]

Wilkinson's Plans, 1788.—When Wilkinson first visited Louisiana, he discovered that colonization projects occupied the mind of Gardoquí and he determined to make use of this knowledge for his own "personal emolument" or for the "interest of his fellow

[22]Morgan to Miró, May 23 and 24, 1789, A. G. I., Sto. Dom., 86-6-17, September 1, 1788-June 12, 1789, and McCully, Dodge, and others to Miró, April 14, 1789, A. G. I., Sto. Dom., 86-6-17, October 4, 1788-May 20, 1789.

[23]Miró to D'Arges, March 4, 1789, A. G. I., Sto. Dom., 86-6-17, March 4-15, 1789.

[24]Houck, *The Spanish Régime in Missouri*, I, xxi.

citizens." With this in mind, he asked Gardoquí for 6000 acres of land and presented to the government a colonization plan whose main outlines can be gathered from the decision thereon. It provided that all Kentuckians desiring to settle in Spanish territory should be received whether coming of their own initiative or upon the solicitation of Wilkinson. They were to be required to bring their families, property, and stock and were to be allowed the enjoyment of whatever religious faith they might profess, though not public observance of it, for all churches had to be Catholic churches, ministered to by Irish clergy. All property introduced was to be exempt from duty. This, of course, favored Wilkinson to the detriment of D'Arges. But instructions were given that D'Arges should not be abandoned and Miró was instructed to wean him from the idea of bringing immigrants by the assurance that the government would reward him as his conduct might warrant.[25]

In September, 1789, Wilkinson advised Miró to abandon for the present the idea of annexing Kentucky, but at the same time to encourage, on the one hand Kentuckians and other Westerners to immigrate to Louisiana, for the purpose of building up a strong pro-Spanish party among the Americans, and, on the other hand, to stimulate the secession of the West from the United States. The West, once independent of the United States, would, he said, ally itself with Spain to the exclusion of any other power. This arrangement, he declared, would be advantageous to Spain since the Americans of the West, under the control of Spain, would serve as a barrier against the advance of Great Britain and of the United States. He recommended that emigration be given the preference over all other plans for detaching the West because it could be carried on without peril to individuals and without prejudice to the relations of Spain and the United States. He believed that, if Louisiana became populous, the misgivings excited by the settlements on the Ohio would disappear and the Spanish government would then be able to vary its policy as it might see fit. He thought that the existing regulations for the admission of immigrants were very favorable but wished them modified to meet the approval of prominent men of Virginia, who might desire as much as 3000 acres because they owned anywhere from 100 to 300 slaves

[25]Decision of the Council of State on Wilkinson's First Memorial, William R. Shepherd (contributor), *American Historical Review*, IX, 749-750.

and had been accustomed to large grants since the first settlements of North America. He insisted that no person should be received who did not bring with him visible property and give ample evidence of good character. He wished each immigrant to be compelled to take the oath of allegiance and to be left free in regard to his private religious beliefs.[26] As Wilkinson was more intent upon his commercial and separation schemes than upon immigration, he could not have introduced any large number of settlers. Nevertheless, he had been able to handicap D'Arges and Morgan who, soon becoming discouraged, abandoned the field to a colonizer of still another nation.

Pennsylvania Dutch Colonizer, Paulus, 1788.—Upon the suggestion of Morgan and Gardoquí, Pedro Paulus, an obscure innkeeper of Philadelphia, and a member of the militia of Pennsylvania, offered to bring in 3000 Dutch and German families from the region lying to the north of Kentucky. He did so believing that the government would reimburse him for his labors by a gift of lands, pay the transportation expenses of such immigrants as he might secure, and grant each of them 600 *arpents* of land. In addition, he asked that his settlers be granted religious toleration, be furnished an English and German speaking priest, be permitted to exercise local self-government, be exempt from military service save in defense of the country, and be allowed to plant tobacco, establish manufacturies, and export flour.[27] As in Morgan's case, Miró opposed the granting of large quantities of land to a proprietor, on the grounds that the system had been unsuccessful in the United States and that the granting of virtual independence would lead the settlers to revolt from the Spanish Dominions. However, he consented to the introduction of one thousand families who were to be given lands. Paulus, himself, was to be rewarded by the bestowal of military rank. He accepted these conditions, but whether or not he ever brought more than the thirty-four persons who accompanied him to Louisiana at the time he presented his proposal can not be determined. Since he held a commission from "2000 persons who were very anxious to

[26]*Ibid.*, 751-764.

[27]Petition of Paulus, December 12, 1788, and Miró to Váldez, March 15, 1789, A G. I., Sto. Dom., 86-6-17, December 8, 1788-March 6, 1789.

immigrate," it is quite possible that he introduced a much larger number.

Prussian Colonizer, 1788, Baron von Steuben.—But not all those favored by Gardoquí were able to secure from superior authorities the necessary approval of their colonization plans. According to Fortier, Gardoquí "accepted the proposition of the Baron de Steuben to settle on the banks of the Mississippi and form a colony of persons who had lately been in the army," but the Spanish government refused its approval.[28] From the detailed information given by Frederick Kapp, Steuben's biographer, a full account is secured. In 1788, Baron von Steuben, who had rendered such valiant service to the United States in the achievement of independence, applied to Gardoquí for permission "to plant a colony within the Dominions of the king of Spain, on the Mississippi, partly agricultural, partly military, in order to secure the King of Spain against an invasion of his neighbors, and to grant to the American settlers on the western Alleghanies a free outlet for their produce." Kapp summarizes the plan as follows:

1st. Baron Steuben engages to plant a colony of farmers and artificers, not exceeding in number of four thousand two hundred persons, within the Spanish province of Louisiana.

2d. For this purpose a concession of two hundred thousand acres of land, in such place as, in military view and relation to the principles of the project may be hereafter agreed upon, is made to the said Baron Steuben and his associates.

3d. As a further encouragement the Spanish government allows to each person, a farmer or artificer, brought to locate himself in good faith within the said tract, the sum of one hundred Spanish dollars as a bounty.

4th. Baron Steuben and his associates will, to every such settler, make conveyance in fee of two hundred and thirty acres of good and arable land within the concession aforesaid, free of all expenses such as may arise upon the writing of the deed.

5th. The settlers from the said tract will be drawn from the United States, or other foreign countries, and no person now a Spanish subject will be taken from his present settlement to make a part of this.

6th. On the part of the government it will be agreed that the inhabitants of this tract be allowed to possess and exercise such mode of religious worship as they may think proper, and that no

[28]Fortier, *History of Louisiana*, II, 128.

penalty, forfeiture, disqualification, etc., be incurred by any difference in faith or practice from those established within his Catholic Majesty's dominions.

7th. The laws of the United States relative to the tenure, transfer or descent of property will be granted to the inhabitants of the said tract, and they will be allowed to institute such process, offices and courts touching these subjects as may be proper and necessary; provided only, that this will be done at their expense and without charge to the government; and provided further, that in all cases when the parties in suit on these subjects signify their consent and desire to have decision according to the Spanish laws, it will be granted to them.

8th. In all other respects the said subjects will be entirely, and without qualification, subject to the Spanish laws and usages. This part of the colony will be formed into a militia and liable to military service within the province when any exigency of government may require it.

9th. In addition to this colony the baron will engage to raise a corps of eight hundred men to be formed into four batallions, three of musketry, and one of riflemen. This corps will in all respects be subject to the discipline and service of his Catholic Majesty's troops, save only that in questions of property and religion, the privileges granted to the other part of the colony will be exended to this also.

10th. The power of nominating all officers of the regular corps will be exclusively within the general thereof, and when approved by the king, commissions will be issued to them accordingly, and vacancies supplied in the same manner.

11th. The same bounty will be given to the soldiers as to the farmers and artificers.

12th. Such colonists and recruits as may be engaged in Germany, will be paid and provided at the king's expense, from the day of their enlistments or engagements respectively, and for the purpose of safe and easy transportation, it will be agreed between the courts of Madrid and Versailles, that they be allowed a free and unmolested passage from St. Esprit in France to Carthagena in Spain, where they are to embark in royal vessels for New Orleans in Louisiana.

Kapp continues:

Steuben presented this plan to Diego Gardoquí, who dispatched it to Madrid; but it does not appear that the court engaged in any negotiations about it. Its rejection is too natural when we consider the absolute form of government in Spain. It could not suit them, that one of their colonies should be more free than the rest, and if not the thorough appreciation of the case, at least the instinct of self-preservation taught the Spanish ministry, that admitting American laws even on a small scale, would by and by have opened and subjected the entire colony to the American pioneers, as has been subsequently shown in the instance of Texas.

It is, nevertheless, interesting to examine the motives of Steuben's plan. They show us the statesman and soldier who anticipates the future and tries to found a building on materials loose in themselves, but grand in the hands of a political talent, the execution of which was only delayed and reserved to the succeeding generation. It is at the same time gratifying to observe that Steuben understood perfectly well the secret of the growth of this rising American empire in the self-government of the commonwealth; a principle more antagonistic to the prerogative of the Spanish autocrat could not be found.

As in the following year Steuben's prospects cleared up and the favorable settlement of his claims became certain, he gave up the idea of removing to the far West, and devoted his whole attention to the cultivation of his own lands in Oneida County.[29]

After the failure of this plan, several years passed before other colonizers appeared.

French Colonizers, Tardiveau, Maison Rouge, Delassus, Dublanc, 1792-1795.—In 1792, Bartholomew Tardiveau, who for fifteen years had lived in the United States, laid before the Spanish government his plans for establishing a numerous population on the west bank of the Mississippi as a means of developing the country, opposing the rapid expansion of the Americans in the West, and of erecting "a barrier between this bold people and the Spanish possessions," especially in Missouri and New Mexico. He suggested that a large part of the necessary men could be secured in the United States. However, he advised that only a limited number of this class of immigrants be received as it was essential to the preservation of the Spanish Dominions of America to keep them in the minority because of their inventive genius and their tendency to assume the reins of government. He drew attention to the fact that conditions in France and in the Low Countries presented the most favorable opportunity for procuring a sufficient number of settlers from that region to erect an effective barrier against the United States. He declared that certain French emigrants who had left their native country because of political conditions there, who had later settled on the Ohio, and who were con-

[29]Kapp, *Life of William Frederick von Steuben*, 687-689.

stantly in danger of Indian attacks and displeased at "the innumerable snares and rogueries of which they had been the victims from the moment when they struck America" would adopt with enthusiasm "the idea of settling near the Illinois river." He reported that he had received a communication from a friend who was acting upon the instruction of the French Company, asking if he could arrange for the reception of these colonists and for those who were to come from Europe. They desired lands and were willing to pay for them. The leaders, likewise, proposed to pay their own expenses and to advance money for such families as needed assistance. Tardiveau proposed to go to France, *via* New Orleans and Philadelphia, for the purpose of arranging all necessary details. He expected also to visit Savoy, the Swiss Cantons, Germany, Flanders, Holland, and, finally, "all countries where Frenchmen were found assembled." He engaged to secure those who by their condition, fortune, standing, and influence, were capable of contributing to the attainment of the proposed plan. He estimated the number who might be obtained at between two and three hundred thousand, unless they should be forced to take up their residence in the United States because of the failure of the Spaniards to push the proposed plan. He asked that the expense of this voyage be paid and that he be given certain commercial concessions. In his final recommendation he suggested that the matter be kept a secret until everything was ready for the execution of the plan.[30] But due to a new revolution in France, Tardiveau was compelled to change his plans and to make an agreement with Duhault Delassus and Pedro Audrain by which they bound themselves to establish flour mills near St. Genevieve and to introduce one hundred families from Gallipolis. This new settlement was to be given the name of Nueva Bourbon as a compliment to royalists and as a warning to those who had followed the fortunes of the revolutionary party. In regard to this plan, Baron de Carondelet, the new governor of Louisiana, who was particularly partial to the French, said:

The importance of the matter, the necessity for speedy decision, the numberless advantages which it represents, the well known character of the commissioners, their ability and fortunes, the im-

[30]Tardiveau to Aranda, July 17, 1792, Houck, *The Spanish Régime in Missouri*, 359-368.

possibility of consulting the captain-general about it, and the absence of any risk resulting to the royal treasury—these seemed to me sufficient reasons for concluding the transaction, in the manner which is made clear in the contract. M. Audrain having set out on the 22nd. for Philadelphia from which city he will go to collect the families from Gallipolis and bring them down by way of the Ohio to Nueva Madrid, Messrs. Lassus and Tardiveau returned up the Mississippi in order to wait for those people and conduct them to the new settlement. It is evident that this scattered seed will produce a hundred fold for the state. From the brief relation which accompanies this . . ., in behalf of the inhabitants of Gallipolis, it is evident that they are persons of education and good standing, and desirable [as colonists]. The poor who remain among them will follow the leading families, who will advance the necessary funds for their first settlement. The prosperity and tranquility which they all enjoy under the mild government of España; their relation with all the principal emigrants from France; the publicity which the removal of all these people from Gallipolis to Spanish territory can not fail to occasion; the certainty that they will find immediate market for their wheat, by means of the contract which has been made with Messrs. Lassus, Audrain, and Tardiveau; the interest which these gentlemen (who now are in possession of a considerable fortune) have in increasing the cultivation and settlement of these lands upon the Misury and Mississippi; the similarity of religion, language, and customs between the old colonists and the new; the resentment of the latter against the Americans, who have not fulfilled any of the promises that they made to them; all these things promise us that the enormous immigration which thus far has flowed to the American territory of the north will be directed to the Spanish territory. And the latter will have this additional advantage, that those vast regions of Illinois, hitherto undefended and almost abandoned, on account of their distance at five hundred leagues from the capital, will be peopled with French royalists, who will maintain resentment against the Americans for their unfair proceedings, and will continue against the English of Canada that opposition and rivalry which is innate in the French nation—forming a considerable barrier against both nations, on the Misury as well as on the Misipi.[31]

As a result of Carondelet's policies here outlined a number of other French royalists were granted lands.

The principal one of these was Maison Rouge, a French marques, who offered to bring down from the banks of the Ohio thirty agri-

[31]Carondolet to Gardoquí, April 26, 1793; Houck, *The Spanish Régime in Missouri*, II, 376-377, and *American State Papers, Public Lands*, 520, 521, 660, 684, 714; III, 342.

culturists who were anxious to form a settlement on the Ouishita, where they hoped to raise wheat and to manufacture flour. A contract was entered into between Maison Rouge and the local authorities.[32] In addition to the gift of land, the governor promised to pay to every family, consisting of at least two members, two hundred *pesos,* to those consisting of four laborers, four hundred *pesos,* etc., in proportion to the number of laborers. The immigrants were to be furnished provisions and a guide for the trip from New Madrid to Ouishita. The smallest amount of land to be granted was four hundred acres. One of the provisions of the contract required that the emigrants should be permitted to bring with them indentured European servants who, after the expiration of their term of service, should be entitled to a grant of land.[33]

The project of inducing French royalists to migrate to Louisiana continued to be a favorite one with the Baron, and, with a view of promoting it, extensive grants of land were made. A grant was made to James Ceran Delassus de St. Vrain, who had lost his fortune during the French Revolution. He had been compelled to abandon his native country and seek refuge in Louisiana. Here he had earned the good will of Carondelet by assisting him to defeat the plans of Genet against the Spanish dominions on the Mississippi. Delassus's grant contained 10,000 square *arpents,* and he proposed to repay the government for this concession by discovering and working lead mines. He, therefore, did not obligate himself to make any settlements.[34]

Julien Dubuc had already formed certain settlements on the frontier of the province on lands which he had purchased from the Indians. He had also discovered and worked several lead mines. Carondelet now rewarded him by a grant of six leagues of land on the west bank of the Mississippi.[35] The census reports available for this period show that a heavy French immigration took place, but no indication is found to show which of the colonizers named deserves the greatest credit for the movement.

[32]Morales to the King, June 30, 1797, A. G. I., Sto. Dom., 86-7-17, May 8, 1797-July 9, 1797.

[33]See the Report of the Committee on Land Claims in Louisiana, *American State Papers, Public Lands*, IV, 52 and 431-434; V, 442-443.

[34]Martin, *History of Louisiana*, 268.

[35]*Ibid.;* see also *American State Papers, Public Lands*. II, 675, and VIII, 387.

Indian Immigrants.—The immigration movement toward the Spanish Dominions was not confined to the whites. According to Moráles, Intendent of Louisiana, certain Indians in American territory, angered by the terms of the Jay Treaty, began to show their dislike for the United States even before any posts had been delivered or any steps taken to run the boundary line fixed by its terms. One hundred and seventy Cherokees applied to the commandant of New Madrid asking for lands; while the chief of the Alabamas in the name of three hundred and ninety-four of his tribe applied to the governor at New Orleans for a similar concession. He declared that practically his entire nation would follow. He testified that he did not wish to live close to the Americans or to be separated from his friends, the Spaniards, who had never harmed the Redman. In response to this appeal, the governor distributed a large number of presents among the petitioners and gave them permission to settle near Opelousas. Other nations also appeared at New Orleans and seemed inclined to follow the example of the Alibamus in case the Americans should offend them in any way. This disposition was not entirely to the liking of Moráles who did not desire to incur the expense connected with these frequent and prolonged visits. However, he consoled himself with the thought that should the Spaniards of Louisiana have any trouble with the Americans, they would find useful allies in these Redmen.[36]

Dutch Colonizers, Bastrop and Fooey, 1797-1798.—The governor was anxious to secure as many friends as possible who could be depended upon to aid the Spaniards in case of trouble with the United States should arise. He, therefore, conceived the idea of attracting numbers of Germans and Dutch. First in importance among the Dutch who offered their services to the governor of Louisiana may be mentioned Baron de Bastrop. But before giving an account of his work, it will be well to mention one of his countrymen who was at this time interested in colonization.

Benjamin Fooey, a Spanish interpreter, was authorized in 1798 to form a Dutch or German settlement near Campo Esperanza, not far from Memphis in what is now Arkansas.[37] No informa-

[36]Moráles to Ulloa, March 31, 1797, A. G. I., Sto. Dom., 87-1-24, March 31, 1797.

[37]Houck, *The Spanish Régime in Louisiana*, II, 114.

tion has been found to indicate that he took any steps to carry out this plan. But Bastrop made greater progress.

Philipe Enrique Neri, Baron de Bastrop, had fled from Holland in 1795 to escape the invading French army and had taken refuge in Louisiana. There he had taken the oath of allegiance and was offered by Governor Carondelet a grant as a reward for the establishment of a colony on the Ouishita river which should serve as a barrier against the Americans who had secured possession of Natchez and who were eager for the gold and silver mines in the Spanish territory, especially in the Ouchita region which lay next in their pathway. Carondelet favored the plan of giving lands to all settlers introduced into Lower Louisiana since, in spite of the fact that Upper Louisiana was being rapidly settled without special concessions, the climate of Lower Louisiana was such that attractive inducements were necessary to secure immigrants. He, therefore, felt justified in offering to pay the transportation expenses of such persons as Bastrop could manage to secure in the United States and to support them for six months after their arrival. Bastrop himself insisted that no large grants be made to immigrants for fear that negroes would be introduced and the cultivation of indigo be undertaken by other *empresarios* and his own plans for the cultivation of wheat in sufficient quantities to supply the flour mills he expected to erect be defeated. He wished also to export the flour thus manufactured after the necessities of the province had been supplied. Upon the receipt of a promise from Carondelet that these privileges would be granted and that he would receive twelve square leagues of land on the Ouchita, Baron de Bastrop departed for the United States in search of settlers.[38] But before he arrived again at New Orleans with ninety-nine persons whom he had persuaded to join him, Moses Austin, who had been an importer in Philadelphia, a shot and button manufacturer in Richmond, and a miner and a merchant at Austinville, Virginia, had decided to settle in Upper Louisiana.

American Colonization Contract, Austin, 1797.—In 1797, finding that his mines in Virginia were less productive than he had expected, and obtaining information from a man who had visited the lead mines in the vicinity of St. Genevieve and who gave a

[38]Morâles to Bastrop, June 16, 1797, A. G. I., Sto. Dom. La. and Fla., 86-7-12, May 8, 1797-July 7, 1799.

favorable report of prospects there, he resolved to visit the region.[39] The following interesting description of his journey to Louisiana and the success of his mission is furnished by Schoolcraft:

Here [at Austinville] he formed a design of migrating into upper Louisiana,—a county which he foresaw must at no remote period, fall within the limits of the United States, and which presented to his sanguine imagination the most flattering prospective as well as immediate advantages. He began his first journey to this country in the autumn of 1797[40] being then in his thirty-first year, and performing the entire journey on horseback, reached St. Louis the succeeding winter. This was an arduous and hazardous journey, and at that early period, before the vast country west of the Ohio had been opened to emigration, was looked upon as an extraordinary feat of hardihood. Indian hostility, though ostensibly terminated by the treaty of Greenville a few years before, was still to be dreaded, and an unprotected traveler passing through the Indian territories ran an imminent risk both of property and life. . . .

The little intercourse subsisting between Louisiana and the American States, partly owing to a dread of Republican principles, from which it has ever been a leading point, in the policy of Spain, to defend her trans-Atlantic colonies, precluded Mr. Austin almost wholly from the customary advantage of introductory letters; and, indeed, he placed his chief reliance for success upon his own personal address,—a qualification which he possessed in no ordinary degree. He knew the weakness of the Spanish character, and resolved to profit by this. I have it from his own lips, that when he came near St. Louis, where the commandant, who was generally called Governor resided; he thought it necessary to enter the town with as large a retinue, and as much parade as possible. He led the way himself, on the best horse he could muster clothed in a long blue mantel, lined with scarlet and embroidered with lace, and rode through the principal streets, where the governor resided, followed by his servants, guides and others. So extraordinary a cavalcade in a place so little frequented by strangers, and at such a season of the year, could not fail, as he had supposed, to attract the particular attention of the local authorities, and the Governor sent an orderly to enquire his character and rank. Being answered, he soon returned with an invitation for himself and suite to take up their residence at his house, observing, at the same time, in the most polite manner, and with characteristic deference to the rank of his guests, that there was

[39]Wooten, editor, *A Comprehensive History of Texas, 1688 to 1897*, I, 440-441.

[40]Should be December, 1796.

no other house in town that could afford him suitable accommodations during his stay. The favorable impression created by his entree which Mr. Austin, in after life, related to his friends with inimitable glee, led on to his ultimate success. He was recommended to the authorities at St. Genevieve, where it seems that the Indians of the upper province then resided, who approved his design to settle in the country—ordered an escort of soldiers, under command of a national officer to attend him on his visit to the mines—and forwarded his petition for a grant of land to the Governor-General at New Orleans, accompanied with the strongest recommendations this petition was drawn up by the government secretary, to whom Mr. Austin had not, however, intimated the quantity to be asked for, and he once observed to me, that it gave him some surprise on reading it, to find that *twelve leagues square* had been demanded. One twelfth of this quantity was granted *en franc allien,* the crown reserving no other right or dues but those of fealty and liege homage; but it was stipulated on the part of Mr. Austin in an agreement with the intendent, to introduce certain improvements in the process of mining, together with some connected branches of manufacture, which were accordingly introduced.[41]

On January 27, 1797, François Valle, Commandant of St. Genevieve, engaged to grant lands to Austin and to thirty families of agriculturists and artisans whom Austin planned to induce to join him in establishing a new settlement. The newcomers were to be given lands in proportion to the size of their families, their means, and their ability to aid in the development of the country. In addition, they were promised the privilege of locating wherever they might choose.[42] Whether or not any of these families save a small number of Austin's relatives and friends ever settled cannot be determined from the records at hand, but on March 15th of the same year Carondelet granted to Austin a league of land embracing the lead mines at "Mine A Burton."[43] In July, 1797, Austin applied for a passport to Martínez de Yrujo, who had replaced Gardoquí as minister from Spain to the United States, and, after considerable difficulty, he managed to secure the desired document. Armed with this, he removed his family from Virginia to the new grant, reaching there in September.[44] Before

[41]Schoolcraft, *Travels in the Central Portions of the Mississippi Valley,* 241, 243.

[42]Affidavit by Valle. Austin Papers.

[43]*American State Papers, Public Lands,* III, 671.

[44]Wooten, *A Comprehensive History of Texas, 1685 to 1897*, I, 440-441.

his arrival, however, the feeling against the English and the Americans who were hostile to Spain's ally, France, had become very strong, and it will be necessary to trace its effect upon Bastrop's colony, and then upon the general history of colonization into Louisiana.

Suspension of Bastrop's Contract.—On June 20, 1797, Governor Carondelet had entered into a formal contract with Bastrop for the introduction of families, but he was soon replaced by Manuel Gayoso. The situation was immediatelv changed; for the new governor objected strenuously to the introduction of Protestants and suspected that, in defiance of the stipulations of his contract, Bastrop was introducing English and Americans whose fidelity to the Catholic religion and the Spanish king were merely feigned. The contract did not meet with the approval of the intendant of the province. He objected, in the first place, because it provided for the expenditure of a considerable sum from the depleted treasury for the transportation of these families from New Madrid to the new settlement and for their maintenance for some time after their location; and principally he said, "although it was to the advantage to increase the population of Ouchita, it would never be to the advantage to increase the number of English and Americans, and other Protestants, imbued, perhaps, with the maxims of liberty which had caused so much revolution, and to place them even nearer Mexico."[45] As a result, the governor ordered the suspension of Bastrop's contract until the matter could be passed upon by the king. This amounted to a nullification; for Bastrop was never able to secure favorable action, in spite of the fact that he promised to secure his families direct from Europe and to receive none who might have been "contaminated" by even the briefest residence in the United States. Indeed, when considering Bastrop's claims, especially in regard to the sale of a portion of the lands in question to Moorehouse, the king forbade the granting of any more lands in Louisiana to Americans.[46] This feeling against the Americans—or rather against all foreigners—had already been embodied in the laws of Louisiana as the following in-

See *American State Papers, Public Lands*, II, 678; III, 682, 683, and VIII, 850.

[45]Morales to King, June 30, 1797, A. G. I., Sto. Dom., 86-7-17, June 20, 1796-July 9, 1799.

[46]Undated petition of Bastrop (1799?), A. G. I., Sto. Dom., 86-7-17.

structions of the governor to the commandants of posts will indicate:

1. [Commandants] are forbidden to grant lands to a new settler, coming from another post, where he has obtained a grant. Such a one must buy land, or obtain a grant from the governor.
2. If a settler be a foreigner, unmarried and without either slaves, money, or other property, no grant is to be made him until he shall have remained four years in the post, demeaning himself well in some honest and useful occupation.
3. Mechanics are to be protected, but no land is to be granted to them until they shall have acquired some property, and a residence of three years in the exercise of their trade.
4. No grant of land is to be made to any unmarried emigrant who has neither trade nor property, until after a residence of four years, during which time he must have been employed in the culture of ground.
5. But, if after a residence of two years such a person should marry the daughter of an honest farmer, with his consent and be by him recommended, a grant of land may be made to him.
6. Liberty of conscious is not to be extended beyond the first generation: the children of emigrants must be Catholics; and emigrants not agreeing to this must not be admitted, but removed, even when they bring property with them. This is to be explained to settlers who do not profess the Catholic religion.
7. In Upper Louisiana, no settler is to be admitted who is not a farmer or mechanic.
8. It is expressly recommended to commandants to watch that no preacher of any religion but the Catholic comes into the province.
9. To every married immigrant of the above description, two hundred *arpents* may be granted, with the addition of fifty for every child he brings.
10. If he brings negroes, twenty additional *arpents* are to be granted him for each; but in no case are more than eight hundred *arpents* to be granted to an emigrant.
11. No land is to be granted to a trader.
12. Immediately on the arrival of a settler, the oath of allegiance is to be administered to him if he has a wife, proof is to be demanded of their marriage; and if they bring any property, they are to be required to declare what part belongs to either of them; and they are to be informed that the discovery of any wilful falsehood in this declaration will incur the forfeiture of the land granted them, and the improvements made thereon.
13. Without proof of a lawful marriage, or of absolute ownership of negroes, no grant is to be made for any wife or negroes.
14. The grant is to be forfeited, if a settlement be not made

within the year, or one-tenth part of the land put in cultivation within two.

15. No grantee is to be allowed to sell his land until he has produced three crops on a tenth part of it, but in case of death it may pass to an heir in the province, but not to one without, unless he come and settle it.

16. If the grantee owes debts in the province the proceeds of the first four crops are to be applied to their discharge, in preference to that of debts due abroad. If, before the third crop is made, it becomes necessary to evict the grantee on account of his bad conduct, the land shall be given to the young man and woman residing within one mile of it, whose good conduct may show them to be the most deserving of it; and the decision is to be made by an assembly of notable planters, presided by the commandant.

17. Emigrants are to settle contiguous to old establishments, without leaving any vacant land—that the people may then more easily protect each other, in case of an invasion by the Indians; and that the administration of justice, and a compliance with police regulations, may be facilitated.[47]

Several points here set forth deserve especial attention. The old antipathy against foreign traders is shown and the religious tolerance previously granted Protestants was practically withdrawn. Such mechanics and agriculturists as were willing to take the oath of allegiance to the Spanish government were still to be subjected to several years probation before lands could be granted them, while possession of property and the duty of actual settlement and cultivation of lands was made obligatory.[48]

Eleventh Hour Plans.—Immigration into Louisiana was not completely checked by the hostility evinced against the Americans. At the court, projects for settling the province were still favorably received. For instance, in July, 1799, a favorable decision was rendered upon the petition of the Spanish minister at Philadelphia.[49] However, no evidence has been found that the petitioner took any steps to introduce families.

The local authorities may also have granted lands to certain

[47]Martin, *History of Louisiana*, 276-277. In October of this same year the intendant was charged with the entire responsibility of granting lands in Louisiana and thereupon, issued regulations governing titles to same, *American State Papers, Public Lands*, III, 488-496.

[48]——— to Urquijo, July 9, 1799, A. G. I., Sto. Dom., 86-7-17, May 8, 1797-July 9, 1797.

[49]——— to Urquijo, July 9, 1799, A. G. I., Sto. Dom., 86-6-17, July 20, 1797-July 9, 1799.

Americans who, like Daniel Boone, manifested a strong feeling against their native country. According to Violette, Boone was granted 10,000 acres by DeLassus in return for bringing into Upper Louisiana one hundred and fifty families from Virginia and Kentucky, but through failure to secure the necessary legal documents, he was never able to obtain confirmation of his grant.[50] However, the only record of his grant found recites that, on December 26, 1799, he was promised 1000 *arpents* by Trudeau.[51] In this no mention of the families to be brought in is made.

From the records, it is clear that many Americans located in Louisiana prior to its sale to the United States; but no definite figures can be given, as the census reports are fragmentary. However, Viles, who made a careful study of the population of Missouri before 1804, estimates that the increase of white population at New Madrid after 1797 was considerable; that St. Genevieve grew steadily between 1795 and 1800; that Cape Girardeau increased in a fairly constant ratio between 1799 and 1803—fully 200 per year; and that St. Louis added to her population practically 100 persons each year between 1796 and 1800. From actual statistics it is known that by 1800 the population of Upper Louisiana amounted to 4949 and that Lower Louisiana, too, in spite of its unfavorable climate, had increased from 12,500 in 1769 to approximately 27,000 in 1798, when the tide of immigration had reached its height. All authorities agree that this unquestionably represented, for the most part, an immigration of Americans.[52]

We are now in a position to follow the development of the colonization movement from Louisiana to Texas.

[50]*History of Missouri*, 64.

[51]*American State Papers, Public Lands*, III, 332.

[52]Viles, "Population and Extent of Settlement in Missouri Before 1804," in *Missouri Historical Review*, V, 197, 199, 204, and 207; Houck, *The Spanish Régime in Missouri*, II, 414; and Martin, *History of Louisiana*, 206, 240, and 300.

MIRABEAU BUONAPARTE LAMAR

A. K. CHRISTIAN

About the time Treat began his negotiations in Mexico, James Hamilton, who had already been in Europe on a mission for Texas, was appointed a commissioner to secure a loan of five million dollars in Europe. He was to miss no opportunity of securing pacification with Mexico, and was authorized to enter into any treaty of amity, commerce and boundaries with Mexico, using money already agreed upon by Congress and the President in settlement of the claims of Mexican bondholders, with whom he was empowered to enter into an agreement. After numerous delays Hamilton arrived in London on September 27, 1840. He found no possible chance of treating with Mexico at that place. On November 13, 1840, he entered into a treaty of amity, commerce, and navigation with Great Britain, which carried with it recognition of Texan independence.[62] The following day he signed a convention providing for British mediation with Mexico. By this convention Texas agreed that if by means of the mediation of Great Britain, an unlimited truce should be established between Mexico and Texas within thirty days after notice of the convention was communicated to Mexico, and if within six months thereafter Mexico should have concluded a treaty of peace with Texas, then the Republic of Texas would take over five million dollars of Mexican bonds.[63]

These two treaties arrived in Texas and were communicated to the Senate on January 25, 1841, and promptly ratified.[64] As a result of this, hoping that a recognition of Texan independence by Great Britain and a formal convention providing for mediation would influence the attitude of the Mexican government, Lamar determined to send a third mission to Mexico, and this time his choice fell upon James Webb, who had succeeded Bee as secretary of state in February, 1839, and was at that time attorney-general. Lamar was absent from the seat of government when these treaties were ratified, and while unsuccessful efforts were being made to secure the authorization of a force for offensive operations against

[62]Gammel, *Laws of Texas*, II, 880-885.

[63]*Ibid.*, II, 886; *British and Foreign State Papers*, XXIX, 84.

[64]*Secret Journals of the Senate*, 195.

Mexico. He returned about the middle of February and immediately began making preparations for sending the mission.

Webb's commission was dated March 22, 1841. Webb was appointed a minister plenipotentiary, but in case he should not be received an alternative commission was prepared appointing him an agent for the purpose of entering into negotiations. The instructions were similar to those of the preceding agents, the only difference being a reference to the convention with Great Britain providing for mediation. A naval vessel was placed at his disposal, and he was to proceed at once to Vera Cruz, but if Mexico showed no indications that she wished to begin negotiations he was to terminate his mission at once.[65] The usual delay took place, and Webb did not arrive off Vera Cruz until May 31, when he addressed a note to the commandant at Vera Cruz asking permission to land, and that he be furnished with passports to proceed to the city of Mexico. This request was courteously refused.[66]

Upon the refusal of the commandant to allow him to land, Webb addressed a note to Pakenham requesting his intervention with the Mexican authorities.[67] Pakenham was so good as to comply with the request, and wrote to the secretary of state urging that an effort be made to come to agreement with the Texan authorities. The secretary of state responded on June 8, declining to consider any proposal which looked to the dismemberment of Mexico. After expressing appreciation for the friendly interest of the British government, Camacho declared that the President could not depart from the principles of honor and justice which prohibited him from recognizing a dismemberment of the territory.[68] Webb returned to Galveston June 29, and reported his failure to Lamar. Upon receipt of this information, Lamar took immediate steps to enter into an alliance with Yucatan in an offensive war against Mexico.

2. *The Federalists and the Alliance with Yucatan*

The relations of the Texans with the Federalists on the Rio Grande, the battle of Alcantro, in which a number of Texans par-

[65]Garrison, *Dip. Cor. Tex.*, 733-736.

[66]Webb to Mora and Mora to Webb, May 31, 1841, Garrison, *Dip. Cor. Tex.*, II, 752-753.

[67]Webb to Pakenham, June 1, 1841, *Ibid.*, II, 755.

[68]Camacho to Pakenham, June 8, 1841, (Translation) *Dip. Cor. Tex.*, II, 758.

ticipated, and the proclamation of Lamar on December 21, 1839, warning Texans against participating with the Federalists against the Central Government have been noted. That the Government of Texas was really neutral, while perhaps sympathizing with the Federalists, there can be no doubt. In order to get the proclamation of neutrality to the Texans in the Federalist army, the assistant adjutant general, Colonel Benjamin H. Johnson, accompanied by a small body of troops, was sent across the Rio Grande to the Federalist camp, and communicated the sentiments of the Government to the Texans assembled there. On his return he was captured by a body of Mexicans, and he and his party were put to death. In spite of this, however, the Texan authorities refused to begin active hostilities. It was used as another count against Mexico, however, and given as an instance of the desire of Texas to avoid war. Writing to Treat in Mexico City regarding this incident, Burnet said:

> This is an event not calculated to assuage the feelings of a people already provoked by unwarranted and unchristian massacres, or to soften the rigors of the war should it be actively renewed. But inasmuch as this atrocity is reported to have been perpetrated by a desultory band of ruffiens without the express authority of the Government, the President will not regard it as an insuperable obstacle to the proposed negotiation. But it may be considered as an infallible assurance, that if hostilities are to continue, they will be conducted with increased animation by an indignant people who know how to avenge a wrong which they would never commit.[69]

Notwithstanding the public sentiment in favor of joint action with the Federalists, and the participation of a good number of Texans in their campaigns, the attitude of the Government remained perfectly correct. The experiences of the Texans who ignored the advice of their Government was ample justification for the Government's position.[70]

[69]Burnet to Treat, March 12, 1840, Garrison, *Dip. Cor. Tex.*, II, 582.

[70]Yoakum, *History of Texas*, II, 288-299, and Bancroft, *North Mexican States and Texas*, II, 326-332, give a full account of the "Republic of the Rio Grande," the Federalist campaigns of 1840, and their final betrayal of the Texans who were aiding them. I shall not follow in detail the campaigns. The statement of Von Holst that Lamar recognized the "Republic of the Rio Grande," is absurd. He allowed Canales an asylum in Texas when he was defeated, but he certainly did not recognize any claim of the Mexicans to territory east of the Rio Grande.

The most successful of these liberal movements broke out in Yucatan in May, 1839. The weakness of the Government of Mexico, and the remoteness of Yucatan from the capital, made it impossible to take adequate steps to reduce her to submission. By the beginning of the following year the revolutionists were in complete control of Yucatan, and the movement had spread into Tobasco and Campeche. Treat kept his Government informed of the developments there as he learned of them, suggesting the possibility of joint action by Texas and Yucatan in case of the failure of his mission. In June, 1840, Commodore Moore was sent with the fleet to carry dispatches to Treat. While he was to be careful to observe strict neutrality and not to attack any Mexican vessel unless he learned that Treat's mission had failed, he was to "endeavour to ascertain the condition of the State of Yucatan, and the disposition of those functionaries administering their Government, whether friendly or otherwise to us, any manifestation of friendship from them you will reciprocate."[71]

Moore left Galveston in June, immediately after receiving his orders, and considering the most important of his instructions the discovery of the attitude of Yucatan, he dispatched the letters for Treat and Pakenham in the schooner *San Jacinto,* while he continued direct to Yucatan, arriving at Sisal on July 31. He was received with every favor by the authorities. After a short time at Sisal he sailed to Campeche, where he found General Anaya and had a friendly conference with him. He returned to Sisal shortly after, and had an interview with the governor-elect, San tiago Mendez, who informed him that "he was anxious that the most friendly relations should be established at an early period, and assured me that the ports of the State of Yucatan were open to any Texan vessel. . . ."[72] On the same day that he reported these movements to the secretary of the navy, August 28, 1840, Moore addressed a letter to President Lamar in which he urged the policy of active warfare. He wrote in part as follows:

> By reference to my report you will see the disposition of the Federalists of Yucatan towards the Government of Texas and their anxiety for the cooperation of our Naval force; the weight

[71]Lamar to Moore, June 20, 1840, Garrison, *Dip. Cor. Tex.*, II, 652.

[72]Moore to Secretary of the Navy, August 28, 1840, 5 Tex. Cong., 1 Sess., Appendix, 232-237, *House Journal.*

of which, thrown at this time on their side would, I feel confident, be the means of establishing the Federal Constitution throughout Mexico, when we would be acknowledged at once.

The Centralists are allmost prostrate, and single handed with the means already at your Command [the Navy] you might, without the least prospect of being molested by them on the Frontier, dictate to, and no longer *ask* at their hands, that which they can be very soon made to *feel* is ours already, viz our perfect Independence of them; and in my humble opinion they will never acknowledge it until they are made to *feel* it.

With the Navy manned as indifferently as it is, every Mexican can be captured that dare put to sea, and their whole Sea Coast be kept in a perfect state of fear and trembling; why then should we temporize any longer with them, when, if they had the power they would annihilate every male Inhabitant of Texas and spread devastation and ruin throughout our devoted Country.

You may keep *Treating* with them until the expiration of your administration and will, in all probability leave for your successor, whoever he may be, to reap all the advantages of your efforts; now is the time to push them for they never were so prostrate.[73]

The fleet returned to Galveston in April, 1841.[74] Before that Lamar had determined to send the third peace mission to Mexico, the details of which I have just related. That the possibility of an alliance with Yucatan in case of failure was already a part of his policy, is indicated by the alternative instructions to Webb. "If you are not permitted to open negotiations with the Government of Mexico," said the instructions,

or having opened them, should find it necessary to discontinue them, without any beneficial results, you will after notifying this Government of the fact be at liberty, to return by the way of Yucatan and ascertain what part the Government of that country would be willing to take in a war which Texas might be compelled to wage against Mexico. In doing this however it is only expected that you will sound the people of Yucatan on the subject as you are not furnished with authority to enter into any treaty stipulations, but you may suggest to the authorities the propriety of sending an agent to this Government with full powers to treat and you may give them assurances of our friendship and willingness to receive such an agent. . . .[75]

[73]Moore to Lamar, August 28, 1840, Garrison, *Dip. Cor. Tex.*, II, 695.

[74]For a full history of the cruise of the fleet in 1840-1841, and the activities under the alliance with Yucatan, see Dienst "The Navy of the Republic of Texas," in THE QUARTERLY, XIII, 18-43.

[75]Mayfield to Webb, March 22, 1841, Garrison, *Dip. Cor. Tex.*, II, 735.

In June, 1841, Yucatan, which had so far been fighting for the restoration of the Constitution of 1824, declared her independence from Mexico. Webb learned of this while waiting to be admitted to Mexico, and although an accident to his vessel prevented him from returning by way of Yucatan, yet he had learned enough to cause him to urge an immediate treaty of alliance and opening of hostilities with Mexico. "Let Texas enter into arrangements at once, with Yucatan and Tobasco," he wrote,

> and each party mutually recognize the Independence of the other, and then let them conjointly renew and prosecute the War untill the Central Government shall be forced into terms, or put down beyond the hope of resuscitation. In renewing the War conjointly with Yucatan and Tobasco, Texas would only be expected to furnish her Navy,—the whole of the land operations to be carried on by the Federalists, and by which means we would be saved the entire expense of keeping an army in the field. . . .
>
> The Federalists of Yucatan and Tobasco have now everything that is necessary to carry on the War successfully, but a Navy, and they want no assistance from us but such as the Navy would afford. Without a Navy they can make no effectual impression upon the Sea ports, and that is the most essential object to be obtained; because it is through the sea ports and the revenue derived from their Commerce that the Government is sustained—take away that, and you cut off all their resources and render them hopelessly imbecile. Hence the great anxiety of the Federalists to make terms with us, because they believe with our assistance in taking their ports, they can immediately bring the Central party down. . . .[76]

This letter was received on July 5, and on the seventh Samuel A. Roberts, acting secretary of state, wrote to Webb as follows:

> Your Communication . . . was received two days ago, and it, together with the accompanying documents, was immediately laid before the President, and he considers the questions involved of such magnitude as to determine him to go at once in person to Galveston, where he can best determine what will, under all the Circumstances, be most proper to be done. He will accordingly leave here in the morning, and will probably be not more than one day behind Mr. Moore on his arrival at Galveston.[77]

On July 20, 1841, Lamar addressed a letter to the Governor of

[76]Webb to Lamar, June 29, 1841, Garrison, *Dip. Cor. Tex.*, II, 764.
[77]Garrison, *Dip. Cor. Tex.*, II, 766.

the State of Yucatan, and as there has been some question as to who took the initiative in the alliance, I shall quote the letter in full. It is as follows:

In reading over the Correspondence of Commodore Moore while commanding the Texan squadron on its late Cruise in the Gulf of Mexico, I have experienced the most sincere and lively Gratification in discovering the many evidences it affords of the kind and friendly sentiments entertained by the Authorities of the State of Yucatan toward the Government and people of Texas; and I now beg leave to assure you sir, that every expression of friendship and regard which has been uttered in your State towards us is most cordially and sincerely reciprocated on our part.

It has been my earnest desire to establish with the States of Yucatan, Tobasco and such others as may throw off the Yoke of Central despotism in Mexico, relations of amity and friendship, and to show the disposition of this Government to reciprocate in the fullest manner, every evidence of good will manifested by the Federalists of Mexico towards this country, I hereby have the pleasure of declaring to you, and of making known to your Citizens, that the Ports of Texas are open to the vessels and Commerce of Yucatan upon the same terms as we extend to the most favored nations, and that this Govt. will require of its Citizens the faithful performance of all contracts, obligations, or compromises which they may enter into with the citizens and subjects of Yucatan.

Should it be the desire of your Excellency and of the Congress of Yucatan to enter into more permanent and specific relations of Amity friendship and Commerce with the Government and people of Texas, I have only to assure you that we shall be happy to receive from you, an agent duly accredited for that purpose; and that we will be prepared to enter into such negotiations and arrangements with him, as will be mutually beneficial, and result in securing a full and complete acknowledgment of the respective rights of both Countries from those who are now our enemies.[78]

The Governor of Yucatan, Miguel Barbachano, made a prompt response to this letter, and immediately sent a commissioner, Martin Francisco Peraza, fully authorized to treat with Texas on all points. Peraza with his secretary, Donaciano Rejon, arrived in Austin on September 11. On September 16 he submitted a proposal to the Texan Government, which with a slight amendment was the plan adopted. By this agreement Yucatan was to pay

[78]Lamar to Governor of Yucatan, July 20, 1841, Garrison, *Dip. Cor. Tex.*, II, 792.

eight thousand dollars to the Texan authorities for the purpose of getting the fleet ready for sea, and eight thousand dollars per month so long as the government should deem it necessary for the squadron to remain in active service. All captures made by the Texan vessels were to be taken into Texas ports for adjudication, and all captured by Yucatan vessels were to be taken into the ports of Yucatan. Peraza had suggested that the prizes be divided equally, but as the Texas navy was much stronger, and could be depended upon to do the greater part of the fighting, Lamar refused to grant that, and the arrangement was agreed to as stated.[79]

On September 18, 1841, Commodore Moore was ordered to fit and provision his ships for the sea. This required about two months, and on December 13 he sailed from Galveston under sealed orders. Outside of Galveston Bar he opened his secret orders and found that he was to sail direct for Sisal in the State of Yucatan, and to cooperate with the sea and land forces of Yucatan in checking any hostile action of Mexico. He was instructed to capture Mexican towns and levy contributions; and for the purpose of compelling payment, he was authorized to destroy public works and edifices, and seize public property, taking care not to molest private property except in the execution of duty. It was hoped that these acts would "strike terror among the inhabitants, which may be very useful to us should it again be thought advisable to enter into negotiations for peace."[80]

Moore arrived in Sisal on January 8, 1842, and found to his disappointment that a convention had been signed between Yucatan and Mexico on December 28, 1841, the basis of which was a return of Yucatan to her allegiance to Mexico. He complained of the apparent breach of faith on the part of the Yucatan Government, but was informed that no promise had been made by Yucatan as to her action in that regard.[81] The Yucatan Government continued to pay the eight thousand dollars monthly, but on March 29, notice was served on Moore that the Yucatan Gov-

[79]For the provisions of the agreement see Moore, *To the People of Texas*, 15-19. This agreement being in the nature of a military convention was not submitted to Congress, hence it is not to be found in a collection of treaties.

[80]Moore, *To the People of Texas*, 13-15.

[81]Moore, *To the People of Texas*, 26-29. See also Rejon to Texan Secretary of State, January 18, 1842, Garrison, *Dip Cor. Tex.*, II, 799-802.

ernment was willing for the squadron to retire. After a mild protest, Moore departed from the Yucatan coast in the latter part of April, and arrived in Galveston on May 1, 1842.[32]

Lamar's term of office closed on December 12, the day before Moore sailed from Galveston, and Sam Houston began his second term in the presidency. Condemning without discrimination everything that Lamar did, Houston repudiated the contract with Yucatan, and on December 15 issued orders for the return of the fleet to Galveston. From some peculiar cause this order did not reach Moore until March 10, when it was too late to accomplish its purpose. In a speech in the United States Senate, March 15, 1854, in denunciation of Moore, Houston said with regard to the convention with Yucatan, "This was done without any authority or sanction of Congress or Senate of the Republic of Texas. It was a mere act of grace or will on the part of the President." This might be answered by saying that Texas and Mexico were still technically at war, and it is hard to see how it was necessary for the President to submit a military convention to the consideration of Congress.[33]

3. *Relations with the United States*

It has been seen that Lamar had a definite policy towards Mexico; but it cannot be said that he had any specific policy towards the United States differing from that of his predecessor or successors. The first years of the republic of Texas were taken up with the importunings of the Texan agents for admission to the United States, either as a state or a territory, or almost on any terms that the United States might lay down, all of which the United States declined with little ceremony. While it is probable that public sentiment with regard to annexation was not materially changed in Texas when the offer of annexation was withdrawn in October, 1838, it is certain that at the time the new president approved the withdrawal of the offer, which, as he said, he had never seen the benefit of. "Notwithstanding the almost undivided voice of my fellow-citizens at one time in favor of the measure," said Lamar in his inaugural address in December, 1838,

[32]Moore, *To the People of Texas*, 53-58.

[33]*Cong. Globe*, 33 Cong., 1 Sess., App., 1081.

and notwithstanding the decision of the National Congress at its last session, inhibiting the chief magistrate from withdrawing the proposition at the Cabinet of Washington, yet still I have never been able myself to perceive the policy of the desired connection, or discover in it any advantage, either civil, political, or commercial, which could possibly result to Texas. But, on the contrary, a long train of consequences of the most appalling character and magnitude have never failed to present themselves whenever I have entertained the subject, and forced upon my mind the unwelcome conviction that the step once taken would produce a lasting regret, and ultimately prove as disastrous to our liberty and hopes as the triumphant sword of the enemy. And I say this from no irreverence to the character and institutions of my native country—whose welfare I have ever desired, and do still desire above my individual happiness—but a deep and abiding gratitude to the people of Texas, as well as a fervent devotion to those sacred principles of government whose defence invited me to this country, compel me to say that, however strong may be my attachment to the parent land, the land of my adoption must claim my highest allegiance and affection.

The key to this opposition is found in what follows. Texas would yield up the right of declaring war or making peace, of controlling the Indian tribes within her borders, of appropriating the public domain for the benefit of education, of levying her own taxes, regulating her own commerce, and forming her own alliances and treaties. Besides, as an independent republic, Texas would adopt free trade, and not be bound by the "thralldom of tariff restrictions" found in the United States. Concluding this phase of his address, he said:

When I reflect upon these vast and momentous consequences, so fatal to liberty on the one hand, and so fraught with happiness and glory on the other, I cannot regard the annexation of Texas to the American Union in any other light than as the grave of all her hopes of happiness and greatness; and if, contrary to the present aspect of affairs, the amalgamation shall ever hereafter take place, I shall feel that the blood of our martyred heroes had been shed in vain—that we had riven the chains of Mexican despotism only to fetter our country with indissoluble bonds, and that a young republic just rising into high distinction among the nations of the earth had been swallowed up and lost, like a proud bark in a devouring vortex.[84]

[84] *Lamar Papers*, No. 361; *Senate Journal*, 3 Tex. Cong., 1 Sess.

Allowing for his love for high sounding phrases, and for his justifiable objection to the termination of the existence of the republic over which he had just come to preside as chief executive, it is perfectly obvious that Lamar was at that time strongly opposed to annexation; and this opposition of the President, together with the lack of interest in the question in the United States, caused the annexation question to lie dormant throughout Lamar's administration. With this out of the way the main things to interest the two countries were the settlement of the boundary, the border Indians, and commercial relations.

The settlement of the boundary between Texas and the United States has been adequately treated elsewhere,[85] and I shall do no more than outline it here. The statutory boundary as claimed by Texas was the line as defined in the treaty of 1819 between the United States and Spain. The line had not been surveyed when Texas made good her independence and adopted this line as her eastern boundary. Naturally there was considerable confusion, especially on account of Indian incursions from the United States. A controversy was precipitated with the United States shortly after the beginning of Houston's administration by the passage of a law creating land offices, and including in their jurisdiction a part of the territory claimed by the United States.[86] This law was inoperative, because the time when it should go into operation was not fixed. A supplementary act was passed June 12 providing that the act should go into effect on October 1.[87] The possible incursions of Texans into land claimed by Arkansas brought a protest from the governor of Arkansas, which was taken up by the secretary of state of the United States, Forsyth, and presented to the chargé d'affaires of Texas as a protest from the United States.[88]

On the same day that the law was passed providing that the land offices should begin work on October 1, another law was passed providing for the appointment of commissioners to run the boundary line.[89] Before the Texan chargé had received notice of this act, however, he had already urged the United States authori-

[85]Marshall, *Western Boundary of the Louisiana Purchase*, 206-241.
[86]December 22, 1836. Gammel, *Laws of Texas*, I, 1276-1284.
[87]*Ibid.*, 1322-1326.
[88]Forsyth to Catlett, June 17, 1837, *Dip. Cor, Tex.*, I, 230.
[89]Gammel, *Laws of Texas*, I, 1331.

ties to appoint a commissioner for running the boundary line.[90] Without attempting to follow the negotiations in detail, it is sufficient to say that after long delay and the presentation of claims and counter claims the Texan minister, Memucan Hunt, on April 28, 1838, signed a convention for running the boundary line.[91] Ratifications were not exchanged until October 12, so the carrying out the convention devolved on the Lamar administration.[92]

There was delay on both sides in appointing commissioners and providing for their needs, and it was not until August, 1839, that the joint commission met in New Orleans, when, on account of the prevalence of yellow fever, and the hostility of the border Indians, the commissioners decided to postpone the beginning of the work until October 15. They did not assemble again until November 12, when they went into camp at Green's Bluff on the Sabine about thirty-five miles from its mouth. They were joined by the Texan commissioner, Memucan Hunt, on January 20, 1840, but the Texans lacked instruments, so there was another delay in beginning. While waiting for instruments for the Texans the commissioners with much difficulty came to a decision as to the method to be pursued under the Treaty of 1819 and the convention of 1838. On May 21, 1840, the survey actually began, the Texans conceding that Sabine gulf should be considered a part of Sabine river, and consenting to the boundary along the western side of that stream.[93] Work was interrupted on June 3, and it was not until February 14, 1841, that the commissioners assembled to renew work, and not until June 24, 1841, that the work was completed.

There was always an Indian question between the two governments. After the recognition of Texan independence by the United States, the treaty of 1831 between the United States and Mexico was considered as binding on Texas and the United States. Periodically the Texas government sent complaints to the United States that efforts were being made to stir up the United States Indians to act with their neighbors in Texas, and as often the authorities of the United States responded, usually courteously, but sometimes coolly, saying they would investigate, and always the re-

[90]Catlett to Anderson, June 17, 1837, *Dip. Cor. Tex.*, I, 229.
[91]Hunt to Irion, April 28, 1838, *Dip. Cor. Tex.*, I, 325-326.
[92]Malloy, *Treaties, Conventions, etc.*, II, 1779.
[93]Marshall, *Western Boundary of the Louisiana Purchase*, 230-235.

sult of their investigation was to show that the Texan fears were without foundation. This procedure had its beginning in the summer of 1836, when Gaines was urged to send forces into Texas for the purpose of keeping the Indians quiet; and ever after that in case of a threat of Indian war, or after any atrocities committed by the Indians as individuals or in small groups, the customary complaint was registered, and the customary answer returned.

The administration of Lamar was not different from any other period of the history of the republic in this respect, and an adequate discussion would require too full a consideration of the whole Indian question for the purposes of this paper. I shall touch on the Indian question only incidentally as I discuss the efforts on the part of Texas to abrogate the Treaty of 1831 and form a new treaty with the United States.

On February 17, 1838, the comptroller of the treasury of the United States issued a circular, in part as follows:

> Referring to the circular from this office, of the 2nd. instant, I have to communicate for your Government that, by information received from the Department of State, it appears the fifth and sixth articles of the treaty with Mexico are held obligatory on the Republic of Texas. It results, therefore, that the vessels and productions of the latter, being placed on equal footing in carrying on its commercial intercourse with the United States, are to be treated with reciprocal favour, and enjoy the like privileges and exemptions that are extended to the productions and vessels of Mexico.[94]

This order was communicated to the Texan secretary of state on March 23, and on the 26th was answered by John Birdsall, stating that

> While the undersigned assures Mr. La Branche of the earnest desire of this Republic to cultivate the most friendly intercourse with the United States, and especially upon those principles of equality and reciprocal favour which should always characterise the commercial relations of friendly States, he cannot yield his assent to the proposition that the commercial stipulations of the treaty with Mexico are obligatory upon the Government of this Republic.
>
> The events of our Revolution, the great changes in territorial and political organization incident to it, necessarily make the application of the treaty, to the new order of things, a question of

[94] *Dip. Cor. Tex.*, I, 313, 314.

mere expediancy addressed to the discretion and reciprocal interests of the two countries.

Not doubting however that the measures of this Government will meet the expectations of the United States, in regard to the commercial intercourse between them, The undersigned will lay before the President who is yet absent, the note of Mr La Branche, and the accompanying Circular at the earliest opportunity after his return, in order that this Government may take the necessary action upon the subject.[95]

That the arrangement proposed proved satisfactory to the President is to be presumed, as there was no further correspondence on the matter. The reservation of Birdsall was natural as the Texan minister was at that time trying to secure a commercial treaty with the United States, and it would have been unwise to prejudice the case by acknowledging without reservation that the Mexican treaty was binding. Besides, the notice of the application of the treaty to Texan vessels came from the treasury department of the United States and did not represent a joint agreement between Texan agents and agents of the United States; and it might have been considered beneath the dignity of Texas to accept this without reservation. This arrangement was put into effect without Texas ever conceding its binding nature, except when the United States was urged to restrain their Indians, and as there was no commercial treaty ever ratified between Texas and the United States, it continued to be the basis of trade between the two countries.

Notwithstanding the Texan authorities had early attempted to form commercial treaties with European countries, it was not until early in 1841 that steps were taken looking to the establishment of commercial arrangements with the United States. On February 17, the secretary of state wrote to Barnard E. Bee, Texan chargé d'affaires in Washington, announcing the receipt of a number of communications from Washington in relation to the construction of the treaty between the United States and Mexico, and the obligations of the United States under that treaty to restrain the border Indians from incursions into Texas. "The President instructs me to inform you," he wrote,

that in all probability it will be the most advisable to defer for

[95]*Ibid.*, 322.

the present any further discussion of that subject: That you will avail yourself of the most favorable opportunity to suggest, to the Secretary of State of the United States the importance, and mutual advantages to be derived to the respective Governments by establishing more definitely our relations and intercourse by farther Treaty stipulations. Independent of the high commercial advantages consequent upon reciprocal Treaty obligations, the civil and criminal administration of the laws of the respective Governments would be very much facilitated by properly tempered regulations relative to fugitives from justice, and public defaulters.[96]

In December Lamar had obtained leave of absence on account of bad health, and at the time this letter was sent he was still away from the seat of government, convalescing at the home of Doctor Hoxie, at Independence, Texas. It seems that Mayfield had instructions from him before suggesting a general treaty with the United States. Some time about March 1, 1841, Lamar returned to the seat of government and took up his duties, and on March 22 Mayfield addressed another letter on the subject of negotiating a treaty.[97] In announcing the return of Lamar to Austin and the resumption of his duties, Mayfield wrote:

His views were known upon the subject of opening a negotiation with the Government of the United States: for forming a definite treaty of Amity, Commerce and Navigation; and embracing such other subjects as may mutually interest both Nations. It is the wish of the President that you should, without delay represent in the most respectful and urgent manner to the Government of the United States the importance of an early Negotiation relative to the several objects contained in my former note, in which the several matters now under consideration and discussion between the two Governments may be embraced, and definitely adjusted upon principles of entire reciprocity.

No specific plan was proposed for the reason that it was hoped that the negotiations would be held in Texas, and Bee was urged to request that they be held there;[98] though some of the argu-

[96]Mayfield to Bee, February 17, 1841, *Dip. Cor. Tex.*, II, 76.

[97]It is necessary to correct a false impression that several of the histories of Texas give. Yoakum, Bancroft, Thrall, Crane, Lester, Gouge, and others state that Lamar retired from the presidency, and that throughout the remainder of his term the office was administered by Burnet. Gouge is particularly caustic, referring to the financial and other failures, and saying Lamar did not have the courage to remain with his office after failure. Even a slight acquaintance with the newspapers and other records of the period should have made impossible this error.

[98]Mayfield to Bee, March 22, 1841, *Dip. Cor. Tex.*, II, 77-78.

ments Bee should advance for the beginning of negotiations were suggested, one of which was the settlement of the right of citizens of each country to carry their body servants with them when traveling in the country of the other. Another reason given was the necessity for coming to some agreement as to the meaning of the treaty of 1831 with regard to the control of the Indians.

By the treaty between Mexico and the United States in 1831, it was agreed that each country should take upon itself the duty of restraining the Indians from crossing the boundary and attacking the citizens of the other, even to the point of using force. The term used was the prevention of "incursions." The Texan government and the government of the United States developed diametrically opposite views with regard to the interpretation of this treaty. The Texan authorities interpreted it to mean that the United States government would prevent the peaceful emigration of United States Indians into Texas, and even went so far as to demand that the United States prevent the immigrant Indians, such as the Cherokees, Caddoes, and others from taking any part in Mexican conspiracies, or even to send a force to assist in ejecting them from Texas. The attitude of the United States was that the treaty meant that the United States would prevent any hostile incursions into the territory of Texas, or if unable to prevent the incursion, she would remunerate the Texas citizens for any loss sustained at the hands of Indian marauders.

The action of the United States government in sending military forces into Texas in the summer of 1836 with the ostensible purpose of keeping the Indians quiet, created a precedent on which the Texans attempted to act from this time forward. Every time an outbreak appeared imminent, the Texan authorities sent the documents proving the conspiracy, and requested some action. These documents were usually submitted to the secretary of war, who at this time was J. R. Poinsett, for investigation. The attitude of the United States government is expressed in a report of Poinsett to the secretary of state on July 18, 1839, after the Texan minister had laid before the secretary of state documents showing that the Mexicans were conspiring with the Cherokees against the Texans.[69] Poinsett wrote:

[69]I have discussed these Indian wars in Chapter IV, and shall not give more here than the international aspect. The documents referred to here were those showing the conspiracy of 1839, resulting in the expulsion of the Cherokees from Texas.

Having carefully examined the documents accompanying that communication [Mr. Dunlap's], I do not find any evidence of a disposition on the part of the Indians within the United States to make war upon the citizens of Texas. The letters of the Mexican authorities allude clearly to the Indians residing within the Texan territory; and the circular is addressed to chiefs who live without the limits of the United States.[100]

This position does not appear to have had a formal answer until December 15, 1840, when Bee in a letter to Forsyth called attention to additional atrocities, and took issue with the position of Poinsett. He claimed that as the Cherokees, Kickapoos, Delawares, Choctaws, Pottawatomies, Shawnees, and Caddoes had come to Texas from the United States without ever securing rights of settlement there, it was the duty of the United States to keep them quiet as well as those which still remained in the United States. Besides, he said, the Indians in the United States mingled indiscriminately with their kindred in Texas, and participated in the atrocities which were complained of. His contention was that the removal of any tribe of Indians into Texas without the permission of the Texan authorities, did not affect the duties of the United States under the treaty.[101]

The response of Forsyth to this communication, January 23, 1841, is what precipitated the demand of the Texan government for the abrogation of the treaty of 1831. He wrote that as usual with anything dealing with Indian affairs, Bee's communication had been submitted to the war department, and that as usual, the conclusion arrived at was, "that the Executive of the United States has no legal power to check or restrain by force the voluntary and peaceable migrations of Indians from the United States to any other country whatsoever." The sole object of the article in the treaty referred to, he said, was to make it the duty of the parties to do everything in their power towards preserving peace among the Indians on their frontiers, and preventing them from attacking the citizens of either party. He claimed that the United States had scrupulously carried out her part of the contract, and stood ready to continue to do so in case of proof that any United States Indians were making marauding expeditions into Texas.[102]

[100]*Senate Documents*, 32 Cong., 2 Sess., No. 14, p. 42.
[101]*Ibid.*, 52.
[102]*Ibid.*, 55.

The death of President Harrison prevented the Texan legation from submitting the request of its government for a treaty until April 23, 1841. On that date Nathaniel Amory, secretary of legation, expressed verbally to Webster the desire of the Texan government to enter into a treaty covering the Indian question, commerce, and other matters at issue between the two governments, and also expressing the desire that negotiations be held in Austin. To the last proposal Webster interposed a negative, though he was non-committal as to the necessity for a treaty.[103] Before this interview took place a letter had gone forward on April 20, signed by the secretary of state, but apparently written by President Lamar, in which the whole Texan contention was defended strongly.

An interesting phase of the arguments used in this communication, which was characteristic of Lamar's methods, is the balancing of the benefits to the United States of the fifth and sixth articles against the duties assumed by the United States under the thirty-third article.[104] I shall quote at some length from this document, without pointing out the fallacies, to give some idea of the methods employed by Lamar. After mentioning the fact that the United States had seen fit in 1838 to adapt the treaty to Texas so far as commerce was concerned, and that Texas had acquiesced in that interpretation of international law, he continued:

Under the Construction given by Mr. Forsyth to the 33rd article of the Treaty Texas would not be receiving an equivalent, for the sacrifices she suffers in her revenues; by allowing Vessels belonging to the United States to enter our Ports free of Tonnage duty. To arrive at a fair interpretation of that instrument the whole should be construed by its several parts and articles, by which means its true spirit and intention may be more accurately defined. It will be found that concessions, and privileges are contained in many of its clauses and provisions in many of its articles of which there cannot be found a sufficient guarantee or equivalent

[103]Amory to Mayfield, April 23, 1841, *Dip. Cor. Tex.*, I, 489.

[104]Articles 5 and 6 of the treaty provided for complete reciprocal tonnage and other local dues, and that the same duties should be charged whether the goods were brought in Mexican or American vessels.

Article 33 provided "that the two contracting parties, shall by all means in their power maintain peace and harmony among the several Indian Nations who inhabit the land adjacent to the lines and rivers which form the boundaries of the two countries;" and it was stipulated that the necessary force would be employed to restrain all incursions on the part of the Indians living within their respective boundaries. *Treaties and Conventions of the United States* (Malloy, ed.), I, 1085-1097.

secured in the same article. This naturally arose from the relative strength, commerce, and political condition of the contracting parties at the time of making the Treaty, as will be seen by reference to the articles cited.

The United States at the time had an extended commerce, and heavy Shipping. Mexico on the contrary (and with but remote prospects of improvement) was limited in her commerce, and yet more in her shipping. The mutual guarantee then as to tonnage and other charges enumerated in the "5th and 6th" articles of the Treaty cannot be said to secure to Mexico an equivalent, as it was apparent and must for years Continue that the whole trade of Mexico with the United States upon the Gulf would be carried in American bottoms.

On the other hand, the United States was well established, with a strong standing army, an organized militia, and an overflowing treasury, and her contribution to this balanced document was a guarantee to protect Mexico from her Indian neighbors. But independent of those considerations, the United States was bound upon principles of justice aside from any treaty stipulations upon the subject, to guard the government of Mexico, her citizens or territory, from hostilities or incursions from those various tribes of Indians, which by her policy she was establishing on the immediate borders of the latter. He did not agree with Forsyth's interpretation of the thirty-third article, and insisted that the United States was obligated to use force to restrain her Indians from making incursions, either peaceful or otherwise, into Texas. Finally, since the United States refused to carry out the plain obligations of the thirty-third article, the minister was to announce to the American secretary of state that Texas had determined to terminate the stipulations of the fifth and sixth articles as provided for by the treaty.[105] These instructions were complied with on May 19, when the secretary of legation informed the American secretary of state that the treaty would terminate a year from that date.[106]

This elicited no response from the United States government, though there continued to be a one-sided correspondence on the subject thereafter. On September 15 Amory submitted a rough draft of a treaty as follows:

[105]Mayfield to Bee, April 20, 1841, *Dip. Cor. Tex.*, II, 82-86.
[106]Amory to Webster, May 19, 1841, *Dip. Cor. Tex.*, I, 496.

Article 1: On commerce and navigation. To be nearly the same as that in the Treaty between Texas and Great Britain, or as the 2nd Article of the convention between Texas and the Netherlands.

2nd. Artc: As regards what shall be considered Texas vessels to be like the 7th Article of the Treaty between Texas and the Netherlands.

3rd. Tonage duties the same on vessels of both countries as in the second Article of the Treaty with Great Britain. Insert provisions for calling upon justices of the Peace, Judges and courts for warrants and other process to apprehend deserters from the Commercial and Naval Service.

4th The flag to protect the ships and goods, and no right of search to be permitted under penalty of damages to be restored by the Government of the officer or officers offending.

Artic 5th Provide for right and obligation of convoy in case of mutual war with a third power, as provided in the 20th article of the Treaty with the Netherlands, the free navigation by each party of the bordering or coterminous rivers and above and below the boundaries.

Artic: 7. The right of each party to land the products of its soil within the territory of the other free of all duty, when the same is intended to be and is actually shipped to any other country.

Artic: 8. To provide for the Indian relations as in the 23rd [33rd] Article of the Treaty between the United States and Mexico, and for removal of Indians from Texas.

Art: 9. Provisions for consular rights.

Art: 10. The right of succession and inheritance to the estates of deceased citizens dying intestate to be preserved as in the country of which they were the subjects, tho' temporarily domiciled abroad.

Art: 11. The Treaty to continue for ten years.[107]

To this communication Webster replied on September 20, stating that on account of a press of other matters he would not be able at that time to discuss the matter of a treaty with Texas, and that on account of his absence in the North it would not be possible to take the matter up before December,[108] so the administration of Lamar came to a close without any definite action having been taken on the proposals of Texas.

The succeeding administration took up the same policy, however, and a brief statement is necessary to complete the story of the negotiations. Bee, who had absented himself from Washing-

[107] *Dip. Cor. Tex.* I, 517.

[108] *Ibid.*, I, 517-518.

ton for the greater part of the summer and fall of 1841, was recalled in a sharp letter of censure, and James Reily was sent armed with full powers to negotiate a treaty. For a good part of this year Webster was engaged in the Webster-Ashburton negotiations over the Northeast boundary, and it was not until July 30, 1842, that the draft of a treaty was signed by the Texan chargé d'affaires and the American secretary of state.[109] The draft of the treaty contained twenty-two articles, and followed generally the subjects suggested by the Texan chargé d'affaires in September, 1841. Freedom of commercial intercourse was to be guaranteed, and duties were to be reciprocal; the use of the Red River, and all rivers having their sources or origin in Texas, and emptying into the Mississippi, and even the Mississippi, were free to the navigation of both parties; right of deposit was allowed without duties while reshipment was being made, and raw cotton was to be imported into each countrv for five years free of duty. Other articles dealt with blockade, rights of neutrals, prizes, and transference of property. A consular service was provided for, and a final article provided for extradition of criminals.

The main cause for demanding a treaty on the part of Texas was the unsatisfactory situation with regard to the border Indians. It will be remembered that the Texans desired that the United States guarantee Texas against the peaceable immigration of United States Indians, and that the United States should remove those which had come into Texas from the United States. Before negotiations got under way, however, Texas had surrendered that point, and the agreement was according to the contention of the United States, with ambiguities removed. It was agreed "that the two contracting parties, by all the means in their power, maintain peace and harmony among the several Indian tribes who inhabit the lands adjacent to the lines and rivers which form the boundaries of the two countries," and in order to attain that result force was to be used, "so that Texas will not permit the Indians residing within her territory, to attack the citizens of the United States or the Indians residing within the limits of the United States, nor will the United States suffer their Indians to attack the citizens of Texas nor the Indians inhabiting her terri-

[109]Reiley to Jones, August 3, 1842, *Dip. Cor. Tex.*, I, 576.

tory, in any manner whatsoever." Captives were to be returned by the two governments.[110]

This treaty was never binding on the two governments as ratifications were never exchanged. The Texas Senate on January 16, 1843, ratified it with an amendment to article V, which permitted free importation of raw cotton,[111] while in March, 1843, the United States Senate ratified it after striking out articles IV and V, which provided for freedom of navigation of the rivers, including the Mississippi, and right of deposit at New Orleans and other points. No further action was taken by either country, as by this time the annexation issue was becoming of supreme interest again.

Another topic that requires some discussion here, and which I have already mentioned in a discussion of the relations of Mexico and Texas, is the attitude assumed by the United States during the efforts of Texas to establish peace with Mexico. When Dunlap was sent to the United States in the place of Bee, who was sent to Mexico, he was instructed to ask for the mediation of the United States between Texas and Mexico.[112] Forsyth gave a limited agreement to this policy, while acting at all times cautiously. The purport of the instructions was that through the mediation of the American secretary of state, Dunlap should get into communication with the Mexican minister, and by some means agree on a treaty with him. It appears that Forsyth did speak to the Spanish minister, without taking any decided stand one way or another. In a private letter to Lamar, May 16, 1839, Dunlap wrote:

I am requested by Mr. Forsythe to give you a private letter relative to our interview this day, concerning the mediation of this Govt. with our Mexican difficulties—as the result may not be subject to a call of Congress. He said to the Mexican minister that the Govet. of Texas had asked the mediation of his Govet. with the hope of settling on amicable terms, by a treaty of peace and limits the present difficulties between Texas and Mexico—and that his Govet. would be very happy to interpose, should it be the wish of Mexico.[113]

[110]The complete text of the treaty can be found in *Dip. Cor. Tex.*, I, 622-628.

[111]*Secret Journals of the Senate*, 276.

[112]*Dip. Cor. Tex.*, I, 369.

[113]*Dip. Cor. Tex.*, I, 383.

This was certainly non-committal enough; but the instructions to Ellis, who was just being sent as minister to Mexico, were less in harmony with the desires of Texas. Ellis was instructed to be ready, while observing strict neutrality, to interpose his good offices between Mexico and Texas, but not until Mexico should ask for them. There is no evidence that Mexico asked for the mediation of Ellis, and none that he ever offered mediation. But the Texan minister was characteristically optimistic, and read into Forsyth's attitude a solicitude for Texas which was unjustified. "Mr. Ellis will be instructed to say to Prest Santa Anna that should Mexico desire the mediation of this Govnt," he wrote, "that nothing will give her more pleasure than to interpose"; but Ellis was not instructed to make any such statement. Apparently, from the instructions, all advances were to come from the Mexicans before Ellis would have been expected to offer the good offices of the United States.

No further developments came on this line until April, 1840. Bee, who had succeeded Dunlap as minister in Washington, communicated to Forsyth information concerning the killing of Colonel Johnson and his party while returning from the Rio Grande country after promulgating Lamar's proclamation of neutrality as between the Centralists and Federalists, and again asked the United States to mediate between Mexico and Texas.[114] In answer, Forsyth informed Mr. Bee "that although he is entirely correct in supposing that the United States desire that the relations between Texas and Mexico may be established upon a friendly footing, nothing has occurred since the communications on that subject from this Department to the Predecessors of Mr. Bee as the Representatives of Texas here, to render a change of the determination of this Government expedient."[115] This cool response effectively closed the matter, and it did not reappear until after the close of Lamar's administration.

Another way in which the United States showed a correct conception of neutrality, was in refusing to allow seamen for the Texas navy to be recruited in American ports. At the beginning of Lamar's administration, as I have shown in another chapter, the vessels contracted for by his predecessor began to arrive, but they

[114] Bee to Forsyth, April 5, 1840, *Dip. Cor. Tex.*, I, 451.

[115] Forsyth to Bee (copy), May 4, 1840, *Dip. Cor Tex.*, I, 453.

were not manned, and it was hoped to secure seamen from the United States. Lieutenant Moore, commander of the sloop *Boston* in the United States navy, resigned his commission and was appointed as commander of the Texan navy. In reporting this resignation to the Texan authorities, Dunlap wrote, July 21, 1839, suggesting that the best plan to obtain tried seamen was to send the vessels back to New York or some other port, and let the commanding officer announce the number of men desired. He said that was the method advised by those most skilled in the matter. He stated that no notice would be taken when the ships left, concluding, "This is the best port for such an enterprise as concealment is more certain amidst such large and busy masses as continually throng this city."[116]

The government of Texas accepted the guarantees of Dunlap. and followed his advice, sending the ships to various American ports for recruits, Moore himself proceeding to New York. It seems, however, that the authorities of the United States were not so blind as Dunlap anticipated. A letter from Forsyth to Dunlap on January 15, 1840, enclosing documents showing that Moore had been violating the neutrality law of 1818, and announcing his purpose to begin legal proceedings against Moore, said, "As you will without doubt promptly inform your Government of the grounds and motives for the proceedings against Mr Moore and his confederates, no erroneous impressions in regard to them can be received but it will understand that they have originated in the desire and determination of the Executive of the United States to use all legal means to preserve our neutrality between Texas and Mexico, and to maintain relations of friendship and good will with both governments." He also announced the determination of his government to exclude Texan vessels of war from American ports in case of any future violation of the law.[117]

The charge against Moore, substantially supported by documents, was that for some time he had been engaged in hiring and retaining within the territory of the United States, citizens of the United States and other persons to enlist themselves in the service of the Republic of Texas as mariners or seamen on board the brig of war, *Colorado*. In spite of his suggestion that this

[116]Dunlap to Lamar, July 21, 1839, *Dip. Cor. Tex.*, 411.

[117]Forsyth to Dunlap, January 15, 1840 (copy enclosed in Dunlap to Burnet, January 27, 1840), *Dip. Cor. Tex.*, I, 437.

procedure be followed in securing mariners and seamen, Dunlap expressed great surprise that any attempt was being made to evade the laws of the United States. He felt confident, he said, that his government would not do any act inconsistent with that spirit of conciliation and good will which she had so fondly cherished towards both the government and citizens of the United States. He protested that the exclusion of Texan vessels from American ports was threatened without giving Moore a fair and complete trial. On January 27, 1840, he sent a note to the secretary of state for the United States enclosing a copy of one from Commodore Moore disclaiming having enlisted any seamen in violation of an act of Congress. To this Forsyth replied, calling attention to the discrepancy between Moore's letter and the documents already presented, and stating that since Moore had left the waters of the United States of his own accord, no further action on the part of the United States *was necessary.* Thus the matter closed.[118]

4. *Relations with France and England*

When William H. Wharton was sent as minister to the United States in November, 1836, he was instructed, if the United States should be indifferent or adverse to the claims of Texas to recognition or annexation, to keep in touch with the ministers of England and France, "explaining to them the great commercial advantages that will result to their nations from our cotton, etc., and finding a market here for their merchandise, and an outlet for their surplus population, on the basis of low duties and liberal encouragement which it will be our interest to establish." In a postscript the Texan secretary of state, Stephen F. Austin, repeated his instructions that in no case was the minister to look for support to other quarters unless the United States should give evidence of a lack of friendly interest.[1] In February, 1837, Wharton became discouraged at the prospect of recognition by the United States, and wrote that he had put the British and French ministers in possession of documents explanatory of the objects of the contest with Mexico, and that he had requested them to ascertain whether or not their countries would receive a diplomatic

[118]For this correspondence see *Dip. Cor. Tex.*, I, 436-442.

[1]Austin to Wharton, November 18, 1836, *Dip. Cor. Tex.*, I, 137, 140.

agent from Texas for the purpose of entering into a treaty of commerce.[2]

Partly as a result of the obvious indifference of the United States to annexation, and to encourage a more favorable attitude by appealing to European countries, and partly from a desire to strengthen the financial system by securing recognition abroad, the Congress which assembled in May, 1837, passed a resolution requesting the President to appoint an agent to Great Britain, and later in a secret joint resolution, it authorized the President to instruct the agent to visit France, in order to secure recognition of their independence by those powers, and to form a commercial treaty.[3] J. Pinckney Henderson, who had acted as secretary of state for awhile after the death of Austin, was commissioned on June 20 as agent under these resolutions, and he arrived in London on October 9, 1837.

Texan affairs had been under discussion in Parliament in 1836, when the anti-slavery interests expressed concern over the possible effect of Texan independence on slavery and the slave trade. On June 5, 1836, Mr. Barlow Hoy interrogated the foreign minister, Palmerston, as to whether or not he had received any communication relative to the establishment of slavery in Texas. Palmerston responded that he had not, but that Texas was in a state of revolt from Mexico, and that no action could be taken until the outcome of that revolt was known. Two months later, August 5, while the supply bill was under discussion, Hoy moved an address to the crown praying "that such measures may be taken as may seem proper to secure fulfillment of the existing treaty between this country and Mexico; and to prevent the establishment of slavery and traffic in slaves in the province of Texas in the Mexican territory." He supported this motion in a long speech in which he emphasized three points, first, the large amount of money invested in Mexican bonds; secondly, the danger of annexation by the United States; and thirdly, the probability that slavery would be permanently established in Texas. He urged Palmerston to send a naval force for the purpose of assisting Mexico in regaining control of the revolted province.

Palmerston in opposing the motion disposed of the fears of Hoy

[2]Wharton to Rusk, February 12, 1837, *Ibid.*, I, 185.

[3]Gammel, *Laws of Texas*, I, 1287; *Secret Journals of the Senate*, 315.

and the other abolitionists by saying that if there were a prospect of annexation to the United States, it would be time for England to interest herself, but that the message of the President of the United States indicated that annexation was unlikely; that if Mexico reconquered Texas the laws of Mexico would apply, and the treaty would be enforced, so that there was no necessity to interfere on that account; and finally, that if Texas should in the future become a part of the United States there might be importation of slaves from other states, but importation from Africa was unlikely.[4] Palmerston's speech satisfied Hoy, and he withdrew his motion; but, as will be seen, the question of slavery and the slave trade continued to operate against recognition of Texan independence by England.

Henderson held his first conversation with Palmerston on October 13, and urged upon him the desire of Texas for recognition by England. Palmerston promised no more than that the matter would be considered by the cabinet as a whole. The conversation included such topics as the commercial benefits to England from recognition, the question of annexation, slavery and the slave trade, the possibility of reconquest of Texas by Mexico.[5] On October 26 Henderson addressed a long letter to Palmerston in which he traced the history of Texas for several years past, and again urged recognition by England, receiving only the promise that the matter would be laid before the cabinet. On December 21 Palmerston announced the decision of the cabinet that they were not ready to give a definite decision at that time, as there seemed still a possibility that Mexico would succeed in reconquering Texas. Henderson attempted to secure a promise that if Mexico had not succeeded in subjugating Texas within a few months England would recognize the independence of Texas, but Palmerston refused to make that promise, advising the Texans to look well to slavery conditions if they desired any consideration from England. Henderson regarded this as final and proceeded to France, after securing an agreement that Texan vessels would be admitted into British ports under the treaty between Mexico and Great Britain.[6]

[4]Hansard, *Parliamentary History of England*, 3d Ser., XXXIV, 1107; XXXV, 928-942.

[5]Henderson to Irion, October 14, 1837, *Dip. Cor. Tex.*, III, 812.

[6]Henderson to Irion, December 22, 1837, January 5, 30, April 12, 1838, *Dip. Cor. Tex.*, III, 831, 839, 843, 853.

Before proceeding with a discussion of later efforts on the part of the Texas government to secure recognition, it will be well to notice briefly a few episodes that caused some friction between the new republic and England, and perhaps served in a measure to delay recognition. In the summer of 1837 a British schooner, *Little Penn,* bound from Liverpool to Tabasco loaded with British goods ran aground on the Yucatan coast. Two Mexican vessels, the *Paz* and the *Abispa,* were sent to salvage the cargo, the *Paz* returning safely to port, but the *Abispa* falling in with two Texan vessels and being captured. The owners of the cargo, F. Lizardi and Company, submitted a claim to the British Government for the sum of £3640. On August 3, 1837, a Texan vessel of war took as a prize the British schooner *Eliza Russell,* commanded by Captain Joseph Russell, and brought her into port at Galveston. The Texan Government immediately ordered her release, but the delay gave Russell grounds for a claim against the government for £865. The Texas Government immediately acknowledged the justness of the claim for the *Eliza Russell,* though there was considerable delay in making an appropriation for settlement of the claim, which resulted in a threat on the part of Palmerston to send a warship to Texas to collect the claims.[7] This threat brought about the appropriation of a sum to settle the claim for the *Eliza Russell,* but the claim for the *Little Penn* was never recognized by Texas.

Just before Henderson arrived in London an agreement was reached on September 15, by the British holders of Mexican bonds and agents of the Mexican Government by which it was proposed to pay a part of the bonds by lands to be located in Texas. The Lizardi Company, a Mexican company in London, which was the chief holder of Mexican bonds, advertised a meeting on October 16 and from day to day thereafter for the purpose of carrying into effect the agreement. Henderson secured from Palmerston a disclaimer on the part of the British Government of any interest in the matter, and on October 16 wrote a formal protest to Lizardi and Company, stating that Texas was no longer under the sovereignty of Mexico, and that the agreement was void.[8] Few of

[7]Palmerston to Henderson, October 23, 1839, 4 Tex. Cong., *House Journal*, 33-34.

[8]Henderson to Irion, November 5, 1838, enclosing Henderson to Lizardi and Company, October 16, 1838, *Dip. Cor. Tex.*, III, 830.

the bondholders took advantage of the offer at that time. This illustrates, however, the difficulties in the way of securing recognition. Later, as we have already seen, an effort was made to secure the acknowledgment of Texan independence by Mexico in return for an assumption of a part of the Mexican debt by Texas.

Two other obstacles in the way of recognition were the possibility that Texas would encourage the slave trade, if she made good her independence, and the desire of Great Britain to pose as the friend of Mexico. The interest of Great Britain in slavery in Texas I shall refer to later. From commercial reasons Great Britain desired to maintain the friendship of Mexico, and until the independence of Texas was unquestionably established, Palmerston felt it inexpedient to recognize it; and it was not until Texas had so proved her independence that failure to acknowledge its independence would have caused greater loss than the straining of Mexican friendship, that recognition was extended. During 1838 the British Government secretly connived at the French blockade of the Mexican ports, the British naval commander being instructed to leave Mexican waters before hostilities could take place; and when hostilities did begin the British Government offered to mediate between the French and the Mexicans, and the conduct of the British mediators convinced the Mexicans of the sincere friendship of the British Government. An effort was made to mediate between Mexico and Texas, also, the British Government, while refusing to recognize the independence of Texas, urging Mexico to acknowledge independence.

With the withdrawal of Henderson from London in April, 1838, the direct connection between the Texan Government and Great Britain was interrupted until the fall of 1839. In the meantime, however, Palmerston showed himself not indifferent to the claims of Texas, and urged on Mexico the necessity of recognizing Texan independence. As I have already stated, Palmerston instructed Pakenham, the British minister to Mexico, in October, 1838, to urge Mexico to acknowledge the independence of Texas, laying stress upon the importance of creating a barrier state between Mexico and the United States. At that time Gorostiza, the Mexican foreign minister, refused to entertain the suggestion because of its unpopularity, but suggested that an armistice might be granted if some European country would undertake to guarantee the boundary. These instructions were verbal, but in April, 1839,

Palmerston sent written instructions to the same effect.[9] The further efforts of the British minister to mediate I have shown adequately in another connection.

In the summer of 1839, Christopher Hughes, American chargé d'affaires in Sweden, returned from a vacation in the United States by way of London. On June 10, 1839, he addressed a note to Lord Palmerston submitting a memorandum prepared by Anson Jones, as Texan minister to the United States, giving reasons for the recognition of Texan independence. Hughes supported the claims with a brief note on his own account. The action of Hughes was entirely on his own account, and without the knowledge of his government. It is interesting only because it drew from Palmerston a brief reply, in which he said, "Thank you for your letter about Texas, which I have sent to Lord Melbourne. The subject, to which it relates is important, but not without difficulties."[10] No doubt the chief difficulty referred to was the opposition of the abolition party in parliament led by O'Connell. On July 9, 1839, O'Connell interrogated the foreign minister as to whether anything had been done toward the recognition of Texas. Palmerston replied that application had been made the preceding year by persons from Texas, but that he had stated that the ministry were not yet ready to recognize Texas, but that he had instructed the minister to Mexico to endeavor to bring about some understanding between Texas and Mexico. He did not inform the House that the instructions called for a recognition of Texan independence by Mexico.[11] Henderson was convinced that the opposition of O'Connell was the only obstacle to recognition, and wrote to Anson Jones, September 27, 1839, from Paris:

> I shall go to England in a few days and urge that Government to recognize or refuse, and give their reasons for so doing. I scarcely hope they will comply with my main request, inasmuch as Mr. O'Connell has threatened them with his vengeance if they do recognize. That threat he made in a speech in Parliament a few days before it adjourned, and you know the present ministry of England dare not run counter to his wishes.[12]

[9]Adams, *British Interests and Activities in Texas*, 28, 29.

[10]Hughes to Jones, June 10, 1839. Jones, *Memoranda and Official Correspondence Relating to the Republic of Texas*, 148-152.

[11]Hansard, 3d Series, XLIX, 82.

[12]Jones, *Memoranda, etc.*, 148.

In May, 1839, James Hamilton was appointed as a loan commissioner under the five million dollar loan act, to dispose of the bonds of Texas in the United States and Europe. He was also commissioned as a joint agent with Henderson to secure the recognition of Texas by Great Britain and France, and to enter into a treaty of amity, commerce, and navigation. Hamilton had become interested in Texas as early as 1836, and in the fall of 1838 he hoped for the appointment by President Houston as loan commissioner, but his desires were not realized. As soon as it was known that Lamar was to be the successor of Houston Hamilton wrote numerous letters to him suggesting means of floating a loan, and as soon as practicable after his inauguration Lamar appointed him to the place mentioned. Hamilton proved prolific in schemes for securing financial aid and recognition, and it is likely that his arguments appealed to Palmerston, resulting finally in several treaties between Texas and Great Britain.

On May 20, 1839, the same day on which his commission was signed, he wrote a letter to H. S. Fox, British minister at Washington, for transmittal to Pakenham, British minister at Mexico, outlining his views as to the advantage to Great Britain of recognition of Texas. This letter was not transmitted until some months later, but it, with other information concerning Texas and Mexico, was faithfully transmitted to Palmerston by Pakenham, and served to prepare the way for the active negotiations undertaken by Hamilton the following year. The immediate purpose of the letter was to secure the good offices of Pakenham to mediate betwen Mexico and Texas while Bee was still attempting to get into communication with the Mexican authorities. It was in this letter that he adopted a policy, already discussed by Bee and Gordon, representative of Lizardi and Company in New Orleans,—offering the payment by Texas of a sum of money to be applied to the payment of Mexican bonds in return for a recognition of her independence within the boundaries demanded. After expressing his desire that Pakenham mediate between Mexico and Texas, he proceeded to give arguments to show the advantage to Great Britain if Texan independence should be accomplished through British mediation. In the first place, he said, the impending blockade of Mexican ports by Texan vessels might cause serious difficulty as Great Britain would hesitate to recognize the blockade, and bloodshed might ensue; secondly, Great Britain had an incalculable interest in the trade of Texas; thirdly, Great Britain might feel a delicacy in recognizing Texas until Mexico had recognized; fourthly, as soon as Great Britain recognized Texas she could obtain through the value of her commerce with Texas, the concurrence of Texas in suppressing the slave trade, which Texas had prohibited by her Constitution.[13]

Hamilton left New York on August 1, arriving in London in September. He had a conference with Palmerston, but nothing definite came of it, and he proceeded to the continent to attempt to secure the loan. Receiving little encouragement, he returned to the United States, and in December he was in Texas, where he secured a resolution of Congress permitting him to asume five million dollars of the Mexican bonds in case recognition by Mexico were secured, and authorizing him to borrow money for the purpose. Henderson having been recalled Hamilton was commissioned as agent to Great Britain, and authorized to sign a treaty of amity, commerce, and navigation. He was also authorized to enter into an agreement with the holders of Mexican bonds.[14] Before returning to Europe Hamilton wrote a letter to Palmerston, February 10, 1840, repeating his arguments for British mediation, and suggested further that Great Britain should threaten to recognize Texas if Mexico refused to agree to British mediation.[15]

On April 18, 1840, Hamilton was given a commission as diplomatic commissioner to the Netherlands and Belgium for the purpose of negotiating a treaty of recognition, and to conclude commercial treaties with those two countries. He proceeded direct to The Hague, where he concluded a treaty of amity, commerce and navigation with the Netherlands on September 18, 1840. He went from there to Brussels and initiated a treaty with the Belgium Government, which was broken off at that time, and he proceeded to England, arriving in London on September 27, when he found Palmerston so busily engaged on the Eastern question that no attention could then be paid to the claims of Texas.[16]

[13]Hamilton to Fox, May 20, 1839, *Dip. Cor. Tex.*, III, 867-871.

[14]The commission is dated December 20, 1839. *Dip. Cor. Tex.*, III, 877.

[15]Hamilton to Palmerston, February 10, 1840, enclosed in Hamilton to Lipscomb, February 25, 1840, *Dip. Cor. Tex.*, III, 887.

[16]See Hamilton to Jones, February 18, 1842, *Dip. Cor. Tex.*, III, 945, for a brief history of Hamilton's procedure.

It is evident that Palmerston had made up his mind to recognize Texas before the arrival of Hamilton, and when negotiations did begin they proceeded rapidly to a conclusion. On October 1 Hamilton addressed a brief formal note to Palmerston laying his credentials before the foreign minister, and asking for recognition on the grounds that Texas had *de facto* achieved her independence, and that she had established a government.[17] On the 14th he laid before the British Government the arguments on which he based the claim of Texas to recognition. The reasons for the recognition and the consequences of failure, which Hamilton thought would appeal to Palmerston, were as follows:

Reasons why Great Britain ought to recognize the Independence of Texas & form a treaty with her.

1st. The future & rapidly increasing value of the Trade with Texas, under a judicious commercial Convention.

2nd. By this means she secures a great Cotton producer and important consumer of her Manufactures, as her customer & a friendly neutral in the event of a war with the United States—

3rd. The Recognition of Texas by Great Britain inevitably Superinduces peace between Mexico & Texas.

4th. Peace at this moment between Mexico & Texas will inevitably insure the payment of a portion of the Mexican debt by Texas.

5th. It likewise insures under the friendly mediation of England a permanent Boundary Line between Mexico & Texas, which will be inviolably observed by Texas, & repress the spirit of future conquest on the part of the Anglo-American race—

In case England does not recognize the following consequences are likely to follow—

1st. In sixty days from this day Vera Cruz, Tampico & Matamoras will be blockaded by the Texian Squadron, which consists of one Corvette, two Brigs, three Schooners & one naval Steamer, now off the Coast of Mexico, while Mexico will be destitute of all naval force whatsoever.

2nd. If Texas is informed that Great Britain will not recognize her Independence & that consequently there is no hope of peace with Mexico, she will forthwith join the Federalists, revolutionize the northern provinces of Mexico & make such additions to her territory as the laws of war would justify under the usages of civilized nations.

3rd. Great Britain has an obvious interest in avoiding a discriminating duty which will be levied against the productions of

[17]*Dip. Cor. Tex.*, III, 925.

all nations which have not recognized Texas & formed Commercial Treaties with her on or before the 1st of Feby. next.

4th. If Her Majesty's Government should decline recognizing I must avail myself of the present situation of public affairs in Europe & make the most beneficial arrangements I can with some continental nation giving it exclusive commercial advantages for a valuable equivalent.

5th. Texas greatly prefers a friendly alliance with England from all those considerations which are connected with a common origin— But if Great Britain refuses all international companionship with her, she will be driven to seek friendly & profitable associations elsewhere.[18]

Four days later Palmerston responded that Great Britain was willing to enter into negotiation for a treaty of commerce and navigation between Great Britain and Texas, "believing the time to be now come when the independence of Texas may be considered as being, *de facto,* fully established; and, when the interests of Great Britain require, that the commercial intercourse between Great Britain and Texas shall be placed under the security to be afforded by a Treaty." Having announced the willingness of his Government to negotiate a treaty, he laid down the condition that Texas at the same time should enter into a treaty to suppress the slave trade. The peculiar geographical position and internal arrangements of Texas, he said, made it incumbent on the British Government to make the conclusion of such a treaty a *sine qua non* condition of any other treaty between Great Britain and Texas. He sent with his letter the draft of a convention in which reciprocal right of search by naval vessels was provided for. The draft of the treaty, which was accepted by Hamilton with only slight modification, provided for the right of search by certain cruisers of merchant vessels, which might on reasonable grounds be suspected of being engaged in the slave trade, in order that, if found guilty they might be sent to their own country for adjudication before their own tribunals. The search should take place only on a specific warrant of the government to which the vessel to be searched belonged.

Hamilton's commission did not authorize him to sign such a convention, but he felt that the importance of recognition and a commercial treaty with Great Britain justified him in going beyond his instructions, and on the 20th he wrote Palmerston of his

[18]Adams, *British Interests and Activities in Texas,* 53.

willingness to sign the convention with minor changes, which was not so difficult to do since the Texan merchant vessel could engage in the slave trade and be under no danger of seizure except on warrant of the Texas authorities, and upon seizure it would be tried only in Texas courts.[19] Preliminary articles for a treaty of amity, commerce, and navigation were agreed upon on November 5, and on the 13th the completed treaty was signed by Palmerston and Hamilton. On the following day a convention was signed which bound Texas to assume a million pounds sterling of the Mexican debt, if within six months Mexico had acknowledged the independence of Texas through British mediation. On the 16th the slave trade treaty was signed.[20]

The commercial treaty and the mediation convention were sent out on December 3 by a special messenger, Arthur Ikin, and arrived in Texas early in January. They were laid before the Senate and promptly ratified without opposition. The slave trade treaty was sent by another messenger, A. T. Burnley, who was associated with Hamilton as loan commissioner. Burnley went by another route, and did not arrive in Texas until February 21, 1841, after the adjournment of Congress, and the ratification of that treaty was delayed until the following session. The British Government refused to exchange ratifications until all three of the treaties had been ratified by Texas, and it was not until June 28, 1842, that ratification was finally exchanged, the Texas Senate having ratified the slave trade treaty in January of that year.

It has been charged reasonably that Hamilton sent the slave trade treaty by a different messenger and by a different route in order to delay its receipt in Texas, for the reason that he feared the action of the Texas Senate on that convention. In his letter transmitting the commercial treaty and mediation convention he made no mention of the other treaty. It was a month later, January 4, 1841, when the slave trade treaty was transmitted. In his letter of transmittal to the secretary of state Hamilton went into considerable detail in explaining the reasons for his exceeding his instructions in the matter of the treaty. The trepidation that he

[19]Palmerston to Hamilton, October 18, 1840, and Hamilton to Palmerston, October 20, 1840, *British and Foreign State Papers*, XXIX, 617-621; *Telegraph and Texas Register*, January 12, 1842.

[20]For the text of these treaties see Gammel, *Laws of Texas*, II, 880-885, 886-904; *British and Foreign State Papers*, XXIX, 80-83, 84-85, 85-96.

felt is also indicated by the letter he wrote to Lamar on the same date. After giving a history of the negotiations, he wrote:

> I did not apprise you of the slave trade convention which I had to conclude with Lord Palmerston to ensure recognition, because I was fearful unattended by those explanations Mr Burnley might afford, it would be liable to misconstruction. Referring you to my letter to the Secretary of State, and my correspondence with Lord Palmerston, I have only to add that I am sure you will concur in the necessity of my acquiescing in such a convention, when Mr Burnley shows you the opinion of the Solicitor of the Bank of England, who advised us that no valid contract could be made in the security of the bonds of an unrecognized Government.[21]

Why Ikin could not have made the suitable explanations does not appear, though Hamilton informed Aberdeen, who had succeeded Palmerston in the foreign office, that he had sent the document by a man well qualified to press it on the people of Texas, and that the illness of his messenger in New York had prevented his arrival in time. He proceeded to press upon the British Government the negotiation of a new treaty granting extensive commercial privileges to Great Britain, but as this was in nowise a policy of the Texan Government, and was rejected out of hand by the British Government, I shall not discuss it here.[22]

The failure of ratification of the treaties left the relations between Texas and Great Britain in the same situation as from the beginning. Though Hamilton was commissioned as minister plenipotentiary, he was unable to assume that dignity and was forced to continue only as diplomatic agent. The British Government did, however, in anticipation of the ratification of the Slave Trade Treaty appoint Charles Elliot, as consul-general to Texas, and toward the close of the year 1841, William Kennedy was sent as an agent to secure the ratification of the Slave Trade Treaty.[23]

The treaty with the Netherlands negotiated by Hamilton in September, 1840, was promptly ratified by the Texan Senate. I have noted that Hamilton was negotiating a treaty with Belgium

[21]Hamilton to Lamar, January 4, 1841, *Dip. Cor. Tex.*, III, 929.

[22]For the terms offered by Hamilton, see Adams, *British Interests and Activities in Texas*, 68-69.

[23]*Dip. Cor. Tex.*, III, 942; Adams, ed., *British Correspondence Concerning Texas*, THE QUARTERLY, XV, 251, 252.

when it became necessary for him to leave for London. No satisfactory basis of agreement was reached between Hamilton and the Belgian Government until the fall of 1841. Under this agreement Texas would admit cotton and woolen goods, iron, and linen manufactured in Belgium at one-half the existing duty, while the same articles from other countries should be required to pay at the rate of 50 per cent ad valorem. Arms and ammunition were to be admitted free for the Belgians, while other countries were to pay a duty of 100 per cent ad valorem. The coasting trade was to be free to Belgian ships the same as to Texan. In return for all these concessions, Belgium was to guarantee a loan of 37,000,000 francs by a specific endorsement of the bonds of the republic of Texas. This extremely disadvantageous treaty was rejected promptly by the Texan Senate on October 20, 1841.[24]

The other European country that showed active interest in Texas was France, and it was to France that the new republic turned for finances when other sources failed them. The fact that France was never able to contribute to the financial needs of Texas by either furnishing or guaranteeing a loan did not for a long time dampen the ardor of the loan commissioners, who were prolific with schemes for securing a loan. But the first interest of Texas was in securing the recognition of independence by France, as well as by the other European powers.

When Henderson withdrew from London in April, 1838, he went immediately to Paris, where he found a much less indifferent attitude than he had found in London. It will be remembered that France was just entering upon the blockade of Mexican ports, which might be expected to create an interest on the part of France in the claims of Texas. On account of the interest of the Government in the Mexican matter, Henderson was not received until May 31, and at that time he was given no assurance that his request for recognition would be favorably acted upon; but the Government immediately instructed the French minister at Washington to send one of his secretaries to Texas in order to report on the conditions there. Alphonse de Saligny was sent, though he did not make his report until late summer of 1839. On October 1 the foreign minister, Count Molé informed Henderson that the Government was disposed to wait until the re-

[24] *Secret Journals of the Senate*, 222, 224.

ceipt of the report of their agent before extending recognition. At the same time Molé requested Henderson to remain in Paris, as France was desirous of making a commercial arrangement with Texas that would serve to encourage commerce until the time of recognition, to which Henderson readily assented.[25] Early in November Henderson signed on the part of his Government an agreement similar to that entered into with Great Britain—"Until the mutual relations of France and Texas are regulated in a complete and definitive manner, the Citizens, the vessels and the Merchandize of the two Countries shall enjoy in every respect in each of the Countries the treatment accorded, or which may eventually be accorded to the most favored Nation, conformably moreover to the Respective Usages."[26]

In April, 1839, Admiral Baudin, minister plenipotentiary to Mexico and commander of the French naval forces in the Gulf of Mexico, who had been blockading the Mexican ports while treating with the Mexican Government, sent the Abbé M. B. Anduze to Texas for the purpose of agreeing to joint action on the part of Texas and France should hostilities between France and Mexico be renewed. This action was in response to an informal expression of Lamar to the French consul at New Orleans before he had determined to send a diplomatic agent to Mexico. "You will perceive, Mr. President," he wrote,

by the letter of the Admiral, which I have the honor to deliver to your Excellency, that I am authorized to enquire into that matter. With every disposition of the Admiral to meet the Government of Texas in an agreement, which shall be mutually beneficial and satisfactory, permit me therefore to ask.

First, What would be the nature of the co-operation of Texas in the event of a new war between France and Mexico?

Second, What would be the extent of your demands, in money, war ammunitions, means of transportation, etc.?

Third, What would be the guarantees offered for the reimbursement of the advances thus made?

. . . .

Though this Mission of mine, Mr. President does not proceed directly from the French Government, as the propositions will, I hope, be mutually advantageous, both to you and to France, The

[25]Henderson to Irion (and enclosures), October 5, 1838, *Dip. Cor. Tex.*, III, 1220.

[26]*Dip. Cor. Tex.*, III, 1233-1234.

Admiral Baudine will feel it his duty to obtain the approbation and sanction of his Government.[27]

To this communication Lamar responded through the secretary of state that until the result of the peace mission to Mexico should be known no agreement could be made for future hostilities; but that in the event of hostilities in the future Texas would gladly co-operate with France, and would bring into the field at the shortest notice twenty thousand soldiers and more if required—which, of course, was impossible—provided France advance the money necessary to a successful prosecution of the war.[28] Admiral Baudin visited Texas in May and was received with much honor and ceremony, which materially advanced the cordial relations of Texas and France.

Saligny, who had been sent as agent to Texas in 1838, made his report in the summer of 1839. This report has not been found, but it must have been favorable as Marshal Soult, who had succeeded Molé as minister of foreign affairs, in July informed Henderson that the French Government had determined to recognize the independence of Texas, but that they preferred to do it in the nature of a commercial treaty. Henderson demurred at this, preferring to receive recognition before entering into negotiations for a commercial treaty, as it would give him a better chance to negotiate as an equal. He was unable to change the French ministry, however, and in September signed a treaty of commerce which carried with it the recognition of Texan independence. Thus France was the first European country to recognize the independence of Texas. The treaty was promptly ratified by the Texas Senate, and Alphonse de Saligny was sent as chargé d'affaires to the newly recognized republic.[29]

From this time until the close of the Lamar administration there were few striking developments in the relations between France and Texas. France did not find it necessary to go to war with Mexico again, and Texas adopted her own policy toward

[27]Anduze to Lamar, April 18, 1839, *Dip. Cor. Tex.*, III, 1244-1245.

[28]Webb to Baudin, April 25, 1839, *Dip. Cor. Tex.*, III, 1246.

[29]Christian, "Tariff History of the Republic of Texas," THE QUARTERLY, XX, 336-337; Gammel, *Laws of Texas*, II, 655. This treaty was signed by the plenipotentiaries on September 25, by the King of France, October 2, and ratified by the Texas Senate on January 14, 1840. Ratification was exchanged on February 14, 1840, the certificate of ratification being signed by Saligny and Abner S. Lipscomb, Texan secretary of state.

Mexico. In the winter of 1840-1841 Saligny made himself obnoxious to the Government by his strenuous advocacy of the notorious Franco-Texienne bill, which the Houston party was attempting to pass over the opposition of the administration. The opposition of the Government to the bill induced a coolness on the part of Saligny, and the assault by a Mr. Bullock on the servant of Saligny led to a disgraceful quarrel between Saligny and the secretary of state, resulting in a request for the recall of the French chargé d'affaires. It had no other effect than the possible one of defeating the loan negotiations in France. Saligny calmly waited until the close of Lamar's administration, when he knew the new President would be more friendly to himself and his colonization projects.

To conclude, in foreign affairs the Lamar administration was notably successful. At its beginning only the United States had acknowledged the independence of Texas, and no commercial rights were recognized by any country; while at its close independence had been recognized by France, the Netherlands, Great Britain, and Belgium, and favorable commercial treaties had been adopted with France, Great Britain, and the Netherlands. A notable failure was the attempt to conciliate Mexico, but in that case the failure does not prove the policy unwise. The policy was advised and abetted by the United States and Great Britain, and though the Houston party criticised it, Houston found it necessary to adopt a similar policy after the beginning of his second administration.

(To be concluded.)

A RAY OF LIGHT ON THE GADSDEN TREATY

J. FRED RIPPY

There is scarcely a topic in American history about which so little is known as the negotiations connected with the Gadsden Treaty. The great secrecy with which they were conducted gave rise to a suspicion which is likely to continue until their nature has been made public. It may be that when all is revealed the discredit which has tended to rest upon the whole affair will prove unfounded. At any rate, the historian's curiosity regarding the matter is well-nigh irresistible.

It is known that there were several important questions to be settled when Gadsden was dispatched to Mexico in the summer of 1853. By the eleventh article of the Treaty of Guadalupe Hidalgo the United States government had been made responsible for the conduct of the Indians residing upon the borders of the two countries. This obligation had proved burdensome and the correspondence regarding the subject had been somewhat irritating. Difficulties regarding the survey of the boundary as laid down in the fifth article of the same treaty had culminated in the spring of 1853 in a grave dispute regarding the southern limits of New Mexico. The acquisition of Pacific possessions had rendered the routes adapted to interoceanic communication very important to the United States. One of these lay across the Isthmus of Tehuantepec within Mexican territory, and citizens of the United States had acquired concessions there, but the Mexican government had nullified the grant upon which their claims were based. This, too, gave rise to much protest and dissatisfaction. Moreover, the entire situation was complicated by the loud proclamations of manifest destiny on the part of a large group of Anglo-Americans, by the voracious appetites of the land-hungry, and by the filibuster raids which were constantly being launched against the Hispanic states to the south.

Gadsden's instructions embraced the boundary dispute, the question of responsibility for the incursions of the Indians into Mexico, and the right of way across the Isthmus of Tehuantepec. With reference to the last he was ordered not to resume negotiations, but to await further advices. His instructions regarding the first two are not known. He was presented to the Mexican government on August 17,[1] and three days later Bonilla, the Mexican Minister of Relations, addressed a complaint to him regarding filibuster preparations in California.[2] He replied to this note two days afterwards, and then communications were exchanged regarding the depredation claims.[3]

This is virtually all that is definitely known regarding the negotiations, as the correspondence has never been published. If Gadsden ever revealed what took place, no record of such revelation has been found. But upon two occasions after the treaty had been concluded Santa Anna referred to the transaction, and his statements are here presented. The first (Document A) is taken from the address issued to his fellow-citizens while he was in exile at Santo Tomás;[4] the second (Document B) is from his memoirs as published by Genaro García.[5] The well-known character of Santa Anna, and the circumstances under which the statements were made will cause the historian to accept them *cum granu saltis,* but they are, nevertheless, interesting as almost the only light we have on this affair. In the translation I have striven to be literal, even at the expense of the best English.

Document A[6]

One of the motives which has served my opponents to wound me cruelly has been the boundary treaty with the United States. I shall therefore make the proper explanations on this point, referring to the data which are in the hands of the Minister of Relations, and to the testimony of six honorable ministers with whom I sufficiently discussed this grave affair.

The government was forced to give preference to the disagreements which the United States was stirring up over the boundary which the unfortunate treaty of Guadalupe Hidalgo marked out;

[1]Moore, *Digest of International Law*, I, 462.

[2]Bolton MSS. (Bancroft Library, University of California).

[3]Moore, *op. et loc. cit.*

[4]This address is entitled as follows: "El General Antonio L. de Santa Anna a sus Compatriotas, San Thomas, Abril 12 de 1858."

[5]*Documentos Inéditos ó muy raros para la Historia de Méjico*, II, 106-111. The main body of the memoirs is dated Nassau, Bahama Islands, November 23, 1870.

[6]Grateful acknowledgment is due C. M. Montgomery of the Spanish department at the University of California for assistance in the translation of these documents.

for with this motive a considerable Anglo-American force was threatening the Department of Chihuahua, and to evade the war into which we were being provoked was a most urgent matter. The Commandante General in fulfillment of his duty, had collected all the troops at his disposition and was already advancing upon the Americans; but [this force] being insufficient to resist successfully, I ordered him to be warned "that under no circumstances was he to make any hostile demonstration against the troops of the United States, and that with prudence and dissimulation he should fall back to the capital of the Department, where he should remain on the defensive, leaving to the supreme government the affair which was being discussed, since it pertained to it exclusively." Moreover, he was told "that in the situation of the republic any indiscretion which would commit it to a war for which it was not prepared would be a crime."

Indeed, the disarmament of the country could have been no more deplorable. I had just observed with bitterness that the plaza of Vera Cruz, the fortresses of Ulúa and Perote were dismantled and, consequently, incapable of being defended. The national government had done nothing in five years to repair the spoliations and ruin of the invaders, although it had [at its disposal] fifteen million dollars in cash from the so-called indemnity. The other fortifications were no better. There was neither army nor navy, nor any depository. The guns in very small number were old and flint-locked. The frontier at all points of its vast extent was abandoned. Nor was there credit to procure supplies. In total, we had nothing with which to oppose the invaders arrogantly appearing along the frontier but the sad spectacle of our exceeding weakness. Under these circumstances, discretion and true patriotism imperatively counseled not to put aside the only means which would save all,—an immediate arrangement with the Minister Plenipotentiary of the United States recently presented at the capital with this object in view.

The Minister, Mr. Gadsden, in several conferences, said in substance: *that the land comprehended within the boundary marked by their engineers was absolutely necessary to the United States for the construction of a railway to Alta California which would assure them an easy and rapid communication with this state, and, therefore, he would be pleased if Mexico would cede peaceably and for a good indemnity that which possibly did belong to her; for in the end that imperious necessity would compel them to occupy it in one way or another.* Once he made me proposals regarding Baja California, and part of Chihuahua and of Sonora, presenting a draft which showed the line that might be traced. This I rejected immediately, limiting myself to the question of boundaries. From these statements of the minister I understood that the United States was not even satisfied with possessing half of the Mexican territory.

In order to proceed with better knowledge and more accuracy in the business which occupied us, a report was requested from the engineer of the republic who knew the region from experience, which being presented was substantially as follows: "with the exception of the not very extensive valley of Mesilla, the rest [of the territory in question] was rocky mountains inhabited by Apaches, who, according to their custom, made war continually upon the adjacent departments."

After examining and considering everything in the junta of ministers, the principle was adopted that, of the evils, it was prudent and rational to prefer the least. Accordingly, the propositions of Mr. Gadsden relative to the territory in question were accepted with the remuneration of twenty million dollars which the government of the United States was to give to that of Mexico.

It is true that there was included in the treaty the annulment of an article of the treaty of Guadalupe Hidalgo by which the United States was bound to pursue the savages who were ravaging our frontier. But I never believed any criticism would fall upon my government on account of a proceeding which the honor and welfare of the nation counseled. This article, as all know, was put in by the Provisional Government of Querétaro in order that there might not appear only THE HORRIBLE SACRIFICE OF HALF OF THE TERRITORY OF THE REPUBLIC FOR FIFTEEN MILLION DOLLARS, but also something which might mislead, and which could be interpreted by some as favorable to Mexico. For my part, I declare that from the time I learned of its contents, then in a foreign country, I understood perfectly that, along with the sacrifice, there was the farce and the humiliation, besides other consequences fatal to the country. The farce, because that article would not be fulfilled by the United States, as it was not [observed] a single time from the years 1847 to 1853, neither would it ever be, because they have no interest in the protection of our frontier, nor have we forces to hold them to the agreement. Humiliating, because we were begging from a foreign government a service which belonged exclusively to the nation; more humiliating still, because the one which was to perform the duty is the worst enemy of the Mexican government which it has offended and despoiled. [It would have] evil consequences on account of the very fact that the troops of the United States would be able to enter our territory when they desired; because of the introduction of contraband which would injure commerce and the treasury; and by reason of the hot-bed of questions to which the abuse that would be made of such an ominous article would give place,—in all of which Mexico, as usual, would receive the worst of the bargain.

Other factors of no little weight which, when taken into consideration, moved us to accept the proposition of Mr. Gadsden, were the condition of the public treasury until the reforms and retrenchments which were introduced should have their effect, the immediate defence of our national integrity, the demands of foreign creditors, the reorganization of the army which the revolution in the south was likewise demanding, and the urgent and unavoidable expenses of the administration. And, notwithstanding my deep conviction of the fact that the expedient adopted was the only one, absolutely the only one which could have saved the critical situation, I refused for a time to agree to the treaty, and gave a special dissenting opinion to the Minister of Relations by whom I hope it will be brought to light, in order that I may be better judged as to the sentiments which I entertained. My spirit was saddened by contemplating the abuse which was being made of our weakness, yet, of our weakness brought about by fratricidal strife. My heart, my sentiments, my character, and, above all, my love of country were going to be sacrificed by those lines which were traced for us and which I could not agree to without emotion. I should have preferred to reply to them, as at other times, with my sword. Would to heaven that my sufferings on account of this thing might be well understood, so as to merit compassion at least! I declare upon my honor that this was one of the great sacrifices which I have consecrated to the welfare of my country.

The Senate at Washington did not consider the treaty of Mr. Gadsden advantageous, and came near disapproving it unanimously, which is an indication that something more was to be solicited from us. [This body finally] approved it after a long discussion, subtracting five from the twenty millions, and at the same time limiting the territory.

Document B

When in April, 1853, I took charge of the government of the republic, the political and financial horizon presented an unpleasant aspect. On the northern frontier our neighbors were threatening another invasion, if the question of boundaries was not arranged to their satisfaction; the savages and robber bands were freely carrying on their depredations; the army was destroyed, and the respectable military class prostrated; the parties were engaged in a stubborn fight and chaos was the only prospect.

The governments of Herrera and Arista had neglected the important branch of finance when they relied upon the fifteen million dollars from the dishonorable and injurious treaty of Guadalupe Hidalgo, as well as the settlement of the boundary which the security of the new frontier was urgently demanding.

The question of boundary was grave and demanded my attention preeminently. The government at Washington, with knife in hand, was still trying to cut another piece from the body which it had just horribly mutilated, and threatening another invasion. In the deplorable situation of the country, it seemed to me that a break with the colossus would be a foolish act; and I adopted the course which patriotism and prudence counseled,—a pacific settlement.

The Mexican engineers employed in marking the boundary had suspended their work because the disagreement grew threatening. An American division was already treading the soil of the state of Chihuahua, and the Comandante General was asking for orders and reinforcements. At this juncture, the Washington government sent to our capital Mr. Gadsden as Minister Extraordinary with ample powers to settle the question in a final manner.

The timely appearance of this envoy furnished an opportunity for the beginning of a negotiation not without notable occurrences.

In the first conference, the Minister of Foreign Affairs being present, the envoy extraordinary from Washington presented a map upon which appeared a new line retaining for the United States, Baja California, Sonora, Sinaloa, part of Durango and Chihuahua,—another half of the territory which they had left us. Vexed with such pretensions, I refused to look at the map, saying, "this is not the matter which ought to occupy our attention." The minister withdrew the map and courteously offered not to present it again.

In the second conference the envoy presented another map on which the Valley of Mesilla figured as belonging to the United States; and this being the crux of the matter, upon it the discussion was centered. I upheld the well-founded contentions of the Mexican engineers which amounted to this: without violating the treaty of Guadalupe Hidalgo, the Valley of Mesilla can not belong to the United States, since the line of division between the two republics is well marked and the Mexican republic has religiously fulfilled the pact.

In the next conference the Valley of Mesilla was the subject of discussion. The envoy extraordinary, impatient with the opposition which his pretension was encountering, let fall these exact words: "So far as my government is concerned, it cannot make any concession in regard to the matter which occupies us, the railway projected from New York to Alta California must proceed through Mesilla, because there is no other practicable route; the consent of the Mexican government would be splendidly rewarded."

In another session the envoy stood by his definitive resolution; but upon hearing me remark that the affair demanded contemplation, he completely lost control of himself and said emphatically: "Gentlemen, it is now time to recognize that the Valley of Mesilla in question must belong to the United States [either] for a stipulated indemnity, or because we shall take it." Such provocation naturally aroused my ire, but I was able to control myself and to hide it cleverly by dissimulation: mindful of the condition of the country, the head ruled the heart in such moments. And as if I had heard nothing, feigning distraction, I said to the envoy: "Mr. Gadsden, I hear you repeating *splendid indemnity,* and I have a curiosity to know how much it will amount to. I suppose it will not be so paltry as that offered for half of the Mexican territory." Surprised at my manner and language, he was unable to reply [for a moment, but at length] he answered thoughtfully and with stammering words: "Yes, a splendid indemnity," and the dialogue continued as follows:

"I plainly see that you are inclined to the negotiation and in conformity with my way of thinking; this pleases me, because thus we avoid the scandal of seeing two neighboring and sister republics in discord at every step and presenting horrifying scenes of blood."

The envoy with apparent joy asked the government what value it placed upon the territory of Mesilla.

"You shall soon know; in cash I value it at fifty million pesos."

Mr. Gadsden sprang from his seat and, astonished, exclaimed, "Oh! fifty million pesos is a great deal of money!"

"My dear Sir, when a powerful nation has interest in the possession of another, it pays well."

"To-morrow I shall answer," and he left.

On the following day the envoy explained himself thus: "Convinced of the interest of my government in the early settlement of the matter which occupies us, I have determined to use the ample power with which it has invested me, and in its name, I propose that the treasury of the United States shall pay to the government of Mexico at the conclusion of the question of the Valley of Mesilla, twenty million pesos on these terms: upon approval of the treaty, ten million pesos, and the other ten at the end of a year."

The proposition exceeded by far what I had expected and I did not offer any objection: the trade was made. The Minister of Foreign Affairs, Don Manuel María Bonilla, was charged with the duty of arranging the terms of the treaty in agreement with the envoy; concluded, it was examined and approved in a meeting of the cabinet.

In Washington twenty million pesos appeared a high price for the Valley of Mesilla. A senator said, "Mr. Gadsden lost his head, I am acquainted with the territory in question and am able to assure you impartially that it is not worth one-fourth of the stipulated sum." After much debate the Senate approved the treaty, after having subtracted ten million from the price agreed upon and something from the territory purchased.

My government, upon again considering the boundary treaty, reasoning with regard to the reduction made by the Senate at Washington, recognized that if it was impolitic to refuse their consent, there remained the satisfaction of having obtained for a piece of wild country relatively what they [the United States] gave for half of the national territory.

NEWS ITEMS

In the *Galveston News* of October 31, 1920, appeared an excellent biographical sketch of Colonel Edward B. Cushing, by Mr. Hamp Cook.

The organization of the Texas State Teachers' Association at Austin, January 28, 1879, and the connection of this movement with the founding of Sam Houston Normal Institute and of the University of Texas are traced by Mr. R. C. Crane in an article published in the *Dallas News* of December 5, 1920.

The heroic portrait of Sam Houston, painted by Stephen Seymour Thomas, was formally presented to the city of Houston, at the University Club, on January 5, 1921. The *Post* of January 6 published an account of the proceedings and pictures of Mr. Thomas and of the painting. The painting is a gift from the artist.

With the issue of July 15, 1920, the *Breeder's Gazette* began the publication of "A Ranchman's Recollections," dealing with the origin of the cattle industry in the Southwest and of the American packing industry, written by Frank S. Hastings, manager of the S. M. S. Ranch.

Mrs. J. C. Terrell died October 16, 1920. She was deeply interested in the library movement of Texas, and for several years was chairman of the State Library and Historical Commission.

Walter Gresham, of Galveston, died in Washington, D. C., November 6, 1920. For forty years Mr. Gresham was a member of Galveston's deep water committee, and represented that city in the efforts to improve the port.

Major George W. Littlefield, capitalist and philanthropist, died at his home in Austin, November 10, 1920. Major Littlefield was a life member of the Texas State Historical Association. In his will he added $100,000 to his earlier gift of $25,000 to endow a Southern History Fund in the University of Texas.

George W. Brackenridge, wealthy banker and philanthropist, died at his home in San Antonio, December 28, 1920. Mr. Brackenridge was a life member of the Texas State Historical Association.

AFFAIRS OF THE ASSOCIATION

In November, 1920, the President of the Association and the editors of THE QUARTERLY found it necessary to send out the following letter:

In 1918 THE QUARTERLY, containing 108 pages, cost approximately $200 an issue to print. During 1919-20 *eighty pages* cost about $275. Hereafter eighty pages will cost nearly $350 an issue. Most of this increase is chargeable to labor. We have examined the cost sheets of our printers and their charges are reasonable.

There are two things that THE QUARTERLY can do: one is to reduce each issue to sixty pages; the other is to ask subscribers to increase their subscription to $3.00 a year. We have decided to do the latter. About a year ago when the first considerable increase in the cost of printing was made, we debated this step very seriously, but determined to struggle along as best we could at the old price. Now we are forced to act.

THE QUARTERLY has been published for twenty-four years. It is regarded by historians and others whose work requires acquaintance with many periodicals as one of the leading half dozen historical journals in the United States. Through its influence during the past fifteen years, the history of the United States has practically been rewritten at every point where it touches Texas. Won't you help us to maintain the present usefulness and prestige of THE QUARTERLY by agreeing to increase your subscription to $3.00 a year? Every other historical journal in the country, not supported by ample endowment or by State grants, has had to increase its rate.

All the income of the Historical Association goes into the publication of THE QUARTERLY, except a small amount for postage and about $250 to $300 a year for clerical help. No officer receives any salary, commission, or other emolument.

We are enclosing herewith a printed slip which we ask you to sign and return to us in the stamped envelope. Since a busy person frequently neglects to reply to an appeal of this kind, though in full sympathy with it, *we shall regard a failure to reply as an affirmative answer.*

We are gratified to announce that several hundred replies received recognize the inevitableness of the increase and cordially accept it. Less than a dozen opposed it.

Meeting of the Association.—The annual business meeting of the Texas State Historical Association will be held in room 158 of the Main Muilding of the Universitv of Texas, Thursday, April 21, 1921, at 10:30 a. m. This meeting will be preceded by a meeting of the Executive Council at 10 o'clock.

THE
SOUTHWESTERN HISTORICAL
QUARTERLY

VOL. XXIV APRIL, 1921 No. 4

The publication committee and the editors disclaim responsibility for views expressed by contributors to THE QUARTERLY

DONELSON'S MISSION TO TEXAS IN BEHALF OF ANNEXATION*

ANNIE MIDDLETON

I. INTRODUCTORY

1. *Recognition of Texan Independence by the United States*

In the fall of 1835 Texas found herself at war with Mexico. This began as an effort on the part of the Texans to restore the "republican principles" of government overthrown by Santa Anna, but it soon became a struggle for independence. Although the Texans held a consultation at San Felipe in November and organized a provisional government, they remained at least nominally faithful to Mexico until the convention met at Washington, Texas, March 1, 1836. This convention declared the independence of Texas, drew up a constitution, and organized a permanent government. Pending the adoption of the constitution and the election of officers for the new government, the convention created a government *ad interim*.

In December, 1835, Governor Smith had directed Branch T. Arthur, Stephen F. Austin, and William H. Wharton, the commissioners to the United States, to ascertain whether the United States would immediately recognize the independence of Texas if she declared her independence; so, after the March convention

*This is a study of the final stage of the annexation movement from the Texan side. Little remains to be said concerning the international phases of this question, but the local aspect of the movement needed examination. This paper and the one to follow on the Texan convention of 1845 were accepted as the thesis for the Master of Arts degree by the Graduate Council of the University of Texas in June, 1920.

had declared independence and organized a government *ad interim,* it was natural to suppose that the government would push the question of recognition with energy. On March 19, David G. Burnet, president of the government *ad interim,* appointed George Childress and Robert Hamilton as agents to the United States to open negotiations for "a recognition of the Sovereignty and Independence of Texas."[1] However, he recalled them, and appointed James Collinsworth and Peter W. Grayson as commissioners to the United States to solicit the recognition of the independence of Texas by the United States and the annexation of Texas to the United States. Since they did not arrive in Washington until July 8, Congress had adjourned, and President Jackson was on the point of leaving for his home at Nashville, Tennessee, Collinsworth went on to Nashville, to converse more at length with President Jackson. Grayson remained in Washington, hoping to open official communication with the authorities there. However, when he presented his credentials, he found that President Burnet had issued them without the seal of state or even his own private seal; so, accordingly, before anything could be accomplished, it was necessary to secure new credentials. He immediately wrote President Burnet asking that new credentials be forwarded him without delay, but no attention was paid to his request. However, he remained at Washington until November. At this time he received a letter from President Burnet announcing that the September elections had been held, and that the new government would doubtless appoint at an early date commissioners to Washington.[2] Therefore, when the commission of Collinsworth and Grayson expired with that of the provisional government, October 22, 1836, the status of the question of recognition was as yet practically untouched so far as any effort on the part of the Texas agents was concerned.

At the general election in September, General Houston was chosen president, and M. B. Lamar, vice-president; and Houston appointed Henry Smith, secretary of the treasury, and Stephen F. Austin, secretary of state. After the government was organized,

[1]Burnet to Childress, March 19, 1836. Garrison, *Diplomatic Correspondence of the Republic of Texas*, I, 73-74, in Am. Hist. Assn. *Report*, 1907, II.

[2]Burnet to Grayson, September 12, 1836. Garrison, *Diplomatic Correspondence of the Republic of Texas*, I, 123, in Am. Hist. Assn. *Report*, 1907, II.

President Houston appointed Wm. H. Wharton minister to the United States "to enter into negotiations and treaties with the United States government for the recognition of the independence of Texas."[3] On December 21, 1836, just three days after Wharton reached Washington, President Jackson in his message to Congress advised delay in the recognition of Texas independence. However, on January 11, 1837, R. J. Walker offered a resolution that "the independent political existence of said state be acknowledged by the Government of the United States."[4] On March 1, 1837, the Senate, by a vote of twenty-three to nineteen, passed this resolution, and two days later President Jackson appointed Alcée La Branche of Louisiana chargé d'affaires to the Republic of Texas.

2. *Offer of Annexation by Texas*

In November, 1836, President Houston had instructed Wharton to make an effort in behalf of annexation, but as John Forsyth, Secretary of State of the United States, thought that annexation should be the work of a northern president, nothing beyond recognition was gained during President Jackson's administration. Van Buren became president in March, 1837; however, Texas made no effort to secure annexation until August. Then Memucan Hunt, the Texan minister at Washington, in accordance with the instructions of his government, presented to Secretary Forsyth a formal proposition for the annexation of Texas. Nevertheless, because of the "furious opposition of the free States" and the fear of involving the country in a war that would be branded as an unjust war by enemies at home and abroad, President Van Buren would not promise assent to this proposal. The offer remained open until President Houston directed its withdrawal in October, 1838; and from that time the Texans put new energy into the effort to secure recognition in Europe. M. B. Lamar became president of Texas in December, 1838, and in his inaugural address he declared strongly against annexation, and an almost unanimous vote of Congress sustained him.

[3]Austin to Wharton, November 18, 1836. Garrison, *Diplomatic Correspondence of the Republic of Texas*, I. 127.

[4]Wharton to Austin, January 15, 1837. Garrison, *Diplomatic Correspondence of the Republic of Texas*, I, 176.

3. *Negotiation of the Annexation Treaty*

Despite the repulse of Texas in her desire for annexation, she was the first to return to the subject. In March, 1842, President Houston, who began his second term as president of Texas in December, 1841, instructed Isaac Van Zandt, the chargé d'affaires from Texas to the United States, to study the sentiment of Congress and the people relative to annexation and to keep his government advised. The United States continued to be indifferent until a truce between Texas and Mexico was secured in the summer of 1843 by the efforts of the British and French ministers in Mexico. Thereupon, Anson Jones, Texan Secretary of State, instructed Van Zandt to make a formal statement to the authorities at Washington "that the subject of annexation was not open to discussion."[5] In the words of Jones, "This aroused all the dormant jealousies and fears of that government, the apathy of seven years' sleep over the question was shaken off, and a treaty of annexation was proposed to be celebrated."[6]

The uneasiness thus awakened at Washington was much increased by reports that the British were using their influence in Texas to abolish slavery. As these reports continued to reach Washington, President Tyler and A. P. Upshur, the United States Secretary of State, came to the conclusion that British influence was working strongly in Texas, and that the one aim of Great Britain was to secure the abolition of slavery in that republic. Therefore, they decided to forestall such an event by concluding a treaty of annexation. The negotiations, so far as they are on record, began October 16, 1843, with a letter from Upshur to Van Zandt offering to reopen the subject. Van Zandt sent to Texas for instructions, but President Houston assumed an attitude of indifference and caution, as he thought the chances for the ratification of the treaty by the United States Senate were not favorable, and, if it should fail, the alienation of England would leave Texas in an awkward position. Therefore, he demanded that the United States should place troops near the Texas border during the time of the negotiations, and that the United States should guarantee the independence of Texas, if the treaty should fail. W. S. Murphy, the United States chargé to Texas, assented

[5]Jones to Van Zandt. July 6, 1843. *Diplomatic Correspondence of Texas*, MS. Texas State Library.

[6]Jones, *Letters Relating to the History of Annexation*, 8.

to the first condition, but not to the second. Nevertheless, President Houston appointed J. P. Henderson to co-operate with Van Zandt in the negotiation of the proposed treaty. Upshur had been killed by accident on February 28, and President Tyler had appointed John C. Calhoun to succeed him; so, it was with him that the Texan chargés negotiated the treaty. On April 22, President Tyler sent the treaty to the Senate for ratification. Although he urged its adoption in the message accompanying the treaty, it was rejected, June 8, 1844, by a vote of thirty-five to sixteen. The opposition contended that the annexation of Texas would favor the extension and perpetuation of slavery, and that Mexico would consider such a step as a just cause for war.

In the meantime Henry Clay and Martin Van Buren had come out against annexation; the Whig and Democratic conventions had been held; Henry Clay had been nominated for the presidency by the Whigs and James K. Polk by the Democrats; and the annexation question had been made a plank in the Democratic platform.

II. Donelson in Texas

1. *Donelson's Instructions*

Just a few days after the Senate rejected the treaty of annexation, it refused to confirm the appointment of W. S. Murphy, who had been acting as representative to Texas by the president's appointment. Thereupon, President Tyler appointed T. A. Howard, a personal friend of Houston and Jackson, to take his place. The Senate confirmed this appointment, June 12, 1844, and Secretary Calhoun promptly issued his instructions. In these Calhoun said: "The recent rejection of the Treaty of annexation by the Senate of the United States has placed the relation between the United States and Texas in a very delicate and hazardous state, and the great object of your mission is to prevent, by every means in your power, the dangerous consequences to which it may lead. As your initial step, satisfy the Texan government that the loss of the Treaty does not necessarily involve the failure of the great object which it contemplated. It is now admitted that what was sought to be effected by the Treaty submitted to the Senate, may be secured by a joint resolution of the two houses of Congress incorporating all its provisions, and this will require only a majority in each house." Calhoun went on to say that just two days after the Senate rejected the annexation treaty, President Tyler had referred it to the House for consideration. A motion was made to lay the President's message and the documents accompanying the treaty upon the table, but this motion was defeated by a majority of fifty-three votes; and a motion to suspend the rules with a view to printing fifteen thousand copies of these papers was carried by a vote of one hundred and eight to seventy-nine. The sentiment of the people was even more satisfactory, and it was constantly growing better; and it was believed that after meeting their constituents, particularly in the South and West, a sufficient number of Congressmen would change to insure passage of a joint resolution.

Calhoun added that it could not be supposed that the government and the people of Texas would abandon the idea of annexation as long as their was any reasonable hope of success, for that "would imply that they are not only insensible to the feelings and sympathy which belong to a common origin, but blind to their own safety and prosperity. The danger is that the revolution of disappointed hopes, highly excited, may be seized upon by an interested and wily diplomacy, and made the means of seducing them" into forming an alliance with England, which would eventually be disastrous to the United States, to Texas, and to the American continent as well, and "the result, in the end, must be abject submission on the part of Texas." The defeat of the treaty was due to "temporary causes," concluded Calhoun, and the policy of annexation had "taken such deep and general hold upon the public mind that it must ultimately triumph, should it not be abandoned by the Government and People of Texas."[1]

Unfortunately Howard was not permitted to carry out these instructions, as he died after a residence in Texas of only thirteen days. President Tyler received the news of his death, September 16, and immediately appointed Andrew Jackson Donelson,[2] the

[1]Calhoun to Howard, June 18, 1844. Smith, *The Annexation of Texas*, 361-362.

[2]Andrew Jackson Donelson (1800-1871) was educated at the United States Military Academy, and graduated from that institution in 1820. He then served for two years as aide-de-camp to General Andrew Jackson. After resigning from the army he attended Lexington College, and was admitted to the bar in 1823. On Jackson's election to the presidency he became his confidential adviser and private secretary, continuing to serve until the close of his second administration. The annexation treaty between the United States and Texas having been rejected by the Sen-

nephew and former private secretary of Jackson, in his place. On the next day he sent a special messenger to Donelson with the following letter:

The state of things is such as to require that the place of Chargé d'Affaires of the United States to Texas be filled without delay and to select him, who, under all circumstances, may be thought best calculated to bring to successful decision the great question of annexation now pending before the two countries. After full deliberation you have been selected as that individual, and I do hope, my dear Sir, that you will not decline the appointment, however great may be the personal sacrifice of accepting.

That great question must be settled in the next three or four months, and whether it will be decided favorably or not may depend upon him who may fill the mission now tendered to you. Indeed I cannot tell you how much depends upon its decision for weal or woe for our country and perhaps to the whole continent. It is sufficient to say, viewed in all its consequences, it is of the very first magnitude, and it gives to the mission, at this time an importance that raises it to the level with the highest in the gift of the Government.

Assuming, therefore, that you will not decline the appointment, unless some insuperable difficulty should interpose, and in order to avoid delay, a commission is herewith transmitted to you, without the formality of waiting your acceptance and the necessary papers.[3]

Donelson accepted this appointment upon the urgent solicitation of the government and his political friends, but at a great sacrifice of his private interests. *Niles' National Register* (Baltimore), October 26, 1844, congratulated the administration upon having been able to secure the services of one so "eminently qualified in all respects for the station, whose knowledge of the relations then subsisting between the two countries, and his intimate acquaintance with the statesmen of both this and that country places him in the enjoyment of advantages which cannot fail to secure the most desirable results."

ate in April, 1844, Donelson was asked to undertake new negotiations, and accordingly was appointed in September, 1844, as representative to Texas. He later served as minister to both Germany and Prussia. After Pierce was nominated in 1859, he quit the Democratic party and joined the American party. He was nominated for vice-president in 1850, but was defeated in the election which followed. He then retired to private life and spent the rest of his time on his vast estate. Appleton, *Cyclopaedia of American Biography*, II, 99.

[3]Calhoun to Donelson, September 17, 1844. *House Exec. Doc.*, 28th Cong., 2 Sess., I, 36; *Senate Doc.*, 28th Cong., 2 Sess., I, 36.

With no flattering prospects of success, Donelson entered upon the work of Howard, in the execution of which he was to follow out Howard's instructions. Howard had written Calhoun, August 6, that Texas desired aid to repel an anticipated Mexican invasion, since Mexico had been induced to her course by the "negotiations pending between Texas and the United States on the subject of annexation." Upon receiving this message, Calhoun had sent Howard a dispatch, instructing him "to assure the government of Texas that President Tyler feels the full force of the obligations of this government to protect Texas, pending the question of annexation, against the attacks which Mexico may make on her in consequence of her acceptance of the proposition of this government to open negotiations on the subject of annexation to the United States." Moreover, "as far as it relates to the executive department, he is prepared to use all its power for that purpose." In conclusion Calhoun had said that President Tyler would urge Congress to adopt measures to protect Texas effectually against the attacks of Mexico, pending the question of annexation. As this dispatch was not delivered to Howard, a copy of it was sent to Donelson, who was to consider it as a part of his instructions.[4]

After Calhoun had sent this dispatch to Howard, Major Butler, the United States agent for the Cherokee Indians, informed him that Mexican agents were being employed to arouse the Indian tribes on the southwestern frontier of the United States to acts of hostility against the citizens both of the United States and of Texas. Since this was a direct violation of the treaty of amity entered into between the United States and Mexico, May 5, 1831, President Tyler instructed and authorized Donelson to maintain peace and harmony among the border Indians, and to "restrain by force all incursions and hostilities of the Indians living within the United States."

Accordingly, the adjutant general issued orders to the officers in command of the forces at Forts Jesup, Towson, and Washita to comply with any requisition made by Donelson.[5]

[4]Calhoun to Howard, September 10, 1844. *Niles' National Register* (Baltimore), LXVII, 234; 28th Cong., 2 Sess., *Senate Doc.* No. 1, p. 38; *Ibid., House Exec. Doc.* No. 2, p. 50.

[5]Calhoun to Donelson, September 17, 1844. *Niles' National Register* (Baltimore), LXVII, 234; 28th Cong., 2 Sess., *Senate Doc.* No. 1, p. 36; *Ibid., House Exec., Doc.* No. 2, p. 36.

2. *Donelson's First Work in Texas*

Within a month after his appointment, Donelson left home for New Orleans; on November 6, 1844, he sailed for Texas, and was thereafter busy, except for a visit to the United States in December, with the difficult task of keeping track of the diplomatic activities of the Republic of Texas, especially in its relations with Great Britain, France, and Mexico.

On arriving in Texas, Donelson met with little encouragement. He heard much of British and French influence, which every day seemed to increase. President Houston had appointed G. W. Terrell, a well known advocate of independence, as minister to France and England, and Donelson feared that this was an indication of a change in Texas policy.[6] The armistice entered into between Texas and Mexico, June 15, 1843, had expired, and Jones had received reports from Mexico that 15,000 Mexican soldiers would arrive at Matamoras in November. This situation was the more alarming, as there was little doubt that England endorsed the proposed campaign, preferring that Texas be Mexican rather than American. On September 10, Calhoun instructed Wilson Shannon, the United States minister in Mexico, to "protest in the most solemn form against both the invasion at this time and the barbarous and bloody manner in which it is proposed to be conducted." Furthermore, he was instructed to accompany the protest with "a declaration that the President cannot regard them with indifference, but as highly offensive to the United States."[7] During an interview with Houston on November 24, Donelson showed him a copy of these instructions. Houston, nevertheless, complained that Henderson and Van Zandt should not have signed the treaty without fuller pledges of protection. Donelson, thereupon, assured him that the President felt the full force of his obligation, and that he would use all his constitutional power to protect Texas, but, since the co-operation of Congress was essential to effect annexation, any disagreement between the executive and Congress would delay matters. Donelson believed that the remedy in such a case was an appeal to the people. That appeal

[6]Donelson to Calhoun, November 18, 1844. Jameson, *Correspondence of John C. Calhoun*, 996.

[7]Calhoun to Shannon, September 10, 1844. *Niles' National Register*, LXVII, 232-233; Crallé, *Reports and Public Letters of John C. Calhoun*, V, 364-373.

had been made, and the election of Polk would be a national endorsement of Tyler's policy. Since Donelson had not received his credentials, he could not present the views of his government, but he gave Houston the assurance that they were so reasonable and just that they would command his respect. Thereupon, Houston professed that he would be glad to see annexation accomplished during his administration, and that he would adhere to this policy as long as there was a hope of effecting it on terms of honor and justice to his country.[8]

Although the American presidential campaign had revived the hopes of the people of Texas, Donelson still considered the situation critical; for, after talking with many prominent citizens, he became convinced that Texas, without giving up slavery, could obtain recognition from Mexico through British mediation. If, in addition to this, England and France offered unrestricted trade and the American Congress failed to act promptly, a satisfactory result could hardly be expected. His aim, therefore, was to hold the Texan government in a state of willingness until the United States could offer a practical invitation. Donelson emphasized the necessity for haste on the part of Congress, lest Mexico should recognize the independence of Texas before the United States could offer annexation. In his letter to Calhoun, November 23, he said, "Every day's delay is adding strength to the hands of those who are playing the game for the ascendancy of the British influence in the Republic. Delay will increase the difficulties already in our way, if it does not make them insurmountable."[9]

As Donelson delivered his letters of credence to Anson Jones, November 29, he was promptly presented in his official capacity to President Houston. On each of these occasions, complimentary speeches were exchanged. The following sentence illustrates the non-committal attitude of Jones. Donelson had assured him of "the sincere desire of the president of the United States to improve and render stable the good understanding between the two Republics." In reply Jones said, "The sameness of origin and interests of the two countries to which you have so kindly alluded has led the people of this on all occasions to desire the maintenance of the most friendly relations; and if the hope which they

[8]Donelson to Calhoun, November 24, 1844. Report by A. C. McLaughlin on the Diplomatic Archives of the Department of State, 69-73.

[9]Donelson to Calhoun, November 23, 1844. Quoted by Reeves, *American Diplomacy under Tyler and Polk*, 181.

have sometimes indulged, that these considerations might lead to the accomplishment of a common destiny, should be disappointed, I trust they will not be lost in their influence upon either country, in the preservation of those principles which they hold in common keeping." Despite Jones's attitude, Houston in his reply to Donelson's address expressed the sentiment of a majority of the people when he said, "Hitherto, my countrymen have been ready and willing to unite their destinies for weal or woe with those of the people of your own great land. Actuated by the noblest and most honorable feelings and motives, they have sent their ministers to the very door of your Senate house, and have asked for admission more than once. They have done all they could do; and the failure which has occurred is, I assure you, Sir, attributable to no want on their part of the most earnest disposition to see the desired union speedily and fully accomplished."[10]

In his valedictory message to Congress, December 2, Houston, nevertheless, did not give utterance to the annexation views with which he had raised Donelson's hopes. He said, "The attitude of Texas now, in my apprehension, is one of peculiar interest. The United States has spurned her twice already. Let her, therefore, maintain her position firmly as it is and work out her own political salvation." He also dwelt at length upon the splendid prospects of Texas if she "persevered in separate independence," upon the "manifest coolness of the United States," and upon the "friendly attitude of the European nations."[11] In his letter to Jackson a few days later, however, his attitude was somewhat more conciliatory. He said that in his opinion Texas should maintain her present position, and should "act aside from every consideration but that of her nationality," though "if the United States should open the door wide, it might be well for her to accept the invitation."[12]

Although President Houston thus made known his opinion in regard to annexation, President Jones, both in his inaugural address of December 9, and in his message to Congress, remained non-committal. Jones, however, a few days later made a definite advance toward England, when he advised Congress to estab-

[10]*Texas National Register* (Washington), December 14, 1844.

[11]*Texas National Register*, December 14, 1844; *House Journal*, 9th Texas Cong., 10-16.

[12]Houston to Jackson, December 13, 1844. Yoakum, *History of Texas*, II, 433.

lish free trade arrangements with any country that would abolish its tolls on the chief products of Texas.[13] Ebenezer Allen, the Secretary of State, was strongly in favor of independence. Some two months before in a letter to William Kennedy, the British consul at Galveston, he had said, "You are well aware of the fact that I have from the beginning been decidedly opposed to the Annexation of Texas to the United States. It is my first object to defeat, if possible, the consummation of this most obnoxious measure, so decidedly hostile, as I conceive it to be, and fraught with such evil consequences to the ultimate prosperity and high destiny of this Country. If I am successful in the accomplishment of this great result, I shall consider it the proudest period of my life."[14]

Although Donelson knew that Allen opposed annexation, he promptly presented his credentials, and the correspondence between Shannon and the Mexican government pertaining to the renewal of war upon Texas by Mexico. Donelson assured Allen that President Tyler had omitted nothing within his constitutional power to "guard the interests of Texas from injury," and that since the recent election of Polk had shown the strength of the annexationists, in no event could Mexico induce the United States to abandon annexation, for it was of "mutual, equal, and vital benefit and safety to both Republics."[15] However, he added, that while the states of the union were exposing themselves to Mexican hostilities by their faithfulness to Texas, the executive would expect Texas to "maintain her connection with the cause of annexation, so far at least as not to consider it lost or abandoned, on account of the late action of the Senate." In reply to this, President Jones instructed Allen to give assurance to Donelson that the existing relations between the Republics, so far as the subject of annexation was concerned, would not be affected by any opposing or unfavorable action on the part of the executive, but that the result might depend upon causes over which he could

[13] *Senate Journal*, 9th Texas Cong., 34; *House Journal*, 9th Texas Cong. 26-30.

[14] Kennedy to Aberdeen September 9, 1844. Adams, *British Correspondence Concerning Texas*, 363.

[15] Donelson to Allen, December 10, 1844. *Senate Journal*, 9th Texas Cong., 191-195.

exercise no control, as the "strength and ardor" in favor of the measure had been decreased by its delay and apparent defeat.[16]

Confiding in Allen's promise that nothing unfavorable to the cause of annexation would be done by the executive, Donelson left Galveston for the United States, December 24, 1844. On the same day, Captain Charles Elliot, the British chargé, wrote Aberdeen, the British secretary for foreign affairs, that Donelson had exercised a great influence upon the people of Texas, that he had exerted strenuous efforts to keep them from agreeing upon any settlement offered by the British and the French, but that he had tried more to break up any other agreement than to bring about annexation.[17]

When Donelson, upon arriving at New Orleans, was informed that Calhoun had sent him a dispatch on a new steamer, the *McKim,* which was making an experimental trip to Galveston, he felt obliged to return immediately to Galveston. However, before leaving New Orleans, he wrote Calhoun:

> Let us get annexation on any terms we can, taking care not to have anything in form or substance that would render doubtful its ratification by Texas. The battle about slavery, boundary east of the Nuesos, and the number of states, will come up in the Constitution to be hereafter formed by the people of Texas, when there will be no danger of loss of the Territory from British intrigue or other causes.
>
> If you are not able to carry annexation by the vote of the present Congress, I shall despair of the cause, not seeing a certainty of much increase of the strength in the next Congress unless it can be secured by a judicious arrangement of the Cabinet. This should be paramount with Mr. Polk who must of course feel himself instructed to omit nothing that can secure immediate annexation.
>
> Referring to the recent elections in the United States, I have said to Texas that the measure was destined to a speedy consummation, and she has said in reply that she would throw no impediment in the way. This gives us the benefit of a trial in Polk's administration, and is so understood by Texas, but I endeavored to give the phraseology such a turn as to convey the idea also that I relied on the present Congress. It seemed to me that I ought

[16]Allen to Donelson, December 13, 1844. *Senate Journal,* 9th Texas Cong., 195.

[17]Elliot to Aberdeen, December 31. 1844. Adams, *British Correspondence Concerning Texas,* 291.

to risk something to secure the measure to Mr. Tyler's administration.[18]

When the United States Congress met in December, 1844, a contest immediately arose over annexation, as George McDuffie introduced a joint resolution which embodied the provisions of the rejected treaty; namely, that Texas should be annexed as a territory, that her citizens should be "incorporated into the Union," that she should be admitted as a state as soon as was consistent with the principles of the federal constitution, that Texas should surrender her public lands, and that the United States should assume the Texan indebtedness to an amount not exceeding ten million dollars.[19] Since Benton of Missouri objected to the terms of this resolution, he introduced a bill on the following day, the substance of which was that the boundaries of Texas should not include the territory in dispute, that slavery should be prohibited in about half of the territory, and that the assent of Mexico should be obtained. Donelson knew that the Texans would never accept these terms, and wrote Benton while he was at New Orleans exhorting him to modify his course, and not to urge his plan of annexation, which was injuring "his friends and his country," but to accept the measures suggested by Houston. This expostulation doubtless had weight with Benton, for on February 5, he introduced a new bill without any specified terms of annexation.[20]

Duff Green, who had been such a willing instrument for annexation under Upshur, was sent to Galveston in September, 1844, as consul with a further duty as bearer of dispatches to Mexico. During Donelson's absence, Green attempted to have the Texan Congress pass a bill in aid of two land companies, the Texas Land Company and the Del Norte Company. These companies had as objects the conquest and the occupancy in behalf of Texas of the Californias and the northern provinces of Mexico by means of a Texas army aided by Indians introduced from the United States. Green offered stock in these companies to President Jones if he would aid in the scheme. Upon Jones's refusal, Green threatened to revolutionize the country and overthrow the existing gov-

[18]Donelson to Calhoun, December 25, 1844. Jameson, *Correspondence of John C. Calhoun*, 1012.

[19]*Journal of the Senate*, 28th Cong., 1 Sess., I, 10.

[20]Donelson to Calhoun, December 26, 1844. Jameson, *Correspondence of John C. Calhoun*, 1011.

ernment. On December 30, President Jones's cabinet voted that Green be given "a passport out of the limits of the Republic."[21] Thereupon, President Jones revoked Green's *exequatur* by proclamation. Since the President wished to retain the good will of the United States, he instructed Allen to express to Donelson his desire "to preserve and promote the mutual relations of concord and friendship which subsist between the two governments and the harmony which characterizes the intercourse of the two nations."[22] In reply to this letter, Donelson assured Allen that the complaint rested on causes which, "much as they are to be regretted, do not interrupt the friendly relations between the two countries."[23] At the same time Donelson wrote Green and inclosed Allen's letter. In reply Green said, "Nothing was farther from my intention than to offer the slightest disrespect to the President, or to resort to any improper measure to interfere in the conscientious discharge of his public duty."[24] Donelson promptly informed Allen of the voluntary disclaimer on the part of Green, and requested that the personal imputations on his character should be withdrawn, and that friendly relations should be restored.[25] President Jones accepted the disclaimer, and expressed to Donelson an appreciation of his motives, which induced him to become the medium of explanation for Green.[26]

As the Texan Congress, which had been in session since December 2, 1844, decided that, in the event of annexation, the least that could be done, consistently with the administration and preservation of the government would be best, it adjourned February 3, and left the subject in the hands of President Jones. Donelson believing that President Polk would remove all difficulties, and that Congress would adopt a plan of annexation, urged President

[21]Officers of the Government to Jones, December 30, 1844. Jones, *Memoranda and Official Correspondence of the Republic of Texas*, 412.

[22]Allen to Donelson, January 4, 1845. Texan Diplomatic Correspondence, MS. Texas State Library.

[23]Donelson to Allen, January 6, 1845. Texan Diplomatic Correspondence, MS. Texas State Library.

[24]Green to Donelson, January 20, 1845. Texan Diplomatic Correspondence, MS. Texas State Library.

[25]Donelson to Allen, January 20, 1845. Texan Diplomatic Correspondence, MS. Texas State Library.

[26]Allen to Donelson, January 21, 1845. Texan Diplomatic Correspondence, MS. Texas State Library.

Jones to hold himself in readiness to call Congress in a special session.[27]

When Donelson thought that nothing more could be accomplished toward annexation until Congress had taken action, he decided to visit the United States. He was determined, however, that no influence should remain inoperative which might confirm the attachment of the people to annexation. With this purpose in view, he left for publication a letter which he had just received from Jackson.[28]

3. Passage of Joint Resolution by United States Congress

As a basis for the annexation of Texas, President Tyler in his annual message of December, 1844, recommended that Congress adopt the rejected treaty "in the form of a joint resolution, or act, "to be perfected and made binding on the two countries, when adopted in like manner by the government of Texas."[1] Thereupon a contest immediately arose over the form of annexation. Within a week after the session began, C. J. Ingersoll in the House and George McDuffie in the Senate, at the suggestion of President Tyler, introduced the terms of the treaty in the form of a joint resolution. However, because of the strong opposition, especially in the Senate, Congress did not adopt the resolution until February 28, 1845:

> 1. Resolved, by the Senate and House of Representatives of the United States of America in Congress assembled.—That Congress doth consent that the territory properly included within, and rightfully belonging to, the Republic of Texas, may be erected into a new State, to be called the State of Texas, with a republican form of government, to be adopted by the people of the said republic, by deputies in convention assembled, with the consent of the existing government, in order that the same may be admitted as one of the States of this Union.
>
> 2. And be it further resolved,—That the foregoing consent of Congress is given upon the following conditions, and with the following guarantees, to wit:—First, Said State to be formed, subject to the adjustment by this Government of all questions of

[27]Donelson to Jones, January 23, 1845. Jones, *Memoranda and Official Correspondence of the Republic of Texas*, 418.

[28]Donelson to Calhoun, January 27, 1845. Jameson, *Correspondence of John C. Calhoun*, 1021.

[1]Richardson, *Messages and Papers of the Presidents*, IV, 379.

boundary that may arise with other Governments; and the Constitution thereof, with the proper evidence of its adoption by the people of said Republic of Texas, shall be transmitted to the President of the United States, to be laid before Congress for its final action, on or before the first day of January, one thousand eight hundred and forty-six. Second, Said State, when admitted into the Union, after ceding, to the United States all public edifices, fortifications, barracks, ports and harbors, navy and navy yards, docks, magazines, arms, armaments, and all other property and means pertaining to the public defence, belonging to said Republic of Texas, shall retain all the public funds, debts, taxes, and dues of every kind, which may belong to, or be due and owing said republic; and shall also retain all the vacant and unappropriated lands lying within its limits, to be applied to the payment of the debts and liabilities of said Republic of Texas, and the residue of said lands, after discharging said debts and liabilities, to be disposed of as said State may direct; but in no event are said debts and liabilities to become a charge upon the Government of the United States. Third, New States of convenient size, not exceeding four in number, in addition to said State of Texas, and having sufficient population, may hereafter, by the consent of said State, be formed out of the territory thereof, which shall be entitled to admission, under the provisions of the Federal Constitution. And such States as may be formed out of that portion of said territory lying south of thirty-six degrees, thirty minutes north latitude, commonly known as the Missouri Compromise line, shall be admitted into the Union, with or without slavery, as the people of each State, asking admission, may desire. And in such States as shall be formed out of said territory, north of said Missouri Compromise line, slavery, or involuntary servitude (except for crime) shall be prohibited.

3. And be it further resolved,—That if the President of the United States shall in his judgement and discretion, deem it most advisable, instead of proceeding to submit the foregoing resolution to the Republic of Texas, as an overture on the part of the United States for admission, to negotiate with that republic—then, Be it resolved,—That a State, to be formed out of the present Republic of Texas, with suitable extent and boundaries, and with two representatives in Congress, until the next apportionment of representation, shall be admitted into the Union, by virtue of this act, on an equal footing with the existing States, as soon as the terms and conditions of such admission, and the cession of the remaining Texan territory to the United States, shall be agreed upon by the Governments of Texas and the United States; and that the sum of one hundred thousand dollars be, and the same is hereby, appropriated to defray the expenses of missions and negotiations, to agree upon the terms of said admission and cession, either by

treaty to be submitted to the Senate, or by articles to be submitted to the two Houses of Congress, as the President may direct."[2]

Because of the bitter fight in the Senate, the joint resolution, as we see, consisted of two parts: the one, embraced in the first and second sections, the original House resolution; the other, the third section, the amendment passed by the Senate and concurred in by the House, authorizing the President to use his discretion in proposing to Texas a new negotiation.[3]

After deliberately considering the joint resolution and the amendment, President Tyler chose the House resolution, as it could be "more readily and with less difficulty and expense carried into effect." His decisive objection to the amendment was that "it must be submitted to the Senate for approval, and run the hazard of receiving the votes of two-thirds of the members present, which could hardly be expected, if we are to judge from recent experience."[4]

As the joint resolution reached President Tyler just three days before the expiration of his term of office, he was severely criticised for not leaving Polk free to select the method he considered best. In order to justify his action, Tyler said, "I deem it quite important that the facts which transpired during the last three or four days of my administration, relating to the annexation of Texas, should be preserved in authentic form." With this in view, he had his cabinet members endorse this statement:

The resolutions reached me, and received my approval, on the 1st day of March, 1845. Mr. Calhoun called on me . . . the same day. He remarked that the power to make the selection between the alternative resolutions rested on me and he hoped that I would not hesitate to act. I replied that I entertained no doubt in the matter of the selection: that I regarded the resolution which had been moved and adopted by the Senate, by way of amendment to the House resolution, as designed merely to appease the discontent of some one or two members of that body, and for no other purpose; and that my only doubt of the propriety of immediate action arose from a feeling of delicacy to my successor. We both regarded the opening of a new negotiation, as proposed by the

[2]Crallé, *Reports and Public Letters of John C. Calhoun*, V, 395; *Congressional Globe*, 28th Cong., 2 Sess., 358-362.

[3]Tyler, *Letters and Times of the Tylers*, II, 362.

[4]Calhoun to Donelson, March 3, 1845. Crallé, *Reports and Public Letters of John C. Calhoun*, V, 393; 29th Cong., 1 Sess., *House Exec. Doc.* No. 2, pp. 125-127.

Senate resolution, as destined to defeat annexation altogether. . . . Mr. Calhoun urged the necessity of immediate action. . . . It was enough that Congress had given me the power to act by the terms of the resolutions, and that the urgency of the case was imminent. . . . The conversation terminated by my requesting him to call the cabinet the next day.

. . . The whole cabinet assembled: every member gave a decided preference for the House resolution over the Senate amendment. . . . All concurred in the necessity for immediate action. I suggested that Mr. Calhoun should wait on Mr. Polk, inform him of my action on the subject, and explain to him the reasons thereof. The suggestion was fully approved. . . . Mr. Calhoun waited on Mr. Polk . . . but he declined to express any opinion or to make any suggestion in reference to the subject.[5]

4. Donelson's Instructions Concerning the Joint Resolution

Since it could scarcely be doubted that the English would use every effort to "induce Texas to reject the terms proposed," Calhoun instructed Donelson to "proceed at once to Texas" and "urge speedy and prompt action."[6] In order to avoid delay, President Tyler dispatched the joint resolution and the instructions to Donelson by a special messenger, Floyd Waggaman.[7]

This haste, however, did not expedite action, as President Polk, a few days after his inauguration on March 4, sent a private letter to Donelson advising him not to act on Calhoun's orders until further instructed.[8] As President Polk wished the advice of his cabinet, he did not take any action until it met, March 10. At this meeting, James Buchanan, the Secretary of State, read aloud Calhoun's dispatch of March 3, and every member of the cabinet concurred without hesitation in preferring the original House resolution offering annexation by joint resolution rather than the Senate's proposal of a new treaty. Thereupon, Buchanan prepared instructions for Donelson confirming Tyler's choice, which he gave to Governor Yell, who was on the point of leaving for New Orleans, for delivery. In compliance with President Polk's

[5]Tyler, *Letters and Times of the Tylers*, II, 364-365.

[6]Calhoun to Donelson, March 3, 1845. Crallé, *Reports and Letters of John C. Calhoun*, V, 393-395; 29th Cong., 1 Sess., *House Exec. Doc.* No. 2, 125-127.

[7]*Niles' National Register*, LXVIII, 16.

[8]Polk to Donelson, March 7, 1845. *Tennessee Historical Magazine*, III, 62.

request, Buchanan directed Donelson to employ all his ability and energy to induce Texas to accept the joint resolution "without qualifications."[9] With these instructions, Buchanan enclosed a note which J. N. Almonte, the Mexican minister to the United States had addressed to Calhoun, protesting against the annexation of Texas and announcing his intention to withdraw from the United States.[10] To this Buchanan replied that the admission of Texas was "irrevocably decided, so far as the United States is concerned," and nothing but the refusal of Texas to ratify the terms and conditions on which her admission depends, can defeat this object. It is, therefore, too late at present to reopen a discussion."[11]

As Donelson had waited at New Orleans for his instructions, Governor Yell upon his arrival, March 24, promptly delivered them, and in the afternoon Donelson sailed for Texas on the *Marmora.*

5. *Efforts of the French and English to Defeat Annexation*

On arriving at Galveston, Donelson was informed that the English and French ministers, Captain Charles Elliot and Compte de Saligny, after receiving dispatches by an English man-of-war from their respective governments, had hastily set out for Washington, Texas. Moreover, the public believed that the ministers had been instructed to guarantee the recognition of the independence of Texas by Mexico and other favorable propositions in the form of commercial advantages, if Texas would refuse to accept the American propositions. Donelson was, therefore, very anxious to reach Washington as soon as the other gentlemen; accordingly, he chartered a steamer and "put off after them."[12]

The following letter from Ashbel Smith, the Texas chargé in London, to Anson Jones, shows that the English and French had actively opposed the annexation of Texas since the Senate had rejected the treaty, June 8, 1844:

I have had an interview to-day with Lord Aberdeen, at his request, concerning the relations of Texas and chiefly in relation to

[9]Buchanan to Donelson, March 10, 1845. *Senate Doc.* No. 1, 29th Cong., 1 Sess., 35-38.

[10]Almonte to Calhoun, March 10, 1845. *Ibid.*, 38-39.

[11]Buchanan to Almonte, March 10, 1845. *Ibid.*, 39.

[12]Donelson to Buchanan, March 24, and March 28. *Ibid.*, 46.

the negotiations at Washington in the United States for annexation. . . .

Lord Aberdeen observed that Her Britannic Majesty's Government and that of France had communicated with each other touching the "annexation"—that entire harmony of opinions exists, and that they will act in concert in relation to it:—That though the rejection of the annexation treaty by the American Senate was regarded as nearly or quite certain, that nothing would be done by these governments until the American Congress shall have finally disposed of the subject for the present session. He stated that then the British and French governments would be willing, if Texas desired to remain independent, to settle the whole matter by a diplomatic act; this diplomatic act, in which Texas would of course participate, would insure peace. settle boundaries between Texas and Mexico, and guarantee the separate independence of Texas. . . .

Lord Aberdeen did not use the word treaty, but employed the phrase *diplomatic act.* It would have all the obligations of a treaty, and would of course be perpetual. . . .

Such an act would . . . give to the European Governments, parties to it, a perfect right to forbid, for all time to come, the annexation of Texas to the United States. . . .[13]

President Houston, on being informed of this proposition, September 25, 1844, instructed Jones to send a dispatch to Smith authorizing him to "complete the *proposed* arrangements for the settlement of our Mexican difficulties as soon as possible."[14] Jones, however, as president-elect, refused to "obey" Houston's "order," for, according to his indorsement of the instructions, he thought that it would defeat annexation altogether or lead to war between Europe and America, that it would produce disturbances and revolutions in Texas, and that it would make it difficult, if not impossible, for him to administer the government successfully.[15] Smith, however, said that Jones disobeyed the order of President Houston because he desired to make the "diplomatic act" the prominent measure of his own administration, and, judging from the course pursued by him after he became president, this seems to have been his real motive. On Smith's return from Europe, December, 1844, President Jones said to him: "It hardly

[13]Smith to Jones, June 24, 1844. Jones, *Letters Relating to the History of Annexation*, 19.

[14]Houston to Jones, September 25, 1844. Jones, *Letters Relating to the History of Annexation*, 20.

[15]Jones, *Letters Relating to the Annexation of Texas*, 10.

seemed fair to deprive you of the honor of negotiating a treaty in London, but the negotiations shall take place here, and you as Secretary of State shall conduct them for Texas."[16] Accordingly, December, 1844, he requested Elliot, the English minister to Texas, to have the British government transmit to him the proposals of the "diplomatic act" "duly prepared for execution," but before this request reached London, France had withdrawn its consent to participate in such an agreement.[17]

From this time, nevertheless, the British and French cabinets pursued more vigorously their efforts to prevent annexation by procuring peace for Texas. They urged Mexico "by every available argument, and in every practical manner, to recognize without delay the independence of Texas, as the only rational course to be taken for securing the real interests of Mexico, to which country the annexation of Texas to the United States would be ruinous."[18] Moreover, their agents in Texas had worked very energetically to arouse public opinion against annexation. On February 8, 1845, the *Texas National Register* (Washington), the official organ of the government, announced that England and France were willing to enter into commercial treaties with Texas on "the most liberal footing," if Texas would remain independent, and that Texas would soon have an opportunity to choose between recognition by Mexico and a longer period of suspense on the mere chance of being annexed by the United States. Of still greater significance was this excerpt from a letter attributed to "a gentleman of high position in Europe," which appeared in the next edition of this paper:

> Lord Aberdeen, although he will do nothing that can justly give offense to the United States, is still decided to take such measures as will bring about peace between Texas and Mexico: provided the former will give satisfactory assurance of her determination to remain independent.
>
> The British government has enjoined on Mexico, in the most earnest and explicit terms to abstain from any attempt to invade Texas, and they have assured that country that they would afford it no aid or countenance at all in case of such attempted invasion, whatever might be its result or consequences.

[16]Smith, *Reminiscences of the Republic of Texas*, 64-65.

[17]Elliot to Aberdeen, December 21, 1844. Adams, *British Correspondence Concerning Texas*, 395.

[18]Aberdeen to Elliot. December 31, 1844. Adams, *British Correspondence Concerning Texas*, 404.

Furthermore, when the House on January 23, 1845, had passed the joint resolution for the admission of Texas, Elliot had urged Texas for these reasons not to accept these terms if offered as a basis for the admission of Texas: (1) That they were too one-sided as to advantages and little short of insulting to Texas as to language; (2) that the expense of a state government would be as much as that of the present republican form, while all the duties collected would go into the United States treasury; (3) that the United States did not assume the debts; (4) that it was out of the question, since they had to pay the debts by the sale of land, to concede to the United States the right of negotiating away their land, or even to enter into any annexation arrangement unless the integrity of their present limits was effectually guaranteed.

On receiving the joint instructions of Great Britain and France, March 24, 1845, Elliot and Saligny decided to act with energy and vigor to prevent annexation. Accordingly, on the next morning they left Galveston for Washington, as they were very anxious to arrive in advance of authoritative news from the United States that Congress had passed the joint resolution. Moreover, they expected Donelson every hour to arrive at Galveston commissioned to conclude annexation with as much speed as possible.[19]

On arriving at Washington, Elliot and Saligny formally invited President Jones, on behalf of his government, to accept the good offices of France and England with a view to an early and honorable settlement with Mexico upon the basis of independence. After a conference with his cabinet, President Jones instructed Ashbel Smith, the Secretary of State, to accept this intervention. Accordingly Smith prepared a draft preliminary to a treaty of peace between Texas and Mexico: (1) that Mexico should consent to acknowledge the independence of Texas; (2) that limits and other conditions should be arranged in the final treaty; (3) that Texas should be willing to submit disputed points respecting territory and other matters to the arbitration of umpires. Furthermore, that Texas should pledge herself to issue a proclamation announcing the conclusion of the preliminaries of peace with Mexico as soon as Mexico accepted the conditions and returned them to the President of Texas, and that she should agree "not

[19]Elliot to Aberdeen, April 2, 1845. Adams, *British Correspondence Concerning Texas*, 462.

to accept any proposals, or to enter into any negotiations to annex herself to any other country" for a period of ninety days from the date of this memorandum. After a personal pledge on the part of Saligny and Elliot that only the courts of London and Paris, their ministers at Washington, and the Mexican government should know of the agreement, Smith, Elliot, and Saligny signed the document. Thereupon, Elliot offered to make a secret journey to Mexico, in order to secure an exact conformity to the preliminary arrangements. Under a pretext of a journey to Charleston, South Carolina, he left Texas on the *Electra,* and when out of sight of land, was transferred to another British ship bound for Vera Cruz.[20]

While at Washington Elliot and Saligny had insisted that Texas have a representative at the courts of France and England with full powers to conclude any arrangement that might be necessary for the safety of the country. They said that they would consider it as striking proof of the "good disposition of this Government at this crisis, if His Excellency would send back his present Secretary of State, who was known and highly appreciated" both in London and Paris, and, therefore, could be of the "highest use." President Jones complied with their request and appointed Smith to this office. At the request of his cabinet he appointed E. Allen, "a man of excellent sense, high character, and of the best disposition in this matter," to succeed Smith, as Secretary of State, as he knew that it would require a person like Smith with "the utmost firmness and caution," to manage affairs with success.[21]

6. *The Convening of the Texan Congress*

When Donelson arrived at Washington, Texas, March 30, he could find out nothing concerning the mission of Elliot and Saligny. He wrote Buchanan that they remained in the capital but one day, and "if they made a communication to this government, in relation to the question of annexation, it is a secret between them and the President." On the afternoon of his arrival, he called upon Ashbel Smith and presented the substance of the

[20]Elliot to Aberdeen, March 30, 1845. Adams, *British Correspondence Concerning Texas*, 462-473.

[21]Elliot to Aberdeen, April 2, 1845. Adams, *British Correspondence Concerning Texas*, 467-468.

American proposition for the admission of Texas, but he seemed unprepared as to the course the President would pursue. So Donelson, thereupon, presented himself to President Jones, who informed him that he had granted Smith a leave of absence, and that he had appointed E. Allen to carry on the negotiations. During the interview the President said that he had intended to call Congress, but, under the circumstances, as now presented, he believed that a better course would be to refer the subject directly to the people, and let them provide for a convention to effect the changes necessary for admission into the Union. He added, however, "that the gravity of the subject required him not to act in haste; and that, though he had a decided opinion of his own, he would dwell awhile on it, until he was aided by his cabinet." Donelson, in conversation with Allen later in the day, found that he too opposed the convening of Congress, as it was his opinion that the executive department could deal with the matter as well as the legislative, since the whole question was extra-constitutional. Donelson disagreed with Allen as to the power of the executive to act independently of Congress, as the joint resolution provided that the "assent of the existing government of Texas" should be obtained before the resolutions could go into effect. Donelson thought that the term "assent of the existing government" implied the assent of both the executive and the legislative departments, so he accordingly urged the President to call Congress at an early date and to work in concert with it in whatever steps might be taken.[22]

In public estimation the government of Texas had not responded with sufficient promptness to the overtures of the American government; so, while Donelson was wrestling with this great measure in a diplomatic way, enthusiastic annexation meetings were held throughout Texas, and county after county endorsed the terms offered by the United States, and demanded prompt action either by Congress or by a convention.[23] In a mass meeting at Brenham, April 11, the people declared unanimously for annexation, and recommended that all the counties elect representatives to a convention to ratify the joint resolution and form a state con-

[22]Donelson to Buchanan, April 1, 1845. *Senate Doc.* No. 1, 29th Cong., 1 Sess., 47-48.

[23]*Niles' National Register* (Baltimore), LXVII, 146; Lubbock, *Six Decades in Texas*, 165-169.

stitution, if President Jones did not convene Congress on or before the fourth Monday in June.[24] The Brazoria annexation meeting, April 14, was also indicative of the great anxiety of the people to act definitely and promptly. The chairman, Timothy Pilsbury, explained the object of the meeting, and appointed a committee to draft resolutions. While this was in retirement, Tod Robinson addressed the meeting. After this the committee reported the resolutions, which were unanimously adopted. These expressed a desire for immediate annexation, with or without the consent of the Jones administration. They instructed their members of Congress to meet at Washington the third Monday in May and assume conventional powers, and, acting with the members of other counties, to call a convention and apportion the representation according to population so as to represent "the people and not acres." There was, also, a committee appointed to prepare an "Address to the People" calling upon them to meet and to insist upon the President's convening Congress. Guy M. Bryan carried a copy of the proceedings to James Love at Galveston, and a mass meeting in that city a few days later strongly indorsed the action of Brazoria.[25] The meeting at Houston on the ninth anniversary of the battle of San Jacinto showed the attitude of a majority of the Texans toward the Americans. They expressed their willingness to enter the American Union on the basis of the terms offered, and declared their "full confidence in the honor and justice of the American people" and their belief that the people of the United States would ultimately extend to them "every privilege that freemen can grant without dishonor and freemen can accept without disgrace."[26] The news of the American proposal spread like "wild fire" throughout the Republic so that by April 12, almost every county in the Republic had held a public demonstration or had set a day for one. These were almost unanimous in their demands for prompt action, and the papers contained little else than accounts of these enthusiastic annexation meetings.[27]

This excerpt from Ashbel Smith's letter to Jones as he was

[24]*Telegraph and Texas Register* (Houston), April 23, 1845; *Texas National Register* (Washington), April 17, 1845.

[25]Lubbock, *Six Decades in Texas*, 166-167; *Texas National Register*, May 1, 1845.

[26]Lubbock, *Six Decades in Texas*, 164-165.

[27]*The Red Lander* (San Augustine), April 26, 1845.

leaving Galveston as minister to England and France, April 9, is further evidence of the excitement about annexation:

. . . I find everywhere very great, very intense feeling on the subject of annexation. . . . I am forced to believe that an immense majority of the citizens are in favor of annexation—that is, annexation as presented in the resolutions of the American Congress—and that they will continue to be so, in preference to independence, though recognized in the most liberal manner by Mexico. The tranquility at present arises from the confidence in your favorable dispositions towards annexation, and the assurance that you will soon present the matter in some definite form to the country, so as to enable the people to vote in favor of it. This I know is your purpose; but should a suspicion to the contrary arise, and should it be suspected that the matter was to be deferred till the European powers could in any wise be heard from or be consulted, especially England, I am certainly informed that an attempt will be made to convene a convention, by calling on the people in public meetings, for the purpose of overriding the Government,—in other words, an attempt will be made to plunge the country into a revolution. The plan has been matured in Harris, Brazoria, and Galveston counties. . . . When it is known that I am going to Europe, as it will be when I sail from the United States, I feel convinced that public opinion will be inflamed beyond control. . . . Invitations will issue from meetings claiming to represent the popular will, urging the people to meet without delay and elect delegates to a convention, for the purpose of exercising all the powers of government. . . .

On looking over what I have written, I see that I have understated rather than overstated the feeling on this subject and the importance that will be attached to my mission when known. I am sure its tendency will be to prevent the dispassionate consideration by the people of grave matter about to be submitted to them; and I am really apprehensive that an attempt may be made to subvert our institutions. . . .

Should you deem it best to delay my sailing for a short time, or to suspend my mission wholly and to consider my journey a private one, or to proceed without delay to my post, I shall act accordingly, and in all cases I shall faithfully attend to the affairs of my country. . . .[28]

As the people had so unanimously expressed a desire for prompt action on the American proposal, and as Donelson had met with little encouragement at Washington, he decided to go to Huntsville for a conference with Houston, whom he found strongly op-

[28]Smith to Jones, April 9, 1845. Jones, *Memoranda and Official Correspondence of the Republic of Texas*, 446-448.

posed to the joint resolution, but in favor of the negotiations contemplated in the Senate amendment. Donelson tried to satisfy him, but he still insisted upon opening negotiations, feeling that "Texas should have something to say about the matter," which would be impracticable with the resolutions. He further added that if Texas should accept the resolution, this would be impossible, for "the terms are dictated and the conditions absolute," while by the Senate amendment "the terms could be arranged by negotiation, and, if accepted by the people at the annual election in September, Congress could then take the necessary action." In fact, Houston showed so strongly his disapproval of the resolution that Donelson said the "ex-president brought all his influence to bear against our proposal and in favor of resorting to the negotiations contemplated by the Senate amendment."[29]

Though Donelson was never able to concur in the opinion that annexation could be best effected by the negotiations in accord with the Senate amendment, yet the next day Houston wrote him that for the sake of human liberty, for the sake of the future tranquillity of the United States, and for the welfare of Texas, "whose interests, prosperity, and happiness are near to my heart and are cherished by me above every political consideration, I conjure you to use your influence in having presented to this government the alternative suggested by the amendment to Mr. Brown's bill, so that commissioners can act in conjunction upon the points which it may be proper to arrange between the two countries before it is too late, and while there is a remedy, . . . that Texas can exercise some choice as to the conditions of her entry into the Union."

As a substitute for the terms of the joint resolution Houston suggested: (1) that the United States should receive and pay a liberal price for the public property; (2) that Texas should retain her public lands; (3) that the United States should indemnify the citizens of Texas for any lands in territory abandoned by the United States; (4) that arrangements should be made for the United States to purchase the vacant lands of Texas at a price stipulated by commissioners; (5) that lands purchased by the United States should not be sold to any Indian tribe, nor should Indians be permitted to settle within the present limits of Texas

[29]Donelson to Calhoun, April 24, 1845. Jameson, *Correspondence of John C. Calhoun*, 1029-1032.

without the consent of the Senate of Texas; (6) that Texas should pay its national debt; (7) that the United States should pay the Texas citizens for lands within its boundary lines; and (8) that Texas should not form a part of the Union until her Constitution was accepted by the Congress of the United States.[30]

Houston's objections to the joint resolution did not deter Donelson from presenting them on April 12, 1845,[31] formally and finally with these comments:

> If Texas now accepts these proposals, from that moment she becomes virtually a state of the Union, because the faith of the United States is pledged for her admission, and the act of Congress necessary to redeem the pledge is obliged to follow as soon as she presents a republican form of government. All then that is necessary upon this basis is for this government, after expressing its assent to the proposals submitted to it, to call a convention of the people to clothe their deputies with the power to amend their constitution and to adapt the government created by it to the new circumstances under which it will be placed by annexation to the Union. . . .
>
> On the ground . . . of more directness and simplicity in the process, whereby time and much expenditure of money will be saved, and of the entire avoidance of all further risks resulting from possible differences attending efforts to obtain terms more suitable to the separate views of the respective governments, it has been thought best by the President of the United States to rest the question of the joint resolution, as it came from the House of Representatives, which contains propositions, complete and ample, as an overture to Texas, and which, if adopted by her, will place the reunion of the two countries beyond the possibility of defeat.
>
> This great question, then is in the hands of Texas . . . and is submitted with the hope that this government will see the necessity of prompt and decisive action.[32]

Since the people had made known their desire to President Jones in a way too plain to be misunderstood, he became convinced that the only safe thing for him to do was to call Congress

[30]Houston to Donelson, April 9, 1845. Lubbock, *Six Decades in Texas*, 160-161.

[31]On April 1, Donelson handed to President Jones for examination the joint resolution and a note which he had written March 31, but he did not present them formally to the Secretary of State until April 12. Jones, *Letters Relating to the Annexation of Texas*, 14.

[32]Donelson to Allen, March 31, 1845. *Senate Doc.* No. 1, 29th Cong., 1 Sess., 48-50; *Telegraph and Texas Register*, June 25, 1845.

in session. Therefore, in an interview with Donelson on April 12, he assured him that "regardless of his individual opinion," he would submit the proposition "fairly and promptly" to Congress,[33] so that Congress could apportion the districts for the election of the deputies to a convention to test the ratification of the proposals, and to make the corresponding changes in the government."[34] On the same day Allen replied to Donelson's note of March 31, saying that by the "organic law" of the Republic of Texas, the President did not have the power to accept or reject the terms offered, but that at an early date, he would convene Congress and present for consideration the joint resolution and the note transmitted with it.[35] Accordingly, on April 15, President Jones issued a proclamation calling a special session of Congress to meet at Washington, June 16, to "receive such communications as may be made to them, and to consult and determine on such measures as in their wisdom may be deemed necessary for the welfare of Texas."[36]

President Jones caused much dissatisfaction by delaying the convening of Congress until June 16, as the people generally believed that he was waiting for the English and French to have an opportunity to defeat annexation by forcing Mexico to recognize the independence of Texas. However, Jones justified his action on the grounds that the delay was unavoidable, as the members could not have assembled earlier because of the water courses throughout the country having overflowed, and that, furthermore, Donelson had requested him to appoint this date so that in the meantime he could visit the United States.[37]

W. D. Miller, the editor of the *Texas National Register* (Washington), in an editorial on April 24, said:

> . . . The President of our Republic, in convoking Congress in extra session on the 16th of June next, shows that he is animated by a high sense of public duty and has a faithful regard for the will of the people of Texas. No one can doubt that a large majority of our citizens are anxious for annexation, and

[33]Jones, *Letters Relating to the History of Annexation*, 15.

[34]Donelson to Buchanan, April 12, 1845. *Senate Doc.* No. 1, 29th Cong., 1 Sess., 52.

[35]Allen to Donelson, April 14. 1845. *Ibid.*, 53.

[36]*Proclamation by the President of Texas*, April 15, 1845. MS. Proclamations of the Republic of Texas, State Library.

[37]Jones, *Letters Relating to the History of Annexation*, 14.

will accept and ratify the terms proposed for this purpose. The President, therefore, interposing no constitutional obstacle to the fulfilment of their wishes, leaves the question to their calm, peaceful, and enlightened action. Congress, doubtless, will recommend the call of a Convention, after apportioning the districts for the election of the delegates, whose duty it will be to adapt our Constitution and Government to the new circumstances under which we shall be placed as an equal member of the American Union.[38]

In a letter to Aberdeen, April 25, however, William Kennedy, the British Consul at Galveston, said that it was not a "faithful regard for the will of the people of Texas," but "fear of the people" which prompted President Jones to convene Congress.[39]

A few days after President Jones summoned Congress, Donelson left for New Orleans. Polk, however, wrote him on May 6, to be at the seat of government when the Texan Congress should meet, and to insist upon immediate action upon the proposals just as they had been submitted, for he felt sure that the British minister would "interpose every obstacle and hold out every inducement to gain time," with a view of defeating the object which they have so much at heart.[40] In compliance with President Polk's request, Donelson returned from New Orleans to Texas the last of May with a strong determination to put forth every effort to complete the great measure of annexation.[41]

7. *The Calling of the Convention*

As one of the conditions of the joint resolution for the admission of Texas was that Texas might be erected into a new state, to be called the state of Texas, with a republican form of government, to be adopted by the people in convention assembled, the ultra friends of annexation were not content with the call of Congress, but clamored for a convention, since Congress could not apportion the representation or form a new constitution. However, there was a great diversity of opinion relative to the calling of the convention. Some of the counties desired to meet in primary assemblies and elect their delegates to a convention previous to the meeting of Congress; others desired that Congress

[38] *Texas National Register*, April 24, 1845.

[39] Kennedy to Aberdeen, April 25. Adams, *British Correspondence Concerning Texas*, 479.

[40] Polk to Donelson, May 6, 1845. *Tennessee Historical Magazine*, III, 64.

[41] *Texas National Register*, July 9, 1845.

should assemble in May, apportion the representation according to population, and designate the day for the convention; while others preferred that the President should apportion the representation and call a convention. This diversity of opinion threatened to lead to serious difficulties, and the enemies of annexation began to predict that a firebrand would be thrown into Congress as soon as it met and that a contest would begin immediately between the eastern and the western members over representation in the convention.

This disagreement over representation was due to the fact that the general convention at Washington in March, 1836, had designated the membership in Congress before Santa Anna invaded and depopulated the western counties with the result that this section of the Republic, with only about one-third of the whole population, had in Congress a majority over the other two-thirds. Nevertheless, it had been impossible to correct these inequalities, as the constitution forbade a reapportionment of the representatives until a census was taken, which so far the western members had been able to prevent. The West claimed that the present basis was fair and just, as this region had always borne the brunt of the war while its population had been decreased and immigration had been prevented by the Mexican invasion. Regardless of this fact, however, the other parts of the Republic were not satisfied with their representation, as "they had the burden of taxation to bear, while the West received all the benefits."[42]

On January 29, 1845, Mr. Scurry, a member of the House from Red River, in discussing the bill for the enumeration of the inhabitants, said that the representation as it then existed tended to build up an aristocracy in the land, as well as an irresponsible government, for some of the members from the depopulated districts were responsible to no constituency at all. He added, furthermore, that "they legislate as they please, vote as they will, and support any measure regardless of the consequences to our country."[43]

After President Jones issued the proclamation convening Congress, this question of representation became very acute as some of the most influential members of the West declared "that they now had the power in Congress, and would keep it in the State

[42]Jones, *Letters Relating to the History of Annexation*, 16.
[43]*Texas National Register* (Washington), April 17, 1845.

Government by apportioning the members of the Convention in such a manner as to perpetuate the old basis."[44]

As this question of representation carried with it the location of the capital, the West was even more persistent in its demand that the basis then existing should be maintained in the convention, for it desired to make Austin the permanent capital. In March, 1842, the Mexicans invaded Texas and surprised and captured San Antonio, so that President Houston had convened Congress at Washington since October, 1842. There had been much contention over the location of the capital. Both houses of Congress had made numerous efforts to return the seat of government to Austin, while a strong but unsuccessful party had attempted to locate it permanently at Washington.[45] After President Jones issued the proclamation convening Congress, the East, North, and Middle sections offered as a compromise to let Austin remain the capital, if the apportionment of representatives could be made according to population, but as the West did not readily accept this arrangement, it was feared that the basis of representation could not be satisfactorily arranged by Congress.[46] Therefore, many of the advocates of annexation urged President Jones to call a convention and apportion the representation, subject to revision by the convention itself. When he did not comply with their request, indications of dissatisfaction, and even of revolution against the administration, were displayed in different sections of the country, as the annexationists thought that the President was merely waiting for the French and English to guarantee the independence of Texas on the condition that she should remain independent.

As a number of the President's friends suggested to Donelson, as he was leaving Texas for New Orleans, that it would be a judicious step for the President to issue a proclamation calling upon his own responsibility, a convention of the people for the purpose of hastening annexation, Donelson, on arriving at Galveston, April 29, sent him this letter:

Feeling that you might have some embarrassment on the subject in consequence of the intimation to me through Mr. Allen, that it was necessary to convoke Congress in order to have an

[44]Jones, *Letters Relating to the History of Annexation*, 16.

[45]Lubbock, *Six Decades in Texas*, 150.

[46]Jones, *Letters Relating to the History of Annexation*, 16.

apportionment of the elective districts, I have taken the liberty to write this note, and to say to you that I trust you will not consider any declaration made to me as a reason for not adopting such suggestion, should it appear otherwise proper.

The great object is to give effect to the public will of Texas. . . . The call you have made of Congress might be confined to that feature of the proposals which anticipates the consent of the existing Government of Texas; while at the same time, the Convention might be in session framing the new Constitution.

The main difficulty, I suppose, in your mind would be the apportionment of the representation to the Convention, which is, considering the jealousy which exists between the eastern and western portions of the Republic, a heavy responsibility. But may not this responsibility be safely risked by you? Such a classification as you suggested to me, is doubtless near an approach to what would be adopted by Congress, if the duty of making it were left to that body; and it cannot be supposed the people would be less willing to come to an agreement. The whole proceeding is but recommendatory, inasmuch as it is extra-constitutional; and your action as well as that of Congress could no more than indicate a plan of the people, by which they could express their sovereign will with convenience and certainty. . . .

Should your proclamation, therefore, after stating the occasion for its being issued, recommend the people to elect delegates to a Convention, to meet on . . . day of June, and to choose one, two, three, or four members, as the case may be, . . . the Convention thus assembled to be the judge of the competency of its members, with the power to correct what they might decide unequal or unjust in the classification of the counties, it would seem to me that you might safely confide in the people themselves, and in the delegates to sustain you.

P. S.—As well as I remember, your classification was: One member for every county. One additional for every two hundred votes and less than five hundred. One additional for every five hundred and over. Perhaps an additional member to the two counties, Montgomery and Red River which have one thousand two hundred votes.[47]

There was a general demand from the people that President Jones should call a convention, and by the first of May a number of the counties had instructed their senators and representatives to meet at Washington the third Monday in May and to assume conventional powers, and, acting in concert with the members of other counties, to call a convention and apportion the representa-

[47]Donelson to Jones, April 29, 1845. Jones, ***Memoranda and Official Correspondence of the Republic of Texas*****, 453-455.**

tion, with or without the consent of the existing government. Since one of the conditions of the joint resolution was, as we have seen, that the constitution formed by the convention should be adopted "with the consent of the existing government," it was exceedingly important that this revolt against the administration be checked. *The Houston Telegraph* of May 7, therefore, urged the President to call a convention to meet at the same time as Congress, and thus check the opposition to the existing government, for it said, "if we neglect one of the conditions proposed in the bill our enemies in the United States will organize and strain every nerve to shut us out of the Union."

As a further evidence of the demand for a convention these extracts are given from a letter written by E. Allen to President Jones from Galveston, May 4:

From the signs now exhibited, there can be no doubt but that the called session of Congress will be a stormy scene. The opponents of your Administration do not intend to place it in your power to appear as the friend of annexation. They care not whether they place you in a false or true position, so that they can add strength and popularity to their hostility to your Administration. . . .

Under such circumstances, it occurs most forcibly to my mind that a call of a convention, to be assembled under the advisory proclamation of the Executive, would not only neutralize and render harmless all the elements of opposition and defeat the machinations of your enemies, but would even place you in such a position that they themselves, however loath, would be bound to support you, and to sustain your course and administration. Mr. Donelson is greatly in favor of such a call,—so is Governor Yell: and the idea is universally satisfactory so far as I can learn and will be advocated by every paper in the country. Those who oppose it will be considered as opponents of annexation. I do not consider that the measure of annexation is to be hastened or materially affected by the assembly of a convention. That body will be superior to Congress: it will deliberate upon the state of the Republic: it will submit the overture to the people: it will probably frame a new constitution and proper provisions fit to become the organic law, whether annexation shall take place or not. . . . Finally, I doubt not but that the Convention thus assembled would provide effectually against revolution and take efficient measures for the continuance of the Government under the present Administration, until annexation shall be accomplished, and the consequent changes that follow in their course. . . . The timely publication of your proclamation would prevent certain members of Congress from becoming members of the Convention, at which, I, for one, should rejoice. . . . The suggested course will place you at the head of the nation, by position and concurrence of circumstances, as well as by election. . . . The armed, organized, disciplined opposition to your administration will be prostrated; and whether annexation finally occurred or not, your course will be applauded, and yourself sustained. . . .

P. S. I think that Congress, when assembled, in the absence of the call of a convention, will assume conventional powers, and appeal to the people to sanction their usurpation and adopt their acts. A wise, but bold and decisive course by the Executive at this crisis, in controlling the excitement, and turning the revolution, (for such it is) to the permanent benefit of the nation, is what I desire to see successfully accomplished.[48]

Jones, however, did not receive Allen's letter until after he had issued the following proclamation:

Whereas the people of Texas have evinced a decided wish that prompt and definite action should be had upon the proposition for annexation recently submitted by the government of the United States to this government, and that a convention should be assembled for this purpose; and

Whereas it is competent for the people alone to decide finally upon the proposition for annexation, and, by deputies in convention assembled, to adopt a constitution with a view to the admission of Texas as one of the States of the American Union; and

Whereas no authority is given by the constitution of this republic to any branch of the government to call a convention and to change the organic law—this being a right reserved to the people themselves, and which they alone can properly exercise—

Therefore, be it know that I, Anson Jones, President of the republic of Texas, desirous of giving direction and effect to the public will, already so fully expressed, do recommend to the citizens of Texas that an election for "deputies" to a convention be held in the different counties of the republic on Wednesday, the fourth day of June next, upon the following basis, viz: Each county in the republic to elect one deputy, irrespective of the number of voters it contained at the last annual elections; each county voting at that time three hundred, and less than six hundred, to elect two deputies; each county voting at that time six hundred, and less than nine hundred, to elect three deputies; and each county voting at that time nine hundred and upwards, to elect four deputies . . . and that the said deputies so elected

[48]Allen to Jones, May 4, 1845. Jones, *Memoranda and Official Correspondence of the Republic of Texas*, 459-460.

do assemble in convention at the city of Austin, on the "fourth of July" next, for the purpose of considering the proposition for the annexation of Texas to the United States, and any other proposition which may be made concerning the nationality of the Republic, and should they judge it expedient and proper, to adopt, provisionally, a constitution to be submitted to the people for their ratification, with the view to the admission of Texas, as a State, into the American Union, in accordance with the terms of the proposition for annexation already submitted to this government by that of the United States. And the chief justices of the respective counties aforesaid will give due notice of the said elections, appoint a presiding officer in the several precincts, who will appoint the judges and clerks of said elections, and have the same conducted according to the constitution and laws regulating elections, and make due return thereof.[49]

According to Elliot, President Jones "convened Congress and recommended a Convention, clearly perceiving that no other means was left him of averting dangerous and irreparable consequences." Moreover, he said that President Jones assured him that the general state of public excitement in favor of annexation, so little looked for three months ago, would not keep him from fulfilling what he felt to be his obligations toward his own country, towards Mexico, and towards the powers that had interested themselves in the peaceful and honorable adjustment of this struggle; and that he should, therefore, in the course of a day or two, issue a proclamation, making known to the people of this country the actual situation of affairs with Mexico and leaving it to them and their constitutional agents to dispose of the result as they should judge best.[50] However, President Jones in a letter to Hamilton Stuart, the editor of the *Civilian and Gazette,* November 23, 1847, said that he called the convention agreeably, "to the expressed will of the people to hasten and insure the success of the measure of annexation and at the same time to settle and put to rest two very exciting questions,—those of the seat of government and the basis of representation."[51]

When President Jones issued the proclamation convening Congress, Donelson considered the question of annexation settled, so

[49]*Proclamation by the President of the Republic,* May 5, 1845. Proclamations of the Republic of Texas, MS. State Library.

[50]Elliot to Bankhead, June 11, 1845. Adams, *British Correspondence Concerning Texas,* 488-489.

[51]Jones, *Letters Relating to the History of Annexation,* 16.

far as Texas was concerned. He predicted, however, that there would be an "increase in the opposition" when Mexico brought forward her project for independence, aided by the temptation which England might offer in the way of commercial advantages; but that opposition would be powerless, compared with the mass who would favor annexation.[52]

8. *The Petition of Texas for Military Aid*

Another very serious question arose when Allen wrote Donelson, May 19, that an acceptance of the proposition submitted by the United States would more than likely cause a Mexican invasion of Texas if the United States did not give her "aid and protection." He accordingly requested that troops be sent to the western frontier as soon as Texas had accepted the terms.[53] Thereupon, Donelson requested him to make an official application, which could be sent to the United States for approval. He assured the Secretary, however, that the assistance would be given since the invasion would certainly be aimed at the interests of the United States. Allen promptly drafted a note asking for military protection, and Donelson forwarded this to Buchanan with the injunction that until Texas should accept the United States' proposal, the greatest caution should be observed, so as not to give the slightest pretext for the assertion that either the government or the people of Texas had been influenced by the presence of United States forces.[54] In reply Buchanan said that the United States would "avoid even the least appearance of interference with the free action of the people of Texas," and that the government would "refrain from all acts of hostility towards Mexico, unless these should become absolutely necessary in self defense."[55] However, before Buchanan received Allen's request for military aid, he had written Donelson that "as soon as the existing government and the convention of Texas shall have accepted the terms proposed in the first two sections of the joint resolution for annexing Texas to the United States, the President will conceive it both his right and his duty to employ the army of the United States

[52]Donelson to Buchanan, May 6, 1845. *Senate Doc.* No. 1, 29th Cong., 1 Sess., 56-57.

[53]Allen to Donelson, May 19. *Ibid.*, 61.

[54]Donelson to Buchanan, May 24. *Ibid.*, 59-61.

[55]Buchanan to Donelson, June 3, 1845. *Ibid.*, 41-42.

in defending that State against the attacks of any foreign power. This shall be done promptly and efficiently, should any emergency make it necessary. In order to prepare for such a contingency, a force of three thousand men shall immediately be placed upon the border prepared to enter Texas without a moment's delay."[56]

9. *Mexico's Acceptance of the Proposals of Texas*

On May 19, 1845, almost a month after Elliot had arrived in Mexico, the government accepted the conditions preliminary to a treaty of peace with Texas, but President Herrera requested that the person or persons sent to Texas to conclude the treaty of peace should take the name of commissioner or commissioners, and that the instant the negotiations should commence, they should bring forward their title of plenipotentiary. Moreover, Luis Cuevas, the Secretary of State, in an additional declaration asserted that if Texas should consent either directly or indirectly, to the "law passed in the United States on Annexation," then this agreement entered into between Texas and Mexico should be considered "null and void."[57] On May 20, Bankhead, the British minister in Mexico, transmitted to Elliot this document containing the acceptance of the Texan proposals, and instructed him to present it secretly to President Jones as soon as possible. Whereupon, Elliot immediately left Mexico for Texas by the way of Vera Cruz.[58]

Elliott, according to his instructions, had expected to keep the negotiation a secret, but on arriving at Galveston, May 30, he found the strength and unanimity of the annexation cry so great that he made known the terms of the preliminary treaty. Donelson was at Iberville, Louisiana, when he heard that Texas and Mexico had entered into a preliminary treaty recognizing the independence of Texas. Before this he had heard rumors of the intrigue, but he had discredited them, and had repeatedly assured his government that there was nothing in the reports of British interference. However, when he received authentic information that the treaty had been accepted by Mexico, he hastened to Gal-

[56]Buchanan to Donelson, May 23, 1845. *Ibid.*, 41.

[57]Bankhead to Aberdeen, May 20, 1845. Adams, *British Correspondence Concerning Texas*, 489.

[58]Bankhead to Elliot, May 20, 1845. Adams, *British Correspondence Concerning Texas*, 487.

veston. Here he met Elliot, who had just arrived from Mexico, and found out from him the exact terms of the proposal carried to Mexico.[59]

Elliot set out for Washington on the first day of June, and hurried on without even pausing for rest. He reached his destination on June 3, and promptly delivered the documents to President Jones, who assured him that he would not fail to "fulfil what he considered his obligation towards his own country, towards Mexico, and towards the powers who had interested themselves in the peaceful and honorable settlement of this struggle, and that he would, therefore, in the course of a few days issue a proclamation setting forth the actual situation of affairs as they existed between Mexico and the people of this country, and then leave it to them and their constitutional agents to dispose of the result as they should judge best."[60] Accordingly, on June 4, President Jones issued this ploclamation giving an account of the circumstances which preceded and led up to the negotiation with Mexico, and proclaiming a "cessation of hostilities against Mexico":

The Executive is now enabled to declare to the people of Texas the actual state of their affairs with respect to Mexico, to the end that they may direct and dispose them as they shall judge best for the honor and permanent interests of the republic.

During the course of the last winter it reached the knowledge of the Executive, from various sources of information, unofficial indeed, but still worthy of attention and credit, that the late and present government of Mexico were disposed to a peaceful settlement of the difficulties with Texas by the acknowledgment of our independence, upon the understanding that Texas would maintain her separate existence. No action, however, could be taken upon the subject, because nothing authentic was known until the month of March last, when the representatives of France and Great Britain near this government jointly and formally renewed the offer of the good offices of those powers with Mexico for the early and peaceful settlement of this struggle, upon the basis of the acknowledgment of our independence by that republic.

It would have been the imperative duty of the Executive at once to reject these offers if they had been accompanied by conditions of any kind whatever. But, with attentive watchfulness in that respect, and great disinclination to entangling alliances of any

[59]Donelson to Buchanan, June 2, 1845. *Senate Doc.* No. 1, 29th Cong., 1 Sess., 64-66.

[60]Elliot to Bankhead, June 11, 1845. Adams, *British Correspondence Concerning Texas*, 498-499.

description, or with any power, he must declare, in a spirit of justice, that no terms or conditions have ever been proposed by the two governments in question, or either of them, as the consideration of their friendly interposition.

Maturely considering the situation of affairs at that time, the Executive felt that it was incumbent upon him not to reject this opportunity of securing the people of this country, untrammeled by conditions, a peaceful, honorable, and advantageous settlement of their difficulties with Mexico, if they should see fit to adopt that mode of adjustment.

Thus influenced, he accepted the good offices of the two powers, which, with those of the United States, had been previously invoked by Texas, and placed in the hands of their representatives a statement of conditions preliminary to a treaty of peace, which he declared he should be ready to submit to the people of this country for their decision and action as soon as they were adopted by the government of Mexico. But he emphatically reminded those functionaries, for the special notice of their governments, that he was no more than the agent of the people; that he could neither direct, control, nor influence their decision; and that his bounden duty was to carry out their determination, constitutionally ascertained and expressed, be it what it might. Our representative at the courts of France and Great Britain, in addition to the task of strengthening the friendly dispositions of these governments, was also especially instructed to press upon their attention, that, if the people of Texas should determine to put an end to the separate existence of the country, the Executive, so far as depended upon his official action, must and would give immediate and full effect to their will.

The circumstances which preceded and led to an understanding with Mexico, have thus been stated; and the people, speaking through their chosen organs, will now determine as they shall judge right. But in the mean time, and until their pleasure can be lawfully and constitutionally ascertained, it is the duty of the Executive to secure to the nation the exercise of choice between the alternative of peace with the world and independence, or annexation and its contingencies; and he has, therefore, to issue the following proclamation:

Whereas authentic proof has recently been laid before me, to the effect that the Congress of Mexico has authorized the government to open negotiations and conclude a treaty with Texas, subject to the examination and approbation of that body; and further, that the government of Mexico has accepted the conditions prescribed on the part of Texas as preliminary to a final and definitive treaty of peace:

Therefore I, Anson Jones, President of the republic of Texas, and commander-in-chief of the army and navy and militia thereof, do hereby make known these circumstances to the citizens of this republic, till the same can be more fully communicated to the honorable Congress and convention of the people, for their lawful action, at the period of their assembling on the 16th June and 4th July next; and pending the said action, by virtue of the authority in me vested, I do hereby declare and proclaim a cessation of hostilities by land and by sea, against the republic of Mexico, or against the citizens and trade thereof.[61]

10. *Opposition to the Preliminary Treaty with Mexico*

The anti-administration party took the position that President Jones had entered into this negotiation with Mexico to create an issue on which a majority of the people would unite against the American proposal. Therefore, a storm of protest arose. "We are informed," said the editors of the New Orleans *Courier,* June 24, "that the feelings of the whole population are aroused to the highest pitch by the treacherous conduct of Jones and by his intention, if left to himself, to throw the republic into the arms of England." Ashbel Smith said that the people appeared frantic in their hostility to the negotiation.[62]

Donelson thought that the negotiation with Mexico *"was nothing more nor less than a contrivance* of Great Britain to defeat annexation or to involve Mexico in war with the United States," as Elliot on his return announced that hostilities would ensue if Texas accepted the American proposition. To meet this emergency and to counteract the effect of Elliot's reports, Donelson, keeping within the limits of his instructions of May 23, prepared a "paper for the Texas government," in which he again pledged the forces of the United States to protect Texas as soon as the government accepted the proposed terms. He sent this communication to Allen on June 11, and at the same time urged him to adhere strictly to the terms of annexation contained in the first and second sections of the joint resolution, and to include nothing in the new constitution that would create a doubtful issue in the Congress of the United States.[63]

As such a large majority of the friends of annexation condemned

[61]*A Proclamation by the President of the Republic of Texas. Senate Doc.* No. 1, 29th Cong., 1 Sess., 81-82; *Proclamation Papers of the Republic of Texas,* 1845, MS. State Library.

[62]Smith, *Reminiscences of the Republic of Texas,* 72.

[63]Donelson to Buchanan, June 11, 1845. *House Exec. Doc.* No. 1, 29th Cong., 1 Sess., 55-56.

President Jones in unmeasured terms for entering into the negotiation with Mexico, on November 23, 1847, Jones, in defense of his action, wrote to the editor of the *Civilian and Gazette* (Galveston):

In March, 1845, the ministers of France and England waited upon me, and showed me their instructions. The good offices tendered had been frequently invoked by Texas, long before I was connected with the executive government, and whether good policy or not, I did not feel at liberty to refuse them. It was probable that the annexation resolutions had passed in some form or other, but the instructions of these ministers had been sent out from London and Paris at a period when there was but very little hope entertained that those resolutions would succeed in any form at all, or that Texas would accept them. They had been sent in good faith and in a spirit of kindness evidently, and I think I should have been wholly unjustifiable before the people of Texas, and the world, if I had refused them. If jealousy of the European powers had been the efficient cause of the immense change of sentiment in the United States which had taken place in the last two years in its favor, it might be well to keep this jealousy alive a little longer. . . . The annexation measure had carried in the Senate by one vote. A little reaction in public opinion might change many votes perhaps, and the question had to be referred to another Congress for final action, and might therefore be lost. It behoved the friends of the measure to be prodent. The Secretary of State of the United States, Mr. Buchanan, bears testimony to the efficiency of the movement. . . . One of its good effects has been to render us, to a very great extent, a united people on the question of annexation. I was desirous to secure entire harmony in the United States on this subject, and it appears from this emotion of Mr. Buchanan that I succeeded tolerably well.

I accepted the good offices of France and England, thus tendered by their ministers, and prescribed the terms of a preliminary treaty, and promised the ministers that if signed by the executive of Mexico with the consent of the Congress, I would submit the proposition it contained, in good faith to the people of Texas; and would carry out their will when expressed, but nothing more. This pledge I subsequently fulfilled amid a storm of violent abuse.

Had the government of the United States adopted the alternative of negotiations as prescribed by the third section of the joint resolution for annexation instead of the one they did, . . . by the pendency of so favorable an offer for peace and independence, Texas would have been in a position to ask and obtain better terms in a treaty for annexation, than she would otherwise have been so that in every way in which the subject can be viewed the country would have been benefited by this preliminary treaty.

Those who so frequently harp on the words "treason and traitor," in reference to the arrangement with Mexico, forget that I was not at that time acting for the U. S.

Despite the fact that the anti-administration party condemned President Jones so severely for entering into the preliminary treaty with Mexico, Wm. B. Ochiltree, a strong annexationist, of Houston, said that it was the duty of the President to accept the offices of the foreign powers to obtain from Mexico the terms upon which she would be willing to acknowledge the independence of Texas, and that since President Jones had stated the terms, and Mexico had accepted them, that he was in duty bound to submit these propositions to Congress, as the constitution required the President to submit all documents in the nature of a treaty to the Senate. Furthermore, if he had rejected the offer on his own responsibility, that he would have been liable to censure.[65]

11. Congress's Acceptance of the American Proposal

After the President issued the proclamation making known the negotiation with Mexico, nothing else of importance occurred relative to annexation until Congress met, June 16. As soon as Congress was organized, President Jones presented both the American and the Mexican propositions, in accordance with his previous announcement, so the alternative of annexation or independence was thus placed before the people, and their "free, sovereign, and unbiased voice" was to determine "the all important issue." In his message, he assured the members of Congress that in so far as it should depend upon the executive to act, he would give immediate and full effect to their expressed will.[66]

Two bills relative to annexation were introduced in Congress, one in each house, and were unanimously adopted, but, as the bills were different in some respects, neither house was willing to accept the bill of the other. Therefore, a committee of conference was chosen by the two houses to effect a compromise. The substitute

[64]Jones, *Letters Relating to Annexation*, 12-14.

[65]*Telegraph and Texas Register* (Washington), June 11, 1845.

[66]*Message of President Jones*, June 16, 1845. *House Journal*, 9th Texas Cong., 5; *Telegraph and Texas Register* (Washington), July 25, 1845.

bill recommended by this committee was adopted and promptly signed by President Jones.[67]

Since Donelson did not think that it would be necessary for him to remain in Texas after the Texas Congress had accepted the American proposition, he had asked permission of Polk to return to the United States. Polk, however, wrote him that he did not consider it safe for him to leave Texas, as the assent of the existing government was but the initiatory step in accomplishing the object of his mission. As the measure would not be beyond danger until it had been accepted by a convention of the people, it was, therefore, very important that the "minister of the United States should be on the spot ready to counteract any influences or intrigues which might be brought to bear upon annexation."[68]

[67]Allen to Donelson, June 23, 1845. *House Exec. Doc.* No. 1, 29th Cong., 1 Sess., 75-76.

[68]Polk to Donelson, May 26, 1845. *Tennessee Historical Magazine*, III, 66-67.

SOME PRECEDENTS OF THE PERSHING EXPEDITION INTO MEXICO[1]

J. FRED RIPPY

Discussions connected with the recent expedition led by General John J. Pershing into Mexico evince a striking ignoring of antecedents. One searches in vain through the contemporary periodicals for a clear statement of the precedents upon which the enterprise was based. Only now and then can there be found evidence revealing a consciousness on the part of the journalists that Mexican border difficulties have not been confined to the last decade. There are occasional references, for instance, to the brilliant pursuit of Gerónimo into Sonora. For the most part, however, the writers maintain a striking silence regarding the past. Even the diplomatic correspondence connected with the recent punitive expedition has little to say of previous circumstances which have resembled those leading to the dispatch of Pershing. As now published it contains only two or three references to the period prior to 1910.[2]

The works of a historical nature which treat the relations of the United States and Mexico since 1910 likewise fail to present the background necessary to a clear understanding of recent developments, most of them plunging immediately into contemporary difficulties as if they were entirely new.[3] In the opinion of the writer, this neglect of antecedents furnishes sufficient justification for the present article.

The bold, reckless, and lawless elements of society usually drift toward the frontier, where they expect to find adventures suited to their taste and freedom from the restraints of more settled regions. Here they take advantage of the sparsity of population, the international line, the weakness of the local frontier govern-

[1]The writer desires to make grateful acknowledgment to Professor Herbert E. Bolton, whose seminar papers he has freely used.

[2]For the correspondence, see *The American Journal of International Law*, X, Supplement, pp. 179ff.; New York *Times*, July 29, August 5, and November 25, 1916; Washington *Post*, January 3, 1917. These journals also contain the best discussion of the expedition from the historical standpoint.

[3]Among the best discussions of the relations of the United States since 1910 are, W. F. Johnson, *America's Foreign Relations*, II, 334ff.; F. A. Ogg, *National Progress, 1907-1917*, p. 284ff.

ments, race and religious prejudices, and whatever else may shield them from the punishment deserved for their transgressions. International borders are therefore likely to be the scene of numerous irregularities and conflicts which threaten constantly to interrupt the friendly relations of the nations concerned. This has been particularly true in the case of the United States and Mexico, whose frontiers have all the features mentioned, plus, in the past, a large number of wild Indians fond of war and plunder and void of any regard for international obligations. The most important border disturbances have resulted from the raids of filibusters, banditti, and Indians; and the difficulties of dealing with the situation have been magnified by the inability of the two governments to reach satisfactory agreements regarding extradition or mutual crossing of the border in pursuit of marauding bands. In fact, the military and police forces of the two nations have not often been able to co-operate effectively. Agents of the federal government of the United States or local officials of the frontier have accordingly been provoked in times of crisis to send troops across the boundary often without the consent and even in the face of protest on the part of the Mexican government. The most important and conspicuous instance of such invasion was the late Pershing expedition, but it is only one of a series extending back for almost three-quarters of a century.

The Occupation of Nacogdoches, 1836. The first invasion of this type was probably the one which resulted in the occupation of Nacogdoches, Texas, in the summer of 1836, although the United States government erroneously assumed at the time that this town, being east of the Neches River, was within its national domain. The year 1836 opened with the Texan revolution in full progress. In March occurred the fall of the Alamo and the massacre of Goliad, and the following month witnessed the flight of the panic-stricken Texans before Santa Anna's advance. At the same time, the Indians on both sides of the border, apparently instigated by Mexican emissaries, were threatening an outbreak which, once begun, was likely to result in indiscriminate robbery and murder. If other motives for precaution on the part of the Washington government were needed, they could be found in the hostile attitude of the advancing Mexican army toward the United States and in the indications that certain of its citizens on the southwestern frontier entertained designs of aiding Texas in violation of the neutrality laws.[4] Accordingly, as early as January 23, 1836, General Edmund P. Gaines, who was then stationed in Florida, was ordered to repair to some position near the western boundary of Louisiana in order to preserve neutrality, to prevent a violation of United States soil, and to hold the border Indians in check, using force if necessary to accomplish his purpose.[5]

Gaines interpreted his instructions in a rather liberal fashion; but, as the sequel was to show, he merely divined the intention of the Secretary of War. Writing to Cass, who held this post, he declared that in case he found "any disposition on the part of the Mexicans or their red allies to menace our frontier," he would feel called upon to "anticipate their lawless movements, by crossing our supposed or imaginary national boundary, and meeting the savage marauders wherever they were to be found in their approach toward our frontier."[6]

Before this letter reached Washington the administration had already decided upon a line of action similar to that suggested by General Gaines. On April 25 this commander was authorized "to take such position, on either side of the imaginary boundary line," as would be best adapted to "defensive operations." He was cautioned, however, not to "advance farther than old Fort Nacogdoches, which is within the limits of the United States, as claimed by this government."[7]

The governors of Louisiana, Tennessee, and Mississippi were immediately called upon for volunteers, and the military officials of Forts Leavenworth and Gibson were ordered to hold their dragoons in readiness to march to the assistance of Gaines. At the same time, Congress was asked to extend the time of volunteer service to six months.

Meantime, Gaines had reached the frontier and found the state of affairs sufficiently grave to justify his contemplated step. Before his preparations could be completed, however, the situation was modified by the victory of the Texans at San Jacinto; but the

[4]An excellent description of the border situation at this time is given in T. M. Marshall, *A History of the Western Boundary of the Louisiana Purchase,* 141ff.

[5]Cass to Gaines, *House Doc.* No. 256, 24 Cong., 1 Sess. (Ser. 291), pp. 40-41.

[6]Gaines to Cass, March 29, 1836, *House Doc.* No. 351, 25 Cong., 2 Sess. (Ser. 332), p. 768.

[7]*House Doc.* No. 256, 24 Cong., 1 Sess. (Ser. 291), pp. 43-44.

zealous General Gaines soon professed to descry future danger. Opportune Indian atrocities, an appeal from the Texans for protection, and reports that the Mexicans were preparing to rescue their President and instigate a general savage uprising led him to dispatch Colonel Whistler to occupy Nacogdoches while he made another call upon the governors for reinforcements.

The occupation was approved by the Secretary of War, but he intercepted the state militia. The President, on the other hand, assumed a more cautious attitude and questioned the wisdom of Gaines's action. The troops were nevertheless allowed to remain upon what was in reality Mexican soil until near the close of 1836. During this time, however, there occurred no important Indian outbreak and no Mexican invasion. Accordingly nothing of value was accomplished; but the episode did lead to a warm diplomatic contest, which resulted in the withdrawal of the Mexican minister and the intensification of Mexican bitterness and suspicion already aroused by the belief that the United States entertained covert designs upon Texas.[8]

The government of the United States justified Gaines's action upon the ground of international law and of treaty obligations to Mexico. Secretary of State Forsyth maintained that under the 33d article of the treaty of April 5, 1831, the troops of the United States, in order to protect Mexican "territory against the Indians within the United States . . . might justly be sent into the heart of Mexico. Nor could the good faith and friendship of the act be doubted if troops of the United States were sent into Mexican territory to prevent . . . Mexican Indians, justly suspected of such design, from assailing the frontier settlements of the United States."[9] Forsyth declared further that the occupation of Nacogdoches rested "upon principles of the law of nations . . . upon immutable principles of self-defence—upon the principles which justify decisive measures of precaution to prevent irreparable evil to our own or to a neighboring people."[10]

The Callahan Expedition, 1855. Some twenty years after this occurrence there took place an invasion of Mexican soil which had

[8]Marshall, *op. cit.*, 157ff.

[9]Forsyth to Gorostiza, May 10, 1836, *House Doc.* No. 256, 24 Cong., 1 Sess. (Ser. 291), pp. 33-35; quoted also in J. B. Moore, *A Digest of International Law* (1906 ed.), II, 419-420.

[10]Forsyth to Ellis, Dec. 10, 1836, quoted in Moore, *op. et loc. cit.*

more important results. It was occasioned by outrages committed upon the Texan frontier settlements by Indians who had their lodges in Mexico, and partially supported by planters desirous of recovering runaway slaves who were accustomed to find refuge on the south side of the Rio Grande. The expedition consisted of three companies of Texan volunteers, led by J. H. Callahan, a veteran of the Fannin massacre, and under orders of the governor of Texas.[11] They crossed the river early in October, 1855, and soon afterwards had an encounter some distance south of the international line with a combined force of Indians and Mexicans. Defeated and compelled to retreat, they fell back upon Piedras Negras, pillaging and burning the town on October 6 and then withdrawing before a considerable Mexican force into United States territory.[12]

In regard to the expedition, W. L. Marcy, then Secretary of State, took the stand that "if Mexican Indians, whom Mexico is bound to restrain, are permitted to cross its border and commit depredations in the United States they may be chased across the border and there punished." He admitted, however, that the right was reciprocal. "If Indians whom the United States are bound to restrain shall, under the same circumstances, make a hostile incursion into Mexico, this Government will not complain if the Mexican forces who may be sent to repel them shall cross to this side of the line for that purpose, provided that in so doing they abstain from injuring persons and property of citizens of the United States."[13] These statements would seem to indicate that the expedition at least was justified by the United States whether it proceeded under the authority of the federal government or not. It had not been possible for the Texan troops to refrain from "injuring persons and property" of citizens of Mexico, however, and the excesses committed at this time were des-

[11]The governor's instructions have not been found, but Callahan's report to the state executive clearly indicates that the troops proceeded under his orders. See Callahan to Governor Pease, Oct. 13, 1855, State *Gazette* (Texas), Oct. 20, 1855.

[12]For a fuller discussion of this episode, see the present writer's "Border Troubles Along the Rio Grande, 1848-1860," *The Southwestern Historical Quarterly*, XXIII (October, 1919), 99-102.

[13]Francis Wharton, *A Digest of International Law* (1886 ed.) I, 230: Moore, *op. cit.*, II, 421.

tined before the matter was settled to cost the United States thousands of dollars.[14]

President Buchanan's Proposed Occupation of Northern Mexico, 1858, 1859, 1860. Injuries alleged to have been inflicted by Mexican Indians and desperadoes upon citizens of the United States residing in northwestern Texas, New Mexico, and Arizona furnished one of the motives which led President Buchanan, in December, 1858, to ask for the permission of Congress to "assume a temporary protectorate over the northern portions of Chihuahua and Sonora and to establish military posts within the same," the protection to be withdrawn as soon as local Mexican governments sufficiently strong to take over the duty could be established. This request was repeated in 1859 and again in 1860, but Congress refused to grant the desired permission and no action was taken.[15]

Cortina and the Orders of Robert E. Lee, 1859-1860. During this same period there developed upon the northern frontier of Mexico a character somewhat similar to "Pancho" Villa. Juan Nepomucina Cortina—sometimes written "Cortinas"—was of Mexican extraction but of uncertain citizenship. A native of Camargo and probably taught the lesson of hatred for the "Gringos" at an early day, he was old enough to fight in the army of Arista during the war between the United States and Mexico. After the treaty of 1848 he moved with his mother and brother to their ranch a few miles above Brownsville, Texas. Here he not only fell in with the rough company of the frontier, but heard reports of and probably witnessed maltreatment of the Mexicans in the region by the Texans. He seems soon to have earned the reputation of a lawless, dangerous man; and though uneducated, and not very attractive personally, he seems to have exercised great influence over the Mexican population of the section. Because of his value as a political asset, and by virtue of the support of a band of armed desperadoes ready to do his bidding, he managed to escape punishment. Finally, however, in the summer and fall of 1859 several murders committed in Brownsville and threats to burn the

[14]For the awards granted to the persons injured during this raid by Joint Claims Commission which sat under the convention of July, 1868, see *Sen. Ex. Doc.* No. 31, 44 Cong., 2 Sess. (Ser. 1720).

[15]J. D. Richardson, *Messages and Papers of the Presidents* (1898 ed.), V, 521, *passim; Sen. Jour.* 35 Cong., 2 Sess., p. 342; "Mr. Buchanan's Administration," Buchanan, *Works* (J. B. Moore ed.), XII, 251.

town and kill all the Anglo-Saxon population, together with the rifling of the United States mails, led the military authorities to take action.

But Cortina's forces were increased by volunteers and conscripts until he was able to hold out against the Texas Rangers and the volunteers sent to dislodge him. For some three or four months he had things in the region pretty much his own way. When hard pressed he simply crossed over the boundary, where he was received as a hero and furnished needed recruits and supplies—he was the champion of the injured Mexican race. Summing up the results of Cortina's depredations, Major Heintzelman of the United States army said in part: "The whole country from Brownsville to Rio Grande City, one hundred and twenty miles and back to the Arroyo Colorado, has been laid waste. There is not an American [left] or any property belonging to an American that could be destroyed in this large tract of land. . . . There have been fifteen Americans and eighty friendly Mexicans killed."[16]

It required the combined efforts of the federal troops and the local militia, in addition to the co-operation of the Mexican military forces finally to break up and scatter Cortina's band. On December 14, 1859, Major Heintzelman with 165 Regulars and 120 Rangers advanced upon his position. Cortina retreated northward, avoiding a serious engagement until December 27, when his forces were overtaken and routed near Rio Grande City. He then fled into Mexico, leaving his "guns, ammunition and baggage carts, provisions, and everything he could throw away to lighten his flight." About sixty of his troops were killed or drowned in the river, and the rest escaped into Mexico without their arms. Cortina afterwards moved southward along the Mexican frontier, collecting the remnants of his scattered forces and eventually establishing his camp at *La Bolza,* about thirty-five miles above Brownsville, with the intention of capturing the American steamboat *Ranchero* on its way down the river. But when, in February, 1860, he attempted to seize this vessel a party of Rangers who had held themselves in readiness crossed over to the Mexican side of the stream and administered a sound defeat. Cortina then set up at *La Mesa* Ranch, but once more the Rangers, this time ac-

[16]Heintzelman to Lee, March 1, 1860, *House Exec. Doc.* No. 81, 36 Cong., 1 Sess. (Ser. 1056), p. 13.

companied by a detachment of Regulars, entered Mexico and forced him to flee.

The whole Cortina affair gave occasion to many wild rumors and false reports; and although the government at Washington received intimations that the reports were exaggerated, the situation was deemed sufficiently grave to demand special attention. Accordingly, Colonel Robert E. Lee, who was thought to possess superior fitness for the task, was placed in command on the frontier early in 1860. He was instructed to demand that the Mexican authorities break up the bands of Cortina who found lodgment on the south side of the Rio Grande, and in case they failed to accomplish this plain duty, to cross into Mexico and disperse the marauders with the forces under his command.

Contrary to some of the reports which had reached Washington, the Mexican civil and military authorities had already shown a disposition to oppose Cortina. Upon two occasions the national guards of Matamoras had given succor to Brownsville. Both the state government of Matamoras and the Mexican national government not only approved the action of these troops, but instructed the military commander of the line of the Bravo to prevent the followers of Cortina from crossing, and to pursue and punish them in concert with the forces of the United States in case they did. This official seems to have co-operated with the American soldiers when they crossed over in pursuit of Cortina in the month of February; and against these invasions themselves no protest appears to have been made, although alleged acts of violence to Mexican property and firing upon a troop of Mexican soldiers was resented. Therefore, when in April, 1860, Lee entered into communication with the Mexican authorities and made known to them his instructions, he received civil and agreeable replies, followed by vigorous measures which sent Cortina into the Burgos mountains in search of a hiding place, and rendered a punitive expedition on the part of Lee unnecessary.[17]

Conditions Along the Border, 1869-1880. During the some fifteen or sixteen years subsequent to the Civil War in the United States and the fall of Maximilian in Mexico conditions on the international border, and especially along the Rio Grande, were probably more unsettled and irritating than ever before or since.

[17]On this entire affair see Rippy, *op. cit.*, 103ff, and authorities there cited.

The states to the north of the line were suffering from the disorders of the reconstruction and the constant ravages of the Indians, while the states to the south were perturbed by revolutions and counter-revolutions characteristic of the section from the achievement of Mexico's independence to the régime of the iron-handed Díaz. On the right bank of the lower Rio Grande bands of cattle thieves were systematically organized. Many of them were probably American citizens, but others were not; and it was hard to ascertain the truth and to exercise discrimination. Above Laredo, Texas, the American border was being laid waste by Indians, which the inhabitants of the region declared to live in the mountain fastnesses of Coahuila and Chihuahua. It was thought, too, that the savages were often guided in their raids by the superior intelligence of Mexicans. Of course most of the Indians had taken advantage of the disorders of the Civil War to escape from reservations in the United States, and the natives still residing on those reservations often made destructive incursions into Mexico, murdering an average of some forty Mexicans annually;[18] but it was difficult to view the question from both sides, and the United States might obviously argue that the subjugation of the Mexican Indians and the Mexican cattle thieves would be advantageous to both countries.

If the reports of the successive commissions sent by the United States to the border may be relied upon, conditions were little short of appalling. If fifty per cent is subtracted for exaggeration one could still well believe that they were grave. Matters reached their worst stage between 1870 and 1880. At the beginning of this period Cortina came again into prominence on the frontier. The outlaws and cattle thieves were said to have rallied to him with an enthusiastic devotion which rendered him "more powerful in that locality than any other authority, national or state."[19] As an official of the Mexican government, he was reported to have winked at and participated in cattle "lifting." Indeed, it was declared that trade in stolen cattle had enabled him to place on deposit in an English bank the snug sum of three hundred thousand dollars, while he retained enough of them to stock four large ranches. Moreover, if reports of the Americans may

[18] *House Exec. Doc.* No. 1, 43 Cong., 1 Sess. (Ser. 1594), Part I, p. 691, *passim;* H. H. Bancroft, *The North Mexican States and Texas*, II, 704.

[19] *Ho. Rept.* No. 701, 45 Cong., 2 Sess. (Ser. 1824), p. VI.

be relied upon, Mexican authorities of smaller caliber assumed the same attitude.[20]

The number of cattle carried off by the raiders was alleged to be enormous. In southwestern Texas cattle raising was followed on a very large scale during this period, ranches comprising from ten to two hundred thousand acres and stocked with from fifty to seventy-five thousand head not being uncommon. Horse raising was likewise engaged in to a considerable extent along the lower Rio Grande, and on a much larger scale farther to the northwest. The raids of the thieves threatened to destroy these important industries. During the nine years between 1866 and 1875 the number of stock between the Nueces and the Rio Grande and south of Laredo decreased almost 80 per cent. A federal grand jury convened in Texas in the spring of 1872 reckoned that there had been stolen from this section since the close of the Civil War an average of five thousand cattle per month.[21] The records for the customs house at Brownsville during this period were said to show that twenty-five per cent of the hides exported from Mexico into Texas at this point bore brands of Texan stock raisers, while another twenty-five per cent gave evidence of having been altered or otherwise defaced. From this it was judged that a great many of them were stolen from Texas.[22]

While the main object of the raiders who crossed over into the Rio Grande-Nueces region was the theft of cattle, they were inevitably led into the perpetration of even worse outrages. Travelers who chanced to meet them and individuals who were thought likely to give out incriminating information were murdered; thousands of dollars in money, merchandise, and other property were taken; towns were raided; postoffices and customs houses were looted; and numerous public officials were killed. In fact, between 1875 and 1877 the situation in this section amounted to a reign of terror.[23]

Depredations committed by Mexican Indians in the region above Laredo and westward to the borders of Arizona were reported to be equally bad, and it was declared that Arizona was

[20] *Ibid.*, No. 343, 44 Cong., 1 Sess. (Ser. 1709), p. 1ff.

[21] *Ibid.*, App., pp. 78-79, 92, 97-100, 115, *passim*.

[22] *House Exec. Doc.* No. 39, 42 Cong. 3 Sess. (Ser. 1565), p. 20.

[23] For the conditions during this period, see *Ho. Rept.* No. 701, 45 Cong., 2 Sess. (Ser. 1824), and a document bound with the same entitled, "Texas Frontier Troubles."

suffering both from Indians, who made their escape into Sonora, and from Mexican bandits. The savages consisted mainly, however, of stray bands belonging to the Lipan, Comanche, Apache, and Kickapoo tribes, who found shelter in the mountains of Coahuila and Chihuahua. A great many horses and sheep were raised on the frontiers of northwest Texas and of New Mexico; but the ravages of these Indians made such occupations extremely perilous. Indeed, the reports alleged that many of the ranches had been entirely broken up. Thousands of stock were stolen, killed and scattered; frequent murders occurred, and several women and children were carried away into captivity.

The general situation can probably be best set forth by the testimony of three officials of the United States army who were stationed on this frontier. Lieutenant Colonel W. R. Shafter, who had been at Fort Clark, Texas, since 1867, testified in 1878 that there was hardly a family which had dwelt for any length of time in the region without having sacrificed a member to the savages.[24] William Steele, who was Adjutant General of the State of Texas at the time, stated that fifty-seven Indian parties had killed forty citizens of Texas between 1875 and 1878.[25] Colonel Hatch of New Mexico reported in 1879 that twenty-five persons had recently been massacred by Mexican Indians, who had purchased arms, ammunition and supplies from the frontier towns of Chihuahua, and that fourteen soldiers and scouts had been killed in pursuit of the raiders.[26]

The policy of the Mexican government in regard to these raids was ineffective, and in the eyes of the government of the United States, dilatory and indifferent. The historian may explain the Mexican attitude by the inability of the national government of Mexico to enforce its will upon the frontier governments; by hatred and suspicion felt toward the United States because of former aggressions; by the fact that the Indians in question had for the most part escaped from reservations on the northern side of the boundary, and that such Indians had often inflicted injuries upon Mexico; by the exasperation which the formation of Mexican revolutionary parties on American soil occasioned; and,

[24]"Texas Frontier Troubles," p. 23.

[25]*Ibid.*, p. 48.

[26]Summarized in Hunter to Zamacona, Nov. 7, 1879, *Ho. Ex. Doc.* No. 1, 46 Cong., 3 Sess. (Ser. 1951), pp. 780-781.

lastly, by interior disturbances which appeared to the successive Mexican administrations more important than the disorders on the frontier. This side of the question could hardly have been expected to make a strong appeal at the time, however; and such a view of the matter would have afforded small consolation to those inhabitants of the United States frontier who were being injured and outraged by Mexican Indians and bandits. It will not occasion surprise, therefore, when it is learned that numerous punitive expeditions invaded Mexican territory during this period.

Venustiano Carranza's List of Invasions. In fact, the expeditions were so numerous that when the late President Carranza desired to prove that the recent so-called violations of Mexican soil by the United States were not confined to his administration, he did not have to go outside of the decade subsequent to 1873. Within that period he was able to find some twenty-three instances.[27] The remainder of this paper will be confined to a description of the more important of these and the circumstances under which they proceeded, and to a statement of some of the agreements which President Porfirio Díaz and the United States government were able to reach in regard to the mutual crossing of the border in pursuit of depredating bands.

The MacKenzie Raid. Carranza began his list by referring to the Kickapoo troubles which culminated in the MacKenzie raid of 1873. For several years these Indians had made bold incursions far into the interior of western and northwestern Texas, so far indeed as to arouse suspicion that they were being led by white men.[28] In 1869 the United States began urging upon the Mexican government the necessity of co-operation in an attempt to bring the culprits back to their reservation in the United States and the advisability of permitting troops of the United States to cross the line in pursuit of the hostiles. The Mexican foreign office replied that the latter request could only be granted with the consent of the Mexican Congress, and showed great reluctance to ask their consent. The United States first warned Mexico that it might become necessary to pursue the hostile Indians into Mexican territory without the permission of the Mexican government, but later decided, out of consideration for the embarrassment oc-

[27]Message of September 1, 1919.

[28]*Ho. Ex. Doc.* No. 1, 41 Cong., 2 Sess. (Ser. 1412), Part II, p. 143.

casioned by the disturbed political conditions in Mexico, not to press the matter for the time being.[29] The Mexican government did offer its assistance in the "just and humane object" of removing the Indians to the northern side of the boundary; but the agents of the United States who were sent down in the summer of 1871 to accomplish this object met with opposition on the part of the local inhabitants and officials and returned home in disgust.[30] Another attempt made during the following year prove equally futile.[31]

Thus the question stood[32] when in May, 1873, news reached Colonel R. S. MacKenzie, who was stationed at Fort Clark, Texas, that the Kickapoos had made a raid and escaped with a drove of horses. He and Lieutenant Bullis immediately took up the trail, and leading their troops into Coahuila, they fell upon the Indian village of Remolino, killing nineteen of the savages, capturing some forty, and recovering sixty or seventy head of horses.[33]

There are several bits of evidence indicating that MacKenzie may not have been acting contrary to the wishes of the United States government. In the first place, on January 16, 1873, Secretary of State Hamilton Fish wrote the minister of the United States in Mexico that the Mexican government appeared "so apathetic or so powerless to prevent such [Indian] raids that sooner or later this government [i. e., the United States] will have no other alternative than to endeavor to secure quiet on the frontier by seeking the marauders and punishing them in their haunts wherever they may be. Of course we should prefer that this should be done with the consent, if not with the co-operation, of Mexico. It is certain, however, that if the grievances shall be persisted in, the remedy adverted to will not remain untried."[34]

[29]Fish to Nelson, June 26, 1871, quoted in Moore, *op cit.*, II, 435; Nelson to Fish, August 30, 1871, *House Exec. Doc.* No. 1, 42 Cong., 2 Sess. (Ser. 1502), Part I, p. 635; *Ibid*, pp. 662-663.

[30]*House Exec. Doc.* No. 1, 42 Cong., 2 Sess. (Ser. 1502), Part I, pp. 649-650.

[31]*House Exec. Doc.* No. 1, 42 Cong., 3 Sess. (Ser. 1552), Part I, p. 416ff.

[32]In the fall of 1873 some four hundred Kickapoos were removed to the United States, and two years later about one hundred and thirty more were persuaded to return. See *Ho. Ex. Doc.* No. 1, 43 Cong., 2 Sess. (Ser. 1634), Part I, p. 716; and *Ibid.*, 44 Cong., 1 Sess. (Ser. 1673), Part I, p. 896.

[33]*House Misc. Doc.* No. 64, 45 Cong., 2 Sess. (Ser. 1820), pp. 187-188; Mexican Border Commission of 1873, *Report*, p. 424.

[34]*House Exec. Doc.* No. 1, 43 Cong., 1 Sess. (Ser. 1594), Part I, p. 643.

Second, on January 22, 1874, Fish wrote the Secretary of War that an incursion into Mexico when necessary for the dispersal of a band of Indian marauders, was not a violation of the law of nations.[35] Third, Colonel MacKenzie does not appear to have been censured for his act; or if censured, he was certainly not removed from his post.[36] Fourth, when this raid was later referred to as a precedent, the American government seems to have acquiesced.[37]

The McNally-Randlett Invasion, 1875. The next expedition of which definite details have been acquired, but the fifth in the enumeration of Carranza, was that which crossed the international boundary in pursuit of cattle thieves in November, 1875. Captain Randlett of the United States army had been encamped with about eighty men at Edinburg for some time, when he received news that thieves with a herd of cattle were on their way to the Rio Grande. He immediately dispatched a courier to Ringgold Barracks for help and a telegram to Fort Brown for more specific orders, while he sent out scouts to ascertain the ford where the robbers would be most likely to attempt to cross with their booty. From Fort Brown on November 16, he received the command: "If you catch the thieves, hit them hard. If you come up to them while they cross the river, follow them into Mexico." From the scouts which he had sent out he learned, on November 17, that a herd of cattle were being driven toward the river with the probable intention of effecting a crossing near *Las Cuevas* during the

[35]Moore, *op. cit.*, p. 421.

[36]The reports of the Adjutant General show that he continued to remain at Fort Clark.

[37]A large number of murders and robberies committed in Texas in the spring and summer of 1874 and the absence of what appeared to be sufficient protection on the part of the federal army, led the Texas government to raise companies of minute men to protect the frontier. The governor gave at least one of the captains of these companies orders to pursue the marauders into Mexican territory. When questioned in regard to this step by the Washington government, he argued that if troops of the government of the United States had a right to "cross the national boundary and continue pursuit of marauders on Mexican soil, . . . Texas forces which are doing the duty which ought to be performed by the United States troops . . . have the same right." *House Report* No. 343, 44 Cong., 1 Sess. (Ser. 1709), pp. XVI, 161-167. In these conclusions the attorney general seems to have acquiesced. *House Exec. Doc.* No. 13, 45 Cong., 1 Sess. (Ser. 1773), p. 62. The fact that Carranza mentions this affair in his message may indicate that a raid took place in pursuance of the order.

run of the day. Preparations for pursuit were hastily made, and shortly after 4 o'clock the troops reached the river, where they found the thieves forcing the cattle off of a steep bank into the stream. An encounter took place, but it was soon interrupted by darkness. Randlett then wrote the *alcalde* of Las Cuevas demanding the return of the cattle and the delivery of the thieves, whose names he supplied. At the same time, he prepared to move to the Mexican shore early the next morning.

Just before daybreak Major Clendenin of Ringgold Barracks arrived and, taking command, forbade Randlett to cross the river on the ground that it would be bad faith to do so while negotiations were in progress. A little later Randlett received a communication from the *alcalde* which informed him that while a few of the cattle had been recovered the thieves had escaped with most of the herd in the direction of Camargo. Randlett thereupon sent a dispatch to the authorities of Camargo and enclosed a copy of his orders. Clendenin, in the meantime, had reported the situation to the commander at Fort Brown and asked for further instructions; and, in reply, had received the following order: "If you have not crossed when this reaches you, await arrival of Major Alexander, who will be at *Las Cuevas* to-morrow with two companies. General is afraid you have not men enough."

About noon of the 18th, and before Alexander had arrived with reinforcements, Captain McNally of the Texas Rangers came upon the scene and declared his intention of crossing the river as soon as his troop should arrive. Clendenin urged McNally to wait until Alexander came, but the captain of the Rangers remained obdurate. Thereupon Clendenin remarked: "If you are determined to cross, we will cover your return, but cannot cross at present to help you." A Gatling gun was then placed in position on the left bank of the Rio Grande, and Randlett was ordered to protect McNally's return, but not to enter Mexican territory unless it appeared that the Texan troops were on the point of being massacred. Clendenin then departed for Ringgold Barracks, leaving Randlett in charge until Alexander should arrive.

By early morning of the 19th McNally had succeeded in getting his men and five horses across the Rio Grande. A considerable skirmish ensued, and about two hundred and fifty Mexican regulars soon put in their appearance. A part of the fighting took place within sight of the American troops; and Randlett, believing that the Texas Rangers were on the point of annihilation, began to dispatch federal troops to his assistance. After the exchange of several volleys, a truce to last until nine o'clock November 20, was agreed upon. Just at this moment Alexander arrived from Fort Brown and commanded the immediate withdrawal of the United States forces. Although McNally declared that he would not return until the Mexican authorities delivered up the cattle and the thieves in accordance with the terms of the truce, he and his men retired the following day.[38]

There seems to have been some confusion in regard to the orders directing the crossing of the international line in pursuit of the thieves. The telegram of November 16 had plainly said, "follow them into Mexico" in case they were overtaken at the river's bank, while that of November 18 did not forbid the crossing, but merely asked for delay on the ground that the forces then present were not sufficient. These telegrams were signed by Helenus Dodt, Acting Assistant Adjutant General, and they contained the expression, "by order of Colonel J. H. Potter." Yet, on November 19, Potter telegraphed Brigadier General E. O. C. Ord, who had charge of the military department of Texas, that Randlett's action had been taken in violation of orders; and on the following day Ord instructed Potter to notify the Mexican authorities that the troops of the United States were ordered not to cross the Rio Grande. In reply to a protest on the part of General Fuero of the Mexican army, Potter accordingly declared that the troops of the United States had crossed into Mexico in disobedience of orders. Almost two years later the Mexican government complained that it had not been informed of any punishment being inflicted upon the subordinate officials for their disobedience.[39] Moreover, when Mexico made diplomatic protest against the violation of its national soil, the Department of State seems to have made no response.[40]

[38]Nevertheless, these vigorous measures seem to have borne fruit; for on November 21, seventy-six cattle were brought to Ringgold Barracks, and reports alleged that seven of the robbers were killed and several wounded by the Mexicans themselves.

[39]Originals of the telegrams to Randlett and Clendenin have not been seen, but copies are contained in Randlett to Acting Adjutant General, Dec. 1, 1875. On the whole affair see *House Report* No. 343, 44 Cong., 1 Sess. (Ser. 1709), pp. 87-96; and *House Exec. Doc.* No. 13, 45 Cong., 1 Sess. (Ser. 1773), p. 62.

[40]Vallarta to Cuellar, August 18, 1877, *House Doc.* No. 13, 45 Cong., 1 Sess., pp. 62-63.

General Ord Assumes Responsibility. Whatever may be the truth in regard to this invasion, it is certain that the expeditions which took place during the next two years were authorized by General Ord. On December 6, 1877, he testified before the congressional committee on military affairs as follows: "I gave orders nearly two years ago to cross over on a fresh trail, I stated my reasons for giving the order and communicated the orders to the administration, and I received no instructions in regard to the matter. The order was not disapproved and consequently it was tacitly approved.[41] The majority of these expeditions represented attempts to punish Indians who had escaped into Mexico after having raided into United States territory. A brief description of two of them may serve to represent their general nature.

During the months of April and May, 1876, twelve Texans were killed by the Lipans led by their chief, Washo Lobo; and Lieutenant Colonel W. R. Shafter of Fort Duncan, incensed by these outrages, determined to pursue the perpetrators into Coahuila. Accordingly he dispatched Lieutenant Bullis across the Rio Grande at a ford about sixty miles above the mouth of the Pecos, with the purpose of spying out the camp of the savages and falling upon it. But the Indians were warned of his approach, and little was accomplished. A raid made in the following July proved more successful, however. Shafter and Bullis passed over the Rio Grande some twenty-five miles above its junction with the Pecos, and marched southward into Mexico for five or six days. The main army of invasion then halted, and Bullis was sent ahead with twenty scouts and as many soldiers to hunt for a village which was reported to be on the San Antonio River. At dawn on July 30, discovering that they were near a Lipan camp, they made an immediate onslaught, which resulted in the death of fourteen Indians, the capture of four squaws and ninety-six horses and mules, and the destruction of the entire Indian village. Bullis then turned northward, joining Shafter on the following day. Before leaving Mexican soil, however, they had another encounter with a band of Indians who had been marauding in Texas, but with less success than on the former occasion.[42]

In December, 1876, and in January, 1877, the Lipans, accompanied by the Mescalero Apaches, again ventured over into the re-

[41] *House Misc. Doc.* No. 64, 45 Cong., 2 Sess. (Ser. 1820), p. 103.

[42] *Ibid.*, pp. 188-189.

gion around Fort Clark, where they picked up two or three hundred head of cattle and more than sixty horses. Lieutenant Bullis with his company, assisted by Captain Keys with two hundred negro cavalry, pursued the band about one hundred and twenty-five miles into Mexico, without being able to overtake them or to recover any considerable amount of stolen property.[43]

The Ord Orders, June, 1877. In spite of these punitive expeditions the Indian incursions continued, and there seemed less co-operation than ever on the part of Mexico. The lack of co-operation may be explained in part by the political disturbances which were occasioned by the attempt of Porfirio Díaz to depose Lerdo de Tejada and gain control of the government. It was apparently due in part, also, to the unfriendly attitude of a group of frontier governors.[44] At any rate, on March 9, 1877, Shafter was impelled to write that "not the slightest attempt" was being made by the Mexicans to prevent the Indians from making incursions into the United States, but, on the contrary, they were "finding a refuge in the towns when pursued, and a market for their stolen plunder at all times."[45] When General Sheridan forwarded this letter to Washington on March 19, he recommended that "the Mexican government be compelled to prevent these hostile incursions."[46] A few days later the hostility of at least one of the frontier governors was evinced by the proposal to punish as traitors certain of the Mexican guides who had aided the American troops in their pursuit of Indians upon Mexican soil. News soon reached General Ord that two of these were being held at Piedras Negras, and thereupon he dispatched Colonel Shafter and Adjutant General Taylor to rescue them; but the prisoners were hurried away before the jail

[43] *Ibid.*, pp. 190-191.

[44] Speaking of an interview which he had with the foreign minister, Foster wrote: "In connection with the embarassments attending border affairs, I referred to the fact that the governors of all the Mexican States on the Rio Grande were regarded as hostile to the United States. The reputation of Governor Canales, of Tamaulipas, was notorious in both countries. Governor Charles, of Coahuila, was in open opposition to the American officials . . . General Trias, just elected governor of Chihuahua, in a recent letter to a newspaper of this city, has, over his on signature, manifested his hostile sentiments." Foster to Evarts, June 20, 1877, *House Exec. Doc.* No. 1, 45 Cong., 2 Sess. (Ser. 1793), Part I, p. 413.

[45] Shafter to the Assistant Adjutant General *House Exec. Doc.* No. 13, 45 Cong., 1 Sess. (Ser. 1773), pp. 4-5.

[46] *Ibid., loc. cit.*

could be seized. The American forces were then withdrawn and General Ord sent word to the governor of Coahuila that any injury to the guides would be considered as a declaration of the intention to co-operate with the savages in their depredations.[47] Before the close of April, reports of another raid were sent to headquarters; and on May 5, Sheridan repeated his recommendation of the previous March, while it was reiterated by Sherman on the 29th.[48]

These occurrences led the Washington government to issue positive orders for the crossing of the Mexican border in the pursuit of Indian and Mexican marauders. On June 1, 1877, General Sherman was instructed in regard to the southwestern frontier as follows:

The President desires that the utmost vigilence on the part of the military forces in Texas be exercised for the suppression of these raids. It is very desirable that efforts to this end . . . be made with the co-operation of the Mexican authorities; and you will instruct General Ord, commanding in Texas, to invite such co-operation on the part of the local Mexican authorities, and to inform them that while the President is anxious to avoid giving offense to Mexico, he is nevertheless convinced that the invasion of our territory by armed and organized bodies of thieves and robbers to prey upon our citizens should not be longer endured.

General Ord will at once notify the Mexican authorities along the Texan border, of the great desire of the President to unite with them in efforts to suppress the long continued lawlessness. At the same time he will inform those authorities that if the Government of Mexico shall continue to neglect the duty of suppressing these outrages, that duty will devolve upon this government, and will be performed, even if its performance should render necessary the occasional crossing of the border by our troops. You will, therefore, direct General Ord that in case the lawless incursions continue he will be at liberty, in the use of his own discretion, when in pursuit of a band of marauders, and when his troops are either in sight of them or upon a fresh trail, to follow them across the Rio Grande, and to overtake and punish them, as well as retake stolen property taken from our citizens and found in their hands on the Mexican side of the line.[49]

These instructions provoked loud protests from the Mexican government. The invasions which the military forces of the United States had made during the past four years had already occasioned

[47] *Ibid.*, pp. 9-12.
[48] *Ibid.*, pp. 13-14.
[49] *Ibid.*, pp. 13-14.

considerable irritation and given the Mexican newspaper press materials which they used to create the impression that the United States was desirous of stirring up trouble. This irritation was increased by the report[50] of the House Committee, made on February 29, 1876, in favor of the general practice of sending troops across the international line, and it was alleged in Mexico that the purpose of the expeditions was not to put down the raids, but to seize more territory.[51] News of the Ord orders now brought matters to a critical stage. The Díaz government, correctly gaging popular sentiment, instructed General Gerónimo Treviño to advance immediately to the frontier with his division with the view of co-operating with the forces of the United States in putting down the disturbing elements on the frontier, but to "repel force with force" in case of an invasion of Mexican soil by the United States army.[52] This declaration rallied all factions to its support. The newspapers, whether Conservative or Liberal, Lerdista or Porfirista, Spanish or Mexican, called upon every loyal son of Mexico to support the new president in his opposition to the colossus which was merely using the frontier depredations as a pretext for making war on a friendly nation.[53] Moreover, the condition was rendered more tense by the fact that the United States was withholding recognition from the Díaz government until some step should be taken to improve the border situation, while Díaz, apparently under the impression that the government of the United States was being influenced by his enemies, especially Lerdo de Tejada, seemed determined to make the cancellation of the Ord orders a *sine qua non* to any agreement looking toward the final solution of the border difficulties.[54]

Invasions Under the Ord Orders, 1877-1880. In this very delicate state of affairs, a great deal was obviously to depend upon the temper and attitude of General Ord, and he proved equal to the test. Even before Treviño reached the border, Ord was presented an opportunity to make use of his new authority if he had desired. Early in June, 1877, the troops of Díaz pursued a Lerdist

[50]*House Report* No. 343, 44th Cong., 1 Sess. (Ser. 1709).

[51]Foster to Fish, May 4, 1876, and enclosures, *House Exec. Doc.* No. 1, 44th Cong., 2 Sess. (Ser. 1741), pp. 398-400.

[52]Ogazón to Treviño, June 18, 1877, *House Exec. Doc.* No. 13, 45 Cong., 1 Sess. (Ser. 1773), pp. 20-21.

[53]Clippings enclosed in Foster to Evarts, June 22, 1877, *Ibid.*, pp. 20-27.

[54]*Ibid.*, pp. 33-34.

band across the border near the Mexican town of Paso del Norte, and attacked it upon United States soil. As soon as the American authorities heard of the invasion, Captain Kelly started for the scene of the fighting, while Colonel Shafter telegraphed General Ord for instructions as to whether he should cross the Rio Grande in pursuit of the retreating Mexicans. Ord directed him not to cross, and the Washington government approved of his course, but instructed John W. Foster, United States minister to Mexico, to enter a formal complaint against the violation of American soil.[55]

Immediately after Treviño reached the frontier, visits were exchanged between him and General Ord, and the latter wrote his government that they had reached a good understanding. The interview which the commanding officer of Fort Brown had with the commander of the national troops in Tamaulipas at about the same time did not result so hopefully, however. The American officer reported that this commander found the instructions of Ord "not palatable," but that he had expressed in polite and profuse language the desire to maintain friendly relations with the United States.[56]

While these friendly interchanges were taking place along the lower Rio Grande, preparations for crossing the boundary in pursuit of Indians were being made farther up the stream. In the latter part of June a band of savages stole some stock in Kerr County and killed one boy while escaping with their booty. Bullis and his scouts trailed them to a crossing on the Rio Grande some distance above the mouth of the Pecos, and then with about thirty-five men entered Mexico. He overtook the culprits more than a day's ride south of the line, and administering a sound defeat, recovered thirty-three stolen horses and returned to the northern side of the boundary.[57]

By this time, however, Treviño, whose understanding with Ord had been severely criticised in the Mexican press,[58] began to urge Ord not to cross the border, or at least to permit the crossing of regulars under discreet orders only. Ord refused to make any promises, but he telegraphed headquarters for more specific instructions. In reply, he was told that his orders did not contem-

[55] *Ibid.*, pp. 15-18, 156ff.

[56] *Ibid.*, p. 163.

[57] *House Misc. Doc.* No. 64, 45th Cong., 2 Sess. (Ser. 1820), p. 191.

[58] *House Exec. Doc.* No. 1, 45th Cong., 2 Sess. (Ser. 1793), Part I pp. 419, 422.

plate passing the border in pursuit of marauders when there was a "Mexican force ready to execute the duty of suppressing and punishing these predatory incursions into our territory."[59] Thereafter Ord seems to have taken considerable pains to notify the Mexican authorities in regard to the raids, but such co-operation as they gave did not remove the necessity for crossing the border. In the course of the more than two years during which the orders remained in force, some ten or fifteen punitive expeditions were made; and it is perhaps a high compliment to the tact and restraint of the military officials of both countries that they were able to avoid a brush between their respective troops.

Perhaps the nearest approach to a hostile outbreak occurred in September or October, 1877, when Bullis with a company of about ninety soldiers made a raid upon an Indian village near Zaragossa, Mexico. It appears that Shafter suspected that the expedition might result in an unfriendly movement on the part of the Mexican regulars stationed in the region; and he accordingly crossed over with some three hundred men to support Bullis in case of trouble. After attacking and burning the village, and capturing a number of Indian women, Bullis set out on his return to the Rio Grande. On the following day the Mexican forces who had taken his trail came into sight; but Shafter's troops appeared at an opportune moment, and the Mexicans soon retired. Had Bullis been unsupported, or had the total number of United States soldiers been smaller, trouble might have resulted.[60]

Agreements for Mutual Crossing of the Border in Pursuit of Indians. It is unnecessary here to enter into the details of the expeditions made under the Ord orders. It suffices to say that they were sent in pursuit both of Mexican and Indian marauders,[61] and

[59]Vincent to Ord, July 14, 1877, *House Exec. Doc.* No. 13, 45 Cong., 1 Sess., p. 175. Ord had probably already been notified that the Mexican republic was awakening to the importance of "repressing the outlawry on the Texas frontier," and instructed "not to be hasty in pursuit across the border, except in an aggravated case." See Sheridan to Sherman, June 9, 1877, *House Exec. Doc.* No. 1, 45 Cong., 2 Sess., Part I, pp. 419-420.

[60]The somewhat inconsistent accounts of this episode are found in *House Misc. Doc.* No. 64, 45 Cong., 2 Sess., pp. 191, 269; and *House Exec. Doc.* No. 13, 45 Cong., 1 Sess., pp. 53-54.

[61]For a brief summary of each of them, see Carranza's message of September 1, 1919, mentioned above. The writer desires also at this point to call attention to an excellent monograph, prepared by Miss Ethel Jones upon the Mexican border question in the Seminar of Pro-

that such vigorous measures slowly but surely improved the border situation. With this improvement came a better understanding between the two countries concerned. On April 9, 1878, the United States had recognized Díaz,[62] regardless of his stand with reference to the passing of the boundary; and in the course of the next two years he showed such ability to deal with the situation that General Ord himself advised that the orders issued on June 1, 1877, were no longer necessary. They were accordingly revoked in February, 1880.[63] Díaz now began to evince a disposition to come to an agreement in regard to future difficulties of the kind. At the same time, the center of the border disturbances shifted from the Rio Grande to the frontiers of New Mexico and Arizona, where the Apaches were committing fearful depredations.

Certain readjustments which the United States government attempted to make in the location of these Indians led to a series of the most formidable uprisings the southwestern frontier had witnessed in years. Led by such chieftains as Victorio, Nana, Natchez, Juh, and Gerónimo, the various Apache bands kept New Mexico, Arizona, Chihuahua, and Sonora in almost constant terror from 1880 to 1886, and hundreds of lives and thousands of dollars worth of property were destroyed. In order to cope with the situation the United States government again appealed to Mexico for permission to cross the border in pursuit of the marauders,[64] and this time with more success than upon former occasions. In the fall of 1880, President Díaz prevailed upon the Mexican Senate to permit an agreement for reciprocal crossing of the boundary for three months,[65] but the United States government seems not to have taken any immediate steps to render the favor it asked of Mexico mutual.[66] On July 29, 1882, however, such a reciprocal agreement was made, and this was renewed from time to time so

fessor Herbert E. Bolton of the University of California, and found in the library of that university.

[62]John W. Foster, *Diplomatic Memoires*, I, 95.

[63]Secretary of War Ramsey to the General of the Army, February 24, 1880, *House Exec. Doc.* No. 1, 46th Cong., 3 Sess. (Ser. 1951), pp. 735-736.

[64]Hunter to Morgan, September 15, 1880, and Morgan to Evarts, September 21, 1880, *House Exec. Doc.* No. 1, 46th Cong., 3 Sess. (Ser. 1951), Part I, pp. 768, 775.

[65]Fernandez to Morgan, October 15, 1880, *House Exec.* Doc. No. 1, 47 Cong., 1 Sess. (Ser. 2009), pp. 745-746.

[66]Mariscal to Morgan, May 4, 1882, *House Exec. Doc.* No. 1, 47 Cong., 2 Sess. (Ser. 2090), Part I, p. 389.

that troops were permitted to pursue Indian raiders into Mexico from August 18, 1882, to November 1, 1886, with the exception of a brief interval lasting from August 18 to October 31, 1884.[67]

The agreement provided that "regular Federal troops of the two Republics may reciprocally cross the boundary line . . . when they are in close pursuit of a band of savage Indians," such crossing to take place only in "unpopulous or desert" regions; i. e., "all those points which are at least two leagues from any encampment or town of either country." Moreover, "no crossing of the troops of either country" was to take place between Capitán Leal and the mouth of the Rio Grande, and in every instance the commander of the troops engaged in the action was to serve due notice on the nearest military commander of the country invaded.

During this period the United States sent numerous punitive expeditions far into Mexican territory in vigorous and ruthless pursuit of the various bands of Apaches and forced them eventually to lay down their arms and acknowledge the rule of the white man; and the only one instance of unhappy friction between the forces of the neighboring countries occurred. In January, 1886, while giving chase to a group of Chiricahua Apaches, Captain Crawford and his command were attacked near Teopar, Mexico, by a detachment of Mexican soldiers, and Crawford was killed. It was decided in this case, however, that the tragedy was due to an accident, and no demand for indemnity was made.[68]

Again in 1890 Indian difficulties led to a provisional agreement to remain in force not more than a year; and on November 25, 1892, it was renewed for another year in order that the troops of the United States might pursue the band of the Apache "Kid," a notorious outlaw and fugitive from justice, who had escaped into Sonora whence he and his accomplices frequently made destructive raids upon the American frontier. After May, 1893, nothing seems to have been heard of this outlaw for some time; but he apparently put in his appearance again in the summer of 1896, for on June 4 of that year the United States and Mexico signed another agreement to remain in force until "Kid's band" was "wholly exterminated."[69]

Whether there were instances of crossing the international line

[67]W. M. Malloy, *Treaties, Conventions*, etc., II, 1144ff.

[68]Moore, *Digest of International Law*, II, 425.

[69]Malloy, *op. cit.*, II, 1170ff.

between the time when "Kid" ceased to trouble the frontier and the dispatch of the Pershing expedition on March 15, 1916, the writer has been unable to ascertain. It is probable, thanks to the improved conditions along the border, that there were few occasions for such crossing until the outbreak of the revolt against Díaz. It is hoped, however, that whatever may have taken place during this more recent period, this paper has made clear the historical background of that expedition and substantiated the statement made in the beginning to the effect that behind it is a series of precedents extending over seventy-five years. That these precedents have been concerned in the majority of instances with Indian marauders does not materially alter the situation, for under international law is not the Mexican government equally responsible whether the depredations are committed by Indians residing in Mexico or by Mexican citizens?

MIRABEAU BUONAPARTE LAMAR

A. K. CHRISTIAN

CHAPTER VI

CLOSING YEARS

When President Houston's first administration closed in December, 1838, it was well known that he would be a candidate to succeed Lamar in 1841. He entered Congress in October, 1839, and immediately became the spokesman for those opposed to Lamar, and succeeded fairly well in creating an anti-administration party in Congress. He denounced Lamar on every occasion, but Lamar usually contented himself with defending his administration against attack. He took no active part in the campaign in 1841, though it was generally understood that he favored the election of the vice-president, David G. Burnet, who was running against Houston. It cannot be said that there was anything like definite party lines in the contest, and the election of Houston by an overwhelming majority did not indicate a complete repudiation of Lamar. Burnet was unpopular, and his brief tenure of the office of president during Lamar's illness did not make him any more popular. Besides, Houston understood thoroughly the turbulent frontier methods of campaigning, and his status at that time as a military hero was unquestioned.

That Lamar's popularity had declined, however, particularly with Congress, cannot be denied. At the beginning of his administration he had an overwhelming majority of both Houses with him, while at its close the House of Representatives was hostile, and the Senate showed only a small majority in support of his policies. But Houston had been less popular at the close of his first administration. The unpopularity of both executives was natural in a frontier state where each man was largely an individualist and inclined to resist any measure of governmental control. The main acts and failures of the Lamar administration I have already recorded. His attitude toward annexation, his Indian policy, the Santa Fé expedition, all aroused some opposition; but the total failure of the financial system during his administration probably caused more discontent than all the other matters put together. For the better part of his term he was in bad health, and this contributed to a certain personal unpopularity. This led to a certain detachment from or coldness toward his friends. "I am informed," wrote Memucan Hunt,

> that you are cold and repulsive in manners, &c. I plead the constant occupancy of your mind on important matters of State and the impossibility of those courtesies which were to be looked for when your mind is thus engrossed &c, &c. It is however very little trouble to ask a man when he reached the city, &c, &c, &c, &c, and I will take the liberty of recommending to you to tax yourself in this respect.[1]

He did not engage in the usual tricks of the politician, and for this he deserves both praise and blame. He is to be praised for depending on the justice of his policies rather than on political movements to bring their success; but if he could have added to that method a little of the political tact applied with success even today, he would have been more successful, and probably would have stood higher among historians.

His administration came to a close in December, 1841, and he retired to his home in Richmond. In the summer of 1842 he visited Georgia and was received with considerable honor. He was elected to the Phi Gamma Society of Emory College at Covington, Georgia, and made addresses at Columbus, Macon, and other places.[2] He returned to Texas in the spring of 1843, and except for a request that James Webb become a candidate for president in 1844, he took no part in politics. The documents included among his papers indicate that he was busy collecting material for his long-planned history of Texas, an occupation which engaged him from this time on, though he never put his material together. In 1844 he became convinced that separate statehood for Texas was impracticable and he advocated annexation. When annexation was accomplished some of his friends urged him to become a candidate for the United States Senate,[3] but he declined, and Houston and Thomas J. Rusk were elected.

When the Mexican War began Lamar attached himself to the Texas Mounted Volunteers, and participated in the battle of Mon-

[1]Hunt to Lamar, June 5, 1839, *Lamar Papers*, No. 1322.
[2]*Lamar Papers*, No. 2146.
[3]*Lamar Papers*, No. 2192.

terey. The Texas troops were under the command of Governor J. Pinckney Henderson, and Lamar acted as division inspector, and also as adjutant. He was highly commended by General Henderson in his report to General Taylor on the battle. General Henderson wrote:

General Lamar, my division inspector, (acting also as adjutant,) was mainly instrumental in causing my troops to be called into requisition. He had accompanied General Quitman in the occupancy of a point in the lower part of the city, where the battle commenced; and it was at his suggestion that a messenger was despatched for my command. He was found in active co-operation with the Mississippi and Tennessee troops; but rejoined my regiment on its arrival, and acted, during the balance of the fight, with the Texans.[4]

Shortly after the battle of Monterey Lamar was placed in command of an independent company and stationed at Laredo for the purpose of holding that post and restraining the Indians from attacking the Texans. He continued in this position until his command was mustered out at the command of General Taylor in September, 1847, though he frequently urged that he be allowed to accompany the main army in case of further fighting. Anticipating General Taylor's order, he requested and obtained of the Texan Government the authority either to re-enlist his company or raise a new company to be stationed at Laredo to continue the work already undertaken, and it was not until June, 1848, after the definite treaty of peace had been signed, that he mustered out his command and retired permanently from military service.[5]

As soon as the Texan authorities had taken possession of the disputed territory between Nueces and Rio Grande, they proceeded to organize it as a part of the State of Texas. Lamar himself, as commandant at Laredo, on July 3, 1847, called an election for local officers at that place. The counties of San Patricio and Nueces were organized by the Texas Government, and took part in the election of state and county officers for the year 1847. Lamar became a candidate for the House of Representatives from those two counties, and on November 1 was elected without oppo-

[4]*House Executive Document* No. 4, 29 Cong., 2 Sess., p. 98.

[5]For this paragraph see *Lamar Papers*, Nos. 2297-2390.

sition. He served in the session of 1847-1848, while his company was being re-enlisted and reorganized. He was proposed for speaker of the House, but was defeated by J. W. Henderson of Harris county by a vote of 34 to 24. He was chairman of the committee on State Affairs, but took little part in the activities of the House; and as soon as the session was over, he returned to his command in Laredo, where he staid until June, 1848.

From this time until 1857 the records of his movements are scanty. In the summer of 1849 he went again to Georgia on business connected with the eleven-league grant of land to a Georgia company, the business which had taken him to Texas in 1835 and 1836. He remained in Georgia until April, 1851, when he returned to Texas. There he married Miss Henrietta Moffitt of Galveston, after having remained unmarried since the death of his first wife in 1835. While in Georgia he contributed his opinion to the great questions of the time in public addresses and newspaper articles.

On August 1, 1850, a group of Macon citizens wrote a letter requesting that Lamar address a public mass meeting to be held in Macon on Clay's Compromise. Declining their invitation, August 16, he wrote that he was opposed to the Clay Compromise, but also to the Missouri Compromise; he was for all the rights of the South, and opposed to all compromises save those of the Constitution. Clay's and the Missouri Compromise were only capitulations on the part of the South, for if Congress could prohibit slavery north of thirty-six thirty, it could prevent it south of that line. "Naturally connected with these matters," he continued,

is the present position of the affairs of Texas. It forms the most practical issue of the day. I look upon the Santa Fé country as forming the first battle-field between the assailants and defenders of the institutions of the South. The Free Soilers are determined to seize the territory for the purpose of abolishing slavery upon it. It is now lawfully a part of Texas, and subject to the dominion of her institutions. If it can be severed, and united with New Mexico, Abolition will accomplish its ultimate purpose at once within the legitimate limits of a sovereign state.

The title of Texas to the territory in question is indisputable. It was within her designated limits while she was an independent government. She held to the Rio Bravo, by the same right by which she held to the Sabine. When she was admitted into the Union, these boundaries were well defined, and recognized by Congress; and it was out of this very Santa Fé country, that the new states were expected to be formed, which are alluded to in the resolutions of annexation.

He went on to say that it was a violation of that territory by Mexico which had resulted in a declaration of war by the United States, and said that the only remedy for the South was secession. "This is the only course for the South," he said.

There is no safety in the Union as it now exists. It is not the Union of the Constitution—not the Union established by the Sages of the Revolution; not the one that 'ensures domestic peace and tranquility;'—but another great dynasty erected on its ruins—a Russian Empire, which makes a Hungary of the South.

He advised a convention of the Southern States, fully empowered by the State sovereignties, to meet as speedily as possible upon the adjournment of Congress, to organize a Southern Confederacy in case the measures of the abolitionists were adopted. He doubted whether or not the Union could continue, but thought that if the South should withdraw, the North would come to terms; however, he thought the South was too divided to secede. Thus he placed himself among the extremists of the South, which was not strange when we recall his earlier alignment in the Indian and tariff controversies of the Jackson period.[6]

He continued to collect historical material, which he began to organize, and even had one chapter of a work on Long's expedition printed. No record of public activity remains, however, until January, 1855, when he became president of the Southern Commercial Convention held in New Orleans at that time, retiring before the close of the session on account of ill health.[7] In 1857 began his diplomatic career, which I shall discuss in some detail.

At the outset of the Buchanan administration Lamar became an applicant for a diplomatic post, which he considered as justified on account of his record as a States' Rights Democrat, and because his nephew, Howell Cobb, was secretary of the treasury.

[6] *Lamar Papers*, No. 2461; *Columbus Times*, September 10, 1850.
[7] *Lamar Papers*, No. 2489.

It seems that from the beginning Lamar desired an appointment to Nicaragua.[8] On March 6, 1857, Senator Rusk of Texas and J. A. Quitman of Mississippi sent a joint letter to Henry A. Wise, Governor of Virginia, asking for his influence to secure the appointment of Lamar as "resident minister to some of the European or South American Republics," and stating that he would accept a position as governor of a territory. Lamar was recommended as having been devoted to democratic principles throughout a long life, stating that he was induced to make application for such an appointment on account of pecuniary distress.[9] On March 8 Lamar applied in person to President Buchanan, and shortly after it was determined to appoint him as minister to the Argentine Confederation. The formal announcement of the appointment came in a letter from Lewis Cass, secretary of state, on July 23, 1857.[10] Lamar was delayed in setting out on his mission on account of financial difficulties, and when he was about to start, Cass and Buchanan decided to send him to the Central American republics, Nicaragua and Costa Rico as minister plenipotentiary.

In the absence of documentary evidence I am unable to state the cause for this change, but the cause seems reasonably clear. On November 16, 1857, Cass and Yrissari, the minister of several of the Central American States had signed a treaty which was expected to settle all questions between the United States and Nicaragua, and as Lamar had asked for the Nicaraguan post in the beginning, and had been given another one because Nicaragua was still unrecognized, the natural thing to do was to change his commission and send him to Nicaragua for the purpose of securing the ratification of the treaty.

I shall not be able to discuss in this paper the details of the conditions in Nicaragua out of which this treaty developed, nor the connection of Lamar with the negotiations; but I shall briefly outline the conditions as they were in order to show the superhuman task undertaken by Lamar. On August 27, 1849, a contract was entered into between the Nicaragua Government and the American Atlantic and Pacific Ship Company, by which in return

[8]See McLeod to Green, February 25, 1857, *Lamar Papers*, No. 2510.

[9]Rusk and Quitman to Wise, March 6, 1857, *Lamar Papers* (draft), No. 2511.

[10]Cass to Lamar, July 23, 1857, *Lamar Papers*, No. 2522.

for a certain sum of money paid by the company, the company was granted exclusive right to operate the Lake and overland transit from the Atlantic to the Pacific.[11] On August 14, 1851, the contract was amended, the company thereafter styling itself the Accessory Transit Company, though no vital changes were made in the charter. This charter was annulled on February 18, 1856, by a decree of the revolutionary government, because, as it was claimed, the company had failed to carry out the terms of the agreement.[12]

The Walker filibustering expedition, which began in 1855, had come to a close with the expulsion of Walker on May 1, 1857; but the expulsion of Walker did not mean that a stable government would be established any more than that there had been a stable government before he went to Nicaragua. The United States had refused to recognize the Walker government, and the government set up after Walker's expulsion was unable to secure recognition at once. But as the new government failed to restore the ships of the Accessory Transit Company, or to open the transit for any other company, the United States thought it time to take a hand in the matter. Hence Yrissari, who had been minister for several of the Central American republics for a number of years, and had recently been appointed minister for Nicaragua, was received officially on November 16, 1857, for the purpose of signing the treaty mentioned above. This treaty, which probably had been discussed by Cass and Yrissari before this date, provided for the guarantee of the transit route by the United States for the benefit of all nations. The provision was that the United States be authorized to employ troops for the purpose of keeping the transit route open in case Nicaragua should fail. Besides this, there was the usual agreements as to commerce.[13] This was the treaty that Lamar was expected to secure the ratification of by Nicaragua.

Lamar arrived in Nicaragua and spent a little more than a year there in fruitless efforts to secure the ratification of the treaty. The contrary interests of three transit companies that claimed exclusive rights on the isthmus, the interests of Great Britain and

[11] *Senate Document* No. 194, 47 Cong., 1 Sess., p. 49.
[12] *Ibid.*, 88.
[13] *Ibid.*, 117-125.

France, and the natural unwillingness of the Ceneral Americans to deal fairly or openly, prevented the accomplishment of his objects. He arrived less than a year after Walker was driven from Nicaragua, and just a short time after his arrest on his second attempt to revolutionize that republic; hence, his reception was not cordial, and he was never able to secure the confidence of any of the officials. The President went so far as to accuse Lamar of being involved with the filibusters, and of having made threats that unless the treaty should be ratified a new filibuster expedition under the auspices of the United States Government would take place; but he was afterwards forced to retract this charge.[14]

In July, 1859, having become hopeless of any result from his efforts Lamar applied for a recall, which was granted, and the latter part of that month he was back in Washington, having drawn up a treaty which he thought might have proved acceptable to the United States Government, but which was never approved. He remained in Washington only a short time, and then returned to his home in Richmond, Texas. He was there preparing to enjoy the association of his friends, when he died rather suddenly on December 19, 1859.

[14]A complete history of Lamar's experiences in Nicaragua does not come within the purposes of this paper. For the sake of unity I have been compelled to omit the story of his connection with that hotbed of revolution and international rivalries, but I shall in the future publish the result of my investigations in this field of his activities.[15]

[15]See for this paragraph Senate Documents, 35 Cong., 2 Sess., No. 1, p. 19.

NEWS ITEMS

"Presented to the University of Texas by Mrs. James F. Perry, widow of the late James F. Perry, great nephew of General Stephen F. Austin. This book has been in the Perry library at Peach Point since the early thirties. Freeport, Texas, March 18, 1921." This is the inscription on nine ledgers and day books kept by James F. Perry I, brother-in-law of Stephen F. Austin, who came to Texas from Missouri in 1831. One of the books is a plantation record, showing the yield of cotton and corn, the labor of the slaves, and the state of the weather. It covers the years 1837-1853. The other volumes contain the record of Perry's mercantile business in Texas, 1831-1834. The volumes possess great value for the economic historian of the state.

Through the kindness of Mrs. Forest H. Farley, of Austin, the University has been permitted to copy a number of interesting documents and letters handed down to her from her great-grandfathers, Patrick Noble, Governor of South Carolina, and William Calhoun, the elder brother of John C. Calhoun.

Of especial interest is a commission issued on December 14, 1808, by Governor John Drayton naming John C. Calhoun as an aide-de-camp, with the rank of Lieutenant Colonel, two letters from Calhoun to Patrick Noble, one written while serving as Secretary of War, the other soon after he had sent to Governor Hamilton his famous defense of the Doctrine of Nullification.

Among the Noble papers, the earliest is a commission issued on November 10, 1779, by Governor John Rutledge, appointing him Major of the Upper Division of Regiment Ninety-six of the Militia commanded by Andrew Pickens, while the most interesting is Patrick Noble to A Georgia Committee in regard to finding some common means of defense for the Southern States against "the arbitrary, unequal, unconstitutional, and therefore unjust system of federal legislation designed to protect manufacturers."

The student of economic problems will be especially interested in a bill presented to Governor Noble for "the Traveling Expenses of Brian Bateman and J. W. Stuckey employed to go to Georgia after Mina McCay on a charge of stealing negroes, and in a letter of John Noble to Joseph Noble in regard to taking up lands in Alabama and Florida, and the prospect for the cession of these regions by Spain.

Dr. William E. Dunn, formerly Associate Professor of Latin-American History in the University of Texas, is now director of a School of Commerce maintained by the Peruvian government at Lima, Peru.

The *Annual Report* of the American Historical Association for 1918, volume II, has just been issued by the Government Printing Office, Washington, D. C. It is the autobiography of Martin Van Buren (808 pages), an exceptionally interesting and valuable historical document. The greater part of it is devoted to the period of President Jackson's administrations.

The *Lamar Papers,* edited by Charles Gulick, has just been published by the Texas Library and Historical Commission.

The University of London has decided to hold in the week commencing July 11, 1921, an Anglo-American Conference of Professors of History following on the Conference of Professors of English, which was held in July, 1920. That conference proved very effective in promoting cordial relations between the university staffs of the two countries, and its results from the academic point of view are already apparent. An international committee has been established to continue in permanent session for the purpose of interchange of information on matters connected with research, and is likely to result in substantial benefits to British and American scholars in the field of English language and literature. The University of Columbia proposes to follow the precedent by arranging a Conference in English in 1922.

AFFAIRS OF THE ASSOCIATION

The annual meeting of the Texas State Historical Association will be held in Room 158 of the Main Building of the University of Texas, on April 21. Papers will be read by Professor Charles W. Ramsdell, on The Indian Problem in Texas, 1846-1859; by Mr. C. R. Wharton, on The Origin and Jurisdiction of the Alcalde in Colonial Texas; by Mrs. Lola Spell, on The First Teacher of European Music in America; and by Professor J. E. Pearce, on The Function and Importance of Museums in the World of Learning. The program will begin at 3 o'clock. There will be a business meeting at the conclusion of the papers.

INDEX TO VOLUME XXIV

of

in
tes,
rk-

to

of,

on
o,

l-

:,

Lightning Source UK Ltd.
Milton Keynes UK
UKOW07f0747040917
308541UK00006B/343/P

9 781276 095